MW00491909

ICME-13 Monographs

Series Editor

Gabriele Kaiser, Faculty of Education, Didactics of Mathematics, Universität Hamburg, Hamburg, Germany

Each volume in the series presents state-of-the art research on a particular topic in mathematics education and reflects the international debate as broadly as possible, while also incorporating insights into lesser-known areas of the discussion. Each volume is based on the discussions and presentations during the ICME-13 congress and includes the best papers from one of the ICME-13 Topical Study Groups, Discussion Groups or presentations from the thematic afternoon.

More information about this series at http://www.springer.com/series/15585

Marja van den Heuvel-Panhuizen
Editor

International Reflections on the Netherlands Didactics of Mathematics

Visions on and Experiences with Realistic
Mathematics Education

 Springer Open

Editor
Marja van den Heuvel-Panhuizen
Utrecht University
Utrecht, the Netherlands

Nord University
Bodø, Norway

The Open Access publication of this book was made possible in part by generous support from the Utrecht University Open Access Fund, the Nord University Open Access Fund, and the NVORWO (Netherlands Association for the Development of Mathematics Education).

ISSN 2520-8322   ISSN 2520-8330   (electronic)
ICME-13 Monographs
ISBN 978-3-030-20222-4   ISBN 978-3-030-20223-1   (eBook)
https://doi.org/10.1007/978-3-030-20223-1

This Springer imprint is published by the registered company Springer Nature Switzerland AG
The registered company address is: Gewerbestrasse 11, 6330 Cham, Switzerland

Preface

This volume is part of the ICME-13 Monographs and is a spin-off of the Netherlands strand of the ICME-13 Thematic Afternoon on "European Didactic Traditions" held in Hamburg in 2016. In this session, four European countries—France, Italy, Germany and the Netherlands—presented their approach to teaching and learning mathematics in school and in research and development. The session inspired mathematics didacticians familiar with Dutch mathematics education to reflect on the approach to teaching and learning mathematics education in the Netherlands and the role of the Dutch domain-specific instruction theory of Realistic Mathematics Education. This resulted in two volumes: *International Reflections on the Netherlands Didactics of Mathematics—Visions on and Experiences with Realistic Mathematics Education* and *National Reflections on the Netherlands Didactics of Mathematics—Teaching and Learning in the Context of Realistic Mathematics Education.*

The current volume is the *International Reflections* book. In this volume, forty-four authors from fifteen countries outside the Netherlands reflect on Realistic Mathematics Education (RME), the domain-specific instruction theory developed in the Netherlands since the late 1960s. The authors discuss what aspects of RME appealed to them and explain how RME has influenced their thinking on mathematics education, the RME-based projects they are working on, and how RME has sometimes even altered aspects of their countries' tradition in teaching and learning mathematics. Consequently, it will not be a surprise that the chapters in this volume express much appreciation for RME. Yet, in addition to their approval, the authors also articulate the challenges of RME. It is apparent that a particular approach to mathematics education cannot simply be transplanted to another country. This knowledge is not new, but what is new is that the chapters show how a 'local' approach to mathematics education—which, in fact, RME is—has turned out in other countries. The authors have elucidated how they have adapted RME to their circumstances and their view on mathematics education. By showing how others have used RME and made their own interpretations of it, a mirror is held up to RME, which in turn also benefits its further development. The chapters make it clear that looking at RME from abroad and from the perspective of other cultural contexts can put a brighter spotlight on the essence of RME than only reflections and deliberations from inside.

Getting the thought in mind of turning the international life of RME into a volume took little more than a split second. Realising this and creating the volume took years—no need to be precise here. It was a huge enterprise that, thanks to the inspiring chapters of all authors who contributed to this volume, has become reality. However, especially instrumental for this was Nathalie Kuijpers, who together with me checked and double-checked all the texts. Many, many thanks for this.

Utrecht, the Netherlands   Marja van den Heuvel-Panhuizen
March 2019   m.vandenheuvel-panhuizen@uu.nl;
                                                       m.vandenheuvel-panhuizen@nord.no

Contents

Chapter 1
Seen Through Other Eyes—Opening Up New Vistas in Realistic Mathematics Education Through Visions and Experiences from Other Countries

Marja van den Heuvel-Panhuizen

Abstract This chapter is a synthesis of visions on and experiences with Realistic Mathematics Education (RME) described in the eighteen following chapters of this volume by forty-four authors from fifteen different countries. Through a process of synthesizing information from these chapters and combining and contrasting what the authors wrote about RME, a comprehensive image emerged of the theory and practice of RME, together with some new vistas. The chapter is structured around the following themes: making acquaintance with RME, narratives of first experiences with RME, highlighted outstanding features of RME, processes of implementation of RME and their challenges, adaptations of RME, criticisms of RME, and the flavours of RME that can be found in foreign curricula, textbooks, instructional materials, and teaching methods. Finally, to conclude the chapter, I reflect on new insights related to RME and directions for its further development that can be gained from this input from abroad.

Keywords Making acquaintance with Realistic Mathematics Education (RME) · Implementation and adaptation of RME · Challenges and criticisms of RME · Outstanding features of RME · Flavours of RME in foreign instructional material

1.1 Introduction

The story of what Realistic Mathematics Education (RME) is, how it came into existence and how it was developed further, has been described already by several people who are or were, in one way or another, part of the Dutch RME community. In this chapter this story is put under the spotlight again, but from the perspectives of people from abroad. The chapter tells how researchers and designers of mathematics

M. van den Heuvel-Panhuizen (✉)
Freudenthal Group, Faculty of Social and Behavioural Sciences & Freudenthal Institute, Faculty of Science, Utrecht University, Utrecht, the Netherlands
e-mail: m.vandenheuvel-panhuizen@uu.nl

Faculty of Education, Art and Culture, Nord University, Bodø, Norway
e-mail: m.vandenheuvel-panhuizen@nord.no

M. van den Heuvel-Panhuizen (ed.), *International Reflections on the Netherlands Didactics of Mathematics*, ICME-13 Monographs,
https://doi.org/10.1007/978-3-030-20223-1_1

education, mathematics teacher educators, and mathematics teachers from fifteen countries outside the Netherlands, made acquaintance with RME, what they thought of it, what convinced them to adopt it, what aspects of RME they criticised, and what adaptations were required to incorporate RME in their own context. The visions and experiences explored in this chapter are based on Chaps. 2–19 of this volume in which forty-four authors tell their own RME story.

If one thing is unmistakably revealed in these chapters, it is in the first place that RME, although it may appear to be a well-defined unified theory of mathematics education, has many faces and should certainly not be considered a fixed and finished theory of mathematics education. Characteristic for RME is that there exists both internally, within the inner circle of RME developers at the Freudenthal Institute, and externally, including people in the Netherlands at other universities and institutions, differences in the interpretation and the appraisal of particular aspects of RME. The same applies to groups and persons in other countries who were inspired by RME. In addition to these concurrent differences, over time there have also been changes in focal points. For example, students' difficulties in learning mathematics was not really a theme that received special attention in the early years of RME. Only later, the development of a didactics for supporting low-achievers became an important issue, while in the last decade another move was made, but this time in favour of offering more learning opportunities to talented students. A further example of RME as a living theory is the rethinking of teaching and learning mathematics that was necessary when computer technology entered the classroom and provided teachers with new tools for organizing lessons and students with new ways of developing mathematical understanding. After all, in the time that the first ideas of RME were conceptualised there were, for example, no such things as online mini-games for fostering students' multiplicative reasoning ability. So, new didactical tools had to find their way into RME and these in turn opened new didactical approaches in RME.

Characteristic of RME are also the many people involved in its development and the mutual influences among these people. Teacher educators, school advisors, and textbook authors could always freely use RME tasks, ideas for lessons, models and strategies, and teaching-learning trajectories. Furthermore, this helping each other with good ideas also occurred in the opposite direction. RME designs have certainly also been inspired by ideas from teacher educators, school advisors, and textbook authors from outside the Freudenthal Institute. This reciprocal inspiration was also the case during all the joint projects the Dutch have carried out with people in other countries. There have always been exchanges of ideas and development in multiple directions. Bringing the visions and experiences from abroad together in this volume and in this chapter, and seeing the use of RME from different socio-cultural perspectives and educational systems can create new sources for reciprocal inspiration and opportunities for opening up new developments in RME.

1.2 Making Acquaintance with RME

1.2.1 Personal Encounters

Making acquaintance with RME was in most cases the result of a personal encounter at a gathering of mathematicians or mathematics educators somewhere in the world. For Wittmann (Chap. 4) this acquaintance took place in 1967 when he met Freudenthal who was one of the invited speakers at a colloquium held at the University of Erlangen in Germany. Wittmann had developed a strong aversion against the New Math movement and was very eager to speak with Freudenthal because of a paper Freudenthal wrote and published in 1963 in a German journal in which he explained that he saw mathematical activity, and not the learning of readymade axiomatics, as the crucial element of learning mathematics.

In Belgium, where New Math was introduced in the 1960s, an important meeting occurred in 1983 when proponents and opponents of New Math defended their positions. In this colloquium Freudenthal and Goddijn gave lectures about the Dutch approach to mathematics education. As is made clear by De Bock and his colleagues (Chaps. 3 and 11), in Belgium there was then, and even earlier, certainly interest in the RME approach, but after this meeting only some limited changes occurred in the programmes and in the formulation of the learning objectives. Yet for both of these small changes inspiration was found in the Dutch RME materials.

In 1983, Selter (Chap. 13) in Germany, while studying to become a primary school teacher, became aware of a paper by Treffers about teaching written multiplication and division by starting off with context problems containing large numbers. Students could solve these problems by using procedures of repeated addition and subtraction which gradually evolved into the more standard ways of written calculation. Reading this paper was a key event for Selter. He realised that this RME principle of progressive schematisation or progressive mathematisation was not only important for learning written calculation algorithms, but that it also could be considered a comprehensive, generally applicable principle for the organisation of mathematical learning or teaching processes.

Further from home, in China, the introduction to RME happened through Freudenthal's book *Mathematics as an Educational Task*. As described by Sun and He (Chap. 10), it was Jiang who read this book in 1985, which gave him a new perspective on understanding mathematics education. Next, this was followed by a face-to-face meeting of Jiang's former student Wang with Freudenthal at the CIEAEM conference in London in 1986. This meeting is considered the start of a new era of exchange in mathematics education between China and the Netherlands.

Also, in many other countries the exchange and collaboration with the Dutch started with personal meetings. For example, in Argentina (Chap. 9), it was Rosenberg who in 1984 came to the Netherlands to specialise in the didactics of mathematics at Utrecht University. This stay was followed by a return visit by De Lange and Schoemaker who introduced RME to professors at the University of Buenos Aires and the National University of Tucumán.

The long-lasting cooperation in mathematics education between the Netherlands and the United States begun when Romberg, who was involved in the development of the NCTM Standards, invited De Lange to the National Center for Research in Mathematical Sciences Education (NCRMSE) at the University of Wisconsin-Madison in the spring of 1988. In their chapter, Webb and Peck (Chap. 2) do not attempt to conceal that it was a beneficial development that these two mathematics educators on opposite sides of the Atlantic with a passion for reforming mathematics teaching and learning, have become colleagues and partners. In the 1990s Romberg also brought about a connection with Puerto Rico (Chap. 16) by proposing López-Fernández to collaborate with him and De Lange on the development of Spanish versions of the materials of the textbook series *Mathematics in Context* (MiC) that NCRMSE was developing together with the Dutch.

The 1990s were busy times. Apart from the activities with and in the United States and Puerto Rico, in 1994 RME also affected Indonesia when Sembiring from the Institut Teknologi Bandung saw De Lange presenting a keynote about RME at the ICMI conference in Shanghai. As is explained by Zulkardi, Putri, and Wijaya (Chap. 18), Sembiring was a representative of the government of Indonesia. He was inspired by the presentation and asked De Lange whether he could help Indonesia to reform the approach to teaching and learning school mathematics that was influenced by New Math. His first job would be to persuade the Indonesian government that RME is the right approach to reforming mathematics education. Four years later De Lange agreed to take on this task.

1.2.2   Narratives of First RME Experiences

When describing acquaintance with RME, very often the narratives that came to the fore are reflecting the thrilling and emotional feelings that arose when one became aware what RME means. In the United States, for Peck (Chap. 2), who was introduced to RME during his second year as a high school mathematics teacher, this break-through moment came when he saw an RME task in which hot dogs and lemonade were ordered in two different compositions and only the total price of each of the orders was given. The assignment for the students was to find out what one hot dog and one lemonade cost. He acknowledged that until that moment, he had always used Gaussian elimination to solve systems of equations, yet he never had understood why it worked. Now he found himself drawn to the context and combined the orders of the food in various ways to make new combinations, eventually eliminating the hot dogs. At this very moment it was clear for him that this context was not just a dressing-up for formal mathematics, but begged to be mathematised. In Peck's own words: "I finally understood elimination! I was hooked. It was clear to me that RME was a powerful tool for didactical design."

In Israel, Arcavi (Chap. 6) had a similar experience. Whereas he had always enjoyed the highly procedural and rule-oriented mathematics that he was offered in school, especially in algebra in which he liked the ingenuity of transforming expressions and inventing particular rules, his acquaintance with RME provided him with a broader view of mathematics. In his university studies, he always experienced mathematical modelling as an application of an already known piece of pure mathematics. It was a real eye-opener for him that RME inverted the order and that a real-world phenomenon could and should be a springboard for mathematisation. Also, RME allowed him to look with new eyes at his initial fondness for the procedural. It led him to consider that the procedural and the conceptual should be deeply interwoven. This new insight formed the roots of his work on sense making with symbols and with images.

For Abrahamson (Chap. 14), working both in Israel and the United States, the moment that—in his own words—was about to change everything, was when he found a paper published in 1979 by the RME designers and researchers Van den Brink and Streefland. In this paper they described and analysed a conversation between a father (Streefland himself) and his eight-year old son about a poster showing a man and a whale, in which the size of the whale compared to that of the man was exaggerated to make it more sensational. The questions addressed to the child and the analysis of the answers revealed that the child clearly realised that the ratio between the man and the whale was wrong. While Abrahamson was searching in vain in cognitive psychology literature for a grounding of his own ideas on children's early development of multiplicative concepts based on sensorimotor experiences, he was very happy to find this observation and the way the Dutch didacticians interpreted the observation and revealed the boy's thinking.

In the chapter about RME-based work in Argentina, Zolkower, Bressan, Pérez, and Gallego (Chap. 9) show that getting acquainted with RME can indeed change one's view on mathematics and mathematics teaching. A teacher student did not leave any doubt about this when testifying: "My relationship to mathematics changed a lot. It used to be very hard for me. I would often get frustrated... I used to hate it. But this year, I think because of how we approached it in this class, focusing on learning and understanding, it changed completely my view of this subject." A similar voice came from a teacher involved in one of the study groups organised in Argentina: "From the start, what intrigued us the most about RME is how it opens up the classroom doors to common sense, imagination, desire to learn, and the mathematising potential of our students."

For the Manchester Metropolitan University group visiting the Netherlands some ten years ago, what they saw in classrooms came as a revelation. According to Dickinson, Eade, Gough, Hough, and Solomon (Chap. 19), they were not just struck by the confidence with which the Dutch students gave correct answers, but also by the variety of justifications the students gave for them. For example, when comparing the size of fractions some used an appropriate whole number (a mediating quantity, as suggested by Streefland) to argue that 3/4 of 60 was larger than 2/3 of 60. Others used a percentage or a decimal argument or compared the fractions with a whole one, arguing that 3/4 needs only an extra 1/4 to make it up to a whole one and is therefore the larger. The English visitors supposed that such methods would not be available to students in their country at that time. A further characteristic of RME which the Manchester group said gave them a new way of thinking about how to teach mathematics, was the slow route to formal mathematics as explained by the iceberg model developed by Boswinkel and her colleagues. Influenced by RME, they began to define mathematical progress differently in two ways. As well as recognising that progress could be defined through the progressive formalisation of models, they also changed their view of the use of contexts as an aid for abstraction. While earlier their idea was to take the context away in order to work on more formal mathematics, after learning about RME, they saw that adding more contexts could also help students. In their own words the group from Manchester formulated it even better than it was ever done within RME itself: "[A]llowing students to see the 'sameness' of different situations, was actually a far more powerful route to abstraction."

1.2.3   Outstanding Features of RME

As described by Sun and He (Chap. 10), to steer a reform movement and make decisions about how to prepare students for society, and especially how to foster students' creativity, having clearly formulated goals is not enough. Also, theoretical power on which one can rely to guide concrete practice towards these goals is necessary. RME is considered to have contributed to generating such a theory for mathematics education in China. In addition, for Chinese mathematics educators it is seen as an outstanding feature of RME, that, in line with a famous Chinese saying, it keeps pace with the times. It is continuously open to new developments and innovations according to the ever-changing society and accumulated experiences of people. Only when this applies to a theory, can it have lasting vitality and the power to extend without limit in both theoretical and applicable aspects. This is very much appreciated in RME.

Wittmann (Chap. 4) was particularly attracted to the ideas Freudenthal and his colleagues at IOWO (Institute for the Development of Mathematics Education) had about research: they did not regard themselves as researchers, but as producers of instruction, as engineers in the educational field. Another important feature of RME for Wittmann was its focus on mathematics as a field of knowledge, though later RME became, as he sees this, too much focused on application. Wittmann also appreciated the genetic view on teaching and learning. He is, like Freudenthal, against the idea of didactical transpositions in which the higher levels of mathematics for mathematicians are converted into lower levels of mathematics for teaching mathematics. Also, the shift away from the strong fixation on standard algorithms towards various ways of calculating based on arithmetical laws was something he valued in RME. All in all, Wittmann has high regard for the contribution Freudenthal and his IOWO colleagues have delivered to mathematics education as a research domain with didactical analysis of the subject matter as the most important source for designing learning environments and curricula.

In other chapters further aspects of RME are highlighted as rewarding. When talking about the United States, Webb and Peck (Chap. 2) emphasise that RME has recast people's mathematical experience as one that should be meaningful, relevant and accessible. According to Niss (Chap. 17) it was the fact that students' individual conceptions and experiences have to be respected and are taken as points of departure for teaching and learning that made RME resonate with Danish mathematics educators so much. This student-centred approach of RME and its great attention to students' personal developments, as expressed in a paper by Freudenthal published in 1971, also received much praise from Abrahamson, Zolkower and Stone in their RME project at Berkeley (Chap. 14). The idea of connecting the teaching of mathematics to fostering youth independence and empowerment was considered as a great vision.

1.3 Processes of Implementation of RME

Getting to know about RME by meeting a knowledgeable person or reading a mind-altering book or paper is one thing, but what it is really about is how this first encounter continues. After a few pioneers in a country were introduced to RME, often a process followed in which the ideas were shared and many people became involved. For example, in England (Chap. 19), over the past ten years a number of projects developing classroom approaches based on RME, working with teachers and their students, have been carried out. In total over 40 schools, 80 teachers and 2000 students took part in these projects.

In Indonesia (Chap. 18) the coverage of RME-related projects and initiatives was more nationwide. Here, after a period of intensive exchange of Dutch and Indonesian staff and particularly by having master and PhD students coming to the Netherlands, several projects were set up to develop Pendidikan Matematika Realistik Indonesia (PMRI), an Indonesian adaptation of the RME approach to teaching mathematics. In addition, an RME-inspired master and an RME-inspired PhD program were also created, as well as courses for teachers, conferences, a website and a national and local centres for PMRI.

The implementation process in Argentina encompassed from the beginning a high degree of teacher involvement. According to Zolkower and her colleagues (Chap. 9), rather than applying the principles of RME top down as dogmas and using RME instructional materials as ready-made recipes, the Patagonian Group of Mathematics Didactics (GPDM) was engaged in the processes of design, try-outs, reflection, revision, new try-outs, through which they reinvented RME. These processes took place in spiral movements in which the participants interconnected their own mathematising activities with those of students in Grades K–12 and with those used in teacher preparation courses.

In other countries as well, there was a strong demand for developing ownership with the RME approach and getting to grips with this way of teaching. As Hernández-Rodríguez, López-Fernández, Quintero-Rivera, and Velázquez-Estrella (Chap. 16) reported, in Puerto Rico the need to have teachers participate 'as students' in working out together the details of the Spanish versions of the MiC units was recognised immediately. Such sessions were followed by detailed discussions around the mathematics addressed in the units and reflections on the use of paradigmatic situations and, above all, on finding ways to integrate the new materials in the mainstream curriculum and in the Puerto Rican culture.

The process of using RME in the United States, described by Webb and Peck (Chap. 2), also reflects a remarkable epistemological consistency between the characteristics of RME and how it was put into practice. In the same vein as in RME where students' active involvement in the learning process is considered as crucial, and the design of instructional materials is considered as engineering and tinkering, they characterise the past twenty years in which RME in the United States was piloted, disseminated, and integrated into mathematics resources as teacher-centred. In this process, signified as "from tinkering to systematic innovation", the focus was on reconsidering how students learn mathematics by having teachers re-experience mathematics through the lens of progressive formalisation and related didactic approaches. The teachers involved—who were often dedicated, volunteer teachers who wanted to take risks—collaborated with researchers to develop and improve RME lesson sequences and curricula and have become instructional leaders who facilitated professional development on RME.

In South Africa, as is indicated by Julie and Gierdien (Chap. 5), teachers were also considered as major role-players in collaboration with university-based mathematics educators, mathematicians and mathematics curriculum advisors when using RME to improve mathematics education. For the development of local instructional theories, it was essential that there was some alignment with the operative school mathematics curriculum. This is linked to the issue of immediacy in the sense that the appropriation of a teaching innovation by teachers is highly driven by their sense of the direct applicability of the ideas distributed by the innovation for their practice.

Whereas in some countries projects with teachers to apply RME or adaptations thereof in classrooms were started immediately, in China there was first much exchange between representatives of RME and Chinese mathematics educators through lectures. At the beginning the discussions about RME remained more at a theoretical level and there was no direct connection between RME theory and what occurred in Chinese classroom practice. Therefore, for example, the idea of 'free productions' was hard to be understood. It was difficult to imagine how to use it in the Chinese educational context. In contrast, 'mathematisation under the guidance of the teacher' was easier to understand because it was closer to the situation in China. This idea did not only affirm students' primary role of learning mathematics, but also emphasises the importance of teacher guidance during the process of mathematisation. As a result, this idea was quickly accepted and supported by the Chinese audience. As Sun and He (Chap. 10) concluded, knowing how RME was concretised in textbook design and classroom instruction was very necessary for understanding the essence of RME. Many examples mentioned in the lectures have become classical cases used in China for mathematics teachers' professional development. By analysing and reflecting on these cases, many Chinese mathematics teachers gain a better understanding of RME and try to change their former teaching practice of direct transmission.

The attitude of thoroughly studying RME sources was also characteristic for Korea. Lee, Chong, Na, and Park (Chap. 15) in their chapter give many examples of Korean mathematics educators who discussed RME ideas. These discussions already started in 1980 with a critical paper by Woo in which he refuted Freudenthal's criticism on Piaget's point of view. A few years later, Woo changed his mind and suggested mathematics teachers in Korea to focus more on mathematical thinking rather than on the mathematical content itself and taking as a guideline for this Freudenthal's didactical phenomenology. Many doctoral studies followed in which didactical phenomenological analyses were carried out on mathematical concepts such as function, negative number, and proportion. Moreover, researchers reflected on the difficulties underlying the Korean instruction methods of such concepts and proposed instruction methods that were more desirable.

1.4 Challenges in Implementing RME

Like in the Netherlands where moving from mechanistic mathematics teaching to an RME approach meant a break with the regular practice, also in other countries where initiatives were taken aimed at implementing RME this implied a paradigm shift in the teaching of mathematics and coping with the challenges that come with this new approach. That such a paradigm shift in the teachers' mindset is necessary for adopting the RME model was explicitly mentioned by Kaur, Wong, and Govindani (Chap. 7) when discussing differences between the Singapore approach in textbooks to teach equations and the approach in the RME-based textbook series MiC. Although in Singapore a drastic change into teaching methods that promote mathematical reasoning and communication might not be necessary, because they are already used in Singapore classrooms, taking up the RME approach would still require a turn in teachers' thinking on how mathematics learning takes place: 'from content to application' should be transformed to 'content through application'.

To activate and reshape mathematics education in Korea inspired by RME necessitated that several problems connected to the traditional mathematics education had to be overcome. According to Lee and her colleagues (Chap. 15) these problems were students' low understanding of mathematical concepts, the focus on blind memorisation of mathematical rules, procedures, and algorithms, and the existence of a poor connection between school mathematics and out-of-school mathematics and a teacher-centred style of mathematics teaching. The challenge the Korean textbook developers faced was to find and develop appropriate contexts through which students can experience that mathematics is a human activity existing near to them, can learn the principles and concepts of mathematics naturally through their own activities, and can improve their interest in and gain a positive attitude towards mathematics. Feedback from teachers who worked with RME-inspired materials revealed on the one hand that through the contexts the students indeed came to various strategies and they learned to communicate in their own words showing that they fully understood what they were doing instead of using only formal mathematical terms. On the other hand the teachers indicated that teaching in this way was very demanding in terms of class preparation and the continuous care and observations of students. In addition, teachers were concerned about the connection to the overall curriculum and how the students would fare in the usual mathematics classes in subsequent grades.

Since in Puerto Rico also there is a large difference between the principles and design methods used in the development of the Puerto Rican curriculum and those used in the development of RME, the paradigm change required for implementing RME there was a big challenge to overcome as well. Therefore, according to Hernández-Rodríguez and his colleagues (Chap. 16), a major balancing act had to be completed, on one side promoting teachers' inventiveness on how to work with the RME-based materials while on the other side following the official curriculum.

When discussing the development of an RME approach in England, Dickinson and his colleagues (Chap. 19) highlighted that the differences between the Dutch and English education system and the effect of the English system on teachers' and students' experiences and expectations have presented them with considerable challenges. Teachers in England are very aware of the pressure to move towards formal mathematics as quickly as possible. Therefore, they are anxious to see students acquiring formal procedures, and teachers may intervene and demonstrate the formal procedure after only one contextual problem. In RME, the process to working at a formal level may involve many lessons, and may even be spread out over a number of years, thus enabling students to gain conceptual understanding of how the procedure works, where it might be used, and how it connects to other areas of mathematics. However, in England it is often expected that performing a mathematical procedure can and should be achieved within one or two lessons. In addition, moving from the faster rote-learned alternatives to slow learning may also encounter resistance from students. This can also occur in response to the challenge that an RME-based classroom culture presents to students when they have to explain their thinking and make connections, ask questions and generally take more risks than in the case of simply 'learning the rules'.

One of the challenges that reform movements can be faced with is related to political issues. This is clearly the case in England where, as shown by Dickinson and his colleagues (Chap. 19), politically driven accountability pressures result in increasingly frequent assessment and a rigorous inspection regime, offering little scope for modifying education. Conversely, in the Cayman Islands (see also Chap. 19), although influenced by the British tradition, a less strict system provided their colleague Eade with more opportunities to work on developing an RME approach. Even so, he has concerns about the future: "There is still a long way to go and there is still a danger that, if the political/educational climate changes, then it would be very easy to destroy the fragile advances that have been made".

Such a political climate change also happened in Puerto Rico which had great consequences for the implementation of RME. At a particular point when Hernández-Rodríguez and his colleagues (Chap. 16) experienced that all the elements pointed to the possibility that the Puerto Rican version of MiC could become the spearhead of mathematics education in Puerto Rico, they suffered a real setback. Although there was public policy support for using this textbook series, the educational materials were developed, training was given and there was an entire infrastructure to dissem-inate the materials, the scaling up did not occur. An important factor in this was that there was a change in Puerto Rico's governing party and consequently a change in the Puerto Rico Department of Education. Given that the new staff responsible was not as enthusiastic about this new approach to teaching mathematics, the necessary funds for carrying out the dissemination were not allocated.

A completely different situation was the case in South Africa. As set out by Julie and Gierdien (Chap. 5), here the new political system rather opened up opportunities for RME. In fact, RME was introduced in South Africa during a period when curricu-lum changes were introduced to fit the educational ideals of the 'new' South Africa, including fostering learner-centredness and non-authoritarian ways of working class-rooms. This kind of learning and teaching that was desired by the first democratically elected government in the country is exactly where RME stands for.

1.5 Adaptations of RME

Implementing RME, being inspired by RME and coping with the challenges that come with this new approach evidently require that adaptations are made to RME, in order to make it workable in a country's educational context and system. In South Africa, despite the common grounds in general ideas about mathematics education such adaptations were, according to Julie and Gierdien (Chap. 5), necessary because of the tension between the content of the RME-based materials and the 'legitimate school mathematics', that is, the mathematics that is valued in high-stakes examina-tions. There is a strong demand for proximity of the used RME resources. Teachers wanted to be assured of the immediate relevance of innovations to their current responsibilities and accountabilities with respect to the curriculum and accompa-nying activities such as examinations. As a result of this requirement it happened that RME-based modules were not disseminated further after trying them out in the classroom. Such was the case with a module on vision geometry. This particular module was chosen due to problems students in South Africa have with geometry and because the topic of vision geometry was quite in line with the RME perspective to provide students with activities where they can experience mathematics. However, even though the activities in this module were found enjoyable and not above the abilities of the students, after a few trials and notwithstanding some revisions to make it closer to the curriculum, it was not further used.

Adaptations were also necessary in the RME-based materials developed for elementary school in Puerto Rico. Hernández-Rodríguez and his colleagues (Chap. 16) illustrated this by describing what happened to the topic of written algo-rithms. As prescribed by official requirements, the materials had to be aligned to the Puerto Rican mathematics standards released in 2000 and 2007, which include that students learn the digit-based algorithms for addition and subtraction of natural numbers very early in elementary school. This was a fixed standard that the mathe-matics educators involved in the reform had to take into account, even though they were aware that research has shown that direct exposure to these algorithms can lead to serious conceptual errors related to the order of magnitude and the decimal representations of numbers. Postponing the teaching of digit-based algorithms like in the Netherlands was not possible. In Puerto Rico, if these algorithms are not present in the arithmetic lessons for the second grade, teachers and the official educational system will not accept such lessons as adequate for teaching. Therefore, the Puerto Rican team followed the standards, but presented the algorithms in such a way in the materials that their teaching was made more meaningful, which indeed significantly improved the students' understanding of them as was revealed in follow-up research. Another adaptation stemmed from the teachers' wish for didactical material full of interesting and concise contexts, but avoiding general and open-ended tasks. Since findings from previous pilot testing showed that MiC material requires students to do extensive reading, tasks which had much text had to be avoided because it kept teachers from using this material. Instead there was a need for a more piecemeal approach.

In Korea, as Lee and her colleagues (Chap. 15) reported, despite the challenges connected to RME, the teachers were rather positive about it, because they think mathematics instruction based on RME can change students' attitude to mathematics to a positive stance by providing them natural situations and activities that can encourage them to actively participate through diverse thoughts and communications. However, a strong suggestion came from the teachers to shorten the process of mathematisation and include repetitive exercises to make RME workable for the Korean educational context.

The work of Selter and Walter (Chap. 13) in Germany stressed adapting the RME principle of progressive mathematisation by including mathematics conferences. These conferences are meant to stimulate and organise exchanges amongst the students that will promote learning and by developing so-called "mathematics language tools", with the purpose to provide students with an instrument for further developing their ability to verbalise the description and justification of mathematical facts.

As described by De Bock, Van Dooren, and Verschaffel (Chap. 3), the Belgian approach to mathematics education was undoubtedly inspired by the Dutch RME model, which is, for example, reflected by the fact that the general objectives for primary school mathematics in Belgium are almost copies of those that were formulated by Treffers and colleagues in the late 1980s. Nevertheless, Belgian mathematics education is not considered to be RME. References to 'realistic' are purposely avoided and instead expressions are used such as 'meaningful situations', which indicates that other choices have been made in mathematics education. An illustration of this is that in Belgium, in contrast with the Netherlands, attention is paid first to standard arithmetical procedures, and more flexible procedures are only taught afterwards.

1.6 Criticisms of RME and Dissenting Views

Apart from all kinds of adaptations necessary to make a reform inspired by RME in accordance with a country's educational regulations and classroom culture, adaptations can also stem from dissenting views on mathematics education or from disapproval about RME. The RME ideas did not travel around the world without meeting criticism.

The main point of criticism echoed in the chapters is that RME, which strength it is to connect mathematics to the real world, is attaching too much weight to horizontal mathematisation. Concerns about this are expressed seriously by Wittmann (Chap. 4). Of course, he can understand that Freudenthal and his IOWO colleagues in the early days of RME wanted to establish a distinct counterpart to New Math and therefore put a lot of emphasis on applications, but he is more in favour of a balanced approach. Therefore, he welcomed that under the flag of RME recently publications have appeared again, such as from Kindt and De Moor, that are extremely interesting in terms of the mathematical structures they address.

For the Belgian mathematics educators in Flanders, RME could also have been more in balance. This is in line with how they view their own approach to mathematics education. As De Bock, Deprez, and Janssens (Chap. 11) explain, Flemish mathematics education in secondary education is so balanced because it resulted from multiple influences. It contains elements of the more traditional approach, which focuses on calculation drill and algebraic techniques, as well as of more structural elements, which focuses on a logical organisation of content and on proof and argumentation, and elements from RME, which undoubtedly enriched Flemish mathematics education, but which never led to the implementation of an orthodox version of the RME model.

With respect to Belgium primary school mathematics, De Bock, Van Dooren, and Verschaffel (Chap. 3) report even more explicit in criticising regarding particular features of RME; or more precisely expressed: features of which it is assumed they belong to RME. RME is criticised for disregarding the mechanistic aspects of learning, the lack of guidance of the construction of knowledge, the excessive freedom that is given to students to construct their own solution methods, the limited attention for the process of de-contextualising, and finally the insufficient recognition of the value of mathematics as a cultural product. Indeed, for some of these issues, such as neglecting the mechanistic aspects of learning and not viewing mathematics as a cultural product, RME can be criticised for not considering them as spearheads principles of RME. However, for other issues this is certainly not the case. The assumed lack of guidance is the opposite of what RME stands for. The excessive freedom that is supposedly given to students to construct their own solution methods is a wrong interpretation of the RME aim to break with the mechanistic approach of solving particular types of problems always in the same manner, but instead stimulate students to choose a solution strategy that suits the problem the students have to solve.

Having said this, it is unmistakably true that RME is often viewed in the wrong way and that these prejudices are often expressed, and often not in such a professional way as is done in the chapters of this volume. Of course, on the one hand a first reaction may be to rectify these misunderstandings, but on the other hand they also offer RME a mirror to look at itself and see which pitfalls there are when promoting RME and its guiding principles. Thus, even when these statements about RME are not fully true, RME should take them into account. What is true in any case is that Flanders outperforms the Netherlands in international comparisons—whatever value one attaches to these.

The critical remarks of the German mathematics educators Selter and Walter (Chap. 13) correspond to those by Wittmann. Their critique is about the limited interpretation of what is meant by context. According to them pure numerical contexts can also be quite meaningful for students. Moreover, numbers can also be realistic. Here again a statement is voiced as critique while it corroborates completely with the RME point of view. RME did always work with a broad conception of context. Yet later in the chapter of Selter and Walter, their critical remark becomes more distinct when it turns out that their main message is that, although they found in several RME publications that attention is paid to vertical mathematisation and that mathematics is regarded as a context of its own, they think that RME could possibly highlight these aspects more strongly.

Interesting in this respect is that while the message from the mathematics educators in Germany and Belgium is that RME should move more towards mathematics as a context of its own and vertical mathematisation, for Arcavi (Chap. 6) in Israel, RME was a kind of wake-up call to move in the other direction: from highly procedural and rule-oriented mathematics to using the real world as a springboard for mathematisation. RME gave him a broader view in the other direction.

For Niss (Chap. 17), discussing the Danish perspective, the point seems not to be the direction—moving more to this side or to that side of the spectrum. His point is the difference in emphasis in the meaning of 'realistic' in Denmark and in the Netherlands. In the RME interpretation, 'real' and 'realistic' incline to refer to students' experiential or emotional worlds and not necessarily to reality in the external world. In RME, fantasy stories or games are considered real and realistic if they are so to the students. This is in contrast with the Danish position which tends to emphasise the external objective reality of the surroundings in which students live such as family, friends, school, the local, national or global community, and scholarly and scientific fields or areas of practice. In RME, 'realistic' includes both problems based on real world situations and problems that students can experience as real. The latter relates to 'realistic' in the meaning of 'realising'; making a situation 'real' for oneself. Maybe within RME, this second meaning is too much emphasised in order to escape from the paralysing extreme requirement of authenticity that is often attributed to RME, and to make room for problems with powerful contexts that can become a model for developing mathematical concepts. Perhaps RME's focus is too much on contexts that lend themselves particularly well for evolving into a model that can be used for solving other problems or for eliciting helpful strategies, instead of on really complex daily life situations that require modelling and where mathematics has to be used to solve them. This different approach to 'realistic' is also reflected in the Danish view on the RME concept of horizontal and vertical mathematisation. According to Niss, the distinction between these two ways of mathematisation never got a foot in the door in Danish mathematics education, because in Denmark modelling involving the extra-mathematical domain, and internal mathematical transformations and processes are considered as very different. In the words of Niss, RME means "modelling for the sake of mathematics (learning)" while "[t]he Danish position tends to put emphasis on the reverse goal, namely mathematics (learning) for the sake of modelling." Although these differences, as Niss acknowledged, are not fundamental, but lie rather in priorities and emphases, it might be fruitful for RME to explore its further development more in this latter direction. Actually, the point to take away from Niss' chapter is again that there should be more balance in RME.

1.7 RME Flavours in Foreign Curricula, Textbooks, Instructional Materials, and Teaching Methods

Despite the fact that there is criticism and that at some points other choices are made, in many of the countries that made acquaintance with RME, ideas, principles and designs that have been developed in the Netherlands can be recognised in the countries' curricula, textbooks, instructional materials, and teaching methods.

The conclusion of Lee and colleagues (Chap. 15) is that in Korea, RME has become one of the major perspectives on mathematics education which has been widely discussed and applied by mathematics educators and mathematics teachers to reform Korean mathematics education over the past 35 years. The careful studies of the RME theory and the MiC textbook series that have been carried out in Korea have exercised a concrete influence on the mathematics curriculum and the textbook development since 2000, both implicitly and explicitly. In particular progressive mathematisation is considered as a potential perspective that would improve and complement Korean mathematics education. Therefore, the changes in the 2015 Mathematics Curriculum intended, for example, to implement the approach of progressive mathematisation for the concept of function.

Although in Argentina, as explained by Zolkower and her colleagues (Chap. 9), the design activities of the Patagonian Group of Mathematics Didactics (GPDM) did not use the RME-based materials of the textbook series MiC and the RME-based project Mathematics in the City as ready-made recipes, many RME designs such as the bus context, the percentage bar and the double number line appeared in Argentinean materials. Also, the described way of teaching is quite in line with RME, reflecting the approach of progressive mathematising, the use of tools and contexts to support this mathematisation process, the idea of guided reinvention, dealing with heterogeneous classrooms, the relevance of reflection, and making room for students' productions and constructions and using them in their teaching. As a result of the many seminars and teaching experiments throughout Argentina and the invitations many GPDM members got to lead teacher-training seminars, offer thematic workshops, present at research conferences, and elaborate or evaluate curriculum documents and instructional materials, the GPDM has become an important referent on RME within Spanish speaking South America and in this way exerts its influence on mathematics education.

Following the report of Selter and Walter (Chap. 13), nowadays mathematisation is seen in Germany also as a guiding principle within the didactics of mathematics for primary school. Moreover, similarities with RME can be recognised in the basic keystones formulated for mathematics education as well. In particular they can be found in considering learning as a (re)constructive activity facilitated by reflection on one's own thought processes and those of others, in viewing teaching as guiding students from their informal, context-bound methods to formal mathematics, and in offering students opportunities for communication and cooperation in small group work or whole-class discussion. However, Scherer's (Chap. 8) concern is that this approach to teaching mathematics does not apply to the German practice of teaching special needs students. Inspired by RME, she thinks that low achievers in mathematics should be offered opportunities to show what they are able to do. Through her studies she collects evidence that low achievers can also benefit from an open approach and are able to choose their own strategies, make use of structures and relations, find patterns and show creative and effective work.

Regarding their experiences in England, Dickinson and his colleagues (Chap. 19) report that although they cannot claim that RME has been implemented fully in schools, they are quite sure that it is the case for many of its principles. The mathematics departments with which they have worked are now far more likely to use models such as the ratio table and the empty number line, and to use contexts throughout a topic, for example, to use the context of a sandwich for teaching fractions, which eventually becomes a model for the formal comparison of fractions. Also, teachers are more apt to invoke visualisations and imagery in their lessons. In addition, there seems to be a slight move in schools to delay the journey to more formal mathematics, and embracing progressive formalisation.

Belgium, which has its own balanced approach to mathematics education resulting from multiple influences, also has elements of RME. An example given by De Bock and colleagues (Chap. 11) for secondary school is related to the teaching of derivates which was inspired by the Dutch HEWET materials in which the derivative was distilled from different real-world contexts in which (rate of) change had to be measured. In addition also a number of RME-inspired didactical innovations have ended up in the Belgian secondary school programme. Of these, perhaps the most important one is the role given to modelling and applications. Furthermore, more attention is given to (guided) self-discovery and active learning processes in the teaching and learning of mathematics; instead of only confronting students with 'end products' of mathematical activity. As discussed earlier, in the Flemish post-New-Math curricula and standards for the primary level (Chap. 3) much can also be recognised from the Dutch RME model, but at the same time valuable elements of the strong Belgian tradition in developing calculation skills and some New Math accents can be found.

According to Ponte and Brocardo (Chap. 12), in Portugal, RME has clearly influenced the mathematics curriculum for elementary school, notably in the topic of numbers and operations. For example, like in RME, much importance is attached to delaying the introduction of the standard algorithms and progressively developing more high-level abbreviated strategies and coming to generalisation and formalisation. Further, the influence of RME is also reflected in using the context of tasks as a starting point and source for modelling, the use of representations and models such as the empty number line, and the emphasis on the flexible use of mental calculation strategies. Here, similar to the RME teaching-learning trajectory for calculating with whole number, stringing strategies (with movements along the counting row), splitting strategies (processing the numbers based on the ten's structure) and varying strategies (based on arithmetic properties) are taught. Research groups in Portugal also make frequent references to key ideas of RME and use the method of didactical phenomenology to explore in depth a mathematical topic with great attention to everyday situations in which such a topic can be traced.

In the United States, Webb and Peck (Chap. 2) estimated the influence of RME on mathematics education as significant. The use of context and models has affected state and national curricula, including the recent *Common core standards for school mathematics*. Models such as the empty number line, percentage bar and ratio table are now common elements in instructional materials and assessments. Moreover, teachers continue to incorporate RME instructional principles into their classrooms and strive to find meaningful ways to engage students in the human activity of mathematising. However, the design principles that give the models such power—didactical phenomenology, emergent modelling and progressive formalisation, and guided reinvention—are often unknown to teachers and thus are incorporated only sparingly.

RME left its fingerprints in China as well. As explained by Sun and He (Chap. 10), from the 2001 Curriculum Standards document it is evident that the design of the standards was influenced by RME, because many keywords and expressions which echo the basic characteristics of RME had never appeared in similar official documents before 2001. Moreover, after this curriculum reform, the basic structure in most textbooks series used in primary and secondary mathematics started with a context problem, followed by a series of questions to lead students to what they are supposed to learn. This way of structuring textbooks was to a great extent inspired by RME. In addition, there was also a change in content. For example, geometry in traditional primary school textbooks involves measurement, including the definition of area and volume with the main focus on calculation, while after the reform in line with the RME approach the important concept of space was also included in mathematics textbooks.

For Denmark, according to Niss (Chap. 17) it is clear that RME in its broadest sense has had an impact on Danish mathematics education, but there are, as discussed earlier, also differences with respect to the meaning of 'realistic' and the role of mathematical modelling. What was, however, in any case an inspiration for several Danish mathematics educators was the method of design research as integrating research and development.

1.8   A Reflection to Conclude

My aim with this chapter was to bring together visions on RME and experiences with it from outside the Dutch circle of RME as they are laid down in the remaining eighteen chapters of this volume covering fifteen countries. Of course, this is not a random sample of countries. The chapters have been written by people who are supporters of RME or who have at least an interest in RME, but despite this the authors did not really display a prejudice towards RME in the sense that they were expressing that RME is the one and only way of teaching mathematics. They did not hold back when airing criticism, and did not mince their words when writing about what they think of RME. The merits of RME were recognised very well, but so were blind spots and unbalanced aspects.

Reviewing all that RME has set in motion it is hard to avoid the conclusion that, since its conception at the end of the 1960s, RME has gained a designated place in the theories of teaching and learning of mathematics. A significant moment of its recognition, as reported by Webb and Peck (Chap. 2), came in 1999 when the RME-based textbook series *Mathematics in Contexts* was described in the seminal book *How People Learn* as an example of a new approach to teaching mathematics that supports learning with understanding. Furthermore, the dispersion to so many and diverse countries worldwide, including countries in western, eastern, northern and southern regions, as well as the different socio-cultural contexts and educational systems which were receptive to RME ideas, can be considered as an illustration of both its robustness and its flexibility. The way mathematics educators in other countries see RME, how they made and make it work, how they talk about it, has let RME rise above a particular personal preference of teaching mathematics. RME has become a multifaceted approach to mathematics education with a joint ownership of many.

This engagement from abroad is very essential to keep RME a living theory. Visions and experiences of others can open our eyes to possible improvement. In this way the following chapters can also provide an impetus for sharpening and revising particular aspects of RME. For example, inspired by Arcavi (Chap. 6) we might elaborate more on the connections between the conceptual and the procedural, and on linking the different representations of mathematical entities. Furthermore, the experiences in England described by Dickinson and his colleagues (Chap. 19) give grounds for reconsidering the RME focus on slow learning and investigating whether there is also room for having quicker routes to formalisation without playing down the fundamental principle of progressive schematisation or mathematisation, as is also suggested by Puerto Rico (Chap. 16) and Korea (Chap. 15).

Creating more space for formal mathematics was a message that could be heard regularly. For Wittmann (Chap. 4) this touches the fundaments of the basis that Freudenthal and his IOWO colleagues have laid for RME. In his eyes, more attention should be paid to vertical mathematisation and to mathematical structures and thinking. A preference for a more balanced approach to mathematics education is, for example, also the sound that is heard from Belgium as expressed by De Bock and colleagues (Chaps. 3 and 11).

A further point that Dickinson and his colleagues (Chap. 19) brought to the fore, which is interesting for further exploration, is that a more formal, abstract level of understanding cannot only be reached by taking away the context, but also by adding more contexts. The latter would allow students to see the 'sameness' of different situations and this might also provide a route to abstraction. Although stemming from a different point of departure, namely his critique on the limited meaning of 'realistic' in RME, Niss (Chap. 17) pointed in a way to the same argument of bringing in more context. According to him, RME tends to insufficiently emphasise the external objective reality of students' surroundings, and the modelling of reality in RME is especially meant for the purpose of the learning of mathematics. This contrasts with the approach in Denmark where the focus is rather on the reverse, namely on learning mathematics to model a problem situation and solve it. Again, this is a suggestion to RME not to concentrate merely on ingenious contexts that can evolve into models intended to serve as a didactical aid for learning mathematics. In fact, this (once more) means bringing more balance between the context as a source and the context as a domain of application.

A last issue that struck me was that of all the characteristics of RME, there was one that was mentioned only sparsely as being relevant when a country was inspired by RME. This is the idea of didactical phenomenology or mathe-didactical analysis as a foundation for developing and researching mathematics education. Webb and Peck (Chap. 2) also noticed in their chapter that while certain RME models are widely used by teachers in the United States, most of them are not familiar with, for example, the idea of didactical phenomenology. Based on what is written in the chapters, this RME idea is not used as widely. Yet there are three prominent exceptions. The first one is Wittmann (Chap. 4) for whom the didactical analysis of the subject matter is the most important source for designing learning environments and curricula. Therefore, he thinks that Freudenthal's book *Didactical Phenomenology of Mathematical Structures* is of overriding importance. The second exception is the use of RME in Portugal. In the chapter of Ponte and Brocardo (Chap. 12) it is clearly shown that didactical phenomenology is considered an important RME idea that is present in several of their research studies. Using this idea means that a given mathematical topic is explored in depth, with great attention to everyday situations in which it can be traced. The third exception was found in Korea. As reported by Lee and colleagues (Chap. 15), in Korea, from the introduction to RME on, the perspective of Freudenthal's didactical phenomenology was taken on board and didactical phenomenological analyses were carried out on mathematical concepts which, among other things, influenced the adoption of progressive mathematisation.

Finally, a warning and an expression of hope. Although all chapters in this volume show RME as a vivid and promising theory with a lot of potential, there are also some concerns about its further development. Wittmann (Chap. 4) is worried about loosening the engagement in mathematics and Niss (Chap. 17) is wondering whether the changes of the Freudenthal Institute, including the split in organisational structure, will undermine the contributions of the Dutch to the further development of mathematics education. These concerns should be a wake-up call to all who wish to make more of the potential of RME. Now that the RME fire is kindled in so many countries, fuelled by the common goal of making mathematics accessible, meaningful, and relevant for all students, I hope that we can keep the essential flame alive and elaborate on it.

Chapter 2
From Tinkering to Practice—The Role of Teachers in the Application of Realistic Mathematics Education Principles in the United States

David C. Webb and Frederick A. Peck

Abstract The history of Realistic Mathematics Education (RME) in the United States has positioned teachers at the centre of innovation from its early years to present day. From the first proof-of-concept study at a high school in Milwaukee to localised professional development opportunities, the application and spread of RME is best characterised as a teacher-centred approach to principled reconsideration of how students learn mathematics. Such reconsideration of beliefs and conceptions is often motivated when teachers re-experience mathematics through the lens of progressive formalisation and related didactic approaches. Through a series of cases that articulate teacher interpretation and application of RME in U.S. classrooms, we highlight how teacher participation has led to greater exploration of student-centred practices. These efforts, while inspired and supported by professional development and curricula, have been inspired and sustained by teachers who provide colleagues a proof-of-concept in local contexts.

Keywords Design principles · Teacher beliefs · Professional development · Mathematics instruction · Progressive formalisation

2.1 Introduction

Mathematics education in the United States is not typically perceived as a field that has demonstrated significant innovation in teaching. Many who experienced mathematics as students speak of the predictability in how it was presented, the boredom, and the limited relevance. "When are we ever going to use this?" is an all-too-common refrain shared by students to their teachers. With great consistency

D. C. Webb (✉)
University of Colorado Boulder, Boulder, USA
e-mail: dcwebb@colorado.edu

F. A. Peck
University of Montana, Missoula, USA
e-mail: frederick.peck@umontana.edu

© The Author(s) 2020
M. van den Heuvel-Panhuizen (ed.), *International Reflections
on the Netherlands Didactics of Mathematics*, ICME-13 Monographs,
https://doi.org/10.1007/978-3-030-20223-1_2

students' mathematical experience is one that has been described as hard and boring, an unfortunate combination that rarely leads to future pursuits in mathematics. It is in this context that Realistic Mathematics Education (RME), and its design principles for curriculum, instruction and assessment, recast the mathematical experience as one that should be meaningful, relevant, and accessible.

In this chapter, we describe the case of how some teachers in the United States have been influenced by and have benefitted from contemporary Dutch principles of mathematics education, specifically RME. Our collective experience includes professional development, curriculum development, educational research, and the role of the teacher. Even though there are many others who could articulate similar cases about their experience with RME, our stance is focused primarily on the characteristic teacher-centred approach that we have observed and experienced over the past twenty years through which RME was piloted, disseminated, and integrated into various mathematics resources in the United States.

2.1.1   The Role of Teachers in Advancing RME in the United States

There are several challenges against advancing mathematics teaching beyond the prevailing transmission model of instruction towards more student-centred approaches that are called for in RME. The challenges that are relevant to this chapter include the apprenticeship of observation, the inherent complexity of ambitious teaching, and the system nature of teaching. While these three constructs are not specific to mathematics education nor education in the United States, these aspects of schooling all involve teachers and the ways in which their classroom practices are envisioned and enacted.

In a classic study of teaching in K–12 schools, Lortie (1975) proposed the hypothesis that teachers emulate practices that they experienced as students. During this 'apprenticeship of observation', which Lortie (1975) estimated at 13,000 hours of observed practice, the role of the teacher and the norms and routines of the classroom are interpreted by future teachers and later imitated. Such recollection of teacher practice, modelled repeatedly, serves as a basis for recreating the surface features of classrooms that the novice teacher has come to value as productive. Continuing the argument, if one's experiences as a student supported his or her success with mathematics (successful enough to pursue a career path into teaching), then those same practices should benefit future generations of students. Historically, with respect to K–12 mathematics teaching, this often led to a mathematics that was predominantly procedural, mechanistic, and predictable. From a case study of secondary schools, a typical day in a mathematics classroom was described as follows.

> First, answers were given for the previous day's assignment. The more difficult problems were worked by the teacher or a student at the chalkboard. A brief explanation, sometimes none at all, was given of the new material, and problems were assigned for the next day. The remainder of the class was devoted to working on the homework while the teacher moved

about the room answering questions. The most noticeable thing about math classes was the repetition of this routine. (Welsh, 1978, p. 391)

What is remarkable is that even though this case study was published almost 40 years ago, the persistence of this routine of review, lesson and practice can be found when observing U.S. mathematics classrooms today despite major policy initiatives and significant resources invested in curricula and professional development. The apprenticeship of observation hypotheses provides one possible (if controversial; see Mewborn & Tyminski, 2006) reason for this.

From an RME perspective, the prevailing routine of school mathematics reflects what Hans Freudenthal (1983) critiqued as the 'anti-didactical inversion' of teaching the results of mathematical activity, rather than engaging students in the activity itself. Why should problem solving in realistic contexts be presented as an afterthought, deferred until the end of skill and concept development as applications when, historically, authentic problem solving was a motivation for developing new mathematics? From this, the central tenet of RME was born: Mathematics should be thought of, first and foremost, as the human activity of mathematising the world.

Supporting student engagement in authentic problem solving requires new models of teaching. One such model is ambitious teaching (Lampert & Graziani, 2009), which "requires that teachers teach in response to what students do as they engage in problem solving performances, all while holding students accountable to learning goals that include procedural fluency, strategic competence, adaptive reasoning, and productive dispositions" (Kazemi, Franke, & Lampert, 2009, p. 11). Ambitious teaching is improvisational, student-centred, and focussed on the development of the full range of learning goals for mathematical reasoning. This resonates with another tenet of RME, in that mathematising the world requires authentic problem solving for students and student-centred instruction by teachers. Ambitious teaching is complex and requires nothing less than a complete overhaul of the prevailing routine in school mathematics.

Changing this routine is challenged by the system nature of teaching (Hiebert & Grouws, 2007). Teachers' decisions and actions are influenced by a milieu of personal and contextual factors that include teachers' prior experiences (including the apprenticeship of observation), teachers' beliefs about mathematics and about teaching and learning, local curricular policies, available resources, the expectations of the community, and other factors. The opportunity for innovation lies at the nexus of these teacher and context variables. Thus, policies and administrative directives, on their own, are ineffective approaches to motivate changes in practice. Similarly, professional development and other opportunities for teacher learning, on their own, are also insufficient. Sustained innovation in teaching requires systemic changes that align policies, resources, and activities towards common goals.

In the case of RME, the vision for teaching and learning mathematics that was articulated by Hans Freudenthal found political support in the United States in 1989, when the National Council for Teachers of Mathematics (NCTM) published *Curriculum and Evaluation Standards for School Mathematics* (NCTM, 1989), and related state and national policies were disseminated throughout the United States. The vision found further support in curricular resources that were developed using RME for use in the United States (described in greater detail below). Finally, through activities that integrated professional development, classroom practice, and academic research, teachers played a central role in the dissemination and integration of RME in the United States.

2.1.2   Attractive Features of RME to U.S. Teachers

From years of observing the use and application of RME at all levels of mathematics, and participating in its implementation, we have developed several hypotheses regarding its uptake by teachers in their classrooms.

First, with respect to curriculum, RME offers a different approach to engage students in new mathematics content. RME's unique context-first approach frequently places students' mathematical engagement on a somewhat level playing field for students from a wide variety of experiences. The use of problem contexts to learn new mathematics provides meaningful anchors for student discussions and mathematical activity. Even though this design principle contradicts many U.S. teachers' prior experiences with mathematics when they were students, the accessibility of mathematical principles when they are situated within carefully selected contexts invites more students to participate and contribute to the mathematical discourse. Mathematically engaged students are a powerful motivator for teachers.

In addition, teachers are attracted to the wide variety of 'pre-formal' models and tools—such as double number lines, percentage bars, and combination charts to support simultaneous calculations with two variables—that are explained as ways to promote progressive formalisation from an RME perspective. In the classroom, these models emerge from realistic activity and are made general though subsequent activity. As such, they serve as powerful resources for students to do mathematics and they invite students to make sense of mathematics (Peck & Matassa, 2016; Webb, Boswinkel, & Dekker, 2008). To teachers, these pre-formal models and tools often demonstrate ways in which curricular design can support improved student learning. In professional development, when these models and tools are first used with teachers, we often hear excitement, followed by puzzlement about why this was the first time they were seeing such powerful didactical devices (Webb, 2017).

Finally, RME has been attractive to teachers in the United States due to its robust approach to assessment. Most would recognise that mathematising involves more than working with procedures and algorithms with precision. Mathematising includes several characteristic features that involve modelling, problem solving, inductive and deductive reasoning, developing logical arguments from a set of assumptions, and so forth. To support teachers in achieving these broader goals, RME offers a comprehensive assessment framework (Dekker, 2007; Verhage & De Lange, 1997). This framework, usually illustrated as an assessment pyramid with three dimensions, has been used by teachers to support students' mathematical reasoning in their classrooms.

2.2 Introduction of RME in the United States: Late 1980s—Mid 1990s

During the 1980s, RME was being articulated in primary and secondary school reforms in the Netherlands. During the latter half of that decade, Thomas A. Romberg, a professor from the University of Wisconsin who was deeply interested in curriculum and policy in mathematics education, was chairing a committee that was putting the final touches on *Curriculum and Evaluation Standards for School Mathematics* (NCTM, 1989). In the spring of 1988 Jan de Lange, the director of the Freudenthal Institute was invited to meet Romberg at the National Center for Research in Mathematical Sciences Education (NCRMSE) at the University of Wisconsin-Madison. It was a beneficial development that these two mathematics educators with a passion for reforming mathematics teaching and learning, on opposite sides of the Atlantic, would become colleagues and partners. One might observe that such international partnerships are somewhat rare in mathematics education, with few publications co-authored by colleagues from different countries.

The aforementioned NCTM standards articulated a student-centred model of mathematics education oriented around problem solving. In recounting the story as told by Romberg, it was understood that the release of the 'Standards' would be followed soon after with significant support from the National Science Foundation (NSF) for the development of instructional materials, professional development, and multiple systemic initiatives to support the vision for school mathematics. It is worth noting that decades before, Romberg was a graduate student at Stanford working with Ed Begle and the School Mathematics Study Group in documenting how the post-Sputnik New Math materials impacted teaching and learning (an effort, much of which, was also funded by the NSF). So Romberg was no stranger to the need for exemplar instructional materials that could support teacher practice and student learning at scale. In Romberg's (1997, p. 139) opinion, one of the exemplar cases might be found in the work of the Freudenthal Institute, based on the "international reputation arising from the work of Hans Freudenthal and his colleagues…and the fact that the performance of Dutch students ranked very high on all international comparative studies." This observation led to the first pilot study of RME in the United States—the Whitnall Study.

2.2.1 The Whitnall Study

As an outcome of a meeting of various scholars and curriculum developers hosted by Romberg, De Lange proposed a pilot study of RME in a U.S. school. The content focus would be statistics. The school would be Whitnall High School, located in a suburb of Milwaukee. Six teachers and their classrooms would be involved in the study, including Gail and Jack Burrill. Jan de Lange rallied several Freudenthal Institute faculty who moved to the Milwaukee area for four weeks, to work closely with the Whitnall High School mathematics department and develop instructional materials based on observed classroom activities from the previous day.

Even though a blueprint for the instructional unit was well-established, regular adaptations were made to the daily activities exemplifying the student-centredness of the approach. As Jack Burrill described the process: "Sometimes we would get copies of that day's lesson the night before. Sometimes the same morning!" (personal communication). Much of the Whitnall Study has been recounted elsewhere (Van Reeuwijk, 1992; De Lange, Burrill, Romberg, & Van Reeuwijk, 1993). The more important point to make here is that the initial entrée of RME into the United States was through dedicated teachers who were willing to face the unknown, take risks in front of their students and colleagues, and perhaps be humbled in the process. Both Jack and Gail Burrill had vivid recollections of the experience—in fact, one might say the experience was transformative. Gail Burrill recounted her experience in this way:

> [T]here was still no real anticipation of the radical changes we would be called on to make in our classrooms. We knew about the NCTM 'Curriculum and evaluation standards for school mathematics'. We were prepared for something new but not so different. As we worked throughout the project, however, the 'Standards' came to life. We began to recognize that we not only needed new ways of teaching but a new way of thinking about the mathematics we should teach. (De Lange, Burrill, Romberg, & Van Reeuwijk, 1993, p. 154)

One of the main challenges for the teachers was in shifting from a teacher-centred to a student-centred classroom. The materials were designed to support student inquiry; they were not designed for a teacher to show the students how to do the problems. This transition to 'letting the students do the mathematics' was not easy, as well-established instructional routines by experienced teachers were found to be difficult habits to break. Eventually, the Whitnall teachers began to internalise the approach used by RME and even began to self-correct their practice. As Jack Burrill recalled, later in the study when he finished teaching a lesson he would meet with the Freudenthal group in the back of the class, and before anything else was said, he would ask, "I blew it again, didn't I?" after recognising that he was doing the mathematics for the students, rather than the having the students to the work.

From a researcher/curriculum developer point-of-view, the experience must have been equally exhilarating. Martin van Reeuwijk was one of the Freudenthal researchers who co-designed materials to be used by the Whitnall teachers. As Van Reeuwijk (1992, p. 516) wrote later in an article summarising the experience:

> After the first week of the project, problems with the new mathematics decreased drastically. Students were interested in the class and commented that they liked mathematics now more than before, that it was not so boring, and that they had discovered that mathematics can be used in real-life situations. When questions arose about homework, they came after school to discuss them. Even the low-level and least motivated students got involved in the data-visualisation unit and liked it.

The shift in student engagement and participation observed by Van Reeuwijk did not go unnoticed by the teachers. The students' response to the RME experiment motivated the teachers to emphasise practices that supported student inquiry and problem solving. One of the key findings from the Whitnall Study was the importance of teacher professional development and support if RME was going to be implemented at scale in the United States. But this is not a challenge unique to the United States. As described further by Van Reeuwijk (1992, p. 517), "[t]he difficulties that students and teachers had in reaction to a new approach to mathematics were the same as those experienced in the Netherlands when the mathematics curriculum was changed." The difference between the Netherlands and the United States is a student population of over 40 million students.

2.2.2 Going to Scale with Mathematics in Context

The Whitnall Study provided a proof-of-concept that RME could work in U.S. classrooms so much so that it motivated Romberg and De Lange to apply for a curriculum development grant at a much larger scale. In the autumn of 1991 the NSF funded the project Mathematics in Context: A Connected Curriculum for Grades 5–8 (MiC), one of thirteen mathematics instructional material development projects funded by NSF in the early 1990s. This project involved a five-year collaboration between research and development teams at the Freudenthal Institute and the University of Wisconsin and scores of elementary and middle school teachers. Focussed on middle grades mathematics, forty units were developed for Grades 5 through 8, which reflected the middle grade band described in the NCTM Standards. Freudenthal researchers were responsible for initial drafts of the units and then these drafts were modified by University of Wisconsin faculty, staff and doctoral students before they were piloted in U.S. schools by teachers and students. To support this work, several Freudenthal researchers moved to Madison, Wisconsin, to work directly with the University of Wisconsin team, and local teachers, as early drafts of the materials were piloted. Given that this project launched before the advent of public email or broadband internet, most communication occurred either in person in Madison, or using trans-Atlantic mail and conference calls.

As the MiC units moved from piloting to field testing, there was a need to recruit many participating teachers across the United States who worked in a diverse set of school contexts. In addition to a significant number of teachers across Wisconsin, field testing of MiC included teachers in California, Florida, Iowa, Massachusetts, Missouri, Puerto Rico, Tennessee and Virginia. Local site coordinators were also recruited to support ongoing communication between research team and teachers, and coordinate classroom level data collection that could be used to inform subsequent revisions of the student books and teacher guides. Encyclopaedia Britannica agreed to publish the materials, and also supported efforts to market the materials even before they were available in their final printed form. Teachers' response to the field testing of MiC was generally positive; however, the challenges observed in the Whitnall Study suggesting a need to support teachers as they transitioned to student-centred practices were magnified further since there were not as many project personnel who worked locally with teachers on a regular basis. Nevertheless, teachers provided copious input from the field, leading to improvements to the student activities and teacher support materials. As the MiC units moved from field testing to the publication of the textbook series *Mathematics in Context* (National Center for Research in Mathematical Sciences Education & Freudenthal Institute, 1997–1998), many of the teachers in the original field test sites decided to adopt MiC after they observed its impact on student engagement and achievement (e.g., Webb et al., 2001; Webb & Meyer, 2002).

Recognition of the need for teacher support led to a commitment on the part of Encyclopaedia Britannica to provide professional development to schools that adopted MiC, which also required the recruitment of lead teachers (many of who piloted and field tested MiC) to facilitate workshops across the United States. It was through this rapidly expanding professional development network that early adopters of MiC were put in the position of communicating RME principles to their colleagues, school administrators, parents and a multitude of teachers who attended MiC workshops. To frame the goals and purpose of MiC, RME was explicitly discussed in these workshops with ample reference to Hans Freudenthal and the historical work of the Freudenthal Institute. Teachers and the co-designers of MiC communicated what RME was, and how it related to the vision of the NCTM Standards. MiC became a U.S. exemplification of RME that demonstrated how formal mathematics could emerge from students' activity in realistic contexts. The careful development of concepts and skills in algebra, number and geometry in MiC became early instantiations of progressive formalisation, and led others to reference these examples in mathematics education research (Driscoll, 1999; Gutstein, 2003). Towards the end of the 1990s, MiC was referenced in the National Academies Press publication *How People Learn* (Bransford, Brown, & Cocking, 1999, p. 137), where it was described as an innovative approach "to the development of curricula that support learning with understanding and encourage sense making". In this widely disseminated book several key principles of RME have been described in lay terms:

> The idea of progressive formalization is exemplified by the algebra strand for middle school students using *Mathematics in Context* (National Center for Research in Mathematical Sciences Education & Freudenthal Institute, 1997–1998). It begins by having students use their own words, pictures, or diagrams to describe mathematical situations to organize their own knowledge and work and to explain their strategies. In later units, students gradually begin to use symbols to describe situations, organize their mathematical work, or express their strategies. At this level, students devise their own symbols or learn some nonconventional notation. Their representations of problem situations and explanations of their work are a mixture of words and symbols. Later, students learn and use standard conventional algebraic notation for writing expressions and equations, for manipulating algebraic expressions and solving equations, and for graphing equations. Movement along this continuum is not necessarily smooth, nor all in one direction. (Bransford et al., 1999, p. 137)

With respect to contributions to mathematics education research, this period also saw the publication of RME related studies in practitioner journals and highly regarded research journals, which offered many cases of the theory and application of RME in U.S. classrooms. During this time there were also a multitude of classroom-based research studies that used RME related materials. These studies were completed as dissertations and focussed on a range of research topics such as curriculum implementation (Brinker, 1996; Clarke, 1995), teacher change (Clarke, 1997), teacher content knowledge (Hutchinson, 1996), student learning (Hung, 1995; Spence, 1997) and classroom assessment (Shafer, 1996; Van den Heuvel-Panhuizen, 1996; Webb, 2001).

2.2.3 Assessing RME

Even though MiC was published and competing for adoption in school districts across the United States, requests for additional support came in from school administrators and teachers regarding assessment. Several assessment initiatives emerged during this time, some funded by the publisher to work directly with teacher in New York City and others funded by the U.S. Department of Education, for example, the RAP (Research in Assessment Practices) project and the CATCH (Classroom Assessment as a Basis of Teacher Change) project. These projects involved a team of Freudenthal researchers, including Jan de Lange, Els Feijs, Truus Dekker, Nanda Querelle, Mieke Abels, Martin van Reeuwijk and Monica Wijers. Working together with several researchers from the University of Wisconsin, and teachers in Philadelphia, Providence (RI), and South Milwaukee, this research project studied ways to support teachers' assessment practices. These projects provided an opportunity to articulate the research domain of classroom assessment as it relates to not only RME, but other scholarly literature regarding mathematical literacy, the use of context in task design, non-routine problem solving and formative assessment. All three of the districts had adopted MiC to some extent, but the research also included teachers who were using other NSF-funded curricula or traditional textbooks. The research team worked closely with teachers as they developed their own classroom assessment experiments, which were opportunities to try new and innovative assessment practices. In many cases this involved using assessment tasks that asked for more than recall of procedures, which revealed other forms of students' mathematical reasoning that had previously been under-addressed in quizzes and tests, or classroom instruction. These classroom assessment experiments were transformative experiences for many of the participating teachers, who emerged as leaders in their district and later shared their findings with other mathematics teachers and school administrators at national conferences. Towards the end of the project, greater attention was given to the ways teachers could support student communication, problem solving, and use of representations through formative assessment.

As we entered the new millennium, mathematics education in the United States was amid a public debate over school mathematics and the way it should be taught (Schoenfeld, 2004). A significant outcome of these so-called 'Math Wars' was a call to draw together mathematics educators, research mathematicians and education psychologists to prepare a revision to the 1989 NCTM Standards. The publication *Principles and Standards for School Mathematics* (NCTM, 2000) subsequently sparked a new wave of revision of NSF-funded instructional materials, and led to a new group of lead teachers and schools being engaged in RME through their involvement in the revision of MiC.

2.2.4   Two Other Collaborations

Two other productive collaborations are worth mentioning here. The first, 'Math in the City', began as a collaboration between Cathy Fosnot from the City College of New York and Maarten Dolk and Willem Uittenbogaard from the Freudenthal Institute. The project had two goals: to learn more about student learning, and to reform both mathematics teaching and the mathematics curriculum. Teacher participation was integral in achieving both goals. The project was centred on teachers, and over 450 teachers participated in courses and summer institutes designed to allow them to re-experience mathematics as mathematising, and to focus on how children learn mathematics. As well, teachers worked with instructional coaches in their classrooms to develop, test, and tinker with instructional activities. These classroom sessions were recorded, and the videos became data that Fosnot and Dolk used to learn more about student learning. Ultimately, this led to innovative developmental progressions that inscribe student learning as movement within metaphorical 'landscapes' of mathematical strategies, big ideas, and models. The collaboration produced a book series written for teachers that shares the activities and the landscapes of learning produced over the five-year project (Fosnot & Dolk, 2001a, 2001b, 2002). The books prominently feature vignettes of teachers engaging their students in RME activities. Moreover, the collected activities that emerged from the collaboration were published as *Contexts for Learning Mathematics* (Fosnot, 2007).

The second collaboration involved Paul Cobb and colleagues in the United States, and Koeno Gravemeijer from the Freudenthal Institute. In the United States, Cobb and colleagues were researching student learning in mathematics classrooms. In looking for heuristics to guide instructional design to promote student learning, they learned about RME and began a collaboration with Gravemeijer to develop, implement, and revise RME-based instructional sequences to promote student learning. In the course of this collaboration, the research team produced instructional sequences for early number (Cobb, Gravemeijer, Yackel, McClain, & Whitenack, 1997; Gravemeijer, 1999) and statistics (Cobb, McClain, & Gravemeijer, 2003; McClain & Cobb, 2001; McClain, Cobb, & Gravemeijer, 2000). In addition, the team made two conceptual shifts in the ways that they viewed student learning in classrooms and in so doing they provided numerous contributions to research on mathematics teaching and learning (e.g., Cobb, Stephan, McClain, & Gravemeijer, 2001). Teachers played a large role in these shifts.

The first conceptual shift occurred when the research team began to view classrooms as activity systems, composed of interdependent means of support, including norms, tools, discourse, and activities. This shift was precipitated by a teacher's question, and the research team's realisation that what counted as an 'answer' was an interactional achievement and not an a priori given nor solely a product of an individual student's personal knowledge (Yackel & Cobb, 1996). In light of this, they shifted their design focus from designing for individual student learning to designing for the mathematical development of classrooms. Because of the central mediating role of teachers in classrooms, this shift entailed a new focus: "[D]evelop[ing] instructional activities that would result in a range of solutions on which the teacher could capitalise as she planned whole class discussions" (Cobb, Zhao, & Visnovska, 2008, p. 117). Hence, teachers assumed a central design role in the interactive constitution of classroom activity systems. In addition, the research team came to view a teacher's enaction of instructional sequences as a fundamentally creative activity, arguing "although designed curricula and textbooks are important instructional resources, teachers are the *designers* of the curricula that are actually enacted in their classrooms" (Visnovska, Cobb, & Dean, 2012, p. 323, emphasis in original). As they came to recognise the creative role of the teacher, the research team made a second conceptual shift: from designing instructional sequences for teachers to implement, to designing supports for teacher learning.

In light of these conceptual shifts, the research team developed three adaptations to RME design theory: (1) a shift in focus, from designing instructional activities and sequences, to designing entire activity systems—including activity sequences but also social norms and classroom discourse; (2) a shift from designing activities to achieve student learning directly, to designing activities that a teacher can use to achieve a class-wide instructional outcome; and (3) incorporating teacher professional development to support teachers' productive adaptations of designed resources (Cobb et al., 2008).

2.2.5 FIUS: Developing RME Networks in the United States

The increasing interest in ways to improve the teaching and learning of mathematics using principles of RME motivated the establishment of the Freudenthal Institute United States (FIUS) at the University of Wisconsin-Madison in 2003. During the early years of FIUS, research proposals were submitted to extend the application of RME into special education and courses typically taught in high schools and community colleges. In 2005, FIUS hosted the first 'Realistic Mathematics Education Conference', which included presentations by Dutch and U.S. researchers and educators describing past, current and emerging use of RME in K–12 curricula, professional development and assessment.

In the autumn of 2005, FIUS relocated to the University of Colorado Boulder. Over the next 10 years, RME was integrated into a number of pre-service and graduate level courses focussed on mathematics and science education, with several of these courses being jointly taught by instructors from the Freudenthal Institute and the University of Colorado Boulder.

In addition, FIUS helped to facilitate several cross-national collaborations involving personnel from the Freudenthal Institute in the Netherlands, FIUS, and U.S. teachers. These collaborations resulted in several classroom studies in middle, high, and post-secondary classrooms that were similar in approach to the Whitnall Study. In post-secondary, Monica Geist and other mathematics faculty at Front Range Community College collaborated with Henk van der Kooij to develop a unit that would deepen students' understanding of exponential and logarithmic functions. The implementation of the unit resulted in a dramatic shift in student engagement and mathematical reasoning in ways that were unexpected for a relatively brief two-week unit (Webb, Van der Kooij, & Geist, 2011). In middle school, a number of productive collaborations were realised. Peter Boon and Mieke Abels worked with middle school teachers in Denver to pilot sequences of applet-based activities organised in the Digital Mathematics Environment. One of the findings from their study was the influence of new contexts and models in the applet sequences; teacher observation of students' productive use of representations resulted in teacher uptake of the same representations during non-tech portions of the unit. A second collaboration involved David Webb from FIUS, Truus Dekker and Mieke Abels from the Freudenthal Institute, mathematics faculty at University of Colorado Boulder, and over thirty teachers in the Boulder Valley (Colorado, U.S.) School District. In this three-year collaboration, teachers designed and redesigned assessments and activity sequences according to RME design principles (Webb, 2009, 2012; Webb et al., 2008). In high school, Fred Peck participated in a series of collaborations with members of the Freudenthal Institute and FIUS as a teacher and researcher.

To give a sense of what these collaborations were like 'from the inside', and the powerful effect that they have for teachers, we now turn to a first-person account of the high school collaborations.

2.3 Guided Reinvention of High School Mathematics: Fred Peck's Personal Account

I was introduced to RME during my second year as a high school mathematics teacher, in a school in the Boulder Valley School District. David Webb had just brought FIUS to the University of Colorado. He came to our school for an afternoon, and introduced the mathematics teachers to Peter Boon and Henk van der Kooij, from the Freudenthal Institute. Peter and Henk were interested in collaborating with teachers in the United States. I was interested in reform mathematics education, including active learning and sense-making, but I had very little design experience. After some brief personal introductions, David passed out the 'Hot dogs and lemonade' task shown in Fig. 2.1, and we all got to work.

What was immediately clear to me as I worked on the problem was the principled use of context. Many of my colleagues set up a system of simultaneous linear equations. This was my first instinct, too. But rather than join my colleagues in formal algebra, I found myself drawn to the context. I combined the orders in various ways to make new combinations, eventually eliminating the hot dogs. By that time in my life, I had used Gaussian elimination to solve systems of equations hundreds of times.

During the summer, many of the residents of Annandale visit Shore Creek Park during the weekend. The park features swimming, boating, bicycling, picnicking and camping.

At Shore Creek Park there is a Hot Dog and Lemonade Stand near the beach. Clara works at the stand on weekends. She has just prepared the two orders below to be served, notice that she writes the prices on the cardboard trays.

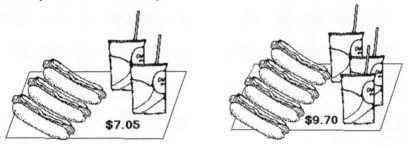

10.   How much would it cost for 1 hot dog and 1 lemonade? Explain your reasoning.

11.   How much does each hot dog cost? Each lemonade?

12.   If Kevin paid $6.20 for an order of hot dogs and lemonade, how many hot dogs and how many cups of lemonade should he receive? Show how you found this.

Fig. 2.1 'Hot dogs and lemonade' task (Webb et al., 2001, p. 5)

But I never understood why it worked. Why can one just combine rows of a matrix to make a new row (or combine two equations to make a third equation)? I knew that elimination worked, but had no idea why. And, of course, someone had to teach the method to me. Nothing about a formal matrix or formal system of equations invited exploration or sense-making.

The 'Hot dogs and lemonade' task was different. The context was not just a 'wrapper' for formal mathematics—something to peel away in order to find the system of linear equations hidden within. Of course, the problem could be interpreted that way, but the context invited mathematical exploration. It was begging to be mathematised. As I engaged in realistic activity in the context, making combinations of hot dogs and lemonade, I finally understood elimination! I was hooked. It was clear to me that RME was a powerful tool for didactical design.

The principled use of contexts—that emerged from Freudenthal's (1983) didactical phenomenology—initially drew me to RME. Soon I learned about guided reinvention and emergent modelling/progressive formalisation (e.g., Freudenthal, 1991; Gravemeijer, 1999; Webb et al., 2008), and I became even more excited about RME. Together, didactical phenomenology, emergent modelling, and guided reinvention offered a set of powerful heuristics to design activity sequences such that formal mathematics can emerge from realistic activity.

For the next six years, I endeavoured to apply these design principles to all my classes. Slowly but surely, I developed a repertoire of activity sequences. In Calculus, I developed an activity sequence involving see-saws and chains of see-saws to guide students to reinvent the chain rule for derivatives, and another involving the path of a 'vomit comet' as it climbs and free-falls to guide students to reinvent the second derivative as a point of inflection (vomit comets are airplanes that engage in a sequence of free falls followed by steep climbs, and are used to simulate zero-gravity). In Probability, I developed activity sequences involving overlapping dart boards and branching rivers to guide students to reinvent joint probability.

I also taught Algebra I with a colleague, Jen Moeller. Jen and I collaborated with David Webb, Peter Boon, and Henk van der Kooij to develop an entire curriculum for Algebra I using RME design principles. We developed a sequence for single-variable equations that guided students to reinvent balance strategies and backtracking strategies, balance models and arrow chain models, and formal expressions as objects to be manipulated and processes to be undone. We developed a sequence for quadratic functions that guided students to reinvent two powerful models for polynomials— an area model and a Cartesian model—and from there to reinvent the fundamental theorem of algebra: that 'line times line equals parabola' and more generally that polynomials are composed of linear factors. Jen and I presented these sequences at local and national conferences (Peck & Moeller, 2010, 2011).

Another colleague, Michael Matassa, joined our school as a mathematics coach, and he and I started to conduct design research in my classroom. We designed, tested, and refined two local instructional theories using RME: one for fractions as they are used in algebra (Peck & Matassa, 2016), and one for slope and linear functions (Peck, 2014). We made theoretical contributions to RME, including a deep analysis of the ways that models transform students' mathematical activity and mathematical understandings (Peck & Matassa, 2016), and a new way of thinking about emergent modelling as a 'cascade of artifacts' (Peck, 2015).

I went to graduate school and wrote my dissertation on RME. I became involved in professional development and conducted workshops for teachers on RME, including emergent modelling and how models transform students' mathematical activity and understanding. Now, I am exploring how cultural theories of learning can contribute to RME, and I am teaching pre-service teachers about RME. I just heard from some former students—now teachers—that they are working together to develop mathematics games using RME design principles.

I still use the 'Hot dogs and lemonade' task.

2.4 Summary Remarks

The influence of RME on mathematics education in the United States has been significant. Its approach to the use of context and models has influenced state and national curricula. Models that were used extensively in early RME resources—such as the empty number line, percentage bar and ratio table—were introduced to many teachers in the United States through RME related instructional materials. RME is also well represented in mathematics education research published in U.S. and international journals.

There are many other stories that could be shared that describe RME's more subtle influence in the non-public space, such as conversations among teachers, school administrators, and university faculty who are seeking ways to improve student engagement with mathematics or impart a more meaningful mathematical experience to the next generation of students. As mentioned previously, at FIUS and the University of Colorado Boulder, principles of RME have influenced undergraduate mathematics and science education and the design of instructional materials to support active learning. RME has been applied elsewhere in the United States by mathematics faculty who are interested in studying and improving student learning in abstract algebra (Larsen, Johnson, & Bartlo, 2013), differential equations (Rasmussen & Kwon, 2007), and other advanced mathematics topics.

In our opinion, what is remarkable about many of these individual stories is the involvement of teachers. From the first pilot study of RME in the United States at Whitnall High to the development of comprehensive curricula, teachers have been central to the dissemination, use, and development of RME in the United States. Teachers have collaborated with researchers to develop and improve RME sequences and curricula, they have become instructional leaders who facilitate professional development on RME, and many continue to participate in the RME community—for example, by sharing their experiences in using RME at the biennial international conference on RME.

Publications such as *Mathematics in Context* and *Contexts for Learning Mathematics* represent the most durable reifications of teachers' participation in RME in the United States. Perhaps even more important, however, are the hidden ways that teachers continue to incorporate RME instructional principles into their classrooms, striving to find meaningful ways to engage students in the human activity of mathematising.

This has been, and continues to be, challenging work. While artefacts of RME have gained wide acceptance in the United States, RME itself is not widely known. Even though *Mathematics in Context* was adopted by several major school districts in New York City, Philadelphia, and Washington DC, its presense as instructional materials has since waned. The extent to which *Contexts for Learning Mathematics* is used presently in U.S. schools is also unclear. Thus, while certain models are widely used, the design principles that give the models such power—didactical phenomenology, emergent modelling/progressive formalisation, and guided reinvention—are often unknown to teachers and thus are incorporated only sparingly. In the U.S. academy, RME remains a niche topic of research and development. Mathematics education scholarship, meanwhile, has taken a sociocultural turn, in which learning is understood as an ontological enterprise and not just an epistemic one. There is a need to continue the theoretical development of RME in light of these advances in learning theory.

As we look towards the future, we are hopeful that these challenges will be recognised as opportunities rather than barriers. As they always have, teachers will play a key role in making that vision a reality.

Acknowledgements We would like to acknowledge the many researchers and teachers who have contributed to the theory and application of RME in the United States, and the vision of Thomas A. Romberg and Jan de Lange to initiate an international partnership that has contributed to mathematics education in numerous ways.

References

Bransford, J. D., Brown, A. L., & Cocking, R. R. (1999). *How people learn: Brain, mind, experience, and school*. Washington, DC: National Academy Press.

Brinker, L. (1996). *Representations and students' rational number reasoning* (Doctoral dissertation). University of Wisconsin–Madison. Dissertation Abstracts International, 57-06, 2340.

Clarke, B. A. (1995). *Expecting the unexpected: Critical incidents in the mathematics classroom* (Doctoral dissertation). University of Wisconsin–Madison. Dissertation Abstracts International, 56-01, 125.

Clarke, D. M. (1997). The changing role of the mathematics teacher. *Journal for Research in Mathematics Education, 28*(3), 278–308.

Cobb, P., Gravemeijer, K., Yackel, E., McClain, K., & Whitenack, J. W. (1997). Mathematizing and symbolizing: The emergence of chains of signification in one first-grade classroom. In D. Kirshner & J. A. Whitson (Eds.), *Situated cognition: Social, semiotic, and psychological perspectives* (pp. 151–233). Mahwah, NJ: Lawrence Erlbaum Associates.

Cobb, P., McClain, K., & Gravemeijer, K. (2003). Learning about statistical covariation. *Cognition and Instruction, 21*(1), 1–78.

Cobb, P., Stephan, M., McClain, K., & Gravemeijer, K. (2001). Participating in classroom mathematical practices. *The Journal of the Learning Sciences, 10*(1–2), 113–163. https://doi.org/10.1207/S15327809JLS10-1-2_6.

Cobb, P., Zhao, Q., & Visnovska, J. (2008). Learning from and adapting the theory of Realistic Mathematics Education. *Éducation & Didactique, 2*(1), 105–124.

De Lange, J., Burrill, G., Romberg, T. A., & Van Reeuwijk, M. (1993). *Learning and testing mathematics in context: The case: Data visualization*. Madison, WI: National Center for Research in Mathematical Sciences Education.

Dekker, T. (2007). A model for constructing higher-level classroom assessments. *Mathematics Teacher, 101*(1), 56–61.

Driscoll, M. (1999). *Fostering algebraic thinking: A guide for teachers, grades 6–10*. Portsmouth, NH: Heinemann.

Fosnot, C. T. (2007). *Contexts for learning mathematics*. Portsmouth, NH: Heinemann. http://www.contextsforlearning.com/.

Fosnot, C. T., & Dolk, M. (2001a). *Young mathematicians at work: Constructing multiplication and division*. Portsmouth, NH: Heinemann.

Fosnot, C. T., & Dolk, M. (2001b). *Young mathematicians at work: Constructing number sense, addition, and subtraction*. Portsmouth, NH: Heinemann.

Fosnot, C. T., & Dolk, M. (2002). *Young mathematicians at work: Constructing fractions, decimals, and percents*. Portsmouth, NH: Heinemann.

Freudenthal, H. (1983). *Didactical phenomenology of mathematical structures*. Dordrecht, the Netherlands: Reidel.

Freudenthal, H. (1991). *Revisiting mathematics education: China lectures*. Dordrecht, the Netherlands: Kluwer Academic Publishers.

Gravemeijer, K. (1999). How emergent models may foster the constitution of formal mathematics. *Mathematical Thinking and Learning, 1*(2), 155–177.

Gutstein, E. (2003). Teaching and learning mathematics for social justice in an urban, Latino school. *Journal for Research in Mathematics Education, 34*(1), 37–73.

Hiebert, J., & Grouws, D. A. (2007). The effects of classroom mathematics teaching on students' learning. In F. Lester (Ed.), *Second handbook of research on mathematics teaching and learning* (pp. 371–404). Charlotte, NC: Information Age Publishing.

Hung, C. C. (1995). *Students' reasoning about functions using dependency ideas in the context of an innovative, middle school mathematics curriculum* (Doctoral dissertation). University of Wisconsin–Madison. Dissertation Abstracts International, 57-01, 87.

Hutchinson, E. J. (1996). *Preservice teacher's knowledge: A contrast of beliefs and knowledge of ratio and proportion* (Doctoral dissertation). University of Wisconsin–Madison. Retrieved from ProQuest Dissertations and Theses A&I (9611421).

Kazemi, E., Franke, M., & Lampert, M. (2009). Developing pedagogies in teacher education to support novice teachers' ability to enact ambitious instruction. In R. Hunter, B. Bicknell, & T. Burgess (Eds.), *Crossing divides: Proceedings of the 32nd Annual Conference of the Mathematics Education Research Group of Australasia* (Vol. 1, pp. 11–30). Palmerston North, NZ: MERGA.

Lampert, M., & Graziani, F. (2009). Instructional activities as a tool for teachers' and teacher educators' learning. *The Elementary School Journal, 109*(5), 491–509.

Larsen, S., Johnson, E., & Bartlo, J. (2013). Designing and scaling up an innovation in abstract algebra. *The Journal of Mathematical Behavior, 32*(4), 693–711.

Lortie, D. C. (1975). *Schoolteacher: A sociological study*. Chicago: University of Chicago Press.

McClain, K., & Cobb, P. (2001). An analysis of development of sociomathematical norms in one first-grade classroom. *Journal for Research in Mathematics Education*, 236–266.

McClain, K., Cobb, P., & Gravemeijer, K. (2000). Supporting students' ways of reasoning about data. In M. J. Burke & R. F. Curcio (Eds.), *Learning mathematics for a new century, 2000 yearbook* (pp. 174–187). Reston, VA: National Council of Teachers of Mathematics.

Mewborn, D. S., & Tyminski, A. M. (2006). Lortie's apprenticeship of observation revisited. *For the Learning of Mathematics, 26*(3), 23–32.

National Center for Research in Mathematical Sciences Education (NCRMSE) & Freudenthal Institute (1997–1998). *Mathematics in context: A connected curriculum for grades 5–8*. Chicago, IL: Encyclopaedia Britannica Educational Corporation.

National Council of Teachers of Mathematics. (1989). *Curriculum and evaluation standards for school mathematics*. Reston, VA: The Author.

National Council of Teachers of Mathematics. (2000). *Principles and standards for school mathematics*. Reston, VA: The Author.

National Governors Association Center for Best Practices & Council of Chief State School Officers. (2010). *Common core state standards for mathematics*. Washington, DC: The Author. Retrieved from http://www.corestandards.org/Math/.

Peck, F.A. (2014). *Beyond rise over run: A local instructional theory for slope*. Presented at the National Council for Teachers of Mathematics Research Conference. New Orleans, LA, April, 2014.

Peck, F.A. (2015). *Emergent modeling: From chains of signification to cascades of artifacts*. Presented at the Fifth International Realistic Mathematics Education Conference, Boulder, CO, September, 2015.

Peck, F. A., & Matassa, M. (2016). Reinventing fractions and division as they are used in algebra: The power of pre-formal productions. *Educational Studies in Mathematics, 92*, 245–278.

Peck, F.A., & Moeller, J. (2010) *From informal models to formal algebra: Using technology to facilitate progressive formalization in Algebra I*. Presented at the Regional Meeting of the National Council of Teachers of Mathematics, Denver, CO, October, 2010.

Peck, F.A., & Moeller, J. (2011). *Length times width equals area and line times line equals parabola: Incorporating two RME models into a cohesive learning trajectory for quadratic functions*. Presented at the Third International Realistic Mathematics Education Conference, Boulder, CO, September, 2011.

Rasmussen, C., & Kwon, O. N. (2007). An inquiry-oriented approach to undergraduate mathematics. *The Journal of Mathematical Behavior, 26*(3), 189–194.

Romberg, T. A. (1997). The influence of programs from other countries on the school mathematics reform curricula in the United States. *American Journal of Education, 106*(1), 127–147.

Schoenfeld, A. H. (2004). The math wars. *Educational Policy, 18*(1), 253–286.

Shafer, M. C. (1996). *Assessment of student growth in a mathematical domain over time* (Doctoral dissertation). University of Wisconsin–Madison. Dissertation Abstracts International, 57-06, 2347.

Spence, M. S. (1997). *Psychologizing algebra: Case studies of knowing in the moment* (Doctoral dissertation). University of Wisconsin–Madison. Dissertation Abstracts International, 57-12, 5091.

Van den Heuvel-Panhuizen, M. (1996). *Assessment and realistic mathematics education* (Doctoral dissertation). Utrecht University. Utrecht, the Netherlands: CD-ß Press, Center for Science and Mathematics Education.

Van Reeuwijk, M. (1992). The standards applied: Teaching data visualization. *Mathematics Teacher, 85*(7), 513–518.

Verhage, H., & De Lange, J. (1997). Mathematics education and assessment. *Pythagoras, 42,* 14–20.

Visnovska, J., Cobb, P., & Dean, C. (2012). Mathematics teacher as instructional designers: What does it take? In G. Gueudet, B. Pepin, & L. Trouche (Eds.), *From text to 'lived' resources* (pp. 323–341). Dordrecht, the Netherlands: Springer. https://doi.org/10.1007/978-94-007-1966-8.

Webb, D. C. (2001). *Instructionally embedded assessment practices of two middle grades mathematics teachers* (Doctoral dissertation). University of Wisconsin–Madison. Retrieved from ProQuest Dissertations and Theses A&I (3020735).

Webb, D. C. (2009). Designing professional development for assessment. *Educational Designer, 1*(2), 1–26. Retrieved from http://www.educationaldesigner.org/ed/volume1/issue2/article6/.

Webb, D. C. (2012). Teacher change in classroom assessment: The role of teacher content knowledge in the design and use of productive classroom assessment. In S. J. Cho (Ed.), *Proceedings of the 12th International Congress of Mathematics Education* (pp. 6773–6782). Cham, Switzerland: Springer.

Webb, D. C. (2017). The Iceberg model: Rethinking mathematics instruction from a student perspective. In L. West & M. Boston (Eds.), *Annual perspectives in mathematics education: Reflective and collaborative processes to improve mathematics teaching* (pp. 201–209). Reston, VA: NCTM.

Webb, D. C., Ford, M. J., Burrill, J., Romberg, T. A., Reif, J., & Kwako, J. (2001). *NCISLA middle school design collaborative third year student achievement technical report.* Madison, WI: University of Wisconsin, National Center for Improving Student Learning and Achievement in Mathematics and Science.

Webb, D. C., & Meyer, M. R. (2002). *Summary report of student achievement data for Mathematics in context: A connected curriculum for grades 5–8.* Madison, WI: University of Wisconsin, School of Education, Wisconsin Center for Educational Research.

Webb, D. C., Boswinkel, N., & Dekker, T. (2008). Beneath the tip of the iceberg: Using representations to support student understanding. *Mathematics Teaching in the Middle School, 14*(2), 110–113.

Webb, D. C., Van der Kooij, H., & Geist, M. R. (2011). Design research in the Netherlands: Introducing logarithms using Realistic Mathematics Education. *Journal of Mathematics Education at Teachers College, 2,* 47–52.

Welsh, W. W. (1978). Science education in Urbanville: A case study. In R. Stake & J. Easley (Eds.), *Case studies in science education* (pp. 383–420). Urbana, IL: University of Illinois. http://files.eric.ed.gov/fulltext/ED166058.pdf.

Yackel, E., & Cobb, P. (1996). Sociomathematical norms, argumentation, and autonomy in mathematics. *Journal for Research in Mathematics Education, 27*(4), 458–477.

Chapter 3
Searching for Alternatives for New Math in Belgian Primary Schools—Influence of the Dutch Model of Realistic Mathematics Education

Dirk De Bock, Wim Van Dooren and Lieven Verschaffel

Abstract We sketch the turbulent history of primary mathematics education in Belgium during the last (half) century. The outline starts with traditional mathematics in the period before and shortly after World War II, an approach that is often, but partly unjustly, labelled as 'mechanistic'. Then we focus on the rise of New Math or 'modern mathematics' in the 1970s. We briefly discuss its roots and describe how this structural approach, which basically followed the development at the secondary level, was implemented in Belgian primary schools. By the early 1980s, New Math was strongly criticised, which paved the way for its fall during the 1990s. This leads us to the current curricula that are strongly inspired by the Dutch model of Realistic Mathematics Education (RME), while maintaining valuable elements of the strong Belgian tradition in developing students' mental and written calculation skills and even some (minor) New Math accents. We describe in some detail the influence of RME on the different mathematical domains in these curricula, as well as some new challenges that arise on the horizon.

Keywords Mechanistic approach · New math · Primary level · Realistic mathematics education · Structural approach

3.1 Traditional Mathematics

The approach that dominated (primary) mathematics education before and in the first decades after World War II is often labelled as 'mechanistic' (Treffers, 1987).

D. De Bock (✉)
Faculty of Economics and Business, KU Leuven, Leuven, Belgium
e-mail: dirk.debock@kuleuven.be

W. Van Dooren · L. Verschaffel
Faculty of Psychology and Educational Sciences, KU Leuven, Leuven, Belgium
e-mail: wim.vandooren@kuleuven.be

L. Verschaffel
e-mail: lieven.verschaffel@kuleuven.be

© The Author(s) 2020
M. van den Heuvel-Panhuizen (ed.), *International Reflections on the Netherlands Didactics of Mathematics*, ICME-13 Monographs, https://doi.org/10.1007/978-3-030-20223-1_3

In a mechanistic approach, the focus of instruction is on factual and procedural knowledge (e.g., knowing how much 6×9 is, to know how to add or multiply multi-digit numbers, to know the formulas for computing the perimeter and the area of regular plane figures, etcetera). Learning is primarily seen as the acquisition of this type of factual and procedural knowledge through basic learning principles such as inculcation, memorising and repeated practice of technical computational skills, principles that were in the same period promoted and theorised by behavioural psychologists (e.g., Thorndike's law of exercise and law of effect). The instruction is heavily teacher directed, with the teacher being the dispenser or transmitter of the distinct specific pieces of knowledge and specific skills to be learned, as well as the taskmaster who decides what information and instruction the learners get, and when and how these are provided. In a mechanistic approach, there is little or no attention for conceptual understanding (the reasons behind the facts and procedures that are taught) and theory development, nor for 'realistic' applications (Freudenthal, 1991). Of course, in a pre-computer era, procedural knowledge and skills were considered more important than today, which partly explains the dominance of this approach in Belgium just like in many other places all over the world. Also in the Netherlands, the mechanistic approach to mathematics education was dominant at that time, but Van den Heuvel-Panhuizen and Drijvers (2014, pp. 521–522) also suggest a link with the science of mathematics (though this may rather apply to the secondary level):

> In the 1960s, mathematics education in the Netherlands was dominated by a mechanistic teaching approach; mathematics was taught directly at a formal level, in an atomized manner, and the mathematical content was derived from the structure of mathematics as a scientific discipline. Students learned procedures step by step with the teacher demonstrating how to solve problems.

To the best of our knowledge, mutual influences between the Belgian and the Dutch primary mathematics educational traditions during the 1960s and before, if there were any, have not yet been investigated.

It would be, however, a mistake to equalise all mathematics education approaches from the first half of the previous century as purely mechanistic. In Belgium, there was, from the 1930s on, a strong focus in primary education in general on child-centredness and on connecting school matter with children's concrete, daily-life experiences. From that time on, the official school curriculum was influenced by the so-called 'Reform Pedagogics', an international pedagogical movement, situated between 1890 and World War II, that strove for a harmonic and broad child development and of which the Belgian teacher and psychologist Dr. Ovide Decroly (1871–1932) was one of the main protagonists (Van Gorp, 2005). For mathematics, this reform-based curriculum involved an approach which showed similarities with what later would be called 'Realistic Mathematics Education' (RME). It was, for example, stated that arithmetic is not a goal in itself, but should always be connected to a concrete reality, that learning should start from observations and from students' own living environment, that long and tedious calculations should be avoided, and that word problems should be inspired by students' activities and interests. Likewise, in the domain of measurement it was recommended to only use measures that

the children would also use in everyday life. Unfortunately, the pedagogical principles that were central to the curriculum were not always faithfully implemented in
practice: Commonly used textbooks still paid a lot of attention to long series of bare
problems, without 'meaning' and apart from any applied context (De Bock, D'hoker,
& Vandenberghe, 2011a).

Growing attention for the student and his learning process was also a main theme
in the work of the International Commission for the Study and Improvement of
Mathematics Teaching (CIEAEM), created by Caleb Gattegno (1911–1988) in the
early 1950s and bringing together leading mathematicians, mathematics educators
and psychologists of that time. A common point of interest within CIEAEM at that
time was related to the use of teaching aids, i.e., semi-concrete materials and models
that could be used to stimulate students' thinking and conceptual understanding (De
Bock & Vanpaemel, 2015; Gattegno et al., 1958; Vanpaemel, De Bock, & Verschaffel,
2012). These teaching aids included cardboard models, light projections, Meccano
constructions, geoboards, films, electrical circuits and the famous Cuisenaire rods,
a set of coloured sticks of different lengths that can be used as a didactical tool to
discover and to explain various arithmetical concepts and their properties. They were
invented by the Belgian primary school teacher Georges Cuisenaire (1891–1975)
(Fig. 3.1) and promoted by no one less than Gattegno himself (Gattegno, 1954,
1988). They were widely used in Belgian primary schools from the end of the 1950s
to support insightful teaching and learning of whole number arithmetic.

Fig. 3.1 Cuisenaire with his famous rods, ca. 1965

3.2   New Math

In the 1960s and 1970s, mathematics education in Belgium—as in many other countries—drastically changed: New Math or 'modern mathematics' broke through. This revolution first took place at the secondary level. From 1968 on, modern mathematics became compulsory in the first year of all secondary schools in Belgium (and from then on gradually in the subsequent years) and remained the prevailing paradigm in secondary mathematics education for about two decades. According to Georges Papy (1920–2011), professor of algebra at the Université Libre de Bruxelles and the figurehead of modern mathematics in Belgium, there were three main reasons to introduce modern mathematics: (1) the failure of traditional mathematics education, (2) the widening gap between mathematics 'as a living science' and mathematics as it was taught at various school levels, and (3) the growing importance of modern mathematics in a variety of other disciplines (Papy, 1976). New Math reacted against traditional, mechanistic approaches and instead emphasised insight in mathematical structure, often through the study of abstract concepts like sets, relations, graphs, algebraic structures, number base systems, etcetera. According to Papy (1976, pp. 20–21), excessive computational drill and practice ("dressage of children") lead to docility instead of free and creative thinking[1]:

> Regardless of the content, there are two main methods to teach mathematics. The most common one submits the students to the subject matter. They are trained and conditioned until they have sufficiently adapted and accept what is offered to them. This is accompanied by ritual and perpetual automatisms for calculating… This dogmatic method subjects the children to algorithms and thus makes frequent drill necessary. A recent document of the Institut de Recherche de l'Enseignement de la Mathématique of the Académie de Marseille recommended 'dressage of children' as an algorithm for subtraction. This method certainly contributes to educate children to become respectful citizens, disciplined soldiers, obedient employees […]. We suggest a diametrically opposite view on education, a method that allows the child to master a situation, to mathematise it, to learn to ask questions about it and to try to solve them, a method that is aimed at the development of personal creative freedom.

A main source of inspiration for the New Math or structural approach was found in the work of Nicolas Bourbaki, a collective pseudonym for a group of (mainly French) mathematicians who, from the late 1930s on, started the ambitious project to rebuild and restructure the mathematical knowledge of that time, a project quite similar to that of Euclid in the 3rd century BC (Bourbaki, 1939). Starting points were basic logical and mathematical structures and Bourbaki's method was a strictly deductive one. Modern mathematics is the application of the model that Bourbaki developed for the science of mathematics as a model for mathematics education (De Bock, Janssens, & Verschaffel, 2004). So, the reasoning by the reformers of that time was more or less as follows: If we start from basic, abstract and empty concepts, such as sets and relations, and we then gradually introduce the more concrete and rich concepts, using a clean deductive method, then students will be better able to understand and appreciate mathematics. To attain this latter goal, however, not only

---

[1] In this chapter, all translations into English were made by the authors.

Fig. 3.2 Papy with a copy of *Mathématique Moderne*, Vol. 1, 1963

a modernisation of the mathematical content was needed, but also a modernisation of didactics and even of the language to communicate about these new mathematical ideas. Venn and arrow diagrams, Logiblocks and all kind of new terms, symbols, and conventions were introduced in the mathematics lessons. At that time Papy's multicoloured textbooks *Mathématique Moderne* (Papy, 1963–1967) were translated in several languages and became quite influential in many European countries and even beyond (Fig. 3.2).

In contrast with the Netherlands, modern mathematics was also introduced at the primary school level in Belgium (and Belgium was even one of the nations that took a leading role and went furthest in this international reform movement at the primary level). In 1976 New Math was introduced in the Belgian primary schools of the Catholic network and two year later in the publicly run schools. Two main reasons were given to make modern mathematics compulsory at the primary level too. First, according to its defenders, the primary level had to prepare students for the modern mathematics of the secondary level. Second, Papy himself argued strongly for starting the teaching of modern mathematics as soon as possible, at an age children are not yet conditioned by the bad habits of the old-fashioned mathematics education. Experiments at that time by Papy and his collaborators (Lenger & Lepropre, 1959; Papy, 1960), coordinated by the Centre Belge de Pédagogie de la Mathématique/Belgisch Centrum voor Methodiek van de Wiskunde, were quite promising in that respect and received ample attention in the international mathematics education community (see also De Bock & Vanpaemel, 2018). For example, Fielker (1961, p. 48) reported:

> Prof. Papy had taught sets to children from eight to twenty-five years old, and it was more difficult with the twenty-five year olds! Undergraduates were conditioned by the bad habits of traditional mathematics [...]. Children of eight or ten were not so conditioned, and most success transpired with some fifteen-year-olds so poor in mathematics that they were uninfluenced by previous courses!

So, at the end of the 1970s, sets and relations became the most important ingredients of mathematics education at the primary level in Belgium, not only as educational goals and contents in themselves, but also as a vehicle to introduce all kinds of 'traditional' mathematical contents and to describe all kind of situations outside mathematics. Probably the most radical change took place in the teaching of geometry. The plane, represented by the symbol π, became an 'infinite set of points' and lines and geometrical figures became 'subsets of π'. In particular, the hierarchical order of the different plane figures was considered as essential (Fig. 3.3). Relations, such as 'all rectangles are parallelograms', were highlighted and visualised in the language of sets. Solving applied problems about geometrical figures was considered less important. Additionally, the correct use of an unequivocal terminology and symbol use was considered of the utmost importance. Therefore, inaccuracies from the pre-New Math programmes were eliminated. For example, a clear distinction was made between a 'circle' and a 'disk'. A circle only referred to the border of the plane figure, and thus its area was no longer πr^2 but 0. The geometry course also provided an introduction to transformation geometry. New topics, such as 'reflection through an axis' and 'axes of symmetry', had to prepare students to an extensive study of transformation geometry at the secondary level.

In the New Math period, primary school children were also introduced to what was called 'logical thinking'. In that part of the mathematics course, children learned to use correctly the connectives 'and' and 'or' and their negation by the logical operator 'not', typically by means of Logiblocks (a set of objects with restricted and well-defined features: rectangle, triangle or disk; yellow, blue or red; small or large, and thick or thin, see Fig. 3.4). They also were trained in correctly using expressions such as 'at least', 'at most', 'not all', 'only if', 'if and only if' and so on. There was even a frisky initiation to algebraic structures at the primary level. This should help students to understand more deeply the basic properties of operations.

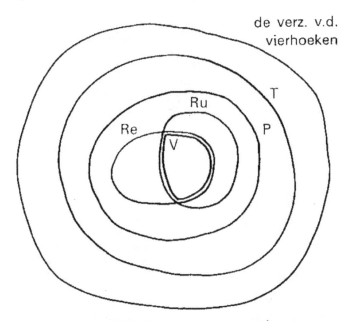

T = de verzameling van de trapezia
P = de verzameling van de parallellogrammen
Re = de verzameling van de rechthoeken
Ru = de verzameling van de ruiten
V = de verzameling van de vierkanten

Fig. 3.3 Venn diagram to classify quadrilaterals ('de verz. v.d. vierhoeken' = the set of quadrilaterals; 'T' = set of trapezoids; 'P' = set of parallelograms; 'Re' = set of rectangles; 'Ru' = set of rhombuses; 'V' = set of squares); taken from *Vernieuwde wiskunde in de basisschool* (Renewed Mathematics in Primary School) (Ministerie van Nationale Opvoeding en Nederlandse Cultuur, 1976, p. 18)

Although the official Belgian primary mathematics curricula were seriously affected by New Math, it is unclear how drastically the daily mathematics lessons were actually affected by it. It is apparent that computation and measurement as well as word problem solving, parts of the 'old' curriculum, were not dropped by primary school teachers during the New Math period (especially not in Flanders and in the Catholic network where the influence of Papy and his collaborators tended to be less strong). These skills were still considered as important, although it was less evident to integrate them in the New Math philosophy.

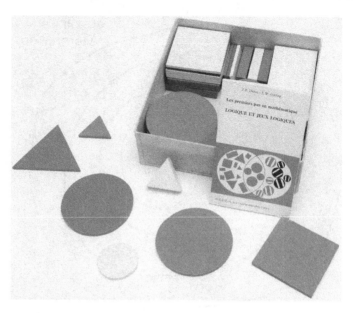

Fig. 3.4 A set of Logiblocks, 1968 (© Les archives de la Fondation Vaudoise du Patrimoine Scolaire—CH 1400 Yverdon-les-Bains)

3.3   Critique on New Math

Although New Math was strongly criticised in international fora since the early 1970s (see, e.g., Kline, 1973), and in the Netherlands Hans Freudenthal (1905–1990) and his team had started the development of a 'realistic' alternative for the teaching and learning of mathematics at the primary level (the Wiskobas[2] project, see, e.g., Treffers, 1993), the Belgian mathematics education community remained remarkably silent. For about twenty years, official curricula in Belgium would follow faithfully the New Math or structural approach. Obviously, several mathematics educators and mathematics teachers were sceptical about this approach, but criticisms were rarely voiced in public (De Bock, D'hoker, & Vandenberghe, 2011b; Verschaffel, 2004). In 1982, this silence was suddenly broken by the Flemish pedagogue Raf Feys. In the *Onderwijskrant*,[3] an innovation-minded, independent and pluralistic journal on education, Feys wrote a virulent pamphlet in which he firmly criticised the starting points of New Math and the way it was introduced and dictated at the primary level (Feys, 1982) (Fig. 3.5). In his close contacts with schools, Feys did not see the appearance of a fascinating world, but "artificial results in a fake reality", and also little enthusiasm in children, but "more disgust, disorientation and desperation" (Feys, 1982, p. 3). He described New Math as "upper-level mathematics" which was in the

---

[2]Wiskunde op de Basisschool (Mathematics in Primary School).
[3]Education newsletter.

Fig. 3.5 Cover of the *Onderwijskrant* in which Feys' (1982) critique on New Math appeared (moderne wiskunde: een vlag op een modderschuit = modern mathematics: a flag on a mud barge)

first place ballast, "i.e. an enormous extension of the programs, concepts that were misunderstood, mechanical learning and pedantry" (ibid., p. 6). Moreover, it created an obstacle for the acquisition of traditional mathematics, which he described as "mathematical-intuitive and practice-oriented lower-level mathematics". He further stated that "three-quarters of the reform involved the introduction of new terms and notations [...], a formal language primary-school teachers are unable to cope with and which complicated the application of mathematics" (ibid., p. 8). The pamphlet ended with a call for a large-scale counter-action, addressed to "teachers, parents,

inspectors 'with free hands', parents' associations, labor movements, teacher training institutes, universities, centres for psychological, medical and social guidance"
(ibid., p. 37).

In his pamphlet, Feys not only criticised New Math, he also suggested how mathematics education at the primary level should evolve, and the model he had in mind
was clearly RME as developed by Freudenthal and his collaborators at the former
IOWO.[4] According to the RME model, the starting point of mathematics education
should not be the structure of mathematics, but children's intuitive, informal and real-
world knowledge and skills, and these should be gradually developed. Feys (1982,
p. 37) wrote:

> When evaluating the renewed mathematics education, we should not only compare with
> the old mathematics, but also with alternatives like the ones that are, e.g., developed in
> the Netherlands by Wiskobas. We need the courage to examine the alternatives thoroughly.
> [...] We opt for an alternative reform along the lines of the Wiskobas approach of the
> IOWO, complemented, however, with a strong emphasis on the social-societal aspect of
> mathematical world orientation.

Although Feys' pamphlet enjoyed some resonance in the Flemish press and the
author received some expressions of support by academics (e.g., by Leen Streefland,
staff member of the IOWO, and by Lieven Verschaffel, whose letters were included
in a subsequent issue of the *Onderwijskrant*), his point of view was not generally
recognised and appreciated. Those responsible for primary mathematics education
wrapped themselves in silence or disqualified Feys' analysis as inflammatory language of irresponsible 'doomsayers' (see, e.g., Verschaffel, 2002). They argued "that
the innovation of mathematics education was a fact and that we, also as parents, could
better express our belief in the revised approach" (quote from an interview of a member of the programme committee of the Catholic network as reported by Heyerick,
1982, p. 5). The discussion had clearly been launched, but the tide had not yet turned!
An important follow-up event was the colloquium What Kind of Mathematics for
5–15 Year Olds? organised in 1983 by the Foundation Lodewijk de Raet, a Flemish
socio-cultural organisation with a pluralist scope (Stichting-Lodewijk de Raet, 1983).
At that occasion, proponents and opponents of New Math defended their positions. A
strong delegation from the Netherlands (in casu from Utrecht) participated, including Aad Goddijn and Hans Freudenthal, who not only gave a lecture, but also firmly
intervened in the discussion afterwards, with significant endorsement addressed to
the opponents of New Math. Obviously, the colloquium elicited opposite points of
views, but also strong dissatisfaction with the current situation ("no one wants to
continue this way"; Stichting-Lodewijk de Raet, 1983, p. 29). It became at least very
clear that something had to be changed and that Belgium (in this case, Flanders)
could not neglect the evolutions that took place in other countries, especially in the
Netherlands. At the end of the colloquium, again a call for action was launched, but
the response to this call was minimal. In the subsequent years, no significant changes
in the Flemish mathematics educational landscape occurred. Although interest in the

---

[4]Instituut voor de Ontwikkeling van het Wiskunde Onderwijs (Institute for the Development of
Mathematics Education).

Dutch alternative did not disappear and the RME approach received strong consideration in academic circles (Verschaffel, 1987) as well as in some so-called 'alternative schools' (based, for example, on the Freinet pedagogy), official curricula were not adjusted. Feys' (1982, p. 3) prediction that "the fateful choice for the New Math approach would also, for a very long time, impede valuable and necessary reforms" came true.

3.4 The 'Realistic' Alternative

At the end of the 1980s, the educational landscape in Belgium changed drastically. Belgium became a Federal State consisting of three Communities: the Flemish, the French and the (small) German-speaking Community. These Communities are based on a common language, or more broadly on 'culture'. Since January 1, 1989, the Communities are responsible for educational matters. We will focus further on the situation in the Flemish Community which has, due to the common language, most affinity with the Netherlands. One of the realisations of the Flemish Community with respect to mainstream education was the development of developmental objectives (for kindergarten) and attainment targets (for the primary and secondary level). Attainment targets are minimum objectives, determined by educational level, which the government considers necessary and attainable for the respective group of students. They are usually related to subjects and refer either to knowledge, to skills or to attitudes. The government determines the attainment targets, but the schools are responsible for reaching these targets with their students. Usually, for that purpose, schools follow the curricula developed by the educational network to which they belong. Hence, the approval of the attainment targets by the Flemish Government on July 15, 1997 was the occasion for the educational networks to develop new curricula for the different school subjects. For mathematics, it was the opportunity to renew this field in line with international developments and to officially break with New Math. The new curricula for mathematics for the three main school networks in Flanders (Gemeenschapsonderwijs, 1998; Onderwijssecretariaat van de Steden en Gemeenten van de Vlaamse Gemeenschap, 1998; Vlaams Verbond van het Katholiek Basisonderwijs, 1998) were implemented in 1998 and are still applicable. They differ slightly from each other, but not significantly. Flanders was (and still is) not ready for a cross-network curriculum for mathematics as advocated by Feys (1987). The curricular innovation of the 1990s was accompanied by new course materials for primary teacher education (Verschaffel & De Corte, 1995a, 1995b, 1995c, 1995d) and by new or renewed textbook series.

In all three networks, the curricula of 1998 differed strongly from the curricula from the New Math era. The typical topics from that period (sets and relations, logical thinking and the initiation to mathematical structures), as well as the abstract and formal spirit of the corresponding didactical approaches, had almost completely disappeared (although some attention for 'relationships between mathematical objects' and 'structuring' was maintained). On the one hand, there was a re-valuation of traditional topics and skills. Curricular objectives again referred to classical mathematical domains such as numbers, operations and computation, measurement and geometry. Traditional skills such as mental calculation and column arithmetic and word problem solving were revised and renewed, and explicit attention was asked for memorisation, automation and repeated practice, elements that characterised the "rich Flemish tradition" (see, e.g., Vlaams Verbond van het Katholiek Basisonderwijs, 1998, p. 10). On the other hand, important new objectives were formulated, objectives that were inspired by the Dutch RME model. For example, the curriculum for the state schools (Gemeenschapsonderwijs, 1998, p. 2) stated that "Mathematics in primary school should focus on mathematising reality. It is therefore necessary to set mathematics education into a natural context". We further read that they want to achieve that "children learn to describe situations derived from their own living environment in the language of mathematics" (ibid., p. 3). In the curriculum for the subsidised public schools (Onderwijssecretariaat van de Steden en Gemeenten van de Vlaamse Gemeenschap, 1998, p. 11), we read that "mathematics starts from real problems, problems that are experienced as 'real' by the students themselves". The new orientation related to content was also accompanied by a plea for opening the range of mathematical solution techniques to more flexible procedures, based on students' insight in the structure of numbers or in the properties of operations, and to informal strategies that students generate themselves. Although the inspiration from the Dutch RME model was manifest—some of the general objectives are actually almost copies of those formulated by Treffers, De Moor and Feijs (1989)—there are also some differences. For example, the programme for the Catholic network (Vlaams Verbond van het Katholiek Basisonderwijs, 1998) avoids using the term 'realistic' and instead speaks about 'meaningful situations'. Moreover, it first asks to pay attention to standard arithmetical procedures and only afterwards to more flexible procedures. Such non-incidental details show that the Dutch realistic vision was not copied blindly, but rather adapted to the Belgian or Flemish (historical) context.

Next to the objectives related to the traditional content domains of mathematics, the curriculum developers introduced some objectives that exceeded these domains. A first type of cross-domain objectives relates to the acquisition of problem-solving skills and strategies and to their use in rich (and applied) problem situations, replacing, in some sense, the traditional culture of word problem solving (Verschaffel et al., 1998; Verschaffel, Greer, & De Corte, 2000). Problem-solving skills and strategies refer to the process that leads to the solution of a problem. Main steps in that process are the analysis of the situation, the selection or building of a mathematical model, the application of mathematical techniques within that model, and the interpretation and evaluation of the results. These steps clearly refer to a modelling perspective, more specifically, to the so-called 'modelling cycle' (Verschaffel, Greer, & De Corte, 2000). Hence, word problems are no longer exclusively seen as a means to apply mathematics that has just been learned, but also to introduce some basic ideas about 'mathematical modelling' at the primary level. Modelling brings a new question to the forefront: Which mathematical model or operation is appropriate in a given situation?

A second type of cross-domain objectives refers to attitudes. Examples are learning to value mathematics as a dimension of human activity, to appreciate smart search strategies in problem-solving activities, to develop a critical disposition towards facts and figures that are used, consciously or not, to inform, to convince, but also to mislead people. The explicit inclusion of cross-domain objectives in the curricula for the primary level implies that schools have to pursue these objectives, without necessarily having to (completely) reach them. These are considered as permanent objectives for mathematics education, even after primary school.

When we look at the actual RME inspired changes in the different mathematical domains, we notice that in numbers and operations, the attention shifted from obtaining insight in the structure of number systems to linking numbers to quantities. That way, numbers are no longer purely abstract entities, but objects that children learn to know and recognise in different forms (e.g., decimal numbers from reading monetary values). With respect to operations, the emphasis shifted from discovering and accurately formulating the commutative, associative and distributive laws to linking operations to concrete and meaningful situations. As well as mental calculation, estimation techniques and the competent use of calculators are also promoted, for example, for solving realistic problems or for checking the result of an operation. Hence, the importance that was previously attached to all kinds of tests for checking computational results (e.g., checking the result of an addition or subtraction by performing the 'inverse operation' or the method of casting out nines for multiplications and divisions) disappeared completely. As mentioned before, in addition to standard computational algorithms, solution methods based on heuristic strategies also acquired their place in the curriculum. A typical example is the use of ratio tables for calculations with proportional quantities (instead of the old 'rule of three').

Also, the domain of measurement changed drastically. While in previous periods, this topic was treated in a rather mechanistic way, with much emphasis on conversion between all kinds of units, often quite artificial ones, current curricula focus on understanding the attributes of length, weight, area, and so on, and on the process of measurement, namely choosing an adequate unit, comparing the unit to the object to be measured and reporting the number of units. Students are invited to visualise the results of their measurement activities in tables and graphs. In addition to standard units, natural units such as body parts are used to come to a better understanding of measurement. Lessons in measurement nowadays are really active ones in which students measure real objects with different tools or create objects of given sizes. Students are also encouraged to use estimations, and activities are provided to develop estimation strategies. To develop some measurement sense, students need some natural references, e.g., the volume of a dessert spoon is about one centilitre, the length of a football pitch is 100 m, or one metric ton is about the weight of a passenger car. There is still some emphasis on metric conversion, but only between natural units or units that are frequently used. Therefore, students can use conversion tables, which are the analogue of ratio tables. As well as gaining inspiration from the Dutch RME model, the new approach to measurement was also strongly influenced by the U.S. standards, published in *Curriculum and Evaluation Standards for School Mathematics* (National Council of Teachers of Mathematics, NCTM, 1989).

With respect to geometry education, Freudenthal (1973, p. 403) wrote:

Geometry is grasping space ... that space in which the child lives, breathes and moves. The space that the child must learn to know, explore, conquer, in order to live, breathe and move better in it.

Starting point in geometry is observation and experience. Students first learn to recognise geometrical shapes in planes and in space by seeing and doing. This experiential geometry that already starts in kindergarten, also matches the Belgian intuitive geometry of the pre-New Math era (Vanpaemel & De Bock, 2017), primarily conceived as a field in which you first see and only then formalise (Ministerie van Openbaar Onderwijs, 1957). A specific RME influence in the curricula of 1998 is particularly evident in various recommendations and clarifications asking to introduce preferably geometrical concepts and methods in realistic contexts. So, for example the concept of an angle is related to the angle made by an opened door, or straight lines first arise as vision lines used to determine an observer's position on a sketch or a picture. The concept of area is introduced intuitively. Starting point is the area of a rectangle that students can determine by counting squares. Area formulas for other regular quadrilaterals are found by cutting and pasting activities. Even the 'difficult' formula for the area of a circle is approximately determined in a similar way. Only later on, this experiential (intuitive, realistic) approach can lead to more abstract notions of geometry, such as parallel and perpendicular lines, equality of shape and size, or symmetry. However, the goal of geometry education is no longer the development of an abstract framework, but teaching students to apply geometry in solving realistic problems in the space in which they live.

In conclusion, we reiterate that the Flemish post-New Math curricula for the primary level were strongly inspired by the Dutch RME model, but did not simply copy that model. One may ask why the Flemish attainment targets (1997) and subsequent curricula (1998) did not choose a more radical implementation of the realistic alternative. Verschaffel (2002, 2004) reports two types of possible explanatory elements. First, since the late 1980s, the RME model was not only praised in Flanders, but critical questions and doubts about the value and feasibility of that model were also raised, and, strikingly enough, it was again Feys who played a pivotal role in these criticisms. Feys' critique focused, among other things, on the neglect of the mechanistic aspects of learning, on the lack of guided construction of knowledge, on the excessive freedom that is given to students to construct their own solution methods, on the limited attention for the process of de-contextualising, and on insufficient recognition of the value of mathematics as a cultural product (Feys, 1998). When comparing new RME methods with traditional Flemish (pre-New Math) methods, he esteemed the latter as superior to the first (Feys, 1989, 1993). Although not all mathematics educators in Flanders agreed with Feys's criticisms, it is likely that his judgments have contributed to the fact that particularly the more extreme elements and aspects of the RME vision were not implemented. Second and complementary to the first element, comparative international research of that period revealed the very high quality of Flemish mathematics education. Actually, Flanders outperformed the Netherlands, not only in large-scale international studies such as TIMSS (Mullis et al., 2000), but also in some small-scale comparative studies only involving the Netherlands and Flanders (see, e.g., Luyten, 2000; Torbeyns et al., 2000). These results not only increased the self-confidence of Flemish mathematics educators, but also strengthened their hesitation to implement a more radical version of the Dutch RME model.

3.5 Math Wars

The negative reaction with respect to the value of the RME model, initiated in Flanders by Feys in the late 1980s, is akin to the position of one of the parties in the Math Wars that emerged around the same time in the United States. These Math Wars refer to a vehement debate held between reformers and traditionalists about mathematics education. This debate was triggered by the publication of the (reform-minded) *Curriculum and Evaluation Standards for School Mathematics* (NCTM, 1989) and the widespread adoption of a new generation of mathematics curricula inspired by these Standards. The vision of the American Standards had much in common with the RME philosophy with, for example, much attention for self-discovery learning via rich interactions between teachers and students and between the students themselves, mathematical connections between the different mathematical domains, continuous vertical learning trajectories (from kindergarten to high school), multiple and flexible problem representations and solution strategies, a meaningful integration of new technologies and a plea to pay less attention to paper-and-pencil calculations and isolated skills. Especially from the side of the professional mathematicians, fierce criticism and even a real counter movement was initiated, blaming the Standards for dumping, without good reason, a number of traditional and tested values of the past, such as the memorisation of facts, the automation of skills and learning through direct classroom instruction. The opposite views between reform-based mathematics educators (of the NCTM) and traditionalists were the basis of the Math Wars in the United States (the further development of which is beyond the scope of this chapter, but which has been discussed by, e.g., Klein, 2007).

The Math War crossed the ocean, and in the Netherlands there also was a heated debate about the quality of mathematics education and its didactical approaches. The debate polarised between two groups that both partly relied on the (interpretation of) results of the Cito studies of the PPON[5] (see, e.g., Janssen, Van der Schoot, & Hemker, 2005) used to assess mathematics achievements of primary students in the Netherlands (Ros, 2009). The Dutch Math Wars were launched by Jan van de Craats, mathematician at the University of Amsterdam and co-founder of the action group Stichting Goed Rekenonderwijs (Foundation for good arithmetic education). Van de Craats (2007) stated that children in the Netherlands are no longer able to calculate, that the RME approach created chaos wherever good mathematics needs calm and abstraction, and that standard algorithms (such as long division) and automatisms—

---

[5]Periodic assessment of education level.

which are, according to the traditionalists, especially helpful for children with medium and weak abilities—have totally disappeared from arithmetic education in the Netherlands. The scholars of the Freudenthal Institute, the successor of the IOWO, had to defend themselves and argue that there is no question of a general decline in the level of computational abilities and that Dutch children, as a result of the RME approach, are doing even better than 10–20 years ago on a number of aspects such as arithmetic in practical contexts, mental calculation, estimation techniques, working with percentages, and that they also have a better conceptual understanding of numbers and computational procedures (Van den Heuvel-Panhuizen, 2010). To clarify this situation, by the end of 2008 Dutch policy makers created a commission, under the auspices of the Royal Dutch Academy of Sciences (KNAW), which scrutinised all available research results. However, although that commission came to the conclusion that there is no demonstrable relationship between the level of computational ability of primary school children and the didactical method that is used ('realistic' or traditional) (KNAW, 2009), the debate in the Netherlands still goes on.

When it rains in Amsterdam, it drips in Brussels... In 2008, Feys and Van Biervliet published a special issue of the *Onderwijskrant*, titled "Mad Math en Math War", in which they informed their readership about the Math Wars in the United States and the Netherlands (Feys & Van Biervliet, 2008, p. 8). Not surprisingly, the authors unambiguously choose the camp of the traditionalists:

> The 'celestial' (too formal) New Math has been replaced by the 'terrestrial', contextual and constructivist approach, having too little attention for calculation skills and readily available knowledge, for generalisation and abstraction, and for mathematics as a cultural product.

The special issue, which also includes a contribution by Van de Craats, is certainly worth reading, but did not have the same strong impact as the 'A flag on a mud barge' issue from 1982. Lamentations about declining educational levels are of all times, but the feeding ground for a Flemish Math Wars seems to be missing. For that, several explanations can be given, but the most important is probably that the Flemish RME variant is less 'realistic' than the Dutch original, as argued above. This is also acknowledged by Feys and Van Biervliet (2008, p. 2) (and reported as their own achievement): "(We) succeeded to slow down the constructivist influence in primary education." Primary mathematics education in Flanders nowadays is eclectic, rather than (extremely) realistic. So, Verschaffel (2002) points out that in Flemish textbooks: (a) less time is spent on the informal, intuitive phase to switch more quickly to abstract, shorter and formal procedures; (b) there is more emphasis on practicing and automatisation; (c) fixed solution methods and schemes are more frequently used in mental arithmetic and word problems; (d) less use is made of new didactical tools and models, such as the reckoning rack and the empty number line, and older materials and models, such as square images, one hundred field and MAB materials,[6] are more frequently deployed; and (e) the principle of progressive schematisation is less consistently applied in the learning of (difficult) number algorithms than in Dutch methods. In conclusion, we can state that today's Flemish mathematics education

---

[6]Multibase arithmetic blocks.

is—according to some people—a colourless mix; according to others a harmonious and workable balance between elements from the mechanistic and realistic traditions, with still some elements of the structural New Math vision.

3.6 Future Developments?

Of course, the fact that Flemish mathematics education seems to have found a good balance between elements from its different traditions does not mean that there is no room for improvement. One of the issues under discussion nowadays in Flanders is how to narrow the gap that exists between primary and secondary mathematics education. These two educational levels are still different worlds, with their own traditions, teachers and teacher education programmes. Students however just continue their school career and what they have learned at the primary level should help them instead of being an obstacle for what they have to learn at the secondary level. We mention three elements that could make the transition from the primary to the secondary level more fluent.

First, at the primary level, problems are typically approached in a purely arithmetical way, while at the secondary level, students switch to an algebraic approach (and an arithmetical approach is typically no longer accepted). Also, teachers at both educational levels make different use of and have different attitudes towards arithmetical and algebraic solutions methods (Van Dooren, Verschaffel, & Onghena, 2001, 2002, 2003). We think that the inclusion of some pre-algebra (methods) in the curricula and/or textbooks for the primary level is worth considering. Moreover, it would re-strengthen the 'structural' element in primary mathematics education, an element that is weakened since the elimination of New Math.

Second, we think that the learning of numbers and operations can be improved by better taking into account the results of recent research in this field. This research has, among other things, shown that prior knowledge about natural numbers often hinders students to understand rational numbers and operations with these numbers. This phenomenon is often referred to as the 'natural number bias'. For example, students may believe that 'multiplication always makes bigger', that $1/4 > 1/3$ because $4 > 3$, or that there are only two numbers between 0.2 and 0.5, namely 0.3 and 0.4 (see, e.g., Van Hoof, Verschaffel, & Van Dooren, 2015). Didactical approaches for both educational levels could better prepare students for this type of differences between natural and rational numbers and related operations, and for errors that may result therefrom.

Third, there is a need for a good, systematic and cross-level learning trajectory for (emergent) mathematical modelling and applied problem solving. This topic is included in the curricula for the (upper) primary level and is supported by a lot of research at that level (Verschaffel et al., 1998), but there is no clear continuation of that trajectory in the first years of secondary school. A revision of the topic of functions (for the first years of secondary school) in the direction of 'functions as models' for various situations and phenomena, an approach that already exists at the upper secondary level in Flanders (Roels et al., 1990), could be considered.

References

Bourbaki, N. (1939). *Éléments de mathématique: Théorie des ensembles* [Elements of mathematics: Set theory]. Paris, France: Hermann.

De Bock, D., D'hoker, M., & Vandenberghe, K. (2011a). *Terugblik op een eeuw wiskundeonderwijs in de Vlaamse lagere scholen – 1: Van 'traditioneel' naar modern* [Looking back over one century of mathematics education in Flemish primary schools—1: From 'traditional' to modern]. *Basis—Schoolwijzer, 118*(19), 13–16.

De Bock, D., D'hoker, M., & Vandenberghe, K. (2011b). *Terugblik op een eeuw wiskundeonderwijs in de Vlaamse lagere scholen – 2: Gematigd realisme of 'eclecticisme'?* [Looking back over one century of mathematics education in Flemish primary schools—2: Moderate realism or 'eclecticism'?]. *Basis—Schoolwijzer, 118*(20), 13–17.

De Bock, D., Janssens, D., & Verschaffel, L. (2004). *Wiskundeonderwijs in Vlaanderen: Van modern naar realistisch?* [Mathematics education in Flanders: From modern to realistic?]. In M. D'hoker & M. Depaepe (Eds.), *Op eigen vleugels: Liber amicorum prof. Dr. An Hermans* [On its own wings: Liber amicorum Prof. Fr. An Hermans] (pp. 157–169). Antwerp, Belgium: Garant.

De Bock, D., & Vanpaemel, G. (2015). The Belgian journal 'Mathematica & Paedagogia' (1953–1974): A forum for the national and international scene in mathematics education. In E. Barbin, U. T. Jankvist, & T. H. Kjeldsen (Eds.), *Proceedings of the Seventh European Summer University on the History and Epistemology in Mathematics Education* (pp. 723–734). Copenhagen, Denmark, Aarhus University, Danish School of Education.

De Bock D., & Vanpaemel G. (2018). Early experiments with modern mathematics in Belgium. Advanced mathematics taught from childhood? In F. Furinghetti & A. Karp (Eds.), *Researching the history of mathematics education: An international overview* (ICME-13 Monographs) (pp. 61–77). New York, NY: Springer.

Feys, R. (1982). *Moderne wiskunde: Een vlag op een modderschuit* [Modern mathematics: A flag on a mud barge]. *Onderwijskrant, 24*, 3–37.

Feys, R. (1987). *Nationaal plan voor het wiskundeonderwijs? Overzicht van de wiskundestandpunten sinds 1983* [National plan for mathematics? Overview of mathematics positions since 1983]. *Onderwijskrant, 48*, 3–17.

Feys, R. (1989). Oerdegelijke kwadraatbeelden en modieuze rekenmannetjes [Solid square images and fashionable little computation men]. *Onderwijskrant, 59*, 2–15.

Feys, R. (1993). Laat het rekenen tot honderd niet in het honderd lopen [Let's not obstruct counting up to one hundred]. *Tijdschrift voor Nascholing en Onderzoek van het Reken/wiskundeonderwijs, 11*(3), 3–16.

Feys, R. (1998). *Rekenen tot honderd. Basisvaardigheden en zorgverbreding* [Arithmetic up to one hundred. Basic skills and extending care]. Mechelen, Belgium: Wolters Plantyn.

Feys, R., & Van Biervliet, P. (Red.). (2008). *Themanummer: Mad Math en Math War* [Special issue: Mad Math and Math War]. *Onderwijskrant & O-ZON-katern, 146*, 2–51.

Fielker, D. (1961). Developments in the teaching of mathematics. Report of the Easter Conference, London, 1961. *Mathematics Teaching, 16*, 32–52.

Freudenthal, H. (1973). *Mathematics as an educational task*. Dordrecht, the Netherlands: Reidel.

Freudenthal, H. (1991). *Revisiting mathematics education: China lectures*. Dordrecht, the Netherlands: Kluwer.

Gattegno, C. (1954). Les nombres en couleurs de Georges Cuisenaire [Coloured numbers by Georges Cuisenaire]. *Mathematica & Paedagogia, 4*, 17–22.

Gattegno, C. (1988). Reflections on forty years of work on mathematics teaching. *For the Learning of Mathematics, 8,* 41–42.

Gattegno, C., Servais, W., Castelnuovo, E., Nicolet, J. L., Fletcher, T. J., Motard, L., et al. (1958). *Le matériel pour l'enseignement des mathématiques* [Materials for the teaching of mathematics]. Neuchâtel, Switzerland: Delachaux et Niestlé.

Gemeenschapsonderwijs. (1998). *Leerplan basisschool aangepast aan de nieuwe eindtermen. Leergebied wiskunde* [Primary school program adapted to the new attainment targets. Learning domain of mathematics]. Brussels, Belgium: Author.

Heyerick, L. (1982). *Moderne wiskunde: Een vlag op een modderschuit. Reacties en vervolg* [Modern mathematics: A flag on a mud barge. Responses and follow-up]. *Onderwijskrant, 26,* 3–5.

Janssen, J., Van der Schoot, F., & Hemker, B. (2005). *Balans van het reken-wiskundeonderwijs aan het einde van de basisschool 4* [Fourth assessment of mathematics education at the end of primary school]. Arnhem, the Netherlands: Cito.

Klein, D. (2007). A quarter century of US 'math wars' and political partisanship. *Journal of the British Society for the History of Mathematics, 22*(1), 22–33.

Kline, M. (1973). *Why Johnny can't add: The failure of the New Math.* New York, NY: St. Martin's Press.

Koninklijke Nederlandse Akademie van Wetenschappen (KNAW). (2009). *Rekenonderwijs op de basisschool. Analyse en sleutels tot verbetering* [Arithmetic education in primary school. Analysis and keys to improvement]. Amsterdam, the Netherlands: Author. Available at: https://www.knaw.nl/nl/actueel/publicaties/rekenonderwijs-op-de-basisschool.

Lenger, F., & Lepropre, M. (1959). Initiation aux mathématiques fondamentales dans une classe de première normale gardienne [Initiation to fundamental mathematics in a first year class of training of kindergarten teachers]. In *Journée d'études 8: L'initiation aux mathématiques – Problèmes psycho-pédagogiques* (pp. 17–24). Brussels, Belgium: Ministère de l'enseignement public, Secrétariat général de la réforme de l'enseignement moyen et normal.

Luyten, H. (2000). Wiskunde in Nederland en Vlaanderen [Mathematics in the Netherlands and Flanders]. *Pedagogische Studiën, 77,* 206–221.

Ministerie van Nationale Opvoeding en Nederlandse Cultuur. (1976). *Vernieuwde wiskunde in de basisschool.* Brussels, Belgium: Author.

Ministerie van Openbaar Onderwijs. (1957). *Leerplan en leidraad voor de eerste drie graden van de lagere scholen* [Program and guidelines for the first three grades of primary schools]. Brussels, Belgium: Author.

Mullis, I., Martin, M., Gonzales, E., Gregory, K., Garden, R., O'Connor, K., et al. (2000). *TIMSS 1999 international mathematics report.* Chestnut Hill, MA: The International Study Center Boston College, International Association for the Evaluation for the Evaluation of Educational Achievement (IEA).

National Council of Teachers of Mathematics (NCTM). (1989). *Curriculum and evaluation standards for school mathematics.* Reston, VA: Author.

Onderwijssecretariaat van de Steden en Gemeenten van de Vlaamse Gemeenschap. (1998). *Leerplan wiskunde voor de basisschool* [Mathematics program for the primary school]. Brussels, Belgium: Author.

Papy, G. (1960). *Premiers éléments de mathématique moderne* [First elements of modern mathematics]. Brussels, Belgium: Author.

Papy, G. (1963–1967). *Mathématique moderne* [Modern mathematics] (Vols. 1, 2, 3, 5, 6). Paris, Bruxelles, Montréal: Editions Didier.

Papy, G. (1976). Het onderwijs in de wiskunde [Mathematics education]. *Nico, 21,* 3–46.

Roels, J., De Bock, D., Deprez, J., Janssens, D., Kesselaers, G., Op de Beeck, R., et al. (1990). *Wiskunde vanuit toepassingen* [Mathematics taught by applications]. Leuven, Belgium: Aggregatie HSO Wiskunde – K. U. Leuven.

Ros, B. (2009). Een pittig tweegesprek over rekenen. Staartdelen of happen? [A lively dialogue about arithmetic. Long division or taking bites?]. *Didaktief, 39*(1–2), 4–8.

Stichting-Lodewijk de Raet. (1983). Verslagboek van het colloquium 'Welke wiskunde voor 5- tot 15-jarigen' [Proceedings of the colloquium 'What kind of mathematics for 5 to 15 year olds']. *Onderwijskrant, 32*, 2–30.

Torbeyns, J., Van de Rijt, B., Van den Noortgate, W., Van Luit, H., Ghesquière, P., & Verschaffel, L. (2000). Ontwikkeling van getalbegrip bij vijf- tot zevenjarigen. Een vergelijking tussen Vlaanderen en Nederland [Development of number concept in five to seven year olds. A comparison between Flanders and the Netherlands]. *Tijdschrift voor Orthopedagogiek, 39*(3), 118–131.

Treffers, A. (1987). *Three dimensions. A model of goal and theory description in mathematics education*. Dordrecht, the Netherlands: Kluwer.

Treffers, A. (1993). Wiskobas and Freudenthal—Realistic mathematics education. *Educational Studies in Mathematics, 25*, 89–108.

Treffers, A., De Moor, E., & Feijs, E. (1989). *Proeve van een nationaal programma voor het reken-wiskundeonderwijs op de basisschool. Deel I. Overzicht einddoelen* [Design for a National Curriculum for mathematics education in primary school. Part I. Overview of goals]. Tilburg, the Netherlands: Zwijsen.

Van de Craats, J. (2007). Waarom Daan en Sanne niet kunnen rekenen [Why Daan and Sanne can't calculate], *Nieuw Archief voor Wiskunde, 5*(2), 132–136.

Van den Heuvel-Panhuizen, M. (2010). Reform under attack—Forty years of working on better mathematics education thrown on the scrapheap? No way! In L. Sparrow, B. Kissane, & C. Hurst (Eds.), *Shaping the future of mathematics education: Proceedings of the 33rd Annual Conference of the Mathematics Education Research Group of Australasia* (pp. 1–25). Fremantle, Australia: MERGA.

Van den Heuvel-Panhuizen, M., & Drijvers, P. (2014). Realistic mathematics education. In S. Lerman (Ed.), *Encyclopedia of mathematics education* (pp. 521–525). Dordrecht, the Netherlands: Springer.

Van Dooren, W., Verschaffel, L., & Onghena, P. (2001). *Rekenen of algebra? Gebruik en houding tegenover rekenkundige en algebraïsche oplossingswijzen bij toekomstige leerkrachten* [Arithmetic or algebra? Use and attitude towards arithmetical and algebraic solution methods by pre-service teachers]. Leuven, Belgium: Universitaire Pers Leuven.

Van Dooren, W., Verschaffel, L., & Onghena, P. (2002). The impact of preservice teachers' content knowledge on their evaluation of students' strategies for solving arithmetic and algebra word problems. *Journal for Research in Mathematics Education, 33*(5), 319–351.

Van Dooren, W., Verschaffel, L., & Onghena, P. (2003). Pre-service teachers' preferred strategies for solving arithmetic and algebra word problems. *Journal of Mathematics Teacher Education, 6*, 27–52.

Van Gorp, A. (2005). *Tussen mythe en wetenschap: Ovide Decroly (1871–1932)* [Between myth and science: Ovide Decroly (1871–1932)]. Leuven, Belgium: Acco.

Van Hoof, J., Verschaffel, L., & Van Dooren, W. (2015). Inappropriately applying natural number properties in rational number tasks: Characterizing the development of the natural number bias through primary and secondary education. *Educational Studies in Mathematics, 90*, 39–56.

Vanpaemel, G., & De Bock, D. (2017). Marxism and mathematics. Paul Libois and intuitive geometry in Belgium. In K. Bjarnadóttir, F. Furinghetti, M. Menghini, J. Prytz, & G. Schubring (Eds.), *"Dig where you stand" 4. Proceedings of the Fourth International Conference on the History of Mathematics Education* (pp. 383–398). Rome, Italy: Edizioni Nuova Cultura.

Vanpaemel, G., De Bock, D., & Verschaffel, L. (2012). Defining modern mathematics: Willy Servais (1913–1979) and mathematical curriculum reform in Belgium. In K. Bjarnadóttir, F. Furinghetti, J. Matos, & G. Schubring (Eds.), *'Dig Where You Stand'—2. Proceedings of the Second International Conference on the History of Mathematics Education* (pp. 485–505). Lisbon, Portugal: New University of Lisbon.

Verschaffel, L. (1987). Realistisch reken/wiskunde-onderwijs in Nederland. Een kennismaking [Realistic arithmetic/mathematics education in the Netherlands. An introduction]. *Christene School. Pedagogisch Periodiek, 94*, 322–334.

Verschaffel, L. (2002). *25 jaar ontwikkelingen in het Nederlandse wiskundeonderwijs op de basisschool vanaf de zijlijn bekeken* [25 years of developments in Dutch mathematics education in primary school viewed from the sidelines]. Lezing gehouden in het kader van het 8ste symposium van de Historische Kring Reken- en Wiskunde Onderwijs over 'De roerige jaren zestig. Van Moderne Wiskunde naar Realistisch Wiskundeonderwijs', 25 mei 2002, Utrecht, the Netherlands.

Verschaffel, L. (2004). All you wanted to know about mathematics education in Flanders, but were afraid to ask. In R. Keijzer & E. De Goeij (Eds.), *Rekenen-wiskunde als rijke bron* [Arithmetic-mathematics as a rich source] (pp. 65–86). Utrecht, the Netherlands: Freudenthal Instituut.

Verschaffel, L., & De Corte, E. (Red.). (1995a). *Naar een nieuwe reken/wiskundedidactiek voor de basisschool en de basiseducatie. Deel 1. Achtergronden* [Towards a new didactic of arithmetic and mathematics for the elementary school and the basic education. Part 1. Backgrounds]. Brussel/Leuven: Studiecentrum Open Hoger Onderwijs/Acco.

Verschaffel, L., & De Corte, E. (Red.). (1995b). *Naar een nieuwe reken/wiskundedidactiek voor de basisschool en de basiseducatie. Deel 2. Vlot en inzichtelijk leren omgaan met getallen en bewerkingen* [Towards a new didactic of arithmetic and mathematics for the elementary school and the basic education. Part 2. To deal fluently and insightfully with numbers and operations]. Brussel/Leuven: Studiecentrum Open Hoger Onderwijs/Acco.

Verschaffel, L., & De Corte, E. (Red.). (1995c). *Naar een nieuwe reken/wiskundedidactiek voor de basisschool en de basiseducatie. Deel 3. Leren omgaan met ruimte en tijd, en uitbreiding van de kennis en vaardigheden rond getallen en bewerkingen* [Towards a new didactic of arithmetic and mathematics for the elementary school and the basic education. Part 3. Learning to deal with space and time, and expanding the knowledge and skills about numbers and operations]. Brussel/Leuven: Studiecentrum Open Hoger Onderwijs/Acco.

Verschaffel, L., & De Corte, E. (Red.). (1995d). *Naar een nieuwe reken/wiskundedidactiek voor de basisschool en de basiseducatie. Deel 4. Leren rekenen in de basiseducatie* [Towards a new didactic of arithmetic and mathematics for the elementary school and the basic education. Part 4. Learning to calculate in basic education]. Brussel/Leuven: Studiecentrum Open Hoger Onderwijs/Acco.

Verschaffel, L., De Corte, E., Van Vaerenbergh, G., Lasure, S., Bogaerts, H., & Ratinckx, E. (1998). *Leren oplossen van wiskundige contextproblemen in de bovenbouw van de basisschool* [Learning to solve mathematical context problems in upper primary school]. Leuven, Belgium: Universitaire Pers Leuven.

Verschaffel, L., Greer, B., & De Corte, E. (2000). *Making sense of word problems*. Lisse, the Netherlands: Swets and Zeitlinger.

Vlaams Verbond van het Katholiek Basisonderwijs. (1998). *Wiskunde leerplan* [Mathematics program]. Brussels, Belgium: Author.

Chapter 4
The Impact of Hans Freudenthal and the Freudenthal Institute on the Project Mathe 2000

Erich Ch. Wittmann

Abstract This chapter is an attempt to describe the direct and indirect influence Hans Freudenthal and his institute had on the developmental research conducted by Mathe 2000. Special attention will be given to the balance of pure and applied mathematics in designing learning environments, where RME and Mathe 2000 differ to some extent, and to the role of mathematics in mathematics education.

Keywords Developmental research · Mathematics as a 'design science' · Structure-genetic didactical analysis · Mathe 2000

4.1 Introduction

In 1967 the department of mathematics at the University of Erlangen organised a colloquium in commemoration of the geometer K. G. Ch. von Staudt (1798–1867). Hans Freudenthal, an international expert also in the foundations of geometry, was one of the invited speakers, and I eagerly awaited to meet him for the following reason: I had just finished my studies as a prospective teacher and was going to submit my doctoral dissertation in the theory of infinite groups. As I was seriously considering the option of moving into mathematics education at a later point of my career, I had also started to read the literature in this rapidly growing field and while doing so I developed a strong aversion against the New Math movement, which at that time seemed to override the teaching of mathematics at both universities and schools.

Erich Ch. Wittmann: Project Mathe 2000

E. Ch. Wittmann (✉)
Technical University of Dortmund, Dortmund, Germany
e-mail: wittmann@math.tu-dortmund.de

In this critical situation one of Freudenthal's papers (Freudenthal, 1963) was an enlightenment for me in several respects. The paper contained a convincing refutation of Bourbaki's architecture of mathematics as a basis for mathematics teaching. Moreover, the paper was written in a style I had never seen before: brilliant, witty and unconventional. For example, the hesitation of a mathematician to publish a paper according to its genesis was compared to the feelings of a man standing in the street in his underwear. The most important point, however, was the picture that was drawn of mathematical learning, namely as a process that passes through different stages, each one a necessary step for the next one. The paper emphasised mathematical activity as the crucial element of learning and described 'local ordering' as a reasonable alternative to readymade axiomatics.

At the colloquium, I had a chance to talk to Hans Freudenthal (Fig. 4.1), and here I learned of his fresh initiatives as the president of the International Commission on Mathematical Instruction (ICMI): the organisation of the First International Congress in Mathematics Education (ICME 1) in Lyon in 1969 and the foundation of an international journal in mathematics education (*Educational Studies in Mathematics Education*, first published in 1968).

What impressed and influenced me likewise was the work that Freudenthal initiated in 1971 at the IOWO[1] in Utrecht. Here he gathered a team of highly creative mathematics educators, among them Aad Goddijn, Fred Goffree, Martin Kindt, Jan de Lange, Ed de Moor, Leen Streefland, George Schoemaker, Adri Treffers, and later Marja van den Heuvel-Panhuizen.

The developmental research conducted at the IOWO (later re-named Freudenthal Institute) served as a source of inspiration for our project Mathe 2000 at the University of Dortmund in many respects. This project was founded in 1987 after Germany had overcome the painful stagnation caused by New Math. For good reasons Hans Freudenthal ranks as one of the five archfathers of Mathe 2000 (see https://www. mathe2000.de/Projektbeschreibung).

In what follows, the influence of 'Utrecht' on 'Dortmund' in four areas is described in a nutshell.

---

[1] Instituut voor de Ontwikkeling van het Wiskunde Onderwijs (Institute for the Development of Mathematics Education).

Fig. 4.1 Hans Freudenthal at the Staudt colloquium in 1967

4.2   Developmental Research

In the preface of the volume *Five Years IOWO* Hans Freudenthal stated:

> IOWO is not a research institute; its members do not regard themselves as researchers but as producers of instruction, as engineers in the educational field, as curriculum developers. Engineering needs background research and can produce research as fall-out. Though both of them will be visible in the present account, its nucleus is our productive work, represented by a few specimens, and embodies our views on mathematics as a human activity and on curriculum development as a classroom activity, guided by curriculum developers, in close contact with all those interested in mathematics education. (IOWO, 1976, p. 189)

In developing didactical units, which nowadays are called learning environments, the Freudenthal Institute has set standards of quality. Many of these environments are just brilliant, particularly those in geometry, and we adopted quite a number of them in the Mathe 2000-curriculum, with a clear preference for those that can be integrated with mathematical structures.

In addition to the contribution that each single learning environment means for teaching a certain content, the work of the Freudenthal Institute has also greatly inspired the view of mathematics education as a 'design science'. The talk given by Edu Wijdeveld (IOWO, 1976, pp. 243–244) on the 'dwarf village' at the colloquium held in 1976 at the occasion of Hans Freudenthal's retirement was particularly pertinent in this respect. The 'dwarf village' represents a substantial application of geometry that is related to combinatorial counting (group operating on a set). When my paper on mathematics education as a 'design science' appeared in English (Wittmann, 1995), I was happy to learn that Adri Treffers called it a "credo of our common work".

As far as the intended close connection of curriculum development with teacher education is concerned, Mathe 2000 had perhaps better boundary conditions than the IOWO as Mathe 2000 did not form an institute of its own but was a kind of virtual project immersed in the official pre-service and in-service teacher education programmes offered by the University of Dortmund. Another clear advance of this structure was that Mathe 2000 was completely independent of any funding.

4.3   The View of Mathematics

Hans Freudenthal, a scholar with an enormous breadth of interests, has taught us to look at mathematics as a field of knowledge that is firmly integrated into our culture and determined by both external ('applied') and internal ('pure') factors. His masterpiece *Mathematics as an Educational Task* (Freudenthal, 1973) bears witness to this conviction. Richness of relationships (*'Beziehungshaltigkeit'*) was a postulate to which Freudenthal frequently referred, and it included both structural relationships ('vertical mathematisation') and relationships with the real world ('horizontal mathematisation'). In his book *Three Dimensions*, Adri Treffers elaborated this approach in detail (Treffers, 1978).

As Freudenthal and the IOWO wanted to establish a distinct counterpart to New Math, it is understandable that a clear emphasis was put on horizontal mathematisation and that the choice of the term 'Realistic Mathematics Education' (RME) was a deliberate one. In Mathe 2000, however, we had the feeling that in the later development of the Freudenthal Institute too much emphasis was put on applications; see, for example, the textbook series *Mathematics in Context* (National Center for Research in Mathematical Sciences Education & Freudenthal Institute, 1997–1998). However, it is only fair to acknowledge that there are also publications by members of the Freudenthal Institute that are extremely interesting in terms of mathematical structures (see, for example, Kindt & De Moor, 2012) and that helped us to shape our own more balanced conception.

4.4   A Genetic View of Teaching and Learning

In Freudenthal's view the learner has no choice but to 're-invent' mathematics under appropriate guidance by starting as a child from most elementary experiences and managing more and more complex structures with growing expertise. Mathematical knowledge can never be transmitted top-down in a readymade form. Even the most perfect lecture can become vital for a student only if he or she makes sense of it by actively re-constructing in personal terms what has been proposed. Hans Freudenthal radically objected to the idea of a didactical transposition from the level of specialists to lower levels. In his talk at the Carbondale Conference on Geometry he put this view in his typical language (Freudenthal, 1971, p. 435):

> Geometry is endangered by dogmatic ideas on mathematical rigor. They express themselves in two different ways: absorbing geometry in a system of mathematics like linear algebra, or strangulating it by rigid axiomatics. So, it is not one devil menacing geometry as suggested in the title of my paper. There are two. The escape that is left is the deep sea. It is a safe escape if you have learned swimming. In fact, that is the way geometry should be taught, just like swimming.

This genetic view is reflected in a series of studies of learning processes conducted at the Freudenthal Institute. Two of them have been of particular importance for Mathe 2000.

In the last e-mail I received from Hans Freudenthal in March 1990, a few months before he passed away, he mentioned a study conducted by a young lady by the name of Marja van den Heuvel-Panhuizen who at that time was unknown to me. This study turned out as fundamentally important for Mathe 2000 for the following reason. According to a long tradition not only in Germany, but also in other European countries, the number space 0–20 and the addition table were introduced in Grade 1 step by step: the students worked with numbers up to 5 or 6, then some months with the numbers up to 10, and only in the last months of the school year the whole space from 0 to 20 was addressed. In Volume 1 of our *Handbook of Productive Practice* (Wittmann & Müller, 1990) we proposed to substitute this step-by-step introduction and the corresponding step-by-step introduction of the addition table by a holistic approach, in which the numbers 0–20, and later the addition table, are introduced in one step. We had a hard time to defend this approach against many critics. Marja van den Heuvel-Panhuizen's empirical findings with her MORE entry-test showed convincingly that the knowledge about numbers that school beginners bring to school is substantial and at the same time strongly underestimated by teachers (Van den Heuvel-Panhuizen, 1996, Chap. 5). These findings, which were corroborated by similar findings in some other European countries, supported the holistic approach of Mathe 2000 on all grounds and helped us to defend our position which in German mathematics education is now widely shared.

In Volume 2 of our *Handbook of Productive Practice* (Wittmann & Müller, 1992) we suggested a similar paradigm shift away from the strong fixation on standard algorithms towards various ways of calculating that are based on the arithmetical laws and represent a kind of early algebra; '*halbschriftliches Rechnen*' (*semiformal strategies)* in the German tradition). We also suggested to use these semiformal strategies as a basis for deriving the standard algorithms (Wittmann & Müller, 1992). We were lucky once more that this approach was strongly supported by another great achievement of a member of the Freudenthal Institute. Adri Treffers' research on 'progressive schematisation' (Treffers, 1987) showed convincingly how naturally students perform the transition from semiformal strategies to the standard algorithms. For us progressive schematisation is so important that we chose it as one of the ten didactical principles on which the conception of Mathe 2000 is based.

4.5 Mathematics Education as a Research Domain

Based on his experiences at the IOWO, Hans Freudenthal has always looked sceptically at mathematics education as a research field, but nevertheless wrote his book *Weeding and Sowing* as a kind of prologue for an emerging research field (Freudenthal, 1978). In this book, he clearly separated the research he had in mind from the research on teaching and learning that is conducted by psychologists, pedagogues, sociologists and other generalists who do not and cannot take the content properly into account. For Freudenthal the didactical analysis of the subject matter was the most important source for designing learning environments and curricula. In this respect his book *Didactical Phenomenology of Mathematical Structures* (Freudenthal, 1983) is of overriding importance. This book is one of the basic references of our attempt to shed some new light on didactical analyses.

In a recent paper, I have tried to combine what I have learned both from Hans Freudenthal and Jean Piaget, another archfather of Mathe 2000 (Wittmann, 2018). My intention with this paper, titled *"Structure-genetic Didactical Analyses—'Empirical Research of the 'First Kind'"*, is also to broaden the scope for empirical evidence. Mathematics, if properly understood, provides not only the contents for teaching but incorporates also processes that are crucial for the teacher-student interaction. After all, mathematics itself is the result of learning processes. When once asked what his motifs as a mathematician were for engaging in mathematics education Hans Freudenthal replied: "I want to understand better what mathematics is." I believe that vice versa it is worthwhile for mathematics educators to engage more deeply in mathematics in order to understand better what mathematics education is or should be about.

References

Freudenthal, H. (1963). Was ist Axiomatik und welchen Bildungswert kann sie haben? [What is axiomatic and what educational value can it have?] *Der Mathematikunterricht, 9,* 5–19.
Freudenthal, H. (1971). Geometry between the devil and the deep sea. *Educational Studies in Mathematics, 3,* 413–435.

Freudenthal, H. (1973). *Mathematics as an educational task*. Dordrecht, the Netherlands: Reidel.
Freudenthal, H. (1978). *Weeding and sowing. Preface to a science of mathematical education*. Dordrecht, the Netherlands: Kluwer Academic Publishers.
Freudenthal, H. (1983). *Didactical phenomenology of mathematical structures*. Dordrecht, the Netherlands: Reidel.
IOWO. (1976). Five years IOWO. *Educational Studies in Mathematics, 7*(3).
Kindt, M., & De Moor, E. (2012). *Wiskunde dat kun je begrijpen [Mathematics you can understand]*. Amsterdam, the Netherlands: Bert Bakker.
National Center for Research in Mathematical Sciences Education & Freudenthal Institute. (1997–1998). *Mathematics in context: A connected curriculum for grades 5–8*. Chicago, IL: Encyclopaedia Britannica Educational Corporation.
Treffers, A. (1978). *Three dimensions: A model of goal and theory description in mathematics instruction—The Wiskobas project*. Dordrecht, the Netherlands: Reidel.
Treffers, A. (1987). Integrated column arithmetic according to progressive schematization. *Educational Studies in Mathematics, 18*, 125–145.
Van den Heuvel-Panhuizen, M. (1996). *Assessment and realistic mathematics education*. Utrecht, the Netherlands: CD-β/Freudenthal Institute.
Wittmann, E. Ch. (1995). Mathematics education as a 'design science'. *Educational Studies in Mathematics, 29*, 355–374.
Wittmann, E. Ch. (2018). Structure-genetic didactical analyses. Empirical research 'of the first kind'. In P. Błaszczyk, & B. Pieronkiewicz (Eds.), *Mathematical transgressions 2015* (pp. 133–150). Kraków, Poland: Universitas.
Wittmann. E. Ch., & Müller, G. N. (1990). *Handbuch produktiver Rechenübungen. Band 1: Vom Einspluseins zum Einmaleins [Handbook of productive practice. From addition tables to multiplication tables]*. Revised edition 2017/18. Seelze, Germany: Klett-Kallmeyer.
Wittmann. E. Ch., & Müller, G. N. (1992). *Handbuch produktiver Rechenübungen. Band 2: Vom halbschriftlichen zum schriftlichen Rechnen [Handbook of productive practice. From semiformal calculations to the standard algorithms]*. Revised edition 2017/18. Seelze, Germany: Klett-Kallmeyer.

Chapter 5
Reflections on Realistic Mathematics Education from a South African Perspective

Cyril Julie and Faaiz Gierdien

Abstract The project Realistic Mathematics Education in South Africa (REMESA) was introduced in South Africa during a period when curriculum changes were introduced to fit the educational ideals of the 'new' South Africa. In this project, modules based on Realistic Mathematics Education were developed by a team comprising staff from the Freudenthal Institute and the Mathematics Education sector of the University of the Western Cape. The modules were implemented in classrooms. In our chapter, we reflect upon the appropriation by practicing teachers of two modules. Teachers viewed the module *Vision Geometry* with scepticism whilst the module *Global Graphs* was more readily accepted. The appropriation was thus differential. In current school mathematics policy documents and learning materials, the major ideas of the module *Vision Geometry* are virtually invisible. The ideas from the module *Global Graphs* are more visible. This can be ascribed to the prominence of graphical representations in South African school mathematics curricula. The two instances point in the direction that the proximity of innovative approaches to the operative curriculum plays an important role with respect to teachers' adoption of the resources for their practice.

Keywords Curriculum change · Innovation and operative curriculum · Vision geometry · Global graphs · Functions, tables and graphs

5.1 Introduction

The project Realistic Mathematics Education in South Africa (REMESA) was introduced in line with local and international or global currents in mathematics education.

C. Julie (✉)
University of the Western Cape, Cape Town, South Africa
e-mail: cjulie@uwc.ac.za

F. Gierdien
University of Stellenbosch, Stellenbosch, South Africa
e-mail: faaiz@sun.ac.za

M. van den Heuvel-Panhuizen (ed.), *International Reflections on the Netherlands Didactics of Mathematics*, ICME-13 Monographs, https://doi.org/10.1007/978-3-030-20223-1_5

71

It took root during a period that saw the first democratic and non-racial elections in South Africa in 1994. This was a period marked by political efforts on behalf of the newly elected South African government to rid the country of its Apartheid past. REMESA thus came at a time where the new state had to work on establishing its legitimacy in the educational sector especially, which was not the case in the past. Not surprisingly, the mid to late 1990s witnessed intense education reform efforts. For example, the National Education and Training Forum (NETF) was formed in 1992 to address the deteriorating schooling system inherited from the Apartheid past. An active sub-committee of the NETF, the Curriculum Technical Sub-Committee (CTSC), embarked on short-term syllabus revision of the different 'field' committees (mathematics, natural sciences, etc.) and 'phase' committees (junior primary, senior primary and secondary) (see Jansen, 1999). In short, these committees had the brief to remove outdated, inaccurate and insensitive content present in the school syllabuses. In addition, during this period there were consultations and negotiations with stakeholders such as student organisations and the South African labour movement. What we ultimately witnessed was the adoption of a school curriculum organised around outcomes-based education. School subjects became known as 'learning areas' wherein there was cross-curricularisation around particular, desired outcomes. Also, at a global level, from the 1960s onwards, there was a quest for cross-curricular work in school mathematics (Julie, 1998). In the case of outcomes-based education, this quest became much more explicit (Julie, 1998). Examples of this global trend can be traced to texts such as "Links Between Mathematics and Other Subjects" (Selkirk, 1982) and "Integrating Mathematics into the Wider Curriculum" (Roper, 1994). The connection to local/national, global forces and cross-curriculum is evident in REMESA publications (Julie et al., 1998; Verhage et al., 2000).

At the (initial) teacher education level, REMESA was semi-inspired by the problem-centred approach at the University of Stellenbosch (Hiebert et al., 1996) which also had underpinnings of Realistic Mathematics Education (RME). Freudenthal's (1973) seminal text, *Mathematics as an Educational Task*, was compulsory reading in graduate courses in mathematics education at University of the Western Cape (UWC) and University of Stellenbosch.

During this period, school mathematics was accorded priority based on the internationally-held belief that quality teaching and learning of school mathematics will contribute towards the economic development of a country. This belief relates to the notion that quality mathematics teaching and learning fosters processes such as group solution-seeking to problems, creativity and the application of mathematics to extra-mathematical situations such as natural, economic, health, cultural and social phenomena. For the South African situation, these were deemed important attributes which should be developed in schools for the country's progress. With these ideas in mind, the Mathematics Education division of UWC entered into a partnership with the Freudenthal Institute (FI) with the objective of introducing RME as a viable approach for school mathematics to work towards the outcomes sought for schooling in the country.

There was thus an awareness of the underlying ideas of RME which provided fertile soil for the partnership entered into.

5.2 The Essences of REMESA

Following the developmental research approach of the FI for the development of local instructional theories, an essential aspect of REMESA was that there must be some alignment of the work done by the project and the operative school mathematics curriculum. The importance of this element is linked to the issue of immediacy in the sense that the differential adoption of a teaching innovation by teachers is highly driven by their sense of the direct applicability of the ideas distributed by the innovation for their practice. Linked to the aforementioned element was that there should be learning resources epitomising RME. These resources should be classroom-tested so that there is evidence of its applicability for the South African context. They should also be in a form that allowed for easy distribution to schools in socially and economically deprived environments in South Africa, which was the empirical domain in which the sector Mathematics Education at UWC operated. A last important component was that a capacity-building element should accompany the project in order to ensure sustainability at the culmination of the project. To realise this, a group of post-graduate students was recruited to research aspects of the implementation of RME in classrooms. The project ran for approximately five years.

A variety of modules (*Vision Geometry*; *Global Graphs*; *Functions, Tables and Graphs*; and *The Exponential Function*) was developed by a team comprising staff from the FI and the sector Mathematics Education at UWC. The FI staff spent time in South Africa for the development of the modules. The reflection in this chapter focuses on the development of two modules: *Vision Geometry* and *Global Graphs*. They were conveniently selected in order to guide discussion on some of the issues involved in adaptation and adoption of instructional design emanating from an educational environment in a highly developed context for use in a late-developing one. The first module discussed below had less influential currency than the second one and reasons for these are discussed.

5.3 Vision Geometry

Vision Geometry was the first module developed and developmentally researched in a classroom (Lewis, 1994). This module was particularly chosen due to problems learners experience with geometry in South Africa. From the RME perspective, developing learning resources where learners are provided with activities where they experience mathematics from Freudenthal's dictum that reality is the source of and the domain of application of mathematics, it was deemed that vision geometry was a sound way manifest the RME approach. The elements or content of vision geometry were: lines of sight, the influence of position when an object is observed, angle of sight, perspective (views), two-dimensional representations of three-dimensional objects and constructions emanating from lines of sight. These elements were encapsulated in activities for learners. One such activity was the 'Thumb jump'. The activity starts with the teacher drawing a line on the chalkboard. A learner is called to the front of the class. With her/his arm stretched out and one eye closed, the thumb has to be positioned so that it is in line with the line drawn on the chalkboard. Once this is fixed, the thumb has to be held in that position, the closed eye is opened and the other eye closed and the position of the line has then to be indicated and drawn. Figure 5.1 depicts the worksheet dealing with the 'Thumb jump' activity.

In Fig. 5.1 the horizontal and skew lines represent the chalkboard. The instructions (which were in Afrikaans) were:

(1) Draw the position of the second line ('streep' in Afrikaans) on the chalkboard. Use a line of sight. [In the teacher guide teachers were encouraged to introduce the concept of 'line of sight'.]
(2) Draw the position of your thumb.
(3) Draw the position of the second line. Stand in a position twice your distance from the first line and draw the second line. What do you observe about the last two lines you have drawn?

Figure 5.2 illustrates a learner doing the 'Thumb jump' activity and Fig. 5.3 shows an example of the drawings that were made when doing this activity. In Fig. 5.3a it can be observed that a learner first drew the entire person holding the stick and illustrated his/her position. After the module designers, who were observing the classroom implementation, alerted learners that they should do the drawing as seen from above, Fig. 5.3b resulted.

An example of a typical response learners offered for the observed phenomenon is given in Fig. 5.4. As is clear from this, the explanations focused on features of the thumb and the seeming 'jumping action' of the eye ("your eye jumps still further").

The other topics covered in the module dealt with hand spans (measuring angles with your hands), views (side and top) and the field of vision.

Of this first encounter with RME, the teacher who implemented the module expressed concern about the time needed for the activities, their impact on curriculum coverage, the connection with the actual content of the curriculum and the manner

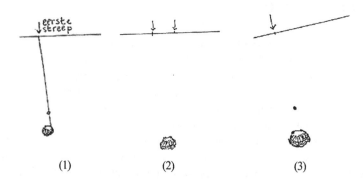

(1)   (2)   (3)

Fig. 5.1 Activities 1, 2 and 3 of the first worksheet on vision geometry ('eerste streep' = first line)

Fig. 5.2 Learner doing the 'Thumb jump' activity

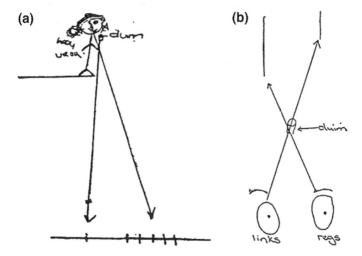

Fig. 5.3 Drawings made by one learner (writing on the left is illegible; 'duim' = thumb; 'links' = left; 'regs' = right]

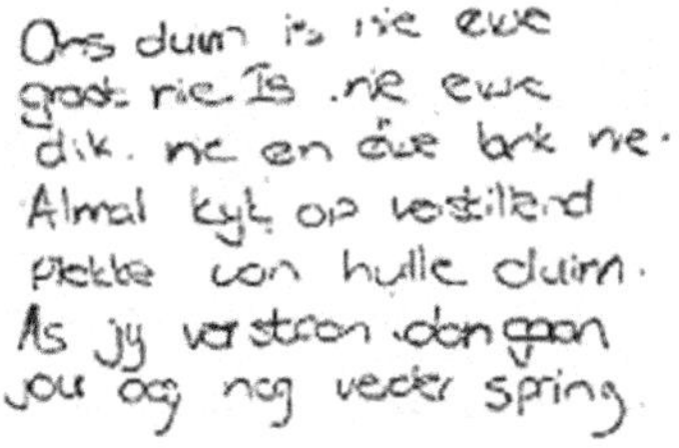

Ons duim is nie ewe
groot nie. Is nie ewe
dik. nc en die bak ne.
Almal kyk op verskillend
plekke van hulle duim.
As jy verstaan con gaan
jou oog nog veder spring.

Our thumps are not the same size.
Not of the same thickness.
Every one looks from different
locations from their thumps. If you
stand further away then your eye
jumps still further.

Fig. 5.4 Explanation of the thumb jump phenomenon

in which the work will be examined since learners will eventually be "confronted with an examination" (Lewis, 1994, p. 69).

Based on the aforementioned feedback from the teacher and observations of the designers, the module was revised, as is characteristic of developmental research. One of the major changes made was to link the experimental work related to vision geometry to aspects of triangle geometry, which is an explicit topic mentioned in the South African curriculum for 12- to 13-year-olds (Grade 8). This led to a starting point different from the 'Thumb jump' activity and was linked to placing an object between two others so that the three are in line as given in Fig. 5.5.

The 'Thumb jump' activity was also more explicitly connected to aspects of the curriculum. One exercise, for example, was "Make a sketch of the thumb jump so that you get two isosceles triangles" and another one was "Make a sketch of the thumb jump so that you get two right-angles triangles." Figure 5.6 is representative of learners' responses to these exercises.

Experimental activities such as the above led to further exercises on classification of triangles. Overall the second cycle of the developmental research activity rendered materials which were more aligned to the curriculum that was operative in South Africa. The time to complete the activities was also addressed through a strategy of

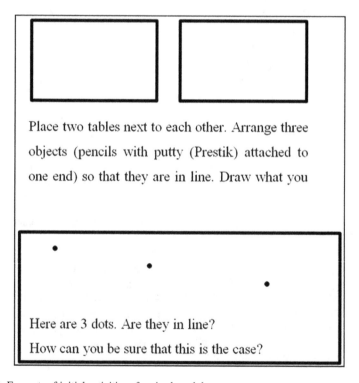

Place two tables next to each other. Arrange three objects (pencils with putty (Prestik) attached to one end) so that they are in line. Draw what you

Here are 3 dots. Are they in line? How can you be sure that this is the case?

Fig. 5.5 Excerpts of initial activities of revised module

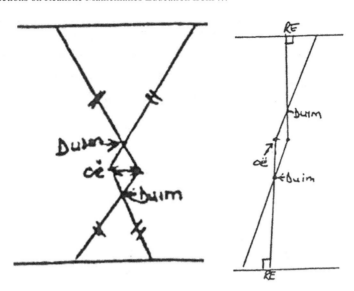

Fig. 5.6 Responses of the learners to the activities about the triangles ('duim' = thump, 'oë' = eyes, 'RE' = right angle)

providing the implementing teacher, different from the one who implemented the first cycle, with more guidance in the teacher guide that accompanied the activities.

The 'Thumb jump' activity was found enjoyable, exciting and not above their abilities by the learners. It was the first time they could use immediate experiences gained through experiments to engage with geometry. The scepticism of the implementing teacher, however, remained and as mentioned above, still revolved around the time needed for the activities, curriculum coverage and examinability of the module's content. Furthermore, there was no dissemination of the module to a wider group of teachers, other than to the two implementing teachers and the teacher who was involved in the development research aspect of this initial encounter with RME. The last-mentioned teacher contended that RME offers great possibilities for the realisation of an education in mathematics for fostering learner-centredness and non-authoritarian ways of working classrooms. This was the kind of learning and teaching that was desired by the first democratically elected government in the country. Despite this, vision geometry had very little traction for impacting on the further curriculum development initiatives in the country. This finding points to tension between the REMESA module content and 'legitimate school mathematics', that is, the mathematics that is valued in high-stakes examinations (Julie, 2012; Kvale, 1993). In current policy documents and learning materials, the major ideas of the module on vision geometry are virtually invisible.

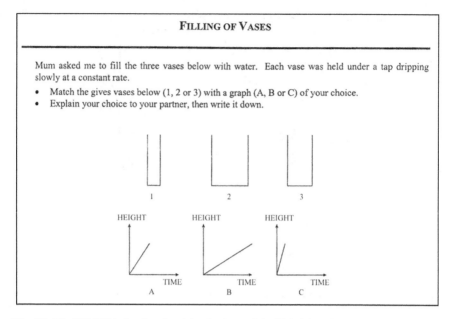

Fig. 5.7   The REMESA-developed activity for the module *Global Graphs*

5.4   Global Graphs

The development of the module *Global Graphs* and the associated teaching experiments occurred when there was a more stable, albeit contested, operative curriculum in the country. For the junior school phase—Grades 7–9 (13- to 15-year-olds) – the name of the subject was changed to Mathematics, Mathematical Literacy and the Mathematical Sciences. This name change was to develop awareness that school mathematics does not only deal with pure mathematics, but also with applied mathematics, mathematical modelling, and probability and statistics. Furthermore, the revised curriculum was still underpinned by an outcomes-based education philosophy and, as alluded to before, 'subjects' were renamed as 'learning areas'. The module *Global Graphs* was an adaptation of activities developed by the Freudenthal Institute on graphs (Roodhardt et al., 1990). This resemblance can be observed in the REMESA activity 'Filling vases' in Fig. 5.7 and Roodhart and his colleagues' activity shown in Fig. 5.8. There are some differences. The REMESA-developed activity, for example, starts by requesting learners to fit graphs to similar vases with different dimensions whilst the activity from the Freudenthal Institute requires the construction of graphs fitting different containers. This difference resulted from discussions between the South African project workers and those from the Freudenthal Institute. The South African participants felt that the graph-fitting situation would be a more appropriate introductory activity for the module of study.

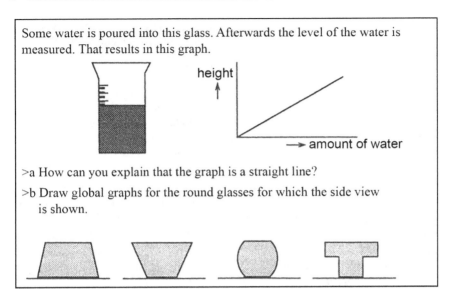

Some water is poured into this glass. Afterwards the level of the water is measured. That results in this graph.

>a How can you explain that the graph is a straight line?
>b Draw global graphs for the round glasses for which the side view is shown.

Fig. 5.8 Activity developed at the Freudenthal Institute for the unit *Tabellen, Grafieken, Formules 2* (Roodhart et al., 1990)

Fig. 5.9 Visual fit of graphs in vases

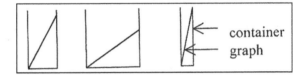

Different from the development of the module *Vision Geometry*, the development of *Global Graphs* was done with a larger group of practising teachers. Some of the teachers involved in the development of the module were also the implementers of the module in their classrooms. The module was implemented in a larger and more diverse classrooms, in terms of language (Afrikaans, IsiXhosa and English-first-language speakers). Julie et al. (1998) describe the development and implementation of the module as follows.

The participating teachers wrote 'stories' about learners' handling of the activity. The major issues emerging regarding learners' dealing with activities from the stories were:

(a) The visual fit of the graphs in the vases as shown in Fig. 5.9.
(b) Reference by learners to a slow and fast rise.
(c) Conjecturing such as "the narrower the glasses the quicker they got filled" (Julie et al., 1998, p. 39).

Overall, teachers expressed satisfaction about the usefulness of the module *Global Graphs*. They wrote:

As teachers we feel that these activities have value for all grades in the secondary school. It opened up meaning of a straight line to those that had dealt with it. It can also be valuable for the introduction of the straight line graph. And lastly, engagement in talking about slow rise, slower rate and faster rate provided learners with the opportunity to grapple with the concept of gradient. (Julie et al., 1998, p. 39)

Furthermore, the module was deemed appropriate for the outcomes-based operative curriculum. Comparing the acceptance of the module *Global Graphs* with that of *Vision Geometry*, the former had more traction. This can be ascribed to the proximity of graphical representations in all versions of the South African curriculum since the transition to a democratic dispensation. For example, in the latest version of the curriculum, the prominence of graphical representations as encapsulated in the module *Global Graphs* is captured as "[I]nvestigate the properties of graphs illustrating real-life relationships e.g., time-distance graphs" (Department of Basic Education, 2010, p. 39). The more readily acceptance of the module *Global Graphs* is also linked to its inclusion in textbooks with possible suggestions for its use in formal assessments. In the textbook *Platinum Mathematics* an activity similar to the vases is included under the section "Interpreting Graphs" (Bowie et al., 2012, p. 165). The formal exemplar test section of the same textbook (ibid., p. 200), also has items which are similar to those dealt with in the module *Global Graphs*.

5.5 Conclusion

Focusing on the design and teaching experiments related to two modules underpinned by the RME philosophy it was demonstrated that the reigning curriculum milieu impacted differentially on the appropriation by teachers of the learning resources. In this regard, the proximity, as perceived by teachers, of the materials to the operative curriculum plays an important role with respect to teachers' adoption of the resources for their practice. This is linked to the idea of immediacy for practice of any innovation. Teachers do want to be assured of the immediate relevance of innovations to their current responsibilities and accountabilities with respect to the curriculum and accompanying activities such as examinations. If this relevance is remote, as with the module *Vision Geometry*, the appropriation is low. On the other hand, if the relevance is near to the operative curriculum and further cemented by other boundary objects such as available textbooks, as it is more the case with the module *Global Graphs*, then the possibility of appropriation is higher.

These considerations led some of the original participants in the REMESA initiative to incorporate these insights into a current initiative related to the development of teaching mathematics in secondary schools. Central to this initiative is the participation of teachers as major role-players in collaboration with university-based mathematics educators, mathematicians and mathematics curriculum advisors. This is in line with Burkhardt's (2006, p. 196) suggestion that "typical teachers in realistic circumstances" participate in initiatives as active and respected participants to work towards the improvement of mathematical education in schools. The initiative referred to is highly driven by the developmental research approach underpinning the work of the Freudenthal Institute. It is thus our contention that the residual effect of the REMESA project is contributing positively to current research and development endeavours to address the issue of high-quality teaching of mathematics in secondary schools in low socio-economic environments in a region in South Africa.

References

Bowie, L., Cronje, E., Heany, F., Maritz, P., Olivier, G., Rossouw, B., & Willemse, S. (2012). *Platinum mathematics*. Cape Town, South Africa: Maskew Miller Longman (PTY) Ltd.

Burkhardt, H. (2006). From design research to large-scale impact: Engineering research in education. In J. van den Akker, K. Gravemeijer, S. McKenney, & N. Nieveen (Eds.), *Educational design research* (pp. 121–150). London, UK: Routledge.

Department of Basic Education. (2010). *Curriculum and assessment policy statement (CAPS) Mathematics: Senior phase*. Pretoria, South Africa: Department of Basic Education.

Freudenthal, H. (1973). *Mathematics as an educational task*. Dordrecht, the Netherlands: Reidel.

Hiebert, J., Carpenter, T., Fennema, F., Fuson, K., Human, P., Murray, H., et al. (1996). Problem solving as a basis for reform in curriculum and instruction: The case for mathematics. *Educational Researcher, 25*(4), 12–21.

Jansen, J. (1999). The school curriculum since apartheid: Intersections of politics and policy in the South African transition. *Journal of Curriculum Studies, 31*(1), 57–67.

Julie, C. (1998). Ideal and reality: Cross-curriculum work in school mathematics in South Africa. *ZDM Mathematics Education, 30*(4), 110–115.

Julie, C. (2012). The primacy of teaching procedures in school mathematics. In S. Nieuwoudt, D. Laubser, & H. Dreyer (Eds.), *Proceedings of the 18th Annual National Congress of the Association for Mathematics Association of South Africa* (pp. 16–31). Potchefstroom, South Africa: North-West University.

Julie, C., Cooper, P., Daniels, M., Fray, B., Fortune, R., Kasana, Z., et al. (1998). Global graphs: A window on the design of learning activities for outcomes-based education. *Pythagoras, 46*(47), 37–44.

Kvale, S. (1993). Examinations re-examined: Certification for students or certification of knowledge? In J. Lave & S. Chaiklin (Eds.), *Understanding practice: Perspectives on activity and context* (pp. 215–240). Cambridge, UK: Cambridge University Press.

Lewis, H. A. (1994). *'n Ontwikkelingsondersoekstudie na realistiese meetkunde on onderig in standard ses [A developmental research study on realistic geometry teaching in standard six (Grade 8)]*. Unpublished master's thesis. Bellville, South Africa: University of the Western Cape.

Roodhardt, A., Hauchart, C., De Jong, J., Van der Kooij, H., De Lange, J., & Van Reeuwijk, M. (1990). *Tabellen, grafieken, formules 2 [Tables, graphs, formulas 2]*. Utrecht, the Netherlands: Freudenthal Institute, Utrecht University.

Roper, T. (1994). Integrating mathematics into the wider curriculum. In A. Orton & G. Wain (Eds.), *Issues in teaching mathematics* (pp. 174–191). London, UK: Cassell.

Selkirk, K. (1982). Links between mathematics and other subjects. In M. Cornelius (Ed.), *Teaching mathematics* (pp. 186–213). London, UK: Croom Helm.

Verhage, H., Adendorff, S., Cooper, P., Engel, M., Kasana, Z., Le Roux, P., et al. (2000). The interrelationship between graphs, formulae and tables: Exploring the relationship between mathematising and outcomes-based education. *Pythagoras, 51*, 33–42.

Chapter 6
Learning to Look at the World Through Mathematical Spectacles—A Personal Tribute to Realistic Mathematics Education

Abraham Arcavi

To Joop van Dormolen,
Who patiently introduced me to the depth, nuances and scope
of Realistic Mathematics Education.

Abstract As professionals of mathematics education, we seldom offer personal accounts of our own learning and development. Although such subjective experiences may be idiosyncratic and hardly generalisable, a brief racconto of what and how one came to know may be useful—firstly, to those from whom we learned (maybe what we learned from them is not what they intended to teach us, and this is worth explicating), secondly, to those whom we teach (for them to know who we are and some of the sources of our learning), and, thirdly, to some colleagues willing to start conversations and to share experiences. This essay subjectively describes aspects of the inspiration generated by the insightful, applicable and effective principles of mathematics instruction that Realistic Mathematics Education has offered to us all, influencing the approaches to teaching and learning and the doing in mathematics education.

Keywords Realistic Mathematics Education · Mathematical gaze · Procedural and conceptual · Modelling

6.1 At the Beginning It Was Symbol Crunching, but with a Bit of Spice

For as long as I can remember, I have enjoyed mathematics. However, the mathematics I enjoyed so much was the only one I was then offered: highly procedural and

A. Arcavi (✉)
Department of Science Teaching, Weizmann Institute of Science, Rehovot, Israel
e-mail: abraham.arcavi@weizmann.ac.il

rule-oriented, especially in Grade 8–9 algebra. I was happy to 'understand' the rules of the game, to be able to eschew the most common calculation mistakes, to play with complicated algebraic expressions and to enjoy the gratification provided by a correct result or the checking and redoing when it was incorrect. Such enjoyment was even greater when the procedural was spiced with even a minimal degree of exploration. For example, I remember myself liking very much the exercises devoted to the rationalisation of denominators (i.e., eliminating irrational terms from the denominator without altering the value of the fraction), both with numbers only and with algebraic expressions. One can hardly say that producing an expression to multiply both numerator and denominator such that the denominator becomes a rational term or a number requires much creativity. Nevertheless, I liked the 'freedom' to search for and to create an appropriate expression (especially when based on the rule $(a - b)(a + b) = a^2 - b^2$). I saw these tasks as requiring some ingenuity and thus they were gratifying. The challenge and the satisfaction of playing with these kinds of tasks led me to try my hand at inventing rules beyond those taught and allowed. I will never forget my elation when, in eighth grade, I realised that $\frac{a+a}{b+b} = \frac{a}{b}$, I was able to explain why and then I proposed the following 'simplification rule' $\frac{a\!\!\!/+a}{b\!\!\!/+b}$. I became even more excited when I noticed that this is true for any number of a's and b's, provided their number is the same. I showed this to my mother (who at the time was also the mathematics teacher of the class) and she smiled; "nice," she said. Later on in life, I learned that many teachers use this 'nice' reaction either for lack of a better one or as a harmless euphemism to avoid discouragement; for other teachers such a 'nice' reaction was perceived by many of my fellow students as worse than a scolding.

I relish these memories, as do many of us with pleasant learning events from childhood. When I was 18, I started to teach. Neither my mathematics nor my didactics were solid, to say the least, but I firmly believed that if I knew something (or at least I thought I did) and I liked it, it was enough to teach it and to teach it well. I had a sense of the satisfaction that students (or at least some of them who were like me) may experience when they solve procedural exercises. I became very skilled at producing loads of such exercises on the spot, and sometimes I even tested the idea that these procedural repetitions may yield interesting 'discoveries'. I remember vividly that while preparing for a lesson, I was amazed to 'discover' (possibly rediscover since I must have seen this in high school) that the results of $a - b$ and $b - a$ were the same number (in absolute value) with opposite signs. I was able to justify this 'insight' formally without too much trouble, but I think this was one of the first opportunities in which the algebraic game-playing did not provide me a satisfactory answer as to the question of why that spoke to my inner sense of intuition. By playing with the number line representation, this discomfort was somehow dispelled. Unfortunately, at the time, as a young teacher I had no mentors who could legitimise the asking of questions, the search for answers and the attempts to reconcile between formal arguments and the inner (highly subjective) conviction about their validity. Also, at the time I disregarded the fact that game-playing which occasionally yields insights for some, may have adverse effects for many other students, and I ignored (double entendre intended) the many other rich facets of mathematics.

With hindsight and many (!) years later, these early mathematical experiences lead me to reflect on three non-trivial issues related to the learning and teaching of rules and procedures in mathematics. Firstly, whereas we often hear (and agree with the claim) that procedural tasks are boring and turn so many students off, and also that procedures are not necessarily at the core of the significant mathematics one wants them to learn, still there are students out there who may find it enjoyable to undertake procedural tasks. As a teacher, I should have been very aware of both types of students. Secondly, there is a widespread tendency to identify the performing of procedures with ritualised mathematics (in the sense of Sfard, 2016), namely tasks that are undertaken by students for social reasons ("we have to", "to please the teacher"), mostly by imitation and usually scaffolded by teachers who point out mistakes and correct them. My own brief stories above can be considered as a counterexample. Creating an expression, inventing a new formula or noticing a new result were undertaken by me to pose new challenges to myself and I was not always scaffolded by others. This insight led me to observe students and teachers over many years, to collect instances of and to elaborate the notion of symbol sense (Arcavi, 1994, 2005a). This was also the main motivation to join my colleague Alex Friedlander, an amazingly creative task designer, in the non-trivial and enjoyable activity of producing tasks to address rules and procedures, which nudge students to de-ritualise their practices and turn them into more explorative ones (Friedlander & Arcavi, 2017). Thirdly, after encountering Realistic Mathematics Education (RME), I was pleased to realise the scope of the main term in its name:

> the adjective 'realistic' is definitely in agreement with how the teaching and learning of mathematics is seen within RME, but on the other hand this term is also confusing. In Dutch, the verb 'zich realiseren' means 'to imagine'. In other words, the term 'realistic' refers more to the intention that students should be offered problem situations which they can imagine ... than that it refers to the 'realness' or authenticity of problems. However, the latter does not mean that the connection to real life is not important. It only implies that the contexts are not necessarily restricted to real-world situations. The fantasy world of fairy tales and *even the formal world of mathematics can be very suitable contexts for problems*, as long as they are 'real' in the students' minds. (Van den Heuvel-Panhuizen, 2003, p. 9–10; emphasis added)

6.2 Starting to Look at the World with Mathematical Spectacles

As mentioned above, during my high school years, most of the mathematics I encountered was oriented towards solving 'pure' mathematical exercises by means of formal procedures. I do not remember many occasions of using mathematics in high school in order to solve a problem from outside mathematics, except perhaps for a few instances of problems in kinematics, but that was in the physics class. To my shame, I heard the term 'mathematical model' for the first time during my university studies. At university, and in many cases supported by the way the mathematics was taught, I still retained my fondness for handling symbols and solving procedural exercises, sometimes pushing them beyond what I was strictly required to do. However, in parallel I started to acknowledge and appreciate the many opportunities to invoke mathematics, especially those arising in everyday life, as demonstrated by the following story (see also Arcavi, 2002).

When I was a first-year undergraduate student in Argentina, I collected bus tickets with palindromes for a friend. The bus tickets bore five-digit numbers (see Fig. 6.1). At that time, it occurred to me to think about the odds of getting a palindrome, and for that I needed to know how many different five-digit palindromes there are. Had this problem been assigned in class, the bus and the tickets would have been omitted as irrelevant frills (if provided at all) and the solution would have looked something like this: in a palindrome, the units, the tens, and the hundreds digits can vary freely, the thousands are the same as the tens, and the ten thousands are the same as the units. There are ten possibilities for each of the varying digits (if numbers like 00100 are considered as a five-digit number), therefore there are 1000 palindromes. My solution during my bus ride was very different from this one, precisely because of the context. In the bus, the tickets were torn from a roll with consecutive numbers. The device from which the bus driver tore the numbers is shown in Fig. 6.1.

It was precisely the sequential appearance of consecutive numbers that led me in producing a solution. If I got, say, 04369, I knew that I had missed a palindrome (04340) by 29 tickets, and that the next would appear only when the 3 changes into 4 (04440), which is 71 tickets away. Similarly, if I got 34221, the previous and next palindromes would be 34143 and 34243 respectively. Thus, I concluded that the palindrome density should be 1 per 100, and since there are 100,000 five digit numbers there must be 1000 palindromes in all. However, I was uncomfortable with this density argument. It took me a while to figure out the source of my doubts. Consider 19991, the next palindrome is 20,002, definitely less than 100 numbers away, or 10901 and its next palindrome 11011 which are more than 100 numbers

Fig. 6.1 Bus tickets (used in Argentina in the 1970s) (Photo by A. Arcavi)

apart! But in analysing the problem further, I found that this does not at all affect the density property; there still is one palindrome for every 100 numbers (namely one palindrome for each change in the middle), although they are not always evenly distributed.

This problem and my proposed solution were a revelation for me. Firstly, it was me who posed a mathematical problem out of the mathematics class and this problem arose from a 'real-world' personal situation: the chances of getting a palindrome. This was one of the first times I experienced that the world out there can be mathematically poor or mathematically rich depending on the ways one looks at it and the questions it may inspire us to pose and solve (I develop this point further in Sect. 6.4). Much later, I also realised that this story has yet another important moral. The context of a problem is not just a mere excuse or a frill to engage students in doing mathematics, the problem can arise from a genuine situation awaiting to be solved. The particular features of a context can also inspire and lead to a solution approach which may be rather different than the method to solve the same problem when presented in 'pure' mathematical terms. Moreover, a context-oriented solution approach can uncover a characteristic of the solution (the irregular distribution of the palindromes although their density is constant). This characteristic of five-digit palindromes emerged as an incidental by-product of a solution method that relied on the contextual features of the problem and which is not at all obvious from the combinatorial solution.

Thus, in my university years, I began to enlarge my mathematical horizons and the types of mathematics that I might encounter, learn and teach.

6.3   Meeting RME

Towards the end of the 1980s and the beginning of the 1990s, I was introduced to RME. At the time, I started my academic career after a post-doctoral fellowship in mathematics education, and my experience with 'applied mathematics' (in curriculum development, teacher education, research on learning) was much richer than in my high school and early university years. Yet, even though procedures and rules were not the only focus of my professional interests (Arcavi, 1994, 2005a), my focus was still on pure mathematics. My acquaintance with Joop van Dormolen started with occasional meetings, which intensified through our collaboration within the International Group for the Psychology of Mathematics Education (PME), when I became Treasurer and Joop was Executive Secretary. Our collaboration grew far beyond mere administrative issues and I started to learn from him about RME. Learning 'live' from one of the persons so deeply involved with all the aspects of RME (curriculum design, teacher development and policy making) was a real treat. Reading and learning from texts is essential to get acquainted with a worldview, but to have an expert nearby to whom one can address questions and discuss answers leads to a faster and deeper learning. These exchanges led us to embark in the joint adventure of co-authoring two volumes of an elementary geometry book which we entitled *Seeing and Doing Geometry* (in Hebrew) (Halevy, Bouhadana, Van Dormolen, &

Arcavi, 1997; Bouhadana, Van Dormolen, & Arcavi, 2000) with its corresponding teacher's guide. This was for me the ultimate experience to learn from within and to enact the RME worldview.

Since I became more knowledgeable about mathematical modelling, and I was better acquainted with its potential to motivate students by appreciating the utility of mathematics, what was there for me to learn from RME? Well, a lot! Mathematical modelling, as I knew it from my own studies and from most school curricula I worked with, presupposed knowledge of pure mathematics which must be properly invoked and applied in order to make a model of a given real situation, solve it mathematically and reinterpret the results in terms of the situation being modelled. This implies that knowing pure mathematics comes before its applications, which seemed to me a natural chronology, and thus it did not occur to me to contest it. RME, as I understood it, inverted the order: the real world and intriguing situations can and should be a springboard to mathematise, first 'horizontally' and then 'vertically' (Treffers & Goffree, 1985; Freudenthal, 1991; Hershkowitz, Parzysz, & Van Dormolen, 1996). In other words, the foundational mathematics education tenet of RME was "to let that rich context of reality serve as a source for learning mathematics." (Treffers, 1993, p. 89)

This key idea was a real eye-opener, because it builds on students' knowledge from outside mathematics as a main resource and it relies on their common sense and their capacity to harness ad hoc intuitive and non-formal strategies as the main stepping stones upon which to build further. Even before Joop and I co-authored the geometry book, a good exercise for me was to co-author with him an article for teachers applying this insightful principle to the nature of two geometrical concepts: circumference and circle. What we did was to gather various real-life appearances that can be a resource for defining these concepts mathematically (Van Dormolen & Arcavi, 2000, 2001). RME proposes such an approach for teaching most topics in mathematics to both the less mathematically-oriented students as well as to the more advanced.

RME had extraordinary achievements both within the Netherlands and abroad. It was founded and directed for many years by Hans Freudenthal, a leading mathematician who dedicated much of his work to mathematics education, its possibilities, as well as its enormous challenges. Freudenthal took special care in understanding the characteristics of the learners, their potential and their difficulties. Not very often do mathematicians engage as deeply with the complexities of mathematics education as Freudenthal did, and thus their contributions tend to remain local or transient. RME under Freudenthal and his many distinguished collaborators and followers covered all levels of school mathematics in a gigantic effort to design, field test and re-design learning and teaching materials taking 'realistic' situations as departure points. RME also developed a systemic implementation that involved a whole country and influenced, directly or indirectly, many curriculum development projects all over the world.

RME's perspective also influenced the world-wide discussions around mathematical literacy and it even inspired the design of items for the PISA examination. The PISA examination can be contentious regarding the negative effects of the test preparation spree it provoked in many countries and the controversial claims regarding correlations between the examination grades and the economic growth of a country (e.g., *The Guardian*, 2014). However, in many cases, due to the prominence and visibility of the examination, it encouraged countries to rethink and to revise their curricula, since it was realised that the kinds of knowledge required for the examination items (mostly inspired by RME) were not appropriately supported or emphasised at school. There are only a few other mathematics education projects that have so wide a scope and that have so strongly influenced mathematics education in the world. There is much to learn from its principles, its implementation and hopefully its lasting effects, even if one does not fully adopt RME.

6.4   Developing a 'Mathematical Gaze'—From Instructional Design to a Learning Goal

The design principles of RME and the heuristics to enact them have been described at length in many sources (e.g., De Lange, 2015), and there is much to be learned from them. In this section, I would like to briefly focus on just one of these heuristics that had an influence on me and which can be described as follows: "I first look for 'images' which can stimulate associative thinking, an approach that has led to many new and surprising discoveries" (De Lange, 2015, pp. 290–291). In other words, looking around for visually salient cues can provide inspiring raw materials from which tasks and problems can be designed in order to lead students to horizontal and vertical mathematisation. This heuristic implies a highly developed eye capable of a 'mathematical gaze'. In my view, such a mathematical gaze would include:

> [...] the predisposition, ability and trust in the usefulness of seeing the non-evident mathematics behind many daily life situations. It also would mean meaningfully imposing the mathematics on these situations by creating and posing problems and questions to which only mathematics can provide an in-depth answer. (Arcavi, 2004, pp. 234–235)

It only takes a quick browsing of the materials of RME to realise that their instructional designers developed a mathematical gaze in amazingly rich ways. It occurred to me that the development of such a gaze could shift its function from a resource for instructional design to a learning goal for students. I witnessed this with myself in the bus story that having a goal in mind (collecting tickets with palindromes on them) may induce the self-posing of some mathematical questions worth pursuing. Why not introduce students to such practices already in elementary school? Consider, for example, the following images and the ensuing questions which can be the object of a classroom discussion (Arcavi, 2016).

Unlike the problem posed about palindromes on the bus tickets, in this case pausing and reflecting on what is the role of the numbers requires more than just pursuing a goal. It requires a certain habit of mind to look at what we take so much for granted and start to ask questions. This is not a trivial switch in the attention (or the lack of it) that we pay to our surroundings, as acknowledged in the following:

Sources of insight can be clogged by automatisms... the question of how and why is not asked any more, cannot be asked any more, and is not even understood any more as a meaningful and relevant question. (Freudenthal, 1983, p. 469)

A number on a license plate or a number indicating a certain building on a street are clearly a way of identification and thus each object is assigned one and only one number. But is this not the basic principle underlying counting? In what sense can we switch from looking at the numbers in a license plate as identifiers, to using them for counting? One way is to realise that one can place an upper bound on the number of cars using the same type of license plates (within a city or a whole country). In the first case, the picture on the left in Fig. 6.2, there are at most ten million cars with these types of license plates. This information was implicit in the license plate number, and a 'mathematical gaze' helped to unfold it. In the second case, we can even ponder about the reason to use letters as well as digits. This may lead to discussions about elementary combinatorics (which we do not need when we use numbers), for example, the English alphabet consists of 26 letters, thus in the position for a letter there are 26 possibilities, and license plates of the type of the picture on the right in Fig. 6.2 can thus accommodate $26 \times 26 \times 26 \times 10 \times 10 \times 10$ cars (much more than with just six digits). This kind of discussion can be scaffolded and supported in upper classes of elementary school and they may even be of interest to junior high school mathematics classes, or teachers in a professional development course, especially if one relates to CCC as a number in base 26.

When we look at numbers that identify addresses in different cities in the world, we may notice that in some of them the numbers are smaller (1–2 digits) than in others (4–5 digits). What could be the reason for that? The urbanisation of many cities adopts the form of a square grid, in which streets are either parallel or perpendicular and they surround 'blocks'. In many cities in Argentina, for example, these blocks are of 100 m by 100 m. Thus a number such as 1363 (see Fig. 6.3) indicates that the address identified is located at 63 m (the ten and the unit digits) from the beginning of the fourteenth block (the thousand and the hundred digits). With such a convention, it is almost impossible to have two neighbouring addresses with consecutive numbers. In other countries, the addresses just use consecutive numbers regardless of the distances and the blocks, and this indeed results in addresses with much smaller numbers. In

Fig. 6.2 What do these numbers indicate? (Photos by A. Arcavi)

Fig. 6.3 What do these numbers indicate? (Photos by A. Arcavi)

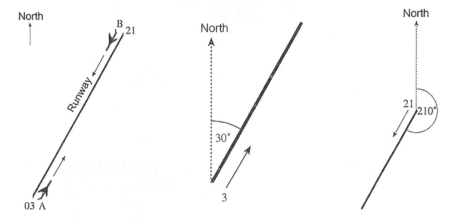

Fig. 6.4 Numbering convention for airport runways

this case, asking a question may lead to looking for information outside mathematics, but which is reflected in the way mathematics is used.

Numbers are everywhere and the unpacking of the question "What does a number indicate?" may yield to practical as well as to mathematical insights. Consider, for example, the numbers at both ends of an airport runway anywhere in the world which express the clockwise measurements of the angle between the runway and the North. Figure 6.4 shows a runway and its two ends which clarify the numbering convention (using two digits only).

This can be the source for a few lessons on the concept of angle, its uses, its measures and more. Consider the road sign in Fig. 6.5.

This sign indicates the steepness of the upcoming part of the road, and can be used to discuss the mathematical concept of slope and the many ways to measure it, including the uses of percentages.

Pairs of numbers seen in elevators around the world (indicating the maximum load and the maximum number of persons allowed) may lead to discussing mathematical concepts such as proportions and averages, and one may even end up suggesting

Fig. 6.5 Road sign indicating the steepness of a road (Photo by A. Arcavi)

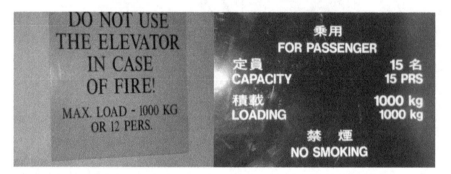

Fig. 6.6 Elevator signs in different countries (Photos by A. Arcavi)

non-mathematical issues like comparing the assumed physical characteristics for the population served by these elevators (Fig. 6.6).

The world out there can provide many opportunities to observe, question, calculate, answer and make conclusions about situations to which many people are blind. Such opportunities may include situations like the following two (Arcavi, 2005b) (Figs. 6.7 and 6.8).

These are just some possible examples which can be used for engaging children in both problem solving around real-life situations and mostly for supporting the development of a mathematical gaze which implies:

Fig. 6.7 How long would it take to you to run the distance that you can walk in 10 min? (Photo by A. Arcavi)

Fig. 6.8 Why are the fish arranged in a circle? (Photo by A. Arcavi)

– A fresh look at situations which are usually taken for granted
– Identifying the 'mathematisable' within situations
– Pondering and asking questions about these situations without expecting them to be given by the teacher or the textbook
– Relating natural language to formal and symbolic language
– Proposing ideas, solutions and conclusions
– Posing problems.

6.5   Coda

By providing an inclusive, educationally sound definition of 'realistic', RME allowed me to look with new eyes at my initial fondness for the procedural and to consider it as an integral part of what can be mathematically valuable. Moreover, it legitimised my perception that the procedural can have a respectable place in what can be 'realistic' for many students. With hindsight, and under the conviction that the procedural and the conceptual (in the sense of Hiebert, 1986) should be deeply interwoven, these were the roots of my work on sense making both with symbols and with images (Arcavi, 1994, 2003).

By re-positioning modelling not only as a way to use mathematics to solve applied problems, but also as a way of using authentic real-life situations as departure points for launching the teaching and learning of mathematical concepts and strategies, RME convinced me of the immense potential of these ideas. Moreover, it inspired me to think that the development of a 'mathematical gaze' is not only a powerful tool for task design, but also an implementable goal even with elementary school students.

By placing the idea of mathematical literacy on the public agenda and by influencing the design of many items in the PISA examination, RME provided me with broader spectacles through which to look at school curricula and caused me to realise what may be missing in them.

Acknowledgements I am very grateful to Marja van den Heuvel-Panhuizen for inviting me to write a chapter for this book and for her openness to accept a personal narrative related to RME rather than insisting on a scholarly research paper. This was an opportunity for me to reflect back on aspects of my own professional development and how parts of it were greatly influenced by RME. I may delude myself in believing that personal accounts of this kind can be useful to our community, but I do hope they will be. Also, I wish to thank Moti Ben-Ari, Joop van Dormolen, Alon Pinto, Ronnie Karsenty, Jason Cooper, Avital Elbaum-Cohen and Gil Schwarts for their careful reading of an earlier version and for their helpful comments and suggestions.

References

Arcavi, A. (1994). Symbol sense: Informal sense-making in formal mathematics. *For the Learning of Mathematics, 14*(3), 24–35.
Arcavi, A. (2002). The everyday and the academic in mathematics. M. Brenner & J. Moschkovich (Eds.), *Everyday and academic mathematics in the classroom. A Monograph of the Journal for Research in Mathematics Education.* (pp. 12–29). Reston, VA: National Council of Teachers of Mathematics.
Arcavi, A. (2003). The role of visual representations in the teaching and learning of mathematics. *Educational Studies in Mathematics, 52*(3), 215–241.
Arcavi, A. (2004). Education of mathematics teachers. In R. Strässer, G. Brandell, B. Grevholm, & O. Helenius (Eds.), *Educating for the future. Proceedings of an International Symposium on Mathematics Teacher Education* (pp. 227–234). Göteborg, Sweden: The Royal Swedish Academy of Sciences.
Arcavi, A. (2005a). Developing and using symbol sense in mathematics. *For the Learning of Mathematics, 25*(2), 50–55.
Arcavi, A. (2005b). Some Japanese mathematical landscapes. http://math-info.criced.tsukuba.ac. jp/museum/arcavi/arcavi_english/. Accessed March 8, 2016.
Arcavi, A. (2016). Miradas matemáticas y pensamiento numérico. *Avances de Investigación en Educación Matemática, 9,* 11–19.
Bouhadana, R., Van Dormolen, J., & Arcavi, A. (2000). *Seeing and doing geometry II (in Hebrew).* Rehovot, Israel: The Weizmann Institute of Science.

De Lange, J. (2015). There is, probably, no need for this presentation. In A. Watson & M. Ohtani (Eds.), *Task design in mathematics education. ICMI study 22* (pp. 287–308). New York, NY: Springer.

ECNAIS. (2014). OECD and Pisa tests are damaging education worldwide—academics. Open letter to Dr. Andreas Schleicher. *The Guardian.* http://www.theguardian.com/education/2014/may/06/ oecd-pisa-tests-damaging-education-academics. Accessed March 8, 2016.

Freudenthal, H. (1983). *The didactical phenomenology of mathematical structures.* Dordrecht, the Netherlands: Reidel.

Freudenthal, H. (1991). *Revisiting mathematics education. China lectures.* Dordrecht, the Netherlands: Kluwer Academic Publishers.

Friedlander, A., & Arcavi, A. (2017). *Tasks & competencies in the teaching and learning of algebra.* Reston, VA: National Council of Teachers of Mathematics.

Halevy, T., Bouhadana, R., Van Dormolen, J., & Arcavi, A. (1997). *Seeing and doing geometry (in Hebrew).* Rehovot, Israel: The Weizmann Institute of Science.

Hershkowitz, R., Parzysz, B., & Van Dormolen, J. (1996). Shape and space. In A. J. Bishop, K. Clements, C. Keitel, J. Kilpatrick, & C. Laborde (Eds.), *International handbook of mathematics education* (pp. 161–204). Dordrecht, the Netherlands: Kluwer Academic Publishers.

Hiebert, J. (Ed.). (1986). *Conceptual and procedural knowledge: The case of mathematics.* Hillsdale, NJ: Lawrence Erlbaum.

Sfard, A. (2016). When words get in your eyes: On challenges of investigating mathematics-in-teaching and on the importance of paying attention to words. https://www.msri.org/workshops/ 793/schedules/20595. Accessed March 8, 2016.

Treffers, A. (1993). Wiskobas and Freudenthal—Realistic mathematics education. *Educational Studies in Mathematics, 25*(1), 89–108.

Treffers, A., & Goffree, F. (1985). Rational analysis of realistic mathematics education. In L. Streefland (Ed.), *Proceedings of the 9th International Conference for the Psychology of Mathematics Education* (Vol. II, pp. 97–123). Utrecht, the Netherlands: OW&OC.

Van den Heuvel-Panhuizen, M. (2003). The didactical use of models in Realistic Mathematics Education: An example from a longitudinal trajectory on percentage. *Educational Studies in Mathematics, 54*(1), 9–35.

Van Dormolen, J., & Arcavi, A. (2000). What is a circle? *Mathematics in School, 29*(5), 15–19.

Van Dormolen, J., & Arcavi, A. (2001). Wat is een cirkel? *Euclides, 76*(5), 182–186.

Chapter 7
Graphing Linear Equations—A Comparison of the Opportunity-to-Learn in Textbooks Using the Singapore and the Dutch Approaches to Teaching Equations

Berinderjeet Kaur, Lai Fong Wong and Simmi Naresh Govindani

Abstract This chapter examines the opportunity-to-learn afforded by two textbooks, one using the Singapore approach and the other the Dutch approach for graphing linear equations. Both textbooks provide opportunities for students to connect mathematical concepts to meaningful real-life situations, practice questions for self-assessment, and reflect on their learning. However, the approaches presented in the two textbooks are different. The Dutch approach textbook has the same context for all the interconnected activities while in the Singapore approach textbook the activities are self-contained and can be carried out independently of each other. In addition, classroom activities, practice questions and prompts for reflection in the Dutch approach textbook provide students with more scope for reasoning and communication. From the reflections of two lead teachers using the Singapore approach textbook it is apparent that they see merit in the Dutch approach textbook, but feel that to adopt the Dutch approach they would need a paradigm shift and adequate support in terms of resources.

Keywords Opportunity-to-learn (OTL) · Dutch approach textbook · Singapore approach textbook · Graphing linear equations

B. Kaur (✉) · L. F. Wong
National Institute of Education, Singapore, Singapore
e-mail: berinderjeet.kaur@nie.edu.sg

L. F. Wong
e-mail: laifong.wong@nie.edu.sg

S. N. Govindani
Yishun Secondary School, Singapore, Singapore
e-mail: simmi_naresh_govindani@moe.edu.sg

M. van den Heuvel-Panhuizen (ed.), *International Reflections on the Netherlands Didactics of Mathematics*, ICME-13 Monographs,
https://doi.org/10.1007/978-3-030-20223-1_7

7.1 Introduction

Carroll (1963) was the first to introduce the concept of opportunity-to-learn (OTL). He asserted that an individual's learning was dependent on the task used and the amount of time devoted to learn. This concept has been particularly useful when comparing student achievement across countries, such as those carried out by studies like Trends in International Mathematics and Science Study (TIMSS). Several approaches have been used by researchers to assess OTL (Brewer & Stasz, 1996; Liu, 2009). Amongst the OTL variables considered by Liu (2009) are content coverage, content exposure, content emphasis and quality of instructional delivery and the OTL categories considered by Brewer and Stasz (1996) are curriculum content, instructional strategies and instructional resources.

The TIMSS textbook study (Foxman, 1999; Schmidt, McKnight, Valverde, Houang, & Wiley, 1997) is one example of examining the OTL based on studies of instructional materials such as textbooks. Recently, Wijaya, Van den Heuvel-Panhuizen, and Doorman (2015) showed how fruitful the concept of OTL is when they investigated the relation between the tasks offered in Indonesian mathematics textbooks and the Indonesian students' difficulties to solve context-based mathematics tasks.

Researchers have generally agreed that textbooks play a dominant and direct role in what is addressed in instruction. Robitaille and Travers (1992, p. 706) noted that a great dependence upon textbooks is "perhaps more characteristic of the teaching of mathematics than of any other subject". This is due to the canonical nature of the mathematics curriculum. Several researchers have noted that the textbooks teachers adopt for their teaching often result in dictating the content they teach and the teaching strategies they adopt (Freeman & Porter, 1989; Reys, Reys, & Chavez, 2004). Therefore, it is not surprising that textbooks may be used as proxies to determine students' OTL (Schmidt, McKnight, & Raizen, 1997; Tornroos, 2005). Inevitably if textbooks implementing a specific curriculum, such as the graphing of equations, differ, students using the respective textbooks will get different OTL (Haggarty & Pepin, 2002). This different OTL have often resulted in different student outcomes as there is a strong relation between textbook used and mathematics performance of students (see, e.g., Tornroos, 2005; Xin, 2007).

7.2 A Study of Teaching Graphing Linear Equations in Textbooks Using the Singapore and Dutch Approach

7.2.1 Objective of This Chapter

The objective of this chapter is to examine the OTL related to graphing linear equations in two textbooks, one of which is using a Singapore approach and the other using a Dutch approach. The book using the Singapore approach is *Discovering*

Fig. 7.1 Textbook *Discovering Mathematics 1B* (Chow, 2013) with approval stamp

Mathematics 1B (Chow, 2013) and the book using the Dutch approach is *Mathematics in Context* (Wisconsin Center for Education Research & Freudenthal Institute, 2010).

7.2.2 Backgrounds of the Contexts of Textbooks Examined

The textbook *Discovering Mathematics* (Chow, 2013) adopts a Singapore approach. It is one of the approved texts that schools may adopt for their instructional needs. Textbooks in Singapore that are approved by the Ministry of Education have an approval stamp, as shown in Fig. 7.1.

These textbooks are closely aligned to the intended curriculum (mathematics syllabuses) issued by the Ministry of Education in Singapore for all schools. The framework for the school mathematics curriculum in Singapore is shown in Fig. 7.2.

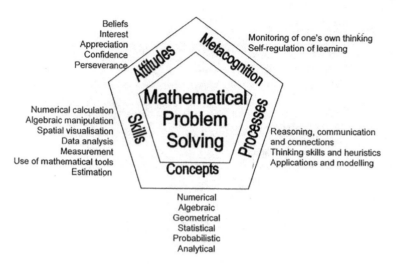

Fig. 7.2 Framework of the school mathematics curriculum (Ministry of Education, 2012)

The primary goal of the curriculum is mathematical problem solving and five inter-related components, namely concepts, skills, processes, metacognition and attitudes, contribute towards it.

The *Discovering Mathematics* textbook includes clear and illustrative examples, class activities and diagrams to help students understand the concepts and apply them. Essentially the textbook advocates a teaching for problem solving approach. In this conception of teaching problem solving, the content is taught for instrumental, relational and conventional understanding (Skemp, 1976) so that students are able to apply them to solve problems associated with content. This is clearly evident from the key features of the textbook, which are a chapter opener, class activities, worked examples to try, exercises that range from direct applications in real-life situations to tasks that demand higher-order thinking.

The *Mathematics in Context* textbook (Wisconsin Center for Education Research & Freudenthal Institute, 2010) written for the U.S. middle school reflects the Dutch approach of Realistic Mathematics Education (RME) (Van den Heuvel-Panhuizen & Drijvers, 2014). The textbook manifests the core teaching principles of RME which are:

- The activity principle—students are active participants in the learning process;
- The reality principle—mathematics education should start from problem situations and students must be able to apply mathematics to solve real-life problems;
- The level principle—learning mathematics involves acquiring levels of under-standing that range from informal context-related solutions to acquiring insights into how concepts and strategies are related;
- The intertwinement principle—mathematics content domains such as number, geometry, measurement, etc. must not be treated as isolated curriculum chapters, but be integrated in rich problems;

- The interactivity principle—learning mathematics is a social activity; and
- The guidance principle—teachers should have a proactive role in students' learning and programmes should be based on coherent long-term teaching-learning trajectories (Van den Heuvel-Panhuizen & Drijvers, 2014, pp. 522–523).

7.2.3 Framework for Analysing the OTL in the Textbooks

The analysis of textbooks can not only be carried out in several ways, but has also evolved with time. This is evident from research studies related to TIMSS. Schmidt et al. (1997) involved in TIMSS, initially focused on examining the content of textbooks, but later Valverde, Bianchi, Wolfe, Schmidt, and Houang (2002) expanded the examination to (i) classroom activities proposed by the textbook, (ii) amount of content covered and mode of presentation—abstract or concrete, (iii) sequencing of content, (iv) physical attributes of the textbooks such as size and number of pages, and (v) complexity of the demands for student performance. Furthermore, non-canonical aspects of mathematics may also be examined. For example, Pepin and Haggarty (2001) in their study on the use of mathematics textbooks in English, French and German classrooms adopted an approach that focused not only on the topics (content) and methods (teaching strategies), but also the sociological contexts and cultural traditions manifested in the books.

In this chapter, we examine the OTL related to graphing linear equations in two textbooks, one of which is using a Singapore approach and the other using a Dutch approach. Our investigation is guided by the following questions:

What are the similarities and differences in the two textbooks with respect to

- sequencing of content in the chapter on graphing equations
- classroom activities proposed by the chapter on graphing equations
- complexity of the demands for student performance in the chapter on equations?

The respective textbook materials examined are Chap. 12, titled "Coordinates and Linear Functions" from the Singapore approach textbook *Discovering Mathematics* (Chow, 2013) and the chapter "Graphing Equations" (Kindt et al., 2010) from the Dutch approach textbook *Mathematics in Context* (Wisconsin Center for Education Research & Freudenthal Institute, 2010).

Table 7.1 Sequencing of content in the two textbooks

Singapore approach in the textbook *Discovering Mathematics 1B—Coordinates and Linear Functions*

Construct the Cartesian coordinate system in two-dimensions and state coordinates of points on it → Plot a graph of a set of ordered pairs as a representation of a relationship between two variables → recognise the idea of functions → recognise linear functions in various forms and draw their graphs → find the gradient of a linear graph as a ratio of the vertical change to the horizontal change

Dutch approach in the textbook *Mathematics in Context—Graphing Equations*

Locate points using compass directions and bearings → locate points on a coordinate system in the context of a forest fire → Starting from steps along a line, investigate the concept of slope → Use the y-intercept as a reference point for graphing linear functions → Draw lines for given equations and write equations for drawn lines → Develop formal algebraic methods for solving linear equations through visualizing frogs jumping towards or away from a path → Learn a formal way of solving equations by simultaneously changing the diagrams and the equations the diagram → Write down the operations performed to keep track of the steps taken in solving an equation → Describe and graph problem situations, which are solved by locating the point of intersection → Combine the graphical method to find a point of intersection with the use of equations → Relate the method for solving frog problems to finding the point of intersection of two lines by linking the lines in the graph to their equations using arrows → Connect the graphical and algebraic method explicitly → Explore the relationship between parallel lines and graphs of lines without intersection points

7.3 Data and Results

7.3.1 The Sequencing of the Content on Graphing Equations in the Two Textbooks

In this section, we tabulate the content in the chapters on graphing equations in the two textbooks. This will allow us to draw out the similarities and differences. Table 7.1 shows the flow of content in the Singapore and the Dutch approach textbook respectively.

From Table 7.1 it is apparent that in the two textbooks the sequence of the content is dissimilar. The books take significantly different pathways in developing the content. In the Singapore approach textbook, students are directly introduced to the terminology (such as Cartesian coordinate system, x- and y-axis, origin, x- and y-coordinates, etc.) and concepts of the topic through some class activities or investigative work. Worked examples are provided next and these are then followed by practice questions on three different levels—simple questions involving direct application of concepts are given on Level 1; more challenging questions on direction application on Level 2; and on Level 3 questions that involve real-life applications, thinking skills, and questions that relate to other disciplines. This is the sequence for each sub-unit, and the chapter ends with a summary, a revision exercise, a real-life context that relates to the topic, and students' reflection.

In the Dutch approach textbook, a real-life context (such as a forest fire) is first introduced and students continuously formalise their knowledge, building on knowledge from previous units (and sub-units). Regarding the context, students gradually adopt the conventional formal vocabulary and notation, such as origin, quadrant, and *x*-axis, as well as the ordered pairs notation (*x*, *y*). In each sub-unit, a summary is provided and some questions are given for students' self-assessment, followed by further reflection.

7.3.2 Classroom Activities Proposed on Graphing Equations in the Two Textbooks

In this section, we tabulate the classroom activities as intended by the two textbooks for the development of knowledge related to the graphing of (linear) equations. Table 7.2 shows the flow of activities in the two chapters in the Singapore and the Dutch approach textbooks respectively. In the Singapore approach textbook, the content is organised as units while in the Dutch approach textbook the content is organised in sections.

From Table 7.2 it is apparent that there are distinct differences in the classroom activities proposed in the two books. Activities in the Singapore approach textbook facilitate the learning of mathematical concepts through exploration and discovery. Some of these activities provide students with opportunities to use ICT tools that encourage interactive learning experiences. While these classroom activities are structured systematically, each activity is complete of itself, and can be carried out independently from the others. There is no one context that runs through all the activities in the chapter. However, in the Dutch approach textbook, students are introduced to the context of locating forest fires from fire towers and this context is used in the activities throughout the chapter. These classroom activities require students to apply their existing knowledge before introducing the formal mathematical concepts, thus providing students with opportunities to make connections between the new concepts and previous knowledge and with applications in real-life situations as well.

7.3.3 Complexity of the Demands for Student Performance on Graphing Equations in the Two Textbooks

In the two textbooks, classroom activities and practice questions comprise questions of two types. The first type is merely about the recall of knowledge and development of skills. These questions contain verbs such as 'find', 'write down', and 'plot/draw'. The second type involves higher-order thinking and these questions ask students to 'explain', 'justify', and 'interpret'. The verbs in the questions refer to the level of cognitive activity the students are invited to be engaged in.

Table 7.2 Classroom activities in the two textbooks

Singapore approach in the textbook *Discovering Mathematics 1B – Coordinates and Linear Functions*
Unit 12.1. Cartesian coordinate system:
State the coordinates of given points on the Cartesian plane and the quadrants in which the points lie → Plot points on the
Cartesian plane → Play a battleship game that involves the use of Cartesian coordinates
Unit 12.2. Idea of a function:
Use a function machine to understand the concept of function and represent a function using verbal, tabular, graphical and
algebraic forms → Practise the different ways a function can be represented → Associate ordered pairs with points on a
coordinate plane to represent a relationship between two variables
Units 12.3. Linear functions and their graphs:
Recognise linear functions and draw graphs of linear functions
Unit 12.4. Gradients of Linear Graphs:
Learn the idea of gradient of a straight line as the ratio of the vertical change to the horizontal change → Interpret the meanings
of positive, negative, zero and undefined gradients → Recognise how the graph of the linear function $y = ax + b$ changes
when either a or b varies → Understand the physical interpretation of the gradient of a linear graph as the rate of change

Dutch approach in the textbook *Mathematics in Context—Graphing Equations*
Section A. Where there's smoke:
Use compass directions and then degree measurements to describe directions → Plot lines that intersect to locate forest fires
on a map → Use coordinates to locate these fires on a computer screen that uses a four-quadrant coordinate grid → Explore
how the coordinates (x, y) change as the fire moves in different directions → Use equations of vertical/horizontal lines to
describe the movement of fires along the vertical/horizontal lines → Draw vertical/horizontal lines described by equation to
represent firebreaks → Use inequalities to describe regions
Section B. Directions as pairs of numbers:
Use direction pairs to describe directions and discover that more than one direction pair can describe the same direction →
Explore the use of direction pairs on a coordinate grid → Investigate direction pairs that describe the same direction and
different directions → Investigate direction pairs that are opposite and discover that they form one line → Learn and apply the
concept of slope through describing a direction as the slope of a line using a single number, the ratio of the vertical component
to the horizontal component → Determine the slope of a graphed line and graph a line give the slope and a starting point →
Determine the slope of graphed lines → Use the slope to determine the point at which two non-parallel lines meet
Section C. An equation of a line:
Investigate how to move along a straight line by taking steps in horizontal and vertical directions on a graphing programme →
Use horizontal and vertical steps to informally investigate the equation of a line in slope-intercept form → Learn and interpret
the meanings of the parameters in an equation in slope-intercept form → Draw the lines using the slope and y-intercept →
Write equations for graphed lines → Investigate the equations of parallel lines → Investigate the relationship between the
slope of a line and the angle that the line makes with the positive x-axis → Learn the relationship between the slope and the
tangent of the angle that a line makes with the positive x-axis
Section D. Solving equations:
Investigate a context involving jumping frogs and compare the effect of different jump lengths on the distance that two frogs
travel from starting points → Compare and use diagrams and equations to determine the unknown length of a frog jump →
Solve equations of the form $ax + b = cx + d$ with reference to the 'frog problem' → Solve 'frog problems' that involve jumps
in opposite directions → Use diagrams to represent expressions and equations and solve an equation → Use a number line to
represent and solve equations → Perform the same operation on each side of an equation to solve it
Section E. Intersecting lines:
Estimate the coordinates where two lines intersect and use the equations for the lines to check the estimate → Solve equations
to determine the coordinates of the point where two lines intersect → Solve problems involving point of intersection for pairs
of lines → Compare and make connections between the graphical and algebraic methods of solving linear equations

In this section, we focus on questions of the second type present in classroom activities and practice questions. Table 7.3 shows the key words and questions stemming from the classroom activities, practice questions and prompts for reflection in the two chapters in the Singapore and the Dutch approach textbook respectively.

From Table 7.3, it is apparent that the classroom activities, practice questions and prompts for reflection in both textbooks do engage students in higher-order thinking. In the Singapore approach textbook questions/instructions such as "What can you observe about the relationship of …?", "What can you say about …?", "Interpret …", "Explain …", and "Describe …" encourage students to integrate information, choose their own strategies, and explain how they solved a problem. However, in the Dutch approach textbook, in addition to the questions/instructions found in the

Table 7.3 Complexity of cognitive demands for student performance in questions in the two textbooks

Approach in textbook	
Singapore approach in the textbook *Discovering Mathematics* 1B—*Coordinates and Linear Functions*	Dutch approach in the textbook *Mathematics in Context*—*Graphing Equations*
• What can you observe about the relationship of ...? • What can you say about ...? • Can we use the equation to ...? Explain briefly. • Describe a real-life example where 2 variables are in a linear relationship and draw a graph to represent the relationship. • Interpret the physical meaning of ...	• Explain why or why not. • What can you say about ...? • Describe what happens ... • How do you ...? Explain your answer. • What do you notice in your answers ...? • Explain how you can conclude this from ... • How did you find out? • What is the simplest way to ...?
	• Explain what each of ... refers to. • Explain the formula. • Does the formula work for ...? • What is the importance of ... for the graph? • Why do you think it is called the ...? • Justify your answer. • What is ... if ...? • Do you agree ...? Explain. • Write down your thinking about this problem. Share your group's method with the other members of your class. • How can you be sure that your answers are correct?
For reflection • Describe in your own words ... • Describe two quantities which have a linear relationship in your daily life.	For reflection • Compare the two ways... • How can similar triangles be used to find the slope of a line? • Describe in your own words what is meant by the word... • Explain why it is important to ... • Think about the three different methods for ... What are the advantages and disadvantages of each method? • Graphs and equations can be used to describe lines and their intersections. Tell which is easier for you to use and explain why.

Singapore approach textbook, there are further questions/instructions such as "What is the simplest way to …?", "What if …?", "Do you agree …?", "How can you be sure …?", "Write down your thinking …", and "Share your method …". These encourage students to analyse, interpret, synthesise, reflect, and develop their own strategies or mathematical models. Therefore, it may be said that the classroom activities, practice questions and prompts for reflection in the Dutch approach textbook span a wider range of higher-order thinking when compared with the Singapore approach textbook.

7.4 Findings and Discussion

In the last section, we examine both the textbooks in three main areas, namely (1) sequencing of content, (2) classroom activities, and (3) complexity of the demands for student performance proposed in the chapter on graphing equations in the two textbooks. Our data and results show that there are similarities and differences in all three of the above areas.

7.4.1 Sequencing of Content

Both the Singapore approach and Dutch approach textbooks provide opportunities for students to connect the mathematical concepts to meaningful real-life situations, practice questions for self-assessment, and reflect on their learning. However, the approaches presented in the two textbooks are different.

In the Singapore approach textbook, students learn the topic in a structured and systematic manner—direct introduction of key concepts, class activities that enhance their learning experiences, worked examples, followed by practice questions and question that allow students to apply mathematical concepts. The application of the mathematical concepts to real-world problems takes place after the acquisition of knowledge in each sub-topic, and reflection of learning takes place at the end of the whole topic.

In the Dutch approach textbook, students learn the mathematical concepts in the topic in an intuitive manner, threaded by a single real-life context. Students learn the concepts through a variety of representations and make connections among these representations. They learn the use of algebra as a tool to solve problems that arise in the real world from a stage where symbolic representations are temporarily freed to a deeper understanding of the concepts. The application of the mathematical concepts to real-world problems takes place as the students acquire the knowledge in each sub-topic, and reflection of learning also takes place at the end of each sub-topic.

7.4.2   Classroom Activities

The classroom activities proposed in both the Singapore approach and Dutch approach textbooks provide opportunities for students to acquire the mathematical knowledge through exploration and discovery. ICT tools are also used appropriately to enhance their interactive learning experiences.

However, the classroom activities proposed in the Singapore approach textbook are typically each complete in themselves and can be carried out independently from the others. There is no one context that runs through all these activities. In the Dutch textbook approach, the context introduced at the beginning of the chapter is used in the classroom activities throughout the chapter. These classroom activities require students to apply their existing knowledge before introducing the formal mathematical concepts, thus providing students with opportunities to make connections between the new concepts and previous knowledge and with applications in real-life situations as well.

7.4.3   Complexity of the Demands for Student Performance

In both the Singapore approach and the Dutch approach textbooks, classroom activities and practice questions comprise questions that (1) require recall of knowledge and development of skills, and (2) require higher-order thinking and make greater cognitive demands of the students. The student learning process is facilitated with questions such as "What can you observe?", "What can you say?", "Explain", "Why do you think?" and "What if?".

However, the classroom activities, practice questions and prompts for reflection in the Dutch approach textbook provide students with more scope for reasoning and communication and promote the development of the disciplinarity orientation of mathematics. There are further questions/instructions that encourage students to analyse, interpret, synthesise, reflect, and develop and share their own strategies or mathematical models.

7.5   Reflections of Two Singapore Mathematics Teachers

Two mathematics teachers who are co-authors of this chapter and are using the Singapore approach textbook in their schools, studied of both textbooks the chapter on graphing equations. There reflections on these chapters were guided by the following questions:

– How do you teach graphing equations to your students?
– Has the Dutch approach textbook provided you with an alternative perspective?

– Would the Dutch approach work in Singapore classrooms? What would it take for it to work in Singapore classrooms?

7.5.1 Profiles of the Two Teachers

Both teachers, Wong Lai Fong (WLF) and Simmi Naresh Govindani (SNG), are lead mathematics teachers. They have been teaching secondary school mathematics for the past two decades. As lead teachers, they have demonstrated a high level of competence in both mathematical content and pedagogical and didactical content knowledge. In addition to their teaching duties they are also responsible for the development of mathematics teachers in their respective schools and other dedicated schools. Teacher WLF teaches in an average ability band school while Teacher SNG teaches in a lower ability band school compared to that of Teacher WLF.

7.5.2 How Do You Teach Graphing Equations to Your Students?

WLF:

Typically, when teaching the topic of graphing equations, I adopt the following sequence. First, I use a real-life example to illustrate the use of the mathematical concepts. Next, I engage students in learning experiences that provide them with opportunities to explore and discover the mathematical concepts, with appropriate scaffolding using questions of higher cognitive demands that require students to reason, communicate and make connections. Lastly, I induct my students in doing practice questions varying from direct application of concepts to application of concepts to real-life problems.

SNG:

Usually when I teach this topic I would first of all use a real-life example to explain the concept of location. To do so, I use the Battleship puzzle (available as a physical board game as well as in an online version) to provide my students with a learning experience and set the context for learning the topic. This puzzle facilitates students in plotting points using coordinates (x, y). Next, I would explain the concept of gradient by linking it to steepness and gentleness of slope of a straight line. An interactive worksheet or an ICT enabled lesson would be used to scaffold learning. Lastly, the concept of equation of a straight line would be explained by plotting points (on graph paper) which lie on a straight line. Students would be engaged in looking for patterns to arrive at the relation between x and y coordinates of any point on a given line. I would highlight and show that every point on the line satisfies the equation and points not on the line do not satisfy the equation. In all of the above, I would ask pertinent questions during the course of the lesson, to check for students' understanding. In addition, I would use mathematical tasks to engage students in reflecting on their learning and addressing students' misconceptions/errors.

7.5.3 Has the Dutch Approach Textbook Provided You with an Alternative Perspective?

WLF:

The Dutch approach has provided me with an alternative perspective where a topic can be taught with the introduction of a real-life context. Moving from informal to formal representations, this approach encourages student to continuously formalise their mathematical knowledge, building on what they already know in real-life and previous topics through mathematical reasoning and communication, thus creating an appreciation and making meaning of what they are learning and how it will be a tool to solve problems that arise in the real world.

SNG:

Yes, the Dutch approach is very interesting because it provides for mathematical reasoning and communication in the classroom throughout the process of learning. Also, teachers are able to help their students in monitoring success and correct errors when appropriate, thus promoting metacognition. These are some of the 21st century competencies that we would like our students to acquire.

7.5.4 Would the Dutch Approach Work in Singapore Classrooms? What Would It Take for It to Work in Singapore Classrooms?

WLF:

When adopting the Dutch approach, the role of a teacher is impetus. The teacher must possess sound pedagogical and didactical content knowledge in order to facilitate student learning with effective questions that promote thinking and make higher-cognitive demands on the students. Through classroom discourse, the teacher has to listen closely to students' responses and observe for evidence of students' under-standing of the mathematics. Besides the mathematical knowledge, the teacher must also possess knowledge of the real-life context so as to help students connect to the context through appropriate questions and discussions.

In order to adopt the Dutch approach in the Singapore classrooms, perhaps a paradigm shift in the teachers' mindset on how mathematics learning takes place is necessary—from 'content to application' to 'content through application'. There may not be a drastic change in the teaching approach or strategies as learning experiences that promote mathematical reasoning and communication are currently taking place in the Singapore classrooms. With appropriate modification to our existing teaching resources, accompanied with well-designed textbooks and teachers' guides, there is definitely a chance of successful implementation of the Dutch approach in our local classrooms.

SNG:

Singapore mathematics teachers may not be adequately skilled in carrying out such lessons. Hence, there is a need for teacher training and a mindset change to explore and embrace the change. Well-designed textbooks and teacher guides could help to alleviate some of the issues.

7.6 Concluding Remarks

This chapter shows how the teaching of graphing equations differs in the Singapore approach and the Dutch approach textbooks. Needless to say, this is the case as both the books are based on different ideas of how best to teach mathematics or how best teachers may facilitate the students' learning of mathematics. It is clearly evident that teachers using the Singapore approach teach for problem solving in which they move 'from content to application', while in the Dutch approach, following the core teaching principles of RME (Van den Heuvel-Panhuizen & Drijvers, 2014) the students are taught 'content through application'. From the reflections of the two lead teachers teaching in Singapore schools and using the Singapore approach it is apparent that they see merit in the Dutch approach but feel that for teachers to adopt the Dutch approach, a paradigm shift in the minds of teachers and adequate support in terms of resources would be necessary.

References

Brewer, D. J., & Stasz, C. (1996). *Enhancing opportunity to learn measures in NCES data.* Santa Monica, CA: RAND.

Carroll, J. (1963). A model of school learning. *Teachers College Record, 64,* 723–733.

Chow, W. K. (2013). *Discovering mathematics 1B* (2nd ed.). Singapore: Star Publishing Pte Ltd.

Foxman, D. (1999). *Mathematics textbooks across the world: Some evidence from the third international mathematics and science study.* Slough, UK: National Foundation for Educational Research (NFER).

Freeman, D., & Porter, A. (1989). Do textbooks dictate the content of mathematics instruction in elementary school? *American Educational Research Journal, 26,* 403–421.

Haggarty, L., & Pepin, B. (2002). An investigation of mathematics textbooks in England, France and Germany: Some challenges for England. *Research in Mathematics Education, 4*(1), 127–144.

Kindt, M., Wijers, M., Spence, M. S., Brinker, L. J., Pligge, M. A., Burrill, J., et al. (2010). Graphing equations. In Wisconsin Center for Education Research & Freudenthal Institute (Eds.), *Mathematics in context*. Chicago, IL: Encyclopaedia Britannica, Inc.

Liu, X. (2009). *Linking competencies to opportunities to learn: Models of competence and data mining*. New York, NY: Springer.

Ministry of Education Singapore. (2012). *O-Level, N(A) Level, N(T) level mathematics teaching and learning syllabuses*. Singapore: Author.

Pepin, B., & Haggarty, L. (2001). Mathematics textbooks and their use in English, French and German classrooms: A way to understand teaching and learning cultures. *ZDM—Mathematics Education, 33*(5), 158–175.

Reys, B. J., Reys, R. E., & Chávez, O. (2004). Why mathematics textbooks matter. *Educational Leadership, 61*(5), 61–66.

Robitaille, D. F., & Travers, K. J. (1992). International studies of achievement in mathematics. In D. A. Grouws (Ed.), *Handbook of research on mathematics teaching and learning* (pp. 687–709). New York, NY: Macmillan Publishing Company.

Schmidt, W. H., McKnight, C. C., & Raizen, S. (1997a). *A splintered vision: An investigation of U.S. science and mathematics education*. Boston, MA: Kluwer Academic Publishers.

Schmidt, W. H., McKnight, C. C., Valverde, G. A., Houang, R. T., & Wiley, D. E. (1997b). *Many visions, many aims: A cross-national investigation of curricular intentions in school mathematics*. Dordrecht, the Netherlands: Kluwer Academic Publishers.

Skemp, R. (1976). Relational understanding and instrumental understanding. *Mathematics Teaching, 77*, 20–26.

Tornroos, J. (2005). Mathematics textbooks, opportunity to learn and student achievement. *Studies in Educational Evaluation, 31*(4), 315–327.

Van den Heuvel-Panhuizen, M., & Drijvers, P. (2014). Realistic mathematics education. In S. Lerman (Ed.), *Encyclopedia of mathematics education* (pp. 521–525). Dordrecht, the Netherlands: Springer.

Valverde, G. A., Bianchi, L. J., Wolfe, R. G., Schmidt, W. H., & Houang, R. T. (2002). *According to the book. Using TIMSS to investigate the translation of policy into practice through the world of textbooks*. Dordrecht, the Netherlands: Kluwer Academic Press.

Wijaya, A., Van den Heuvel-Panhuizen, M., & Doorman, M. (2015). Opportunity-to-learn context-based tasks provided by mathematics textbooks. *Educational Studies in Mathematics, 89*, 41–65.

Wisconsin Center for Education Research & Freudenthal Institute. (2010). *Mathematics in context*. Chicago, IL: Encyclopaedia Britannica Inc.

Xin, Y. P. (2007). Word problem solving tasks in textbooks and their relation to student performance. *Journal of Educational Research, 100*(6), 347–359.

Chapter 8
Low Achievers in Mathematics—Ideas from the Netherlands for Developing a Competence-Oriented View

Petra Scherer

Abstract Although in Germany a competence-oriented view on teaching and learning mathematics has been one of the guiding principles for primary mathematics since the early 1990s, this approach was not appreciated for low achievers or for students in special education. Research in special education mostly focused on diagnosis with regard to deficiencies and not considering individual thinking and interpretations of mathematical tasks and problems. Moreover, the usual teaching practice in special education could be characterised by learning step-by-step in a rather mechanistic and reproductive way. Influenced by research papers and encouraging classroom experiences with low-achieving students in the Netherlands, my research focused on the question to what extent competence-oriented diagnosis followed by an inquiry-based learning approach would be appropriate also for students with special needs, or especially for them. Instead of underestimating these students' abilities, it seemed necessary to give them the opportunity to show what they are capable of, for example, by using more open problems that show the ideas students have in mind. In several projects and studies referring to different mathematical topics it could be shown that even low achievers benefited from a competence-oriented diagnosis and from an open approach and that these students were able to choose individual strategies, make use of structures and relations, find patterns and show creative and effective work.

Keywords Low achievers · Tests · Context-related problems · Open problems · Mathematical competencies · Qualitative research

P. Scherer (✉)
Faculty of Mathematics, University of Duisburg-Essen, Essen, Germany
e-mail: petra.scherer@uni-due.de

113

M. van den Heuvel-Panhuizen (ed.), *International Reflections on the Netherlands Didactics of Mathematics*, ICME-13 Monographs,
https://doi.org/10.1007/978-3-030-20223-1_8

8.1 Introduction

One will always find in any school learners who have learning problems in general or especially with learning mathematics. One might think that it is possible to use specific methods or materials to avoid those difficulties; however, it has turned out that this is not always sufficient. More fundamental research is necessary concerning the concepts for instruction and the way of planning the teaching and learning processes (see also Scherer, Beswick, DeBlois, Healy, & Moser Opitz, 2016). Moreover, to adapt the teaching to the students' needs, substantial information is needed about the learners' difficulties and about the knowledge the students have available. Research is required to reveal this information. The special focus in this chapter is the influence of the Dutch approach to mathematics education on research carried out with students with special needs in Germany.

8.2 Mathematics Education in Special Education in Germany

In Germany, students with special needs either visit special schools for handicapped students or visit regular schools in inclusive settings. Both settings show extremely heterogeneous groups in classroom and the teacher is confronted with various handicaps, for example deficits in language or visual perception, failure of concentration or reduced memory, which means that a high degree of differentiation is needed. Until now there are two types of teacher education programmes: one for special education and one for the regular school system. Teacher education programmes preparing teachers for an inclusive school system are still under development.

In this chapter, the focus will be on students with learning difficulties and learning disabilities. The corresponding approaches for teaching and learning with relevant concepts for instruction in mathematics will be discussed and the influence from abroad will be reported from the early 1990s.

Looking in more detail at the concepts of teaching and learning mathematics it can be stated that special education followed a more traditional view for a long time. Consequently, the concrete situation in classroom for low achievers was quite different from teaching practice in regular schools. Whereas in regular education one could see an approach to the teaching-learning process in which students are active participants and are offered opportunities for guided-discovery learning, in special education this approach was mostly disregarded. Instead, of having a constructivist view on learning, behaviourism remained the central principle.

Although in 1977 the curriculum for mathematics in special education already pointed out that the students should be able to develop their own methods of problem solving, and the danger of getting stuck in purely schematic thinking through mechanistic drill-and-practice was clearly stated (KM, 1977, p. 7), textbooks and classroom practice did not live up to these high expectations. The generally shared opinion was that low achieving students cannot cope with more demanding and complex problems, and the mechanistic teaching methods were rarely called into question.

Thus, very often the demands were lowered, and learners' activities were confined to bare reproduction. Textbooks and most teaching proposals and hence the usual teaching practice in special education could be characterised by learning step-by-step in a rather mechanistic and reproductive way. Mechanistic drill-and-practice often replaced insightful learning (Baier, 1977; Grölz, 1983), and low achievers were too often confronted with a 'mathematical diet': problems containing the discovery of patterns and structures were avoided. Regarding context problems, the students were not challenged to mathematise and to really do mathematics.

These findings were not only true for Germany but could be generalised for other countries (Ahmed, 1987; Moser Opitz, 2000; Trickett & Sulke, 1988). In the Netherlands as well, there is a tradition in special education in which mathematics instruction is dominated by the principles of learning step-by-step, isolation of difficulties and giving prescribed and fixed ways of solutions (Van den Heuvel-Panhuizen, 1991).

In Germany, these more traditional approaches can still be found in the majority of textbooks for special education. Although the situation changed over the years, there still is scepticism with respect to using a reformed approach for low achievers in which there is room for students' own contributions to the teaching-learning process. But from the point of view of mathematics education such an approach is necessary for identifying students' existing difficulties and giving them the opportunity to show what they are capable of. In this sense, the research reported below can be understood as a plea for an ongoing change of teaching practice. With concrete examples, the influence of mathematics education in the Netherlands will be illustrated, starting from the competence-oriented view on low achievers' learning processes.

8.3 Looking at the Netherlands: Looking at a Competence-Oriented Approach

8.3.1 Realistic Mathematics Education

The Dutch approach of Realistic Mathematics Education (RME) (Streefland, 1991; Treffers, 1987; Van den Heuvel-Panhuizen & Drijvers, 2014) propagates an approach to mathematics education in which students are given an active role and can come up with their own solutions based on familiar context situations. This use of contexts is one of the main characteristics of RME, but this should not be misunderstood. RME is not only restricted to context-related problems, but also covers inner-mathematical tasks and problems, as the term 'realistic' is derived from 'to realise' in the meaning of 'to imagine' (Van den Brink, 1991, p. 199).

The active acquisition of knowledge and own solutions for problems allow an intellectual and emotional identification (Streefland & Treffers, 1990, p. 315). The teacher has to offer learning situations that enable the students to make discoveries, but this requires that the student is provided with powerful tools such as (context) models, schemes, symbols (Streefland & Treffers, 1990, p. 313ff.). In the Netherlands, the criteria for a competence-oriented view lead to a critical view on testing procedures formats as well as on learning environments and adequate teaching practices (Streefland, 1990b). As a consequence, different formats for diagnostic procedures as well as teaching and learning situations came into existence.

8.3.2 Diagnostic Procedures: New Assessment Formats

Using diagnostic instruments has a long tradition in special education, as those results should give important information for the next learning steps and expected learning processes. The concrete instruments and methods are of major importance, and there are several possibilities for diagnosing learning difficulties. Many tests show what students *do not know*. But they do not show *why* nor do they give information about *what* the students *are able to do*.

As mentioned above, the German situation in special education in the early 1990s could be characterised by following the paradigm of behaviourism. According to this paradigm, the instruments and procedures for diagnosing mathematical formation were more deficit-oriented than competence-oriented (Scherer, 1999).

At the same time in the Netherlands attempts were made to introduce alternate forms of tests with respect to the test procedures and methods as well as to the construction of problems and items. According to Van den Heuvel-Panhuizen (1990) tests are needed that:

cover the whole spectrum of the arithmetic/mathematics area concerned (p. 57),

give children the opportunity to show what they are able to do (p. 61),

provide information about abilities and strategies (p. 68).

Van den Heuvel-Panhuizen (1991) convincingly presented a Dutch study carried out with low achievers (in Grade 5 and 6) on the topic of ratio—a topic that was usually avoided in special education as it was assumed to be too difficult for low achievers. She developed a written test with context-related items in contrast to the usual formal items. Beyond numerical problems she also integrated qualitative problems that could be solved by estimating or measuring and that allowed individual solution strategies. The results showed a higher rate of correct answers than expected by teachers, school psychologists and school inspectors.

Influenced by this encouraging research, studies have been carried out in Germany as well in which a more competence-oriented approach was taken to assess students than was common in Germany.

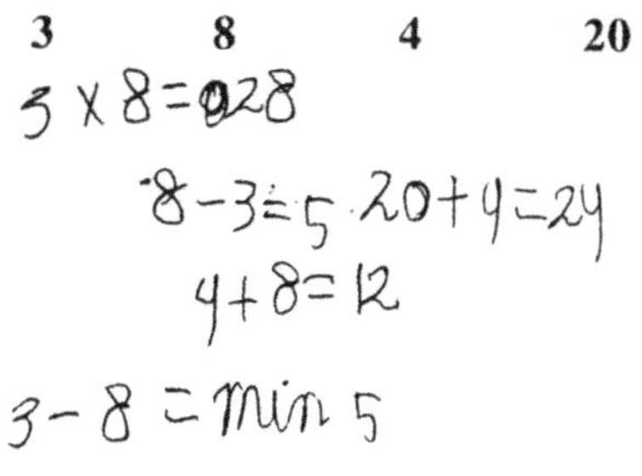

Fig. 8.1 Free production
(Streefland, 1990a, p. 44)

$$3 \qquad 8 \qquad 4 \qquad 20$$

$$3 \times 8 = 028$$

$$8 - 3 = 5 \quad 20 + 4 = 24$$

$$4 + 8 = 12$$

$$3 - 8 = \min 5$$

8.3.3 Students' Own Productions: Open Problems

One central type of problem—for tests as well as for regular teaching—is that of so-called 'own productions' or 'free productions' (Streefland, 1990a). Own productions offer various opportunities for own strategies and solutions and support a suitable differentiation (Streefland & Treffers, 1990, p. 315). An example is given in Fig. 8.1, and other illustrations of this format of open problems can be found in Sect. 8.4.2.

Here, students should make their own problems with the given numbers 3, 8, 4 and 20. They were free to choose the operations and could select particular numbers and decide how many numbers they wanted to use in a problem. The worksheet of an eight-year-old student that is shown in Fig. 8.1 shows that within this format mistakes might occur with operations and tasks that have been dealt with in school (3 × 8 makes 28). But at the same time, the format allows inventions and excursions to new mathematical areas. The worksheet illustrates insights in mathematical operations that have not yet been dealt with in mathematics (subtractions resulting in negative numbers, see also Sect. 8.4.4).

8.3.4 Making Connections Between Problems: Patterns and Structures

Mathematics is often named as the science of patterns and structures (Wittmann & Müller, 2008). For all students and especially for students with problems in mathematics making connections and the use of relationships could be a help for understanding (see Scherer, 1997). An example of the Dutch approach for a test item is illustrated in Fig. 8.2. The aim is to use 'auxiliary problems' or 'support problems' to investigate whether the students have insight into properties of operations and possess the ability to apply them.

Also in Germany, making use of patterns and structures was of great importance for designing learning opportunities for students—probably more emphasis was put on this aspect compared to the Netherlands. In Germany, the operative principle (Wittmann, 1985), that is, the analysis of mathematical objects and operations and their effects, is considered of great importance. The application of this principle

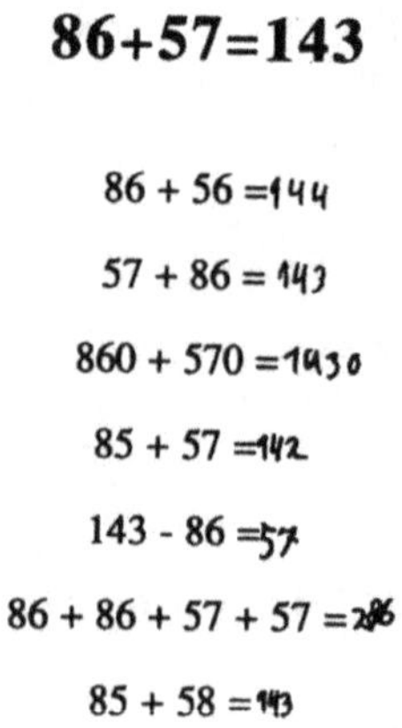

Fig. 8.2 Making use of
'support problems' (Van den
Heuvel-Panhuizen, 1996,
p. 153)

$$86+57=143$$

86 + 56 =144

57 + 86 = 143

860 + 570 =1430

85 + 57 =142

143 - 86 =57

86 + 86 + 57 + 57 =286

85 + 58 =143

can be identified in textbooks in the design of task series and in explicit problems in which students have to look for patterns and structures. For example, students should reflect upon specific modifications for a product when multiplying: What effect can be identified when increasing/decreasing one factor by 1? Is there an effect when changing the order of the two factors? How to reach the same result for a product when the first factor is doubled? This principle is not only true for arithmetic but should also be discussed for geometry. For example, doubling the length of a square side: What effect do you observe for the square area?

8.4   Research in Germany

8.4.1   Competence-Oriented Diagnosis

The guiding principles for diagnostic procedures and ideas for competence-oriented instruments presented above lead to several projects and case studies concerning the diagnosis of existing mathematical knowledge for different mathematical topics: arithmetical knowledge about numbers up to 20 or up to 100, addition and subtraction with numbers up to 20 or 100 (Scherer, 1999, 2005), multiplication and division (Scherer, 2003), understanding of place value (Scherer, 2014). In all studies, the learners were offered a variety of problems for a specific mathematical content with different levels of representation and with context embedded as well as context-free problems. Offering this variety of problems which reflect the competence-oriented view can give deeper insight in the students' competencies while at the same time identifying existing difficulties or misconceptions. The problems were not only administered using a paper-and-pencil test format, but also in interview situations in the sense of Piaget's clinical interview method (Opper, 1977).

With respect to context-embedded problems, two phenomena can be observed. Firstly, low achievers might solve these problems in daily life but not at school (Carraher, Carraher, & Schliemann, 1985). Secondly, low achievers are often afraid of word problems offered at school which often are too artificial (Scherer, 2009). In Germany, low achievers often struggle with the language and the mathematics (Scherer, 1999). They have, for example, difficulties with the calculations and with understanding the word problems. Also, several studies have shown that especially with regard to mathematics in contexts, low achievers have negative attitudes. Other studies showed that a lot of low achieving students are in fear of failing, and missing self-esteem could be stated (Scherer, 1999, 2009). At the same time, it is clear that all students should be able to solve context problems and as a consequence dealing with context problems at school is of great importance.

Generally, everyday experiences are of great importance for mathematics education for all students (Van den Heuvel-Panhuizen, 2005). On the one hand, context situations can serve as starting points for learning mathematics, for illustrating mathematical ideas. On the other hand, mathematical topics can be used in the field of real-life applications. Although context situations should help to understand mathematics, too often the opposite is true. Due to an inappropriate way of using context problems in mathematics education, students might not see any connection between mathematics at school and in real life, and consequently, they cannot use their experiences from daily life.

8.4.1.1 Example 1: Solving a Context-Embedded Multiplication Problem

For testing the operations of multiplication and division several items have been designed covering countable and non-countable problems or different ideas for division as quotative and partitive division (for an overview see Scherer, 2003). Figure 8.3 shows an item for solving a context-related multiplication problem illustrated by a dart game. The scored points are visible by means of (thrown) darts and the question was "How many points did the boy score in the dart game?" (Scherer, 2003, p. 13ff.).

The example is taken from a case study with fourth graders of the school for students with learning disabilities (Scherer, 2003). The topic for this grade in special education is multiplication and division with numbers up to 100, whereas this topic is dealt with in second grade in regular school. With these students written tests as well as individual interviews were carried out and the study showed a great heterogeneity within one class (for details see Scherer, 2003).

Vladimir, a 10-year-old boy, classified as a low achiever, was offered a total of 40 items with the paper-and-pencil test (multiplication problems, division problems, context-free and context-embedded problems). Compared to the whole class he was a below average student solving 13 out of 40 tasks correctly. Referring to different items different dependencies became obvious and the interplay of tests and interview could explain some of the phenomena in detail. Especially the interview could reveal his existing competencies.

Fig. 8.3 Context-related multiplication problem

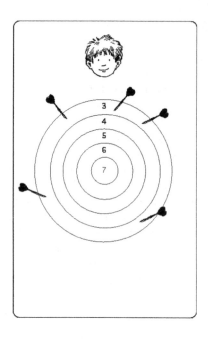

For the context-related multiplication in Fig. 8.3, during the written test Vladimir worked on five similar items with different numbers (the number of arrows and the positions of the arrows varied while the picture of the board with the numbers from 3 to 7 remained the same). For all five items, Vladimir gave the answer 23. Probably, he added all numbers given on the board (calculation error included).

The interview gave more insight in his underlying thinking. Confronted with the item in Fig. 8.3, firstly, Vladimir again added all the numbers on the board (3 + 4 + 5 + 6 + 7). He got the result 24, again including a calculation error. The interviewer asked him about the meaning of the arrows. Vladimir then added 5 to his first result and got 29. The interviewer started anew simulating the game: "Imagine that we both play this dart game. One arrow means 3 points." Vladimir at once calculated the 'threes' together, again with a calculation mistake, and finally got the result 16. So, at first sight the context of the dart game did not have any meaning for Vladimir and one might think that this context was not suitable. But reflecting on the context and the interviewer's stimulation of the real-life connection showed that Vladimir was able to work and argue in the given context correctly.

After working out the new solution, the interviewer reflected on this new result:

I: Why did you do it another way?

Vladimir: Because … We have played now.

I: Yes. … And what's now the correct result? If you want to know how many points the boy scored in this dart game?

Vladimir: Twenty-nine

Obviously, for Vladimir playing a game did mean a specific world, whereas the solution of a mathematical problem took place in another world, probably in a kind of 'mathematical world'. For mathematics instruction Vladimir's reduced framing with the first attempt has to be considered: Teachers should try to make those individual framings explicit and encourage students to express further ideas and conceptions.

What could be seen is that especially low achievers have a lot of difficulties. Not only with calculations, but also with understanding a situation, understanding a given text or picture, with finding a correct representation of their ideas etc. At this point, it has to be emphasised that these difficulties are not necessarily to be understood as features of the students themselves, but they can also be consequences of the kind of instruction the students experienced (Scherer, 1999; Van den Heuvel-Panhuizen, 2001). The implicitly critical remarks mentioned above (referring to textbooks) show that the way of teaching and learning has to change. For all students it is absolutely necessary that they are actively involved in the acquisition of mathematics and that they get a genuine understanding of real and modelled situations and of signs and symbols.

8.4.1.2   Example 2: Working Out the Quantity of Dots

The following example is taken from Scherer (1999) from a study performed with third graders in special education. Part of study was the inquiry of the previous knowledge when starting to work with numbers up to 100. Also in this study, written tests as well as individual interviews were carried out and different types of problems were given. Figure 8.4 shows an item for determining the number of dots presented in a structural arrangement. A part of the field of hundred with the structure of five was used with the question whether the children would make use of the given structure. The problem could be solved by counting one-by one and would show if all counting principles are used correctly (see Gelman & Gallistel, 1978). Moreover, the number 48 offers several possibilities for using the structure of fives or tens: the more or less conventional strategy of reading a field horizontally, but also reading it vertically (Scherer, 1999, p. 178 ff.).

The following interview episode illustrates Mary's (Grade 3) individual strategy:

> Mary: [counts the first column of dots tapping with her finger at every dot] One, two, three, four, five …
>
> [counts with her eyes speaking lowly: ten, twenty, thirty, forty; then one by one] Forty-eight.

The interviewer asked her to explain how she got the result 48.

> Mary: I made like this [points at two columns of five], … those two are ten, then twenty, thirty, forty [points at every two columns of five], and the last I have counted.

For the design of test items in a competence-oriented approach it is also necessary to reflect on concrete numbers and arrangement so that a variety of strategies is possible.

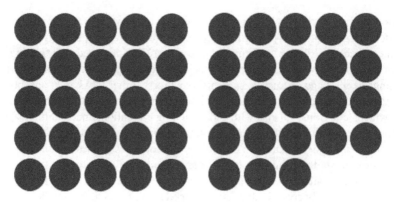

Fig. 8.4 Working out the quantity of dots

8.4.2 Students' Own Productions: Open Problems

As mentioned in Sect. 8.3 the competence-oriented view should also be used for designing teaching and learning situations in mathematics. A possible format is that of so-called own productions realised by open problems as illustrated in Sect. 8.3.3, and other examples will be given in the following.

8.4.2.1 Example 3: Find Problems with Given Numbers!

The task "Find addition and subtraction problems with the numbers 3, 6, 12, 20!" may help to clarify existing misconceptions, but at the same time it enables the child to show his or her abilities: For example, making use of arithmetic structures and properties or the individual extent of systematic work, etcetera. Moreover, this format covers a 'natural differentiation'. It allows to include problems at different levels that are neither fixed nor determined by the teacher (Scherer & Krauthausen, 2010). The students are free to choose three or more numbers, although experiences in school showed that many students chose problems with only two numbers.

The worksheet in Fig. 8.5 is from Marc, a third grader who attended a school for learning disabled students and who had been operating with numbers up to 100 in classroom for a few weeks. In total, Marc wrote down 12 problems which he divided into three groups by himself (he did not explain the reason for that). He made subtraction problems as well as addition problems (including all doubles) and many problems with the result 20. No counting or calculating errors occurred. It is remarkable that he wrote down just four subtractions. Moreover, it came to the fore that Marc had difficulties in notating subtractions. In two of them he used the 'wrong' notation: $3 - 12 = 9$ and $6 - 20 = 14$. This contrasts with the solution showed in Fig. 8.1, where the student solved this problem by 'inventing' negative numbers. An issue that is relevant to note here is that for further diagnosis and figuring out

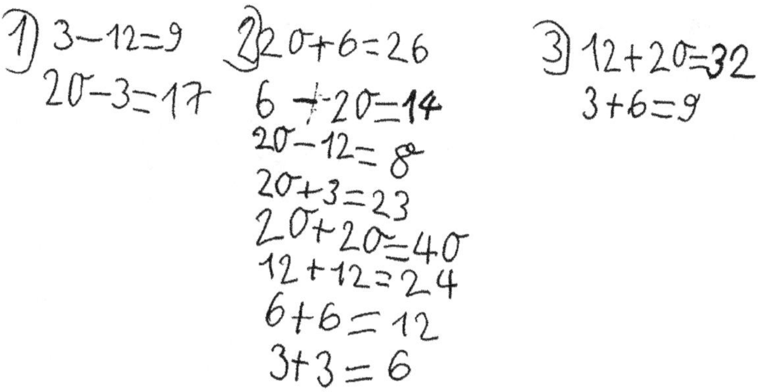

$$1)\ 3-12=9$$
$$20-3=17$$

$$2)\ 20+6=26$$
$$6+20=14$$
$$20-12=8$$
$$20+3=23$$
$$20+20=40$$
$$12+12=24$$
$$6+6=12$$
$$3+3=6$$

$$3)\ 12+20=32$$
$$3+6=9$$

Fig. 8.5 Open problem with pre-given numbers

the consequences for instruction, the teacher's mathematical background is of major importance (see Scherer, 2007, p. 601ff.).

Open problems can be designed for every mathematical topic. Students can also be encouraged to reflect on the problems they have designed themselves or can be stimulated to produce problems within particular categories such as 'My easy problems' or 'My difficult problems' or 'My special problems' (see Krauthausen & Scherer, 2014, p. 144ff.; Van den Heuvel-Panhuizen 1996, p. 144ff.;). Open problems can also be varied in the cognitive demand they ask; some problems are more straightforward and others require real problem solving (see Klavir & Hershkovitz, 2008; Krauthausen & Scherer, 2014, p. 100ff.).

8.4.2.2 Example 4: Open Problems Completely Posed by the Students Themselves

Open problems can also come completely from the students themselves. In a mini project, in which fifth-graders of a school for learning disabled students had figured out that they could walk 4 km an hour. They themselves came with the problem of how many kilometres they might cover in one full day, that is in 24 hours. Problems such as 24 × 4 had not yet been treated in their classroom previously (see also Scherer, 2003). Nevertheless, several students found solutions.

Sandrina wrote down the problems from 1 × 4 up to 24 × 4 without directly calculating them (Fig. 8.6a). She started with the easiest one and worked out the following results one after another, in which the results did not correspond with the multiplication in the same line. Finally, she stopped with this laborious way of working. Jan wanted to split up 24 × 4 into 10 × 4 + 10 × 4 + 4 × 4, which represents an effective way of working out this multiplication. He also started with calculating the results of the multiplication table up to 10 (Fig. 8.6b). Unfortunately,

Fig. 8.6 Solution strategy of
Sandrina (**a**) and Jan (**b**)

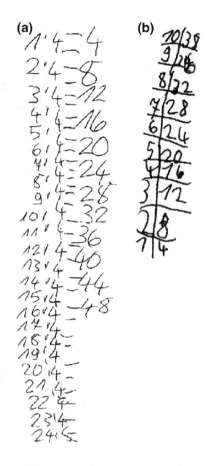

he made a mistake in the multiplication table ($9 \times 4 = 34$), which then continued throughout his calculation ($10 \times 4 = 38$, because of $34 + 4 = 38$).

In this example, it is shown that even the 'simple' and basic problems like 10×4 were not directly written down. Yet, it might be that both students have this knowledge, but do not apply it in this complex situation.

It is necessary that connections are understood on the basis of meaningful representations. Taking the following example: How can you explain the relation between 2×4 and 20×4? Many students come to this extension by the so-called 'step multiplication table' by means of a rather mechanistic use of rules. For the problem 3×70, for example, the problem 3×7 is taken from the multiplication table and then the following rule is derived: "For the new result, one zero has to be appended". Accordingly, two zeroes are appended in the problem 30×70 ("Look at the total of the number of zeroes in the factors and append just as many zeroes to the result"). Such a rule, degenerated in a rather meaningless way, however, can lead to confusion for the students when the result of the original multiplication problem already has a zero at the end. For example, if 50×80 has to be calculated, the reference is

$5 \times 8 = 40$ and many students write down 400 as the result. With calculations beyond 1000 and thus a higher quantity of zeroes, these uncertainties can increase.

In general, certain relations such as 'exchange problems' (e.g., using the commutative property $6 \times 8 = 8 \times 6$) or 'derived problems' (e.g., $6 \times 8 = 5 \times 8 + 1 \times 8$) have to be explicitly practised by offering students problems with numbers by which the making use of these relations is explicitly elicited. Or, as shown earlier, open problems with given numbers may help to reach this goal as the students will use the given numbers inevitably in a more or less systematic way and the patterns become obvious.

A more conscious selection of numbers and taking into account their relations should not be underestimated in instruction. For the students, the use of these relations demands for understanding of connections between problems (Ter Heege, 1999), between operations (multiplication and division, but also between multiplication and addition) as well as having insight in relations between different levels of representation (Scherer, 2003). Only in this way can knowledge about the result of 20×4 which is not immediately accessible be effectively reconstructed by using 2×4.

This, of course, requires that in education much attention is paid to developing understanding of these number relations, and the operative principle is of major importance (see Sect. 8.3.4; Wittmann, 1985; see also Ter Heege, 1999; Van den Heuvel-Panhuizen, 2001, p. 76ff.).

8.4.3   Making Use of Picture Books for Learning Mathematics

The study carried out by my doctoral student Anna Vogtländer on pre-school children's competencies when engaged in picture books reading (Vogtländer, 2015) was also inspired by RME research. This study is in line with the nowadays generally accepted recognition of the importance of early mathematics education (see Van den Heuvel-Panhuizen & Elia, 2014). In Germany, the research on young children's mathematical development was provoked in particular by international comparative studies like TIMSS and PISA and several empirical studies, like the SCHOLASTIK study (e.g., Weinert & Helmke, 1997). The SCHOLASTIK study indicates that school beginners with a low level of achievement maintain their relative position until the end of their primary education, that is, low-achieving students hardly seem to catch up on their peers. Therefore, it is important to create and offer stimulating learning environments, to support young children in their individual learning processes.

One way of supporting children's mathematical competences is making use of picture books. There are interesting research developments concerning the use of such books in relation to young children's learning of mathematics in the Netherlands (Scherer, Van den Heuvel-Panhuizen, & Van den Boogaard, 2007; Van den Heuvel-Panhuizen & Van den Boogaard, 2008; Van den Heuvel-Panhuizen, Van den Boogaard, & Doig, 2009; Van den Heuvel-Panhuizen, Van den Boogaard, & Scherer,

2007). These studies showed that selected picture books, which are not written to teach mathematics explicitly, have the power to stimulate mathematical thinking. The studies illustrated how picture books can offer a meaningful context for learning mathematics and can give children an informal entry to mathematical ideas early on.

These studies were one of the starting points for Vogtländer's research project in the field of early childhood mathematics education (Vogtländer, 2015). The purpose of this study is to investigate the mathematical thinking and learning processes of young children during reading sessions with picture books. Although the authors of the selected picture books did not have the intention of teaching children mathematics, the picture books gave children opportunities to talk about mathematics anyway. Moreover, reading picture books can be an activity that can motivate children to discover and explore mathematical contents by themselves based on their existing competencies.

8.4.4 Primary Students' Preconceptions of Negative Numbers

The study done by my doctoral student Christian Rütten, who focused on primary school students' pre-conceptions of negative numbers (Rütten, 2016) is another example of RME influence on German research on mathematics education, and in particular the recognition within RME that students can already be familiar with mathematical procedures and possess conceptions of mathematical objects before official instruction at school. In Rütten's study it was revealed that whereas in Germany negative numbers are not dealt with in mathematics until the 5th grade, students in the lower primary grades do already know something about negative numbers and integer operations. In his study, the pre-instructional knowledge of integers of nearly 300 German third- and fourth-graders was assessed through a paper-and-pencil test followed by individual interviews. Characteristic of this assessment was that, contrary to the traditional written tests, students were offered room for informal notation and reasoning (Van den Heuvel-Panhuizen, 1990, 1996), which made it possible to recognise more detailed students' knowledge. Related to the RME approach, motivating and supporting task contexts "offer the opportunity to sound out the students' abilities while avoiding obstructions which are causes by formal notation" (Van den Heuvel-Panhuizen & Gravemeijer, 1991, p. 142). A characteristic of the Dutch type of assessment is the use of open problems that allow the students to answer with individual strategies and at different levels, and to show what they are capable of. By offering meaningful pictures and representations, these tasks are nearly self-explanatory, and do not need more information to handle. Furthermore, in all tasks, students are prompted to reason about their answers or write down notes on scrap paper.

Guided by this general characteristic, Rütten (2016) investigated primary students' pre-conceptual knowledge of negative numbers by enabling them to encounter negative numbers in realistic contexts (thermometer, elevator, games, number line, etc.) without using conventional symbols. By means of open problems, the test allows the students to show their own ideas and in part idiosyncratic symbolisation relating to these new mathematical objects.

The results of the administered test showed a wide range of primary students' ideas of integers. Furthermore, the test allowed to specify some phenomena earlier described in other studies, e.g., the idea of a divided number line (Peled, Mukhopadhyay, & Resnick, 1989) or the idea that decimals with zero are less than zero (e.g., Stacey, Helme, & Steinle, 2001). In summary, also in this study the Dutch approach for paper-and-pencil tests provides a productive instrument for a qualitative inquiry.

8.5 Conclusions and Perspectives

As pointed out, the Dutch approach to mathematics education had—and still has—a high impact on German research. In the following I will recapitulate them.

8.5.1 Competence-Oriented Diagnosis and Instruction

With regard to low achievers the diagnosis plays an important role. Diagnosis should be seen in a competence-related view, which means the diagnosis of difficulties and of existing abilities at the same time. This can be realised through interviews, but also through written tests (Van den Heuvel-Panhuizen, 1990, 1991, 1996). Instead of underestimating low achievers' abilities, it is necessary to give them the opportunity to show what they are capable of. If the problems are open, the level is not fixed at the beginning, and that can boost students' confidence. In this chapter, I gave several examples in which specific difficulties with particular mathematical contents were pointed out and the power of students' own work was illustrated. These examples showed that even low achievers can choose alternative strategies, make use of structures and relations, find patterns and show creative and effective work. However, the orientation on competencies and the opportunity of productive work cannot completely solve all the diverse problems of low achievers in mathematics, and the new teaching approach will probably cause a lot of difficulties in the beginning, as the students have to become familiar with working in an active and responsible manner. Yet, by competence-oriented diagnosis and instruction, misconceptions and difficulties can be identified more easily and at an early time. If the students only have to work on problems as regularly presented in textbooks, some specific mistakes as discussed in this chapter will not become apparent.

8.5.2 Own Productions and Open Problems

Students often approach open problems with enthusiasm because the results are assessed not only as right or wrong, and therefore the fear of failure is reduced (Grossman, 1975). The open approach offers the opportunities for natural differentiation, as the students can work on several levels of difficulties and be successful at their own level (Krauthausen & Scherer, 2014). The danger of under- or overestimating the weaker students, as well as the better ones, can be thoroughly reduced (Scherer, 1999; Wittmann, 1990, p. 159). Learning-disabled students are often underestimated or misjudged, and we often limit their potential that would come to the fore with a more open approach. Supporting students means making certain demands on them and aiming at long-term learning processes and not only thinking of short-term success in learning.

To optimally take advantage of students' capabilities it is indispensable for the teacher to be familiar with the mathematics in order to be able to recognise and evaluate the possibly uncommon discoveries of the students.

8.5.3 Support of Own Strategies

For successfully solving problems, also initially unfamiliar problems, it seems especially essential to encourage learning-disabled students to follow their own methods. At the same time, unfamiliar problems should be explicitly made subject of discussion in class. Only in this way, these students learn that they themselves can solve problems with their own ideas (see also Ter Heege, 1985, p. 380). Especially for solving word problems, or context problems in general, own notations and independently developed strategies play a central role. The knowledge gained in this way can be easier remembered and applied and it also contributes to supporting self-confidence and independency (see also Isenbarger & Baroody, 2001, p. 468).

8.5.4 Role of Mistakes

Over and above there is a need for a change in attitude: difficulties and errors should be regarded as natural concomitants of the learning process and not just short-term solutions should be searched for. Difficulties and errors should be cleared for students—whenever possible—in a meaningful way. Then, students will in the end benefit from the ideas, strategies and attempts that initially were not successful. Teaching should not be only oriented on pure results. It is important that students should "feel no shame or embarrassment when they present erroneous solutions in front of the others" (Cobb, Wood, & Yackel, 1991, p. 165).

At this point, it has to be emphasised that specific difficulties are not necessarily to be understood as features of the students themselves, but that they can also be consequences of the kind of instruction they have experienced. With a small-step instruction conception, which can currently still be encountered in German schools for students with learning disabilities, many mathematical topics are usually introduced and worked on in isolation from each other. For example, students learn the task 6 × 8 in the 8-row and at another point in time they learn 8 × 6 in the 6-row. The fact that students do not then use the relation of the commutative law is not a surprise.

8.5.5 Last but Not Least

Overall, for students with learning disabilities the quality of teaching is of great importance:

> Good teaching that emphasises the structure of a subject is probably even more valuable for the less able student than for the gifted one, for it is the former rather than the latter who is most easily thrown off the track by poor teaching. (Bruner, 1969, p. 9)

References

Ahmed, A. (1987). *Better mathematics. A curriculum development study.* London, UK: HMSO.

Baier, H. (1977). Allgemeine Prinzipien der Erziehung und des Unterrichts in der Schule für Lernbehinderte [General principles of education and teaching in schools for learning disabled]. In G. O. Kanter & O. Speck (Eds.), *Handbuch der Sonderpädagogik* (Vol. 4, pp. 252–277). Berlin, Germany: Marhold.

Bruner, J. S. (1969). *The process of education.* Cambridge, MA: Harvard University Press.

Carraher, T. N., Carrahar, D. W., & Schliemann, A. D. (1985). Mathematics in the streets and in schools. *British Journal of Developmental Psychology,* (3), 21–29.

Cobb, P., Wood, T., & Yackel, E. (1991). A constructivist approach to second grade mathematics. In E. von Glasersfeld (Ed.), *Radical constructivism in mathematics education* (pp. 157–176). Dordrecht, the Netherlands: Kluwer.

Gelman, R., & Gallistel, C. R. (1978). *The child's understanding of number.* Cambridge, MA: Harvard University Press.

Grölz, H. (1983). Problemorientierte Unterrichtsmethoden in der Schule für Lernbehinderte [Problem-oriented teaching methods in the school for the learning disabled]. *Zeitschrift für Heilpädagogik, 34*(10), 645–653.

Grossman, R. (1975). Open-ended lessons bring unexpected surprises. *Mathematics Teaching,* (71), 14–15.

Isenbarger, L. M., & Baroody, A. J. (2001). Fostering the mathematical power of children with behavioral difficulties: The case of Carter. *Teaching Children Mathematics, 7*(8), 468–471.

Klavir, R., & Hershkovitz, S. (2008). Teaching and evaluating 'open-ended' problems. *International Journal for Mathematics Teaching and Learning, 20*(5), 23 p.

KM – Kultusminister des Landes NRW (Ed.) (1977). *Richtlinien und Lehrpläne für die Schule für Lernbehinderte (Sonderschule) – Mathematik* [Guidelines and curricula for schools for learning disabled (special schools)—Mathematics]. Köln, Germany: Ritterbach.

Krauthausen, G., & Scherer, P. (2014). *Natürliche Differenzierung im Mathematikunterricht – Konzepte und Praxisbeispiele aus der Grundschule* [Natural differentiation in mathematics education – Concepts and practical examples from primary school]. Seelze, Germany: Kallmeyer.

Moser Opitz, E. (2000). *"Zählen – Zahlbegriff – Rechnen". Theoretische Grundlagen und eine empirische Untersuchung zum mathematischen Erstunterricht in Sonderklassen* ["Counting—number concept—arithmetic". Theoretical foundations and an empirical investigation of mathematical primary education in special classes]. Bern, Switzerland: Haupt.

Opper, S. (1977). Piaget's clinical method. *Journal of Children's Mathematical Behavior, 1*(4), 90–107.

Peled, I., Mukhopadhyay, S., & Resnick, L. B. (1989). Formal and informal sources of mental models for negative numbers. In G. Vergnaud, J. Rogalski, & M. Artigue (Eds.), *Proceedings of the 13th International Conference for the Psychology of Mathematics Education* (Vol. 3, pp. 106–110). Paris: PME.

Rütten, C. (2016). *Sichtweisen von Grundschulkindern auf negative Zahlen. Metaphernanalytisch orientierte Erkundungen im Rahmen didaktischer Rekonstruktion* [Views of primary school children on negative numbers. Metaphore-analytic oriented explorations in the context of didactical reconstruction]. Heidelberg, Germany: Springer.

Scherer, P. (1997). Productive or reproductive exercises—What is appropriate for low attainers? In C. Van den Boer & M. Dolk (Eds.), *Naar een balans in de reken-wiskundeles – Interactie, oefenen, uitleggen en zelfstandig werken* (pp. 35–49). Utrecht, the Netherlands: Utrecht University, Freudenthal Institute.

Scherer, P. (1999). *Entdeckendes Lernen im Mathematikunterricht der Schule für Lernbehinderte – Theoretische Grundlegung und evaluierte unterrichtspraktische Erprobung. 2. Auflage* [Discovery learning in mathematics education for learning disabled—Theoretical foundations and evaluated teaching practices, 2nd ed]. Heidelberg, Germany: Edition Schindele.

Scherer, P. (2003). Different students solving the same problems—The same students solving different problems. *Tijdschrift voor Nascholing en Onderzoek van het Reken-Wiskundeonderwijs, 22*(2), 11–20.

Scherer, P. (2005). *Produktives Lernen für Kinder mit Lernschwächen: Fördern durch Fordern. Band 1* [Productive learning for children with learning disabilities: Supporting through challenging. Part 1]. Horneburg, Germany: Persen.

Scherer, P. (2007). Diagnose und Förderung im Bereich der elementaren Rechenoperationen [Diagnosis and giving support in the domain of elementary arithmetic operations]. In J. Walter & F. B. Wember (Eds.), *Handbuch der Sonderpädagogik, Band 2. Sonderpädagogik des Lernens* (pp. 590–604). Göttingen, Germany: Hogrefe.

Scherer, P. (2009). Low achievers solving context problems—Opportunities and challenges. *Mediterranean Journal for Research in Mathematics Education, 8*(1), 25–40.

Scherer, P. (2014). Low achievers' understanding of place value—Materials, representations and consequences for instruction. In T. Wassong, D. Frischemeier, P. R. Fischer, R. Hochmuth, & P. Bender (Eds.), *Mit Werkzeugen Mathematik und Stochastik lernen* (pp. 43–56). Wiesbaden, Germany: Springer.

Scherer, P., & Krauthausen, G. (2010). Natural differentiation in mathematics—The NaDiMa project. *Reken-wiskundeonderwijs: Onderzoek, Ontwikkeling, Praktijk, 29*(3), 14–26.

Scherer, P., Beswick, K., DeBlois, L., Healy, L., & Moser Opitz, E. (2016). Assistance of students with mathematical learning difficulties: how can research support practice? *ZDM Mathematics Education, 48*(5), 633–649.

Scherer, P., Van den Heuvel-Panhuizen, M., & Van den Boogaard, S. (2007). Einsatz des Bilderbuchs 'Fünfter sein' bei Kindergartenkindern – Erste Ergebnisse eines internationalen Vergleichs [Use of the picture book 'Being fifth' with kindergarten children—First results of an international comparison]. In I. Lehmann (Ed.), *Beiträge zum Mathematikunterricht 2007* (pp. 921–924). Hildesheim, Germany: Franzbecker.

Stacey, K., Helme, S., & Steinle, V. (2001). Confusions between decimals, factions and negative numbers. A consequence of the mirror as a conceptual metaphor in three different ways. In M.

Van den Heuvel-Panhuizen (Ed.). *Proceedings of the 25th Conference of the International Group for the Psychology of Mathematics Education* (Vol. 4, pp. 217–224). Utrecht, the Netherlands: Utrecht University, Freudenthal Institute.

Streefland, L. (1990a). Free productions in learning and teaching mathematics. In K. Gravemeijer, M. Van den Heuvel-Panhuizen, & L. Streefland (Eds.), *Contexts, free productions, tests, and geometry in Realistic Mathematics Education* (pp. 33–52). Utrecht, the Netherlands: Utrecht University, Freudenthal Institute.

Streefland, L. (1990b). Realistic Mathematics Education (RME). What does it mean? In K. Gravemeijer, M. Van den Heuvel-Panhuizen, & L. Streefland (Eds.), *Contexts, free productions, tests, and geometry in Realistic Mathematics Education* (pp. 1–9). Utrecht, the Netherlands: Utrecht University, Freudenthal Institute.

Streefland, L. (Ed.). (1991). *Realistic Mathematics Education in primary school: On the occasion of the opening of the Freudenthal Institute.* Utrecht, the Netherlands: Utrecht University, Freudenthal Institute.

Streefland, L., & Treffers, A. (1990). Produktiver Rechen-Mathematik-Unterricht [Productive arithmetic-mathematics instruction]. *Journal für Mathematik-Didaktik, 11*(4), 297–322.

Ter Heege, H. (1985). The acquisition of basic multiplication skills. *Educational Studies in Mathematics, 16*(4), 375–388.

Ter Heege, H. (1999). Tafelkost: Wat is 'oefenen van elementaire vermenigvuldigen'? [Table issues: What is 'practice of elementary multiplication'?]. *Willem Bartjens, 18*(5), 40–41.

Treffers, A. (1987). *Three dimensions. A model of goal and theory description in mathematics instruction—The Wiscobas project.* Dordrecht, the Netherlands: Kluwer.

Trickett, L., & Sulke, F. (1988). Low attainers can do mathematics. In D. Pimm (Ed.), *Mathematics, teachers and children* (pp. 109–117). London, UK: Hodder and Stoughton.

Van den Brink, J. (1991). Realistic arithmetic education for young children. In L. Streefland (Ed.), *Realistic Mathematics Education in primary School. On the occasion of the opening of the Freudenthal Institute* (pp. 77–92). Utrecht, the Netherlands: Utrecht University, Freudenthal Institute.

Van den Heuvel-Panhuizen, M. (1990). Realistic arithmetic/mathematics instruction and tests. In K. Gravemeijer, M. Van den Heuvel-Panhuizen, & L. Streefland (Eds.), *Contexts, free productions, tests and geometry in Realistic Mathematics Education* (pp. 53–78). Utrecht, the Netherlands: Utrecht University, Freudenthal Institute.

Van den Heuvel-Panhuizen, M. (1991). Ratio in special education. A pilot study on the possibilities of shifting the boundaries. In L. Streefland (Ed.), *Realistic Mathematics Education in primary school. On the occasion of the opening of the Freudenthal Institute* (pp. 157–181). Utrecht, the Netherlands: Utrecht University, Freudenthal Institute.

Van den Heuvel-Panhuizen, M. (1996). *Assessment and Realistic Mathematics Education.* Utrecht, the Netherlands: Utrecht University, Freudenthal Institute.

Van den Heuvel-Panhuizen, M. (Ed.). (2001). *Children learn mathematics.* Utrecht, the Netherlands: Utrecht University, Freudenthal Institute.

Van den Heuvel-Panhuizen, M. (2005). The role of contexts in assessment problems in mathematics. *For the Learning of Mathematics, 25*(2), 2–9 & 23.

Van den Heuvel-Panhuizen, M., & Drijvers, P. (2014). Realistic Mathematics Education. In S. Lerman (Ed.), *Encyclopedia of mathematics education* (pp. 521–525). Dordrecht, the Netherlands: Springer.

Van den Heuvel-Panhuizen, M., & Elia, I. (2014). Early childhood mathematics education. In S. Lerman (Ed.), *Encyclopedia of mathematics education* (pp. 196–201). Dordrecht, the Netherlands: Springer.

Van den Heuvel-Panhuizen, M., & Gravemeijer, K. P. E. (1991). Tests are not all bad. An attempt to change the appearance of written tests in mathematics instruction at primary school level. In L. Streefland (Ed.), *Realistic Mathematics Education in primary school. On the occasion of the opening of the Freudenthal Institute* (pp. 139–155). Utrecht, the Netherlands: Utrecht University, Freudenthal Institute.

Van den Heuvel-Panhuizen, M., & Van den Boogaard, S. (2008). Picture books as an impetus for kindergartners' mathematical thinking. *Mathematical Thinking and Learning, 10*(4), 341–373.

Van den Heuvel-Panhuizen, M., Van den Boogaard, S., & Doig, B. (2009). Picture books stimulate the learning of mathematics. *Australian Journal of Early Childhood, 34*(2), 30–39.

Van den Heuvel-Panhuizen, M., Van den Boogaard, S., & Scherer, P. (2007). A picture book as a prompt for mathematical thinking by kindergartners: When Gaby was read 'Being fifth'. In I. Lehmann (Ed.), *Beiträge zum Mathematikunterricht 2007* (pp. 831–834). Hildesheim, Germany: Franzbecker.

Vogtländer, A. (2015). Mathematische Lerngelegenheiten in Bilderbüchern entdecken und nutzen [Discovering and using mathematical learning opportunities in picture books]. In F. Caluori, H. Linneweber-Lammerskitten, & Ch. Streit (Eds.), *Beiträge zum Mathematikunterricht 2015* (Vol. 2, pp. 952–955). Münster, Germany: WTM.

Weinert, F. E., & Helmke, A. (Eds.). (1997). *Entwicklung im Grundschulalter*. Weinheim, Germany: Beltz/Psychologie Verlags Union.

Wittmann, E. C. (1985). Objekte – Operationen – Wirkungen: Das operative Prinzip in der Mathematikdidaktik [Objects—Operations—Effects: The operative principle in mathematics didactics]. *mathematik lehren,* (11), 7–11.

Wittmann, E. C. (1990). Wider die Flut der 'bunten Hunde' und der 'grauen Päckchen': Die Konzeption des aktiv-entdeckenden Lernens und des produktiven Übens [Against the flood of 'colourful dogs' and 'grey packets': The concept of active-discovery learning and productive practice]. In E. C. Wittmann & G. N. Müller (Eds.), *Handbuch produktiver Rechenübungen* (Vol. 1, pp. 152–166). Stuttgart, Germany: Klett.

Wittmann, E. C., & Müller, G. N. (2008). Muster und Strukturen als fachliches Grundkonzept [Patterns and structures as fundamental mathematical concept]. In G. Walther, M. Van den Heuvel-Panhuizen, D. Granzer & O. Köller (Eds.), *Bildungsstandards für die Grundschule: Mathematik konkret* (pp. 42–65). Frankfurt, Germany: Cornelsen Scriptor.

Chapter 9
From the Bottom Up—Reinventing Realistic Mathematics Education in Southern Argentina

Betina Zolkower, Ana María Bressan, Silvia Pérez and María Fernanda Gallego

Abstract This chapter focuses on the Grupo Patagónico de Didáctica de la Matemática (GPDM), a collective of about twenty teachers and teacher educators in Southern Argentina who, united by a shared interest in making mathematics meaningful, relevant, and accessible to all students, have been learning about, adapting, implementing, and contributing to Realistic Mathematics Education (RME). The chapter is organised as follows. First, we outline the state of mathematics education reform in Argentina in the 1990s. Next, we describe how the GPDM was formed, how participants learned about and implemented RME in their classrooms, and how the group's sphere of influence in Grades K–12 and in pre-service and in-service mathematics teacher education expanded from the local to the regional, the national, and the international level. We close with a reflection on what we have learned throughout this creative appropriation process. Throughout the chapter, a selection of annotated vignettes on the work of GPDM teachers and their students illustrate the manner in which the legacy of Hans Freudenthal materialised and continues to materialise in Argentinean classrooms.

Keywords Realistic mathematics education · K–16 study group · Professional development · Instructional design · (Re)contextualising · Modelling

B. Zolkower (✉)
Secondary Education, Brooklyn College, City University of New York, New York, USA
e-mail: betinaz@brooklyn.cuny.edu

A. M. Bressan
Ministerio de Educación, Viedma, Río Negro, Argentina
e-mail: anamariabressan@gmail.com

S. Pérez · M. F. Gallego
Instituto de Formación Docente Continua, S. C. de Bariloche, Río Negro, Argentina
e-mail: perezdaq@gmail.com

M. F. Gallego
e-mail: marfer.gallego@gmail.com

© The Author(s) 2020
M. van den Heuvel-Panhuizen (ed.), *International Reflections on the Netherlands Didactics of Mathematics*, ICME-13 Monographs,
https://doi.org/10.1007/978-3-030-20223-1_9

9.1   Introduction

The focus of this chapter is the Grupo Patagónico de Didáctica de la Matemática (GPDM),[1] a collective of about twenty teachers and teacher educators in Southern Argentina. For the past fifteen years, this group, united by a shared interest in making mathematics meaningful, relevant, and accessible to all students, has been learning about, adapting/adopting, implementing, contributing to, and disseminating Realistic Mathematics Education (RME) (Freudenthal, 1973, 1983, 1991).

Freudenthal (1991) proposes to view mathematics as the human activity of mathematising that is, organising or structuring subject matter by mathematical means. As described by Freudenthal (1991), Gravemeijer and Terwel (2000), Van den Heuvel-Panhuizen (1996, 2005a, 2005b), Treffers (1991), and Streefland (1991a), the central principles of RME are: (1) realistic, in the sense of realisable or imaginable, contexts and situations as points of departure for *horizontal* mathematising; (2) the central place of students' productions and constructions in the teaching-and-learning process; (3) teacher-guided emergence and development of models that support *vertical* mathematising; (4) intertwining of curriculum strands and connections across school subjects; and (5) interaction aimed at comparing, contrasting, and reflecting upon different ways/levels of schematising, diagramming, modelling, symbolising, and formalising the problematic situations at hand.

The chapter is organised as follows. First, we outline the state of mathematics education reform in Argentina in the 1990s. Next, in a narrative organised chronologically in three phases, we describe how the GPDM was formed, how its participants learned about and implemented RME in their classrooms, and how the group's sphere was of influence in pre- and in-service teacher education, as well as how instructional design increased from the local to the regional, national, and international levels. A collection of vignettes on the work of GPDM teacher participants and their students illustrates the manner in which the legacy of Freudenthal and his colleagues and disciples materialised and continues to materialise in Argentinean classrooms. The chapter ends with a reflection on what we have learned throughout this creative appropriation process.

9.1.1   Curricular Innovation in Mathematics Education

In Argentina, curricular innovation began in the 1990s with the newly released Common Basic Contents (CBC) (Consejo Federal de Cultura y Educación, 1995), which effected radical changes in the content and methods of mathematics education. The CBC signalled a move away from the structuralist approach of the Modern Mathematics or New Math (dominant in Argentina since the late 1960s). The above-mentioned reform documents emphasised not only conceptual development and procedural skills, but also the attitudes and dispositions associated with the practice of

---

[1] Patagonian Group of Mathematics Didactics.

doing mathematics. A second level of curriculum reform materialised in support documents prepared by the National Department of Education and distributed to the 23 provinces and the Autonomous City of Buenos Aires.

The 1990s standards and guidelines were influenced by the French Didactique, an approach that had entered Argentina in the 1980s with the translation of the work of Guy Brousseau and his colleagues at the Bordeaux IREM.[2] Professors of didactics of mathematics travelled to Paris, Strasbourg, and Bordeaux to pursue doctoral research and brought back materials related to their teaching experiments that were then disseminated and adopted nationwide. The degree of comprehension of the French Didactique among mathematics teacher educators and teachers varies significantly, thus resulting in transpositions of not always the same quality as that of the original experiments.

9.1.2   Initial Attempts at Bringing Realistic Mathematics Education to Argentina

In 1984, Diana Rosenberg received a fellowship from the Dutch government to specialise in the didactics of mathematics at OW&OC[3] at Utrecht University. There she participated in two research projects: the HEWET[4] project, aimed at improving mathematics instruction at the secondary level, and the project De Baas over de Computer,[5] which focused on introducing the computer in the early grades of secondary school. In 1986, Jan de Lange and George Schoemaker facilitated workshops for professors at the Universities of Buenos Aires and Tucumán in which they introduced RME and, particularly, ways of using computers to teach various mathematics topics. The next step was to explore the possibility of a collaborative project involving the universities of Buenos Aires and Utrecht. In 1987 a series of seminars was offered at several locations in the Buenos Aires province organised by the Ministry of Education of that province and conducted by Martin Kindt. Among the most successful of these seminars was the one offered in the city of La Plata, in that most participants expressed interest in developing RME-inspired materials adapted to their students' needs. Yet the impossibility of providing one day off per month for each teacher participant to work on that project prevented this initiative from getting off the ground.

In a last attempt at collaborating with the Freudenthal Institute, in 1998 and with the support of the Argentinean National Department of Education, Jan de Lange met with specialists at various public and private institutions and gave a presentation enti-

---

[2]Institut de Recherche sur l'Enseignement des Mathématiques (Research Institute for Mathematics Education).

[3]Onderzoek Wiskundeonderwijs en Onderwijs Computercentrum (Mathematics Education Research and Educational Computer Centre).

[4]Herverkaveling Wiskunde I en II (Re-allotment Mathematics I and II).

[5]Master of the Computer.

tled "Mathematics in Reality" at the Centro de Altos Estudios en Ciencias Exactas. De Lange's work with secondary school teachers spread excitement about RME and its potential for improving mathematics instruction. A series of workshops in the city and province of Buenos Aires as well as in the northern city of Tucumán expanded interest in the RME approach. However, lack of long-term institutional support made it difficult to materialise RME ideas in teacher participants' classrooms.

9.1.3 San Carlos de Bariloche, Birthplace of the Grupo Patagónico de Didáctica de la Matemática

In December of 1998, Ana Bressan[6] and two colleagues from the Curriculum Office of the National Department of Education met Zolkower, who at the time was working at the City College of New York in the project Mathematics in the City, an NSF-funded,[7] RME-inspired in-service teacher education project directed by Catherine T. Fosnot in collaboration with Willem Uittenbogaard and Maarten Dolk (from the Freudenthal Institute). On that occasion, Zolkower shared informally her experience from this project and that immediately sparked Bressan's interest in bringing RME to her hometown, San Carlos de Bariloche.

Located in the Patagonian region, San Carlos de Bariloche (population: circa 140,000 habitants) is an international ski tourism destination and an important centre for research and development in science and technology. The city houses the Balseiro Institute, which offers masters and doctoral degrees in physics and nuclear engineering, and the INVAP, a high-tech centre for the design of nuclear reactors, radars, and satellites. Also located in Bariloche are branches of several public and private universities and the Instituto de Formación Docente Continua (IFDC) which is attended by local students and students from nearby cities and towns. All of the above makes of Bariloche a hub strongly tied to a variety of academic, scientific, and cultural centres notwithstanding its distance (1700 km) from Buenos Aires. Perhaps it is that very distance, coupled by its relatively small size, which makes of Bariloche a fertile ground for innovation in science, technology, and education.

Bariloche is a highly class-stratified town. Middle and upper classes (shop-owners, business and administration workers, professionals, and hotel owners and managers) reside in the centre, east, and west sections of town. More than half of the city's inhabitants live in the southern part; this includes lower and lower middle classes, subsidised workers, immigrants, maids, waiters, and aboriginal people. The educational needs of such a diverse population are served by more than 28 secondary schools, 30 public elementary schools (most with kindergarten annexes), about 30 independent private kindergartens, and 18 private schools (spanning Grades 1 through 12). All

---

[6]Bressan has been working in mathematics curriculum design and teacher education since 1975 and was a central person in preparing the Río Negro Mathematics Curriculum that later became the foundation for the National Curriculum Standards in Mathematics in Argentina.

[7]Funded by the U.S. National Science Foundation.

of the above places, demands on teacher preparation that are hardly met by basic, one-size-fits-all content and methods coursework in that many prospective teachers arrive to those courses with weak foundations in basic literacy and mathematics.

In the winter of 1999, invited by Bressan, Zolkower taught in Bariloche a mini-course for teachers entitled Closing the Gap between School Math and Common Sense: Freudenthal's Realistic Mathematics Education and gave a presentation at the Regional Centre of the University of Comahue. These events led to the formation, in February of 2000, of a study group of more than twenty teachers working in early childhood, elementary, and secondary classrooms of public as well as private schools. The collective, which named itself Grupo Patagónico de Didáctica de la Matemática (GPDM),[8] set off to "improve our practice by approaching the problems of learning and teaching mathematics taking RME as an object of study", as expressed by one of the participants. Another participant reflected: "From the start, what intrigued us the most about RME is how it opens up the classroom doors to common sense, imagination, desire to learn, and the mathematising potential of our students."

Since then, the degree and sphere of influence of the GPDM has been increasing steadily through classroom teaching experiments, workshops, courses, specialisation post-degrees, online seminars, conference presentations, and its web-page (gpdmatematica.org.ar). Group participants have produced more than twenty publications in *Novedades Educativas* (a magazine for teachers widely read throughout Latin America), *Yupana* (a journal of the University of Litoral, Argentina), *Paradigma* (a journal from Venezuela), *Premisa* (a journal of the Argentinean Society of Mathematics Education), *Didáctica* (a journal from Uruguay), and in the GPDM's webpage; two book chapters (Bressan, Zolkower, & Gallego, 2004; Zolkower & Bressan, 2012); two books (Bressan & Bressan, 2008; Brinnitzer et al., 2015); dozens of conference presentations (e.g., Zolkower's presentation at the FIUS in Colorado; Zolkower, 2009); and a myriad of translations of seminal work by RME specialists. Roughly once a year, Zolkower travels to Bariloche to offer thematic workshops on topics such as unpacking the teacher's role in conducting whole-class interaction, and the function of diagrams and diagramming in non-routine problem-based lessons, and to co-present at regional conferences. Meanwhile, from the distance, she shares resources with the group; co-designs teaching experiments; co-authors papers that narrate those experiences; and collaborates on a research study of teacher conduction of whole-class interaction (Shreyar, Zolkower, & Pérez, 2010; Zolkower, Shreyar, & Pérez, 2015).

---

[8]Is part of the Grupo de Educación Bariloche (Fundación GEB), a non-profit organisation devoted to in-service teacher education.

9.2   First Phase (2000–2004): Contexts, Situations, Models, and Strategies

9.2.1   Fractions, Decimals, and Percentages

In the summer of 2000, Zolkower facilitated a four-day workshop in Bariloche on the realistic approach to ratio and proportion, fractions, decimals, and percentages. The decision to start with these topics was motivated by the fact that rational number tends to present difficulties for teachers and students. Typically, fractions, decimals, ratio, proportion, and percentages are taught as separate topics. Students are presented with a set of rules to perform with little emphasis on why those rules work. In particular, with regard to fractions, they are expected to transit rather quickly from fraction as part/whole to fraction as bare number with little attention to fraction as ratio or to the use of the ratio table and open number line as tools for mathematising genuinely problematic situations. This approach often results in the 'multiplication makes bigger, division makes smaller' generalisation leading to errors when operating with rational numbers. Streefland's (1991b) research documents the positive effect of teaching fractions within realistic contexts as antidote to the above misconception.

During the workshop, participants worked on selected activities from the textbook series *Mathematics in Context* (MiC) (Wisconsin Center for Education Research & Freudenthal Institute, 1997–1998), in particular the units *Some of the Parts* (Van Galen, Wijers, Burrill, & Spence, 1997–1998) and *Fraction Times* (Keijzer et al., 1997–1998) and, in so doing, became familiar with Streefland's (1991b) classroom experiments on introducing fraction as ratio via fair sharing situations while guiding the development of level-raising tools (e.g., fraction strips, number line, ratio table, pie chart, and bar model). The collaborative study of MiC activities benefited from the GPDM's heterogeneous composition. Whereas lower grades teachers became aware of weaknesses in their understanding of rational number, those teaching mathematics in upper grades appreciated the pivotal function of contexts and models in supporting students' understanding of and fluency with fractions. Furthermore, comparing and contrasting productions at different levels allowed participants to make sense, through their own experiencing and reflective discussions, of two central notions in RME, namely guided reinvention and progressive mathematising (Freudenthal, 1991).

> Students should "reinvent mathematising rather than mathematics; abstracting rather than abstractions; schematising rather than schemes; formalising rather than formulas; algorithmising rather than algorithms; verbalising rather than language…". (Freudenthal, 1991, p. 49)

The above-described work proved so productive and intriguing that the idea of classroom try-outs emerged almost immediately. Processes and results from those experiences were analysed and discussed in group meetings giving participants the opportunity to consider student-generated strategies, the function of contexts and models, the advantages of heterogeneous grouping, and the paramount role of the teacher in guiding whole-class interaction.

The following is an example of what came out of such a discussion. It is an excerpt from a journal entry in which Silvia Pérez, co-author and GPDM participant, narrates an event in her 5th grade classroom.

> For the whole-class share I posted on the board strips with fractions and we worked together on how to complete the whole starting off with each of the fractions. Next the students had to think about different ways to make a whole by combining 1/2, 1/4, 1/3, 1/8, 1/6, and/or 1/5 (Fig. 9.1). All kinds of calculations were proposed using addition, subtraction, multiplication, and division. And this led to more examples, surprising strategies, unexpected questions, and new discoveries.

The above event and other similar experiments in GPDM classrooms called for revisiting the forms and functions of assessment. From the perspective of RME, assessments are viewed as serving foremost a didactical purpose, namely to gather information about each student's learning which teachers can use, before, during, and after each instructional sequence to guide individual as well as collective learning processes (Van den Heuvel-Panhuizen, 1996, 2005b). For example, the end-of-the-unit assessment Pérez (2004) designed for her 5th graders included bare number and context problems involving fraction as ratio, operator (measuring), part/whole, division, and bare number. In Fig. 9.2 there are four items from that assessment.

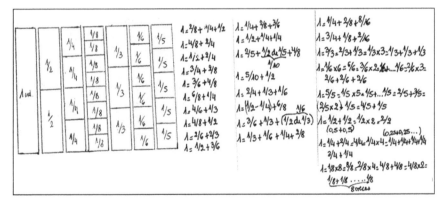

Fig. 9.1 Fraction strips posted on the board by Silvia

- 8 children share 5 pancakes. How much pancake does each child get?
- Can we fit 3/5 of a can and 5/10 of a can in one can? Explain!
- Solve each of the following calculations [...]. Then choose one of them and invent a problem such that that calculation could be used to solve it. 1/2 + 3/5 = 2/3 + 3/4 =
- Compare 9/12 and 5/8 using three different strategies.

Fig. 9.2 Sample items from an end-of-the-unit assessment on fractions

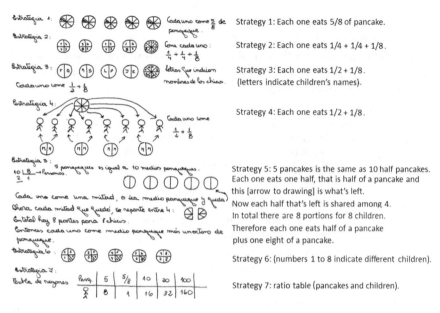

Fig. 9.3 Sample solutions for the problem about 5 pancakes for 8 children

Figure 9.3 shows the strategies students used to solve the pancakes problem. Worth highlighting is the use of circles as a model of the pancakes; different ways of cutting the pancakes leading to different, yet equivalent, expressions for each child's share; and the use of the ratio table with doubling and 'ten times' strategies.

The students' work in Fig. 9.4, concerning the comparison two fractions (9/12 and 5/8), offers further evidence of these 5th graders' appropriation of models for representing, working with, and thinking about fractions (fraction bar, circular model: pie chart and clock, and number line) as well as flexible strategies (e.g., using 3/4 as a benchmark and generating equivalent fractions). This assessment yielded invaluable information about students' strengths and weaknesses that the teacher took into account as she planned subsequent lessons.

The following year, these same students worked with Graciela Méndez, also a GPDM member. At a bi-weekly meeting, Graciela shared her 6th graders' work on problems involving rational numbers that, to everyone's amazement, evidenced their strong number sense, including the flexible use of a variety of tools and strategies. Figure 9.5 presents nine responses to: "7/12 is smaller than 70%. Is that true or false? How do you know?"

Worth underlining in the students' work is their ability to use different representations of rational number, the use of the double number line (G) and strategies such as completing the whole (H), benchmarks (A, C, D, I), equivalent fractions (B, C, E), and approximation and estimation (A, D, H).

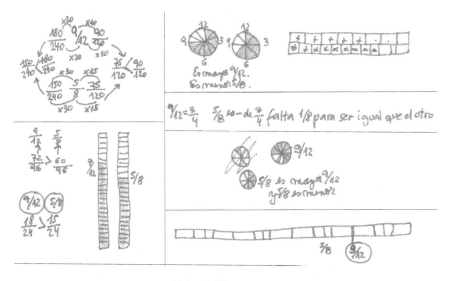

Fig. 9.4 Use of models to compare 9/12 and 5/8

A.	B.	C.
It's true because 50% is 6/12 and 6/12+1.5/12=7.5/12= 62.5% and that's a bit less than 70%.	7/12 → 3.5/6 → 1.75/3 I know that 1.75/3 is smaller than 2/3 and 2/3 is smaller than 70%.	2/3 is less than 70% 2/3=8/12 8/12 is more than 7/12 So, 7/12 is less than 70%
D. 6/12=50% and 1/12 is about 8% So, 7/12 is about 58%, that is less than 70%.	**E.** 70%=7/10 7/12=35/60 7/10=42/60 35<42 So 7/12<70%	**F.** It is less than 70%. To be equal it would need to be 8/12.
G. 6/12 7/12 8/12 9/12 50% 75% 70% is only 5% away from 75%. That's a bit more than 8/12. So, 70% must be more than 7/12.	**H.** If you have 7/12, you need 5/12 to get to 1. That means that 7/12 is more than ½. It's about 65%.	**I.** It is true because 6/12=50% and 1/12 is less than 20%. So, 7/12 cannot be more than 70%.

Fig. 9.5 Sample responses to the 70% and 7/12 comparison

9.2.2 City Buses

Experiences that brought RME into the classroom extended to other topics and grade levels. Inspired by the work of Van den Brink (1991), Mary Collado, another GPDM teacher, introduced to her 1st grade students the city bus as a context for early addition and subtraction. The instructional sequence began with play-acting, the bus conductor (paper hat on his head) circulating around the room picking up and dropping off passengers at various stops (desks). This was followed by a whole-class

Teacher:	How do we show that they got ON the bus? And how do we say they got OFF? What can we put here? [Points to the empty rectangle + vertical stick representing a bus stop.]
Carolina:	Put another bus!
Josefina:	Change the number!
Florencia:	Erase that number.
Jeremy:	WE COULD USE A PLUS!
Teacher:	Why plus?
Jeremy:	Because when they get on, there are more people
Teacher:	And here, did people get ON or they got OFF?
Sebastian:	Somebody got off!
Teacher:	How do I put that?
Sebastian:	MINUS, PUT A MINUS!!

Fig. 9.6 Getting on and off the city bus: emergence of the plus and minus signs (capitals indicate emphasis)

conversation about different ways of drawing bus trajectories, as shown in the brief excerpt below (Fig. 9.6).

The city bus served as a springboard for students to invent their own bus stories and, in the process, learn to use arrow language (dynamic) as a precursor of standard (static) expressions with the = sign. All of the above included teacher-guided opportunities for sharing, comparing, contrasting, and reflecting upon students' constructions and productions geared towards level rising. Figures 9.7a–f show how the city bus evolved from context, to model *of*, to model *for* (Streefland, 1985; Van den Heuvel-Panhuizen, 2003) thereby supporting progressive schematisation towards formal addition and subtraction. It is worth highlighting in the samples below the contrast between the bus stories by Fede (Fig. 9.7a) and Nata (Fig. 9.7f). Whereas Fede's presents a school bus' early morning trajectory picking up children and bringing them to school, Nata's depicts the opposite trajectory, the bus delivering children to their homes at the end of the school day (*todos* in Spanish means *all*).

In Mary Collado's own words:

> The bus context gave meaning to addition and subtraction and served afterwards as a model for the children to fall back to in order to make sense of other homologous situations, or when working with bare number problems. This context was also fruitful to generate a wide range of mathematisable situations including: (1) geometry: trajectories, location via points of reference, distance, sketching the inside of the buses, top and side views, symmetries, and so on; and (2) arithmetic: ticket fares, coin combinations for the ticket machine, numbers on the tickets, capacity of buses, school bus trajectories (first adding on and on, then subtracting on and on), short distance versus long distance buses, and so on. (Collado, Bressan, & Gallego, 2003, p. 15)

9.2.3   From Necklaces to Number Lines

Another RME-inspired context/object appropriated by GPDM teachers in elementary and secondary grade classes was the beads necklace. Necklaces proved invaluable

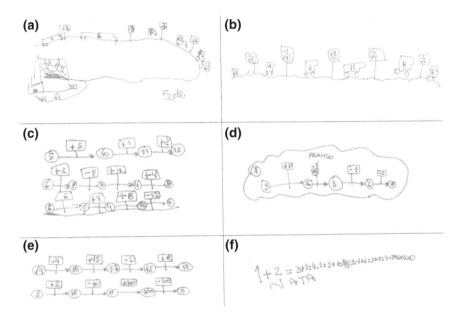

Fig. 9.7 First graders' own productions (bus stories)

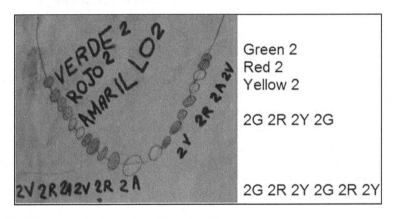

Fig. 9.8 Initial work of a first grader with bead necklaces

artefacts for developing students' mental arithmetic skills; working on ratio, proportion, and fractions; factors, multiples, divisibility, and remainders; and early algebra activities (e.g., describing and symbolising repeating and patterns and generalising those via building formulas). Figure 9.8 shows the initial work of a first grader with necklaces.

Activities involving patterns in necklaces included introducing them as material artefacts, drawing them, describing their structure (e.g., by relating the number of beads in the repeating pattern unit or 'chunk' with the total number of beads), invent-

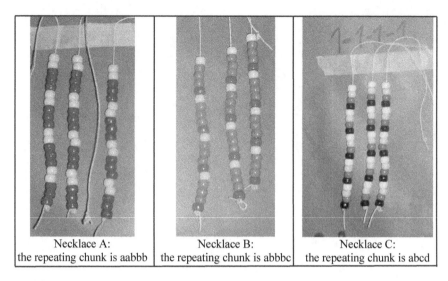

| Necklace A: | Necklace B: | Necklace C: |
| the repeating chunk is aabbb | the repeating chunk is abbbc | the repeating chunk is abcd |

Fig. 9.9   Three student-generated 20-bead necklaces

ing abbreviated descriptions (by means of icons; letter strings; and letters, numbers, and parentheses); creating necklaces with beads of different colour, size, price, or different number of beads; making necklaces that satisfy given constraints (e.g., the number of beads, the repeating chunk or pattern unit, the ratio between different colour beads, the length necklace, or the price).

Called upon to imagine themselves as workers in a necklace factory, students in Carolina Moreno's 2nd grade classroom were asked to design bicolour 20-bead necklaces with a complete repeating pattern. After completing this task, they arrived at the following conclusions: (1) if a necklace has a complete repeating pattern, the colour of the last bead is the same as the colour of the last bead in the chunk; (2) the pattern is complete when the number of beads in the repeating chunk fits an exact number of times in the total number of beads in the necklace; (3) if you have 20 beads, you cannot make a necklace with a pattern of length 3 or 9; and (4) you can make a 20 bead necklace with patterns of length 2, 4, 5, and 10. Also, beginning with a certain amount of beads in the chunk, they played at making different necklaces (Fig. 9.9).

When asked to make all possible 36-bead necklaces with complete repeating patterns, they used the language of multiplication, 'times' (*veces*) and 'goes into' (*entra en*), to describe, explain, and justify their findings. Figure 9.10 shows, summarised by the teacher, how these second graders expressed different decompositions of 36 as the product of two whole numbers.

In line with RME, a bi-colour 100-bead necklace structured in 10 groups of 10 beads with alternating colours served as a flexible (adaptable to each student's level) material artefact and a precursor to the open number line (Fig. 9.11), a schematic and continuous and, thus, more abstract linear model (Van den Heuvel-Panhuizen,

Number of bead sin the pattern unit	Total number of beads
2	2 x 18
3	3 x 12
4	4 x 9
6	6 x 6
9	9 x 4
12	12 x 3
18	18 x 2

Fig. 9.10 Decomposition of 36 in the context of bead necklaces

Fig. 9.11 Locating 37 on the 100-bead necklace

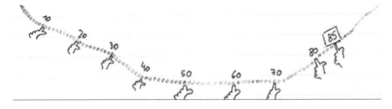

Fig. 9.12 Locating 85 on the 100-bead necklace

2008). This necklace functioned as a context/model for a variety of activities whereby students could attend to, both, the cardinal and ordinal aspect of numbers (37 beads, the 37th bead) as they worked on locating, comparing, and decomposing numbers; counting and calculating; grouping, and so on.

Figure 9.12 shows diagrammatically the way a student located the number 85 on the 100-bead necklace.

Figure 9.13 illustrates the use of the necklace as a tool for solving the following subtraction (difference as distance on the line) problem: "Today is the 5th of March. School begins on the 29th. How many vacation days do you still have?"

Figure 9.14 shows how two 2nd grade students use the open number line to solve 47 + 12 + 21.

In 4th, 5th, and 6th grade GPDM classrooms necklaces and number lines are routinely used for representing, working on, and thinking about problematic situations involving ratio and proportion (Freudenthal, 1983), alongside other tools such as the ratio table, the double number line, and the bar model. On their part, when teaching functions, sequences, and series, upper elementary and secondary grade GPDM teachers take advantage of necklaces as artefacts to support algebraising, for example, describing, symbolising, and generalising repeating as well as recursive patterns.

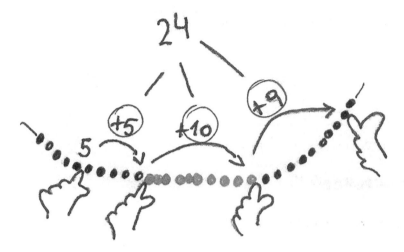

Fig. 9.13 Bead necklace as a tool for subtraction

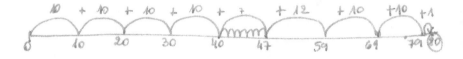

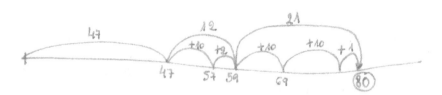

Fig. 9.14 Adding numbers on the open number line

9.2.4   The Function of Contexts in RME

The meaning of 'realistic' and the mathematical-didactical value of realistic contexts and situations intrigued most GPDM teachers. In particular, they debated the issue of how to find 'good' contexts and verify that those are actually fruitful mathematising. These concerns motivated several classroom experiments. One of these (Rabino, Bressan, & Zolkower, 2001), in 8th grade, involved comparing how students solved bare number calculations (multiplying and dividing rational numbers) with how they solved, a week later, context problems that involved those same calculations. The results confirmed the hypothesis that context problems were easier for the students to solve than bare number ones (Van den Heuvel-Panhuizen, 2005b), except when the situations depicted were unfamiliar to them. As shown in Fig. 9.15, the percentage

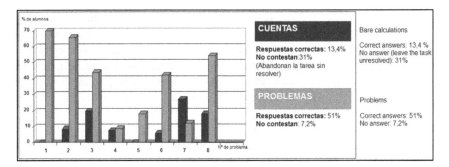

Fig. 9.15 Percentage of correct answers for bare number problems and for the context problems

of correct answers increased greatly for problems involving meaningful situations in familiar contexts. For example, for 60 ÷ 1/2, 83% of the students ($n = 35$) gave a wrong answer whereas for the corresponding context problem (60 L of beer packed in 1/2-L bottles; how many bottles?) almost 70% responded correctly. This experiment was replicated in other classrooms with similar results further confirming the hypothesis that realistic contextualising supports the meaningful construal of mathematical meanings.

Another experiment, in two 5th grade classrooms (Martínez Pérez, da Valle, Zolkower, & Bressan, 2002), aimed at developing in students a disposition to attend to the specifics of the problematic situations and activate their common sense and recall prior experiences about those situations. A third example is "¿Seño, es cierto eso?" (Is that true, miss?) (Pérez, Bressan, & Zolkower, 2001), an essay describing changes in two 6th grade classrooms which resulted from the move away from stereotypical and contrived word problems towards open-ended problematic situations embedded in realistic contexts.

9.2.5 Mental Arithmetic: Models and Strategies

Alongside a continued focus on contextualising and recontextualising, it became a central for GPDM teachers to deepen their own understanding of models in RME (in particular, the function of models in facilitating the transition from situational, to referential, general, and formal level) as well as develop their ability to use those models spontaneously and flexibly. This interest emerged organically, as teachers reflected on their students' use of models emerging in their students' activities around the MiC units they were studying.

In parallel with the work on models, the group focused on developing and strengthening their own as well as their students' mental arithmetic skills. The latter included cycles of design, implementation, documentation (video-recording and transcription), interpretative analysis, and reflection on mental math activities. This effort is in line with a central tenet of RME, namely, that the ability to use a variety of strategies, properties, and tools when solving arithmetic calculations is a central component of number sense. Strings (i.e., sets of interrelated bare number calculation presented horizontally to discourage the mechanical use of standard algorithms and, instead, promote the noticing and taking advantage of those relationships as well as using strategies that are suited to the numbers at hand) and other mental math activities became ubiquitous in GPDM classrooms at all grade levels. The above resulted in the publication of three booklets (for Grades 1–2, 3–4, and 5 through 7) with a wide range of activities for strengthening students' number sense that are currently in use in many classrooms within and beyond the GPDM.

Performing mental computations and comparing and contrasting alternative strategies solidified students' understanding of number and operations serving as a foundation for appropriating standard algorithms via progressive schematising and formalising. As an illustration, Fig. 9.16 shows multiplications of fraction strings done in a 6th grade classroom, with annotations of student strategies (on the left column: arrows linking the various problems; on the right column: description of strategies and supporting calculations) by the teacher, María de los Angeles Biedma.

Another example, shown in Fig. 9.17, presents a sequence of interrelated percentages of 360 supported by the bar model. This is a hybrid tool (double number line plus area model) that allows for finding equivalent ratios while keeping the part-whole relationship in view.

Figure 9.18 shows how a student calculated a series of percentages of 350 by using the double number line.

9.3 Second Phase (2005–2009): Deepening and Solidifying

9.3.1 Mathematising Within the GPDM

In 2005, Oscar Bressan, an Atomic Centre physicist and professor at the Balseiro Institute joined the GPDM. His involvement in the group contributed greatly to strengthen the mathematising abilities of participants with regard to selected topics in number theory, geometry and measurement, and probability and statistics (Bressan & Bressan, 2008). For example, in one of the sessions facilitated by Oscar, the focus was the following question: "Approximately how many digits are there in the product $20 \times 21 \times 22 \times 23 \times 24 \times 25 \times 26 \times 27 \times 28 \times 29 \times 30$?" Figure 9.19 shows the variety of strategies used by teachers to solve the problem.

Another problem tackled by the group session was 'Flowers and grass' (Fried & Amit, 2005):

We want to plant flowers and grass in a 6 m by 10 m rectangular garden. The grass will be planted in the four corners, in the shape of four isosceles right triangles with the right-angle vertex of each coinciding with the angles of the rectangle. The condition is that the two triangles, the one with vertex in D and the one with vertex in

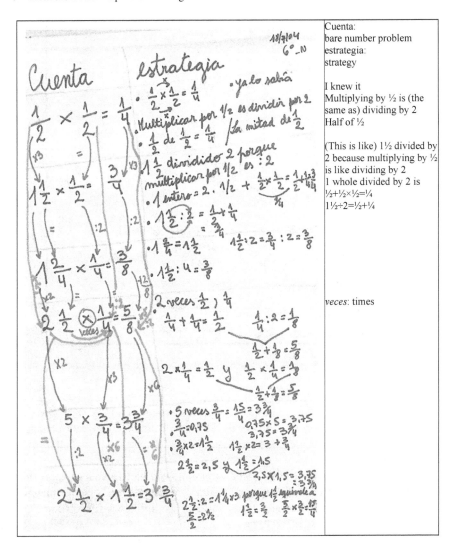

Fig. 9.16 Multiplications of fraction strings

B need to be congruent. The flowers will be planted in the remaining parallelogram-shaped area.

Group participants were presented with, both, the verbal description of the problematic situation and the accompanying diagram (Fig. 9.20) and the request that they write down observations and formulate as many meaningful questions about it as they could. Next the group selected the following three questions to focus on: Assuming that there are different possibilities for the parallelogram to plant flowers in, depending on the length of segment DE, would all of those yield the same area? If not, which

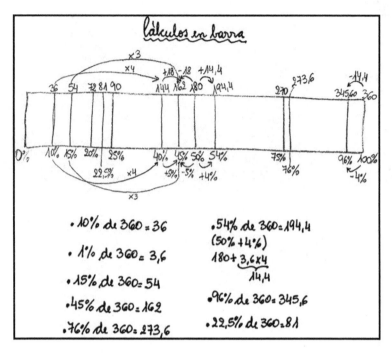

Fig. 9.17 Calculating percentages of 360 with the bar model (Van den Heuvel-Panhuizen, 2003)

parallelogram would maximise the area for planting the flowers? What happens to the area of the triangles in the corners as the area of the parallelogram changes? Figure 9.21 shows the different approaches followed by participants (Zolkower & Bressan, 2012).

Synergically, the heterogeneity of the group allowed participants to appreciate different levels and manners of mathematising including how concrete material (Fig. 9.21a), graph paper diagrams (Fig. 9.21b), function tables (Fig. 9.21c), and calculus tools (function, derivative, graphing the inverted parabola, Fig. 9.21d) all served as tools for representing and/or solving the problem. This modality of working with "spiral tasks" (Fried & Amit, 2005, p. 432) was extended, with great success, to workshops attended by other teachers and teachers-in-training in Bariloche and in surrounding towns and cities.

The pressing need to deepen participants' mathematical-didactical abilities and, at the same time, generate material for the increasing number of courses offered by the GPDM led to translating papers by RME specialists, adapt (recontextualised) MiC units, and design activities and instructional sequences. Among the latter, worth mentioning is the design of materials for: linear functions; ratio and proportion, fractions, decimals, and percentages; congruency and similarity; patterns, symbols, and rules; mental arithmetic; side and top views; and polygons. In designing the above, emphasis was placed on using suitable, familiar, and meaningful contexts,

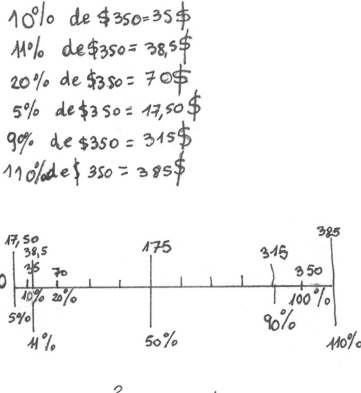

Fig. 9.18 Double number line as a tool for calculating percentages of 350

situations, and artefacts to support mathematising, for example, advertisements, price lists, mandalas, clippings from newspapers and other printed media, photographs, hiking and elevation maps, bus schedules, restaurant menus, dissection and edge-matching puzzles.

The second phase saw an increase in the number of courses offered by the GPDM in Bariloche, rural areas of the provinces of Río Negro, and cities in the provinces of Neuquén, Mendoza, and Buenos Aires. In Neuquén, several GPDM participants collaborated in designing and teaching the post-degree mathematics unit Teaching in Schools Located in Diverse Urban Contexts. This required adapting RME-inspired

Rocío (elementary school teacher) paired up the numbers whose one-digits add to 10 (i.e, 23 x 27, 24 x 26, 22 x 28, and 21 x 29). She noted that those four products, which are a bit more than 600 each, add 3 digits to the overall product but got stuck there.

Oscar continued Rocío's idea:
24x26= (30-6) (30-4) = 900 – (6+4) x 30 + 6x4= 600 +24
23x27= (30-7) (30-3) = 900 – (7+3) x 30 +7x3 = 600 + 21
… and so on with 22 x 28, 21 x 29 and 20 x 30, which gives about 600^5.
600^5 can be expressed as $6^5 x 10^{10}$ that is close to $10^4 x 10^{10}$. Therefore, the product has 14 digits.

Adriana (secondary school teacher) solved the problem by approximation. Using the calculator, she did 20^{10} and got 14 digits; then she did 30^{10} and got 15 digits; then 25^{10} would give between 14 and 15 digits.

Patricia (secondary) also used the calculator but she transformed the expression using factorials. She divided 30! by 19!
(Thus: 30x29x28x27x….x1) ÷ (19x18x17x…x1) and obtained 14 digits.

Oscar worked with logs. He knows that the log of 2 is 0.30, thus the log of 20 is 1.30. This allowed him to estimate 1.30 x 10 (20 appears 10 times in the product) and get 13. He adds 1 to that and concludes that the number of digits is approximately 14.

Ana María made groups of 20 x 20 ignoring the one's place and got $400^5 x30$. That can be expressed as $4^5 x100^5 x30 = 4^5 x10^{10} x30$, which gives a number with approximately 13 digits. If we add back to that 20 times the sum of the ones digits, from 1 to 9, which we ignored initially, we get 900. So, the product in question has about 14 digits.

Fig. 9.19 Solving the 'Large product digits' problem

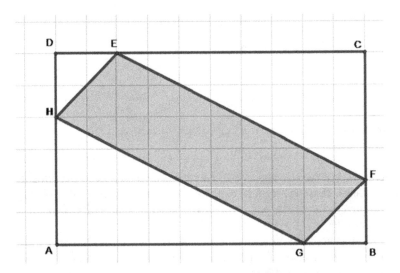

Fig. 9.20 Diagram accompanying the 'Flowers and grass' problem

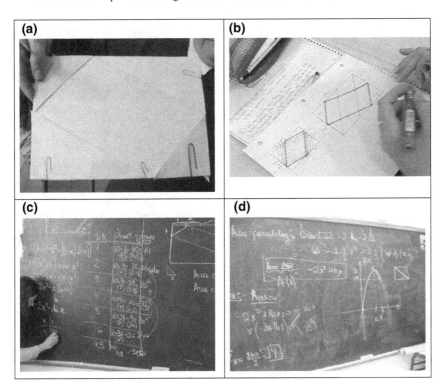

Fig. 9.21 Solving the 'Flowers and grass' problem

materials for working in those schools, trying those out, and gathering classroom-generated artefacts.

9.3.2 Making Connections

In line with the RME principle that intertwining the four curriculum strands and making connections between mathematics and other school subjects gives coherence to instruction and promotes different ways of and tools for mathematising, GPDM participants designed, tried out, and documented many interdisciplinary instructional sequences (see gpdmatematica.org.ar).

For example, a lesson that gave students the opportunity to link mathematics with natural sciences centred on a postcard image of a tiny hummingbird. The experience was framed within the broader theme of using visual images, a sub-type of 'rich contexts' (Freudenthal, 1991), as springboard for students to formulate and tackle meaningful questions in contrast with the ubiquitous reliance on ready-made, stereotypical

Fig. 9.22 Bird on a # 2
pencil

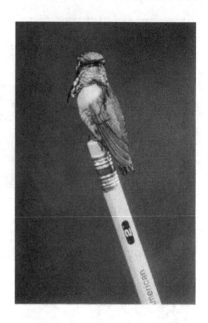

pseudo-narratives known as word or story problems. Figure 9.22 shows the postcard
Silvia Pérez presented to her 5th grade students (Pérez, Bressan, & Zolkower, 2006).

This image, a grandmother's gift to the class on the occasion of the ongoing natural
science project, generated plenty of comments and questions, for example: "It can't
be so small!", "Is that a trick?", "How did they take that picture?" As Silvia asked
her students to organise those questions in some manner, they did so according
to three categories they themselves formulated: questions that could be answered
using information retrievable from the postcard image itself; questions that called
for information not included in the postcard yet available if searched elsewhere; and
questions that could not be answered at all due to the impossibility of accessing the
needed information.

Next, the class agreed to address the following questions: "About how much does
the hummingbird measure?", "Exactly how much does it measure?", "What is the
relationship between the size of the bird and the size of the (#2) pencil?" As they
addressed these questions, students explored the relationship between lengths in
reality and in the picture and, via measuring, estimating, and using the ratio table,
arrived at 4.9 cm. The bird is the *Mellisuga helenae*, the smallest type of hummingbird
in the world, and measures less than 5 cm. As a spin-off of this project, the class visited
a local radio station to talk to listeners about these birds. Along these same lines,
namely the intertwining of mathematics and natural sciences, there was a project,
done in 2005 in two 4th grade mathematics/science classes, around the measuring
of moss (Pérez, 2007).

Similarly, in the winter of 2008 Rocío Alvarez engaged her 7th graders (school
attended by low SES students) in a mathematics/science inquiry around the theme
of snow. The inquiry emerged spontaneously as several students expressed concern

about the shortage of snow expected for that winter, a central preoccupation given that the seasonal work and income of many Bariloche inhabitants depends heavily on snow attracting skiers to the city and its surroundings. While many questions posed by the students concerned snow as a physical-chemical phenomenon, a few expressed curiosity of a geometric kind, as in: "What does a snowflake look like when you look at it close up?" Rocío asked them to draw snowflakes, next those diagrams were checked experimentally (using magnifying glasses) and, honing into the geometric structure of snowflakes, including its multiple symmetries, the work centred the properties of regular hexagons, and how those properties can be used to construct them with ruler and compass (Fig. 9.23).[9] This experience was replicated years later with other groups of 7th grade students (Álvarez, 2015).

Invited to apply what they had learned about how to construct regular hexagons with geometric tools, students generated designs such as the following (Fig. 9.24).

The following year, when her 7th graders expressed interest in ergonomics and its application to the design of furniture, Rocío seised the opportunity to use that as a context for doing some geometry. Motivated by the question of what would be the ideal couch/chair for watching TV, the students tried different seating positions, searched online for types of chairs, and compared and contrasted various models measuring different heights and angles. Finally, they concluded that the best angle formed by the back and the seat is one ranging between 100° and 120°, and that the angle between the top of the back and the edge of the seat should be between 110° and 130°. After working on "Part D: Angles" of the MiC unit *Made to Measure* (De Lange & Wijers, 1997–1998), the students were able to confirm their predictions. Finally, they designed their own couch/chairs, taking into account angle measurement constraints, as shown below (Fig. 9.25).

9.3.3 Fall Seminar: Teachers Teaching Teacher Educators

The increasing visibility and impact of the GPDM soon caught the attention of the education authorities at the national level. In May of 2009, with funding and logistical support from the National Ministry of Education, the group offered in Bariloche a five-day Fall Seminar on RME for teacher educators representing of all of the 23 Argentinean provinces. The seminar was attended by 50 teachers, 38 of them with scholarships given by the INFD,[10] as well as curriculum specialists from the latter. In addition, the seminar benefited from the participation of Willem Uittenbogaard (and his wife Sylvia Eerhart) and Diana Rosenberg, the latter playing a crucial role as guide and simultaneous translator.

---

[9]An additional resource for this inquiry was the collection of snowflake images by Wilson Bentley (1865–1931), http://snowflakebentley.com.

[10]The INFD is part of the National Ministry of Culture and Education and has the function of directing and coordinating teacher education policies and programmes.

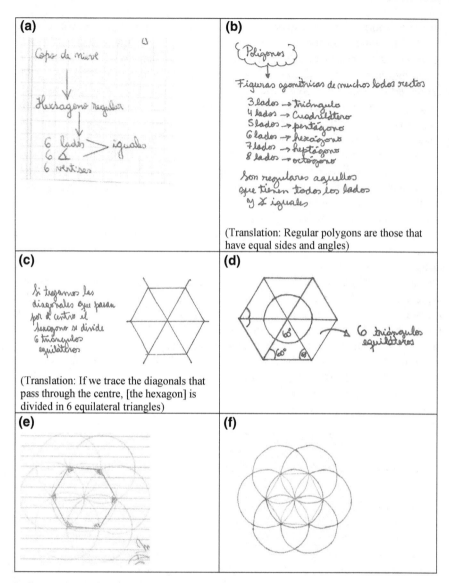

Fig. 9.23 From snowflakes to the properties and construction of regular hexagons

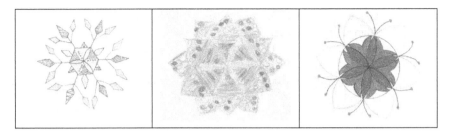

Fig. 9.24 Students' own hexagonal designs

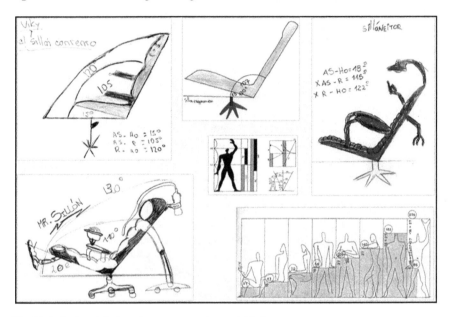

Fig. 9.25 Students' designs for an ergonomic couch/chair

The Fall Seminar was organised as follows: in the morning, teacher-led presentations and thematic workshops on the RME approach to whole number and rational number operations, geometry and measurement, and algebra (specifically, the patterns, symbols, and equations sub-strand); in the afternoon, guided visits to selected GPDM classrooms as well as to the teacher training institute, followed by post-visit debriefing sessions. In line with Freudenthal's (1991) emphasis on the parallel between mathematising and didactising, the seminar was organised around teaching experiments in GPDM classrooms (in Grades 1 through 10 as well as in teacher training courses), with guided opportunities for participants to observe learning and teaching processes, analyse student work, and reflect on all of the above.

Among the lessons planned for and tried out for the occasion were: an adaptation of the 'Barter' problem from *Comparing Quantities* (Kindt, Abels, Meyer, & Pligge, 1997–1998); brick pyramid problems (from the Dutch textbook series *Wis en Reken*;

see also, Zolkower & Rubel, 2015; Abrahamson, Zolkower, & Stone, this volume); an 18-piece regular hexagon dissection puzzle (Bressan, Rabino, & Zolkower, 2014); mental arithmetic mini-lessons (Pérez, Zolkower, & Bressan, 2014); side and top views (inspired by *Side Seeing*, Jonker, Querelle, Clarke, & Cole, 1997–1998); and exploring similarity within the context of making a triangular patchwork quilt for a sofa (adapted from *Triangles and Patchwork*, Roodhardt et al., 1997–1998). As an example, Fig. 9.26 shows the work of 7th grade students' working on the 'Barter' problem:

> Paulo goes to the market with 2 sheep and 1 goat which he wants to barter for corn to bring home for his family. They offer him: 1 bag of salt for 2 chickens, 2 bags of corn for 3 bags of salt, and 6 bags of salt for each sheep. What can Paulo do with his sheep and goat in order to come home with corn?

These and other student productions were posted simultaneously on the board and then compared and contrasted; also, errors were spotted and corrected (Fig. 9.26c). The teacher then engaged her students in a whole-class conversation focused on progressive symbolising which culminated in the conjoined writing, on a new poster (Fig. 9.27), of expressions that included letter symbols signifying the items bartered, arrows connecting fair share exchanges (exchange this for that), and the formal algebraic language of equations.

The Fall Seminar contributed greatly to further disseminating RME throughout Argentina, which can be inferred from the significant increase in the number of visitors to our webpage as well as the plethora of invitations for GPDM members to lead teacher-training seminars, offer thematic workshops, present at research conferences, and elaborate or evaluate curriculum documents and instructional materials.

9.3.4   In the Meanwhile, in Pre-service Teacher Education

The Teacher Training Institute in Bariloche houses three programmes: elementary, early childhood, and special education. Since 2008, GPDM members teach many of the courses offered therein. Pre-service candidates arrive to those programmes with patchy and mostly procedural mathematical content knowledge and limited problem solving skills. Furthermore, many of them have a complex and often troubled relationship to mathematics, a "rigid and strict subject" that is "hard to understand," and which they have had "lots of difficulties" with.

In view of the above, the initial preparation of mathematics teachers aims at helping candidates re-signify, expand, and deepen their mathematical knowledge as well as revisit and transform their beliefs about the subject, how students learn it, and how to teach it. In that respect, RME is a powerful tool for achieving such aims. As an illustration of the impact of RME in teacher education through the work of GPDM teacher educators, below is the testimony of a pre-service teacher candidate:

> My relationship to mathematics changed a lot. It used to be very hard for me. I would often get frustrated… I used to hate it. But this year, I think because of how we approached it in

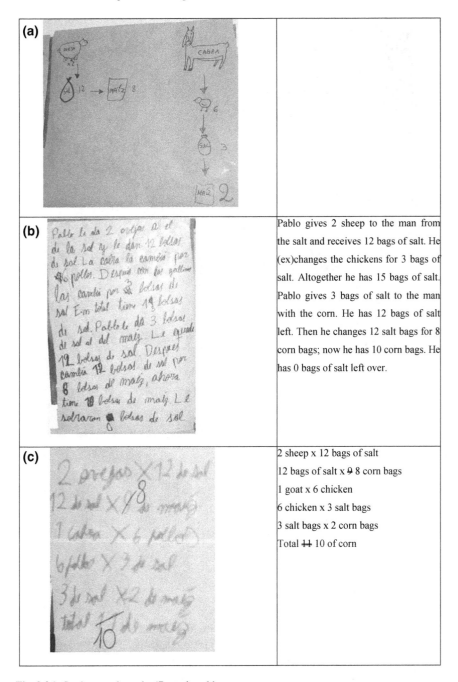

(a)

(b)

Pablo gives 2 sheep to the man from the salt and receives 12 bags of salt. He (ex)changes the chickens for 3 bags of salt. Altogether he has 15 bags of salt. Pablo gives 3 bags of salt to the man with the corn. He has 12 bags of salt left. Then he changes 12 salt bags for 8 corn bags; now he has 10 corn bags. He has 0 bags of salt left over.

(c)

2 sheep x 12 bags of salt
12 bags of salt x 9̶ 8 corn bags
1 goat x 6 chicken
6 chicken x 3 salt bags
3 salt bags x 2 corn bags
Total 1̶1̶ 10 of corn

Fig. 9.26 Student work on the 'Barter' problem

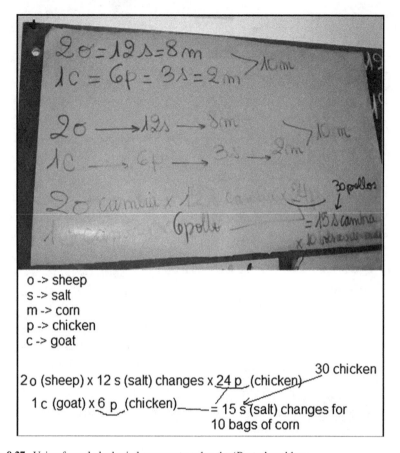

Fig. 9.27 Using formal algebraic language to solve the 'Barter' problem

this class, focusing on learning and understanding, it changed completely my view of this subject. Now I put a lot of enthusiasm when doing math and when I make mistakes I do not feel frustrated because I know I can learn from those mistakes.

9.3.5 Thinking Aloud Together

Mathematising, interacting, and reflecting are tightly connected (Dekker & Elshout-Mohr, 2004; Elbers, 2003; Freudenthal, 1991; Goffree & Dolk, 1995). Yet for interaction and reflection to support progressive mathematising teachers ought to be skilful at guiding whole-class exchanges towards: posing questions about open-ended situations; sharing ideas, connections, productions, constructions, and further questions; practicing the use of models and strategies; and comparing, contrasting, and assessing alternative solution approaches or different ways of diagramming, symbolising, and generalising mathematical relationships.

In most classrooms, the whole-class share and discussion portion of the lesson typically occurs after the students have finished solving the problem at hand, and the interaction focuses on individual students (or groups) presenting their work, with the teacher facilitating the exchanges via follow-up questions (e.g., revoicing, echoing) aimed at level raising, and then closing up with a more or less interactive (and more or less explicit) institutionalisation of the target mathematical idea. Interested in exploring a variation of this approach which we have witnessed in classrooms taught by experienced and highly effective teachers, we framed our research around the following question: "What is the effect on students learning when whole-class conversations are held not when students are done solving the problem but, instead, midway through that process?" The empirical evidence we found (Shreyar, Zolkower, & Pérez, 2010; Zolkower & Pérez, 2007, 2012; Zolkower & Shreyar, 2007; Zolkower, Shreyar, & Pérez, 2015) suggests that these thinking-aloud-together conversations, when skilfully conducted by the teacher, can serve as an interpersonal plane for sharing ideas in statu nascendi thus maximising opportunities for students to appropriate them.

9.4 Third Phase (2011–2015): The GPDM, an Ever-Expanding Endeavour

During this third phase, the GPDM established itself as an important referent for mathematics teacher education in Argentina. Its members are frequently invited to conduct thematic workshops and seminars and present at conferences in the provinces of Catamarca, Córdoba, Buenos Aires, Ciudad Autónoma de Buenos Aires, and Santa Fe as well as in Salto (Uruguay) and, most recently, in Lima (Perú). The GPDM is regularly called to participate in committees on teacher preparation, in-service training, and instruction and assessment design at the provincial and the national levels. Furthermore, input from the group and, through it, from RME ideas have found their way into the curriculum and standards documents for the provinces of Río Negro and Neuquén.

The group's webpage plays a paramount role in disseminating the realistic approach via papers and instructional materials, adaptations of the latter (recontextualised units and activities), newly designed material, and teacher narratives of classroom experiences (many of which are published in *Novedades Educativas*). Increasingly, the group's webpage serves as a venue for receiving requests to serve in thesis committees and evaluate programmes throughout Argentina as well as other countries in the region. All of the above evidenced the place of the GPDM as an important referent on RME within Spanish speaking South America.

9.4.1   More Publications and Translations

Since 2001, RME-inspired lessons and units designed and implemented by GPDM teachers are regularly published in magazines and journals of widespread distribution in Argentina and abroad (see webpage, publications list). Also, the number of translations into Spanish of RME-related material continues to increase. For instance, in 2006 Gallego translated the online publication *Great Assessment Problems* (Dekker & Querelle, 2002); in 2011, Gallego and Zolkower translated *Children Learn Mathematics* (Van den Heuvel-Panhuizen, 2008, 2010); and in 2012, Gallego and da Valle translated *Young Children Learn Measurement and Geometry* (Van den Heuvel-Panhuizen & Buys, 2008, 2012) for a Mexican publisher.

9.4.2   Research Projects

Worth mentioning here are two recent collaborative inquiry projects conducted by group members that bear a strongly RME imprint. The first project, framed within the larger initiative Mathematics For All, focused on using games (e.g., games for teaching divisibility and other number theory topics). The second project, which we have referred to in Sect. 3.5, concerns the study of a teacher's manner of conducting whole-class conversations.

The mathematics games project, financially supported by the INFD, involved an interdisciplinary team that included members of the GPDM who are also professors at the Instituto de Formación Docente Continua.[11] This work resulted in the publication *El Juego en la Enseñanza de la Matemática* (Brinnitzer et al., 2015), a volume consisting of 60 games that can be used to address a wide range of curriculum topics, with variations for different grade levels as well as for meeting the needs of students who perform at various levels in mathematics.

Regarding the second project, over the past eight years, Zolkower and Pérez, together with Sam Shreyar from Teachers College, Columbia University, have been studying whole-class interaction in mathematics classrooms within a theoretical-methodological framework that intertwines tools from Systemic Functional Linguistics (SFL) (Halliday & Matthiessen, 2004) with ideas from Vygotsky, Dewey, and Freudenthal. Treating whole-class conversations as multi-semiotic texts (O'Halloran, 2000; Zolkower & de Freitas, 2012), we use SFL tools to describe and explain the choices of grammar and vocabulary, in addition to gestures and diagrams, made by the teacher in conducting those exchanges (Shreyar et al., 2010; Zolkower & Pérez, 2012; Zolkower, Shreyar, & Pérez, 2015). The main goal of this research is to describe, at a fine-grained level of lexico-grammatical detail, the manner in which

---

[11]The team, called Ludomateca, includes professors who teach courses in different areas (mathematics, arts, student teaching practicum) and levels (early childhood and elementary) as well as students in the elementary education programme.

experienced teachers support progressive mathematising in thinking-aloud-together conversations that involve the class as a whole.

9.5 Closure

Over the past sixteen years, our study and implementation of RME has been an invaluable collective experience in that it allowed us to: (a) experience first-hand the meaning of mathematising; (b) improve our own number sense, symbol sense, and spatial sense; (c) appropriate a wide range of mathematising tools and ways of using those tools; (d) enhance our ability to make, modify, and use diagrams as mathematical thinking devices; (e) understand how to use realistic contexts and situations can be used to support the guided reinvention of mathematising in the different curriculum strands; (f) acquire practice in recognising, finding, inventing, and using realistic problematic situations, including those which involve inter-strand and inter-disciplinary connections; (g) make room for and use students' productions and constructions; (h) acquire practice in organising and guiding students' work attending to informal, semi-formal, and formal levels of mathematising; (i) appreciate and make good didactical use of heterogeneities (i.e., differences in social, cultural, linguistic background as well as academic performance); and (j) become aware of the pivotal role of reflection in mathematising and didactising.

Rather than applying the principles of RME top down as dogmas and using RME instructional materials as ready-made recipes, the GPDM engages in processes of design, try out, reflection, revision, new try outs, and so on, in spiral movements that inter-connected our own mathematising with that of students in Grades K–12 and in teacher preparation courses. Fuelled by the common goal of making mathematics accessible, meaningful, and relevant for all students, we are reconstructing realistic mathematics education from the bottom up and, in so doing, we are contributing, albeit locally, to breach the gap between teachers and mathematics education specialists and the dichotomy between theory and practice.

Acknowledgements The authors wish to acknowledge the GPDM teachers who contributed their classroom work for the vignettes included in this chapter as well as all the other members of our group.

References

Álvarez, R. (2015). La geometría del copo de nieve [Geometry of snowflakes]. *Didáctica*, 2–13.
Bressan, A., & Bressan, O. (2008). *Probabilidad y estadística: Cómo trabajar con niños y jóvenes* [Probability and statistics for working with children and adolescents]. Buenos Aires, Argentina: Novedades Educativas.
Bressan, A., Rabino, A., & Zolkower, B. (2014). El rompecabezas hexagonal: ¿Dónde está la matemática? [The hexagonal puzzle: Where is the math?]. *Didáctica*, 28–35.

Bressan, A., Zolkower, B., & Gallego, M. F. (2004). Los principios de la educación matemática realista [Principles of realistic mathematics education]. In H. Alagia, H., Bressan, A., & Sadovsky, P. (Eds.), *Reflexiones teóricas para la educación matemática* (pp. 69–98). Buenos Aires, Argentina: Libros del Zorzal.

Brinnitzer, E., Collado, M., Fernández Panizza, G., Gallego, M. F., Pérez, S., & Santamaría, F. (2015). *El juego en la enseñanza de la matemática* [The role of play in mathematics teaching]. Buenos Aires, Argentina: Novedades Educativas.

Collado, M., Bressan, A., & Gallego, Ma. F. (2003). El colectivo y las operaciones de suma y resta [City buses and addition and subtraction]. *Novedades Educativas, 15*(149/150), 14–19 and 10–15.

Consejo Federal de Cultura y Educación. (1995). *Contenidos Básicos Comunes para la Educación General Básica* [Common Basic Contents for General Education]. Buenos Aires, Argentina: Ministerio de Cultura y Educacion de la Nación, República Argentina.

De Lange, J., & Wijers, M. (1997–1998). Made to measure. In Wisconsin Center for Education Research & Freudenthal Institute (Eds.), *Mathematics in context*. Chicago, IL: Encyclopedia Britannica.

Dekker, R., & Elshout-Mohr, M. (2004). Teacher interventions aimed at mathematical level-raising during collaborative learning. *Educational Studies in Mathematics, 56*(1), 39–65.

Dekker, T., & Querelle, N. (2002). *Great assessment problems*. Utrecht, the Netherlands: Freudenthal Institute.

Dekker, T., & Querelle, N. (2006). *Grandes problemas de evaluación* [Great assessment problems] (de M. Fernanda Gallego, Trans.). http://www.gpdmatematica.org.ar.

Elbers, E. (2003). Classroom interaction as reflection: Learning and teaching mathematics in a community of inquiry. *Educational Studies in Mathematics, 54*, 77–99.

Freudenthal, H. (1973). *Mathematics as an educational task*. Dordrecht, the Netherlands: D. Reidel Publishing Company.

Freudenthal, H. (1983). *Didactical phenomenology of mathematical structures*. Dordrecht, the Netherlands: D. Reidel Publishing Company.

Freudenthal, H. (1991). *Revisiting mathematics education: China lectures*. Dordrecht, The Netherlands: Kluwer Academic Publishers.

Fried, M. N., & Amit, M. (2005). A spiral task as a model for in-service teacher education. *Journal of Mathematics Teacher Education, 8*(5), 419–436.

Goffree, F., & Dolk, M. (1995). *Standards for primary mathematics teacher education*. Utrecht, the Netherlands: Freudenthal Institute/SLO.

Gravemeijer, K., & Terwel, J. (2000). Hans Freudenthal: A mathematician on didactics and curriculum theory. *Journal of Curriculum Studies, 32*(6), 777–796.

Halliday, M. A. K., & Matthiessen, C. M. I. M. (2004). *An introduction to functional grammar* (3rd ed.). London, UK: Hodder Arnold.

Jonker, V., Querelle, N., Clarke, B., & Cole, B. R. (1997–1998). Side seeing. In Wisconsin Center for Education Research & Freudenthal Institute (Eds.), *Mathematics in context*. Chicago, IL: Encyclopaedia Britannica.

Keijzer, R., Van Galen, F., Gravemeijer, K., Shew, J. A., Cole, B. R., & Brendefur, J. (1997–1998). Fraction times. In Wisconsin Center for Education Research & Freudenthal Institute (Eds.), *Mathematics in context: A connected curriculum for grade 5–8*. Chicago, IL: Encyclopedia Britannica.

Kindt, M., Abels, M., Meyer, M., R., & Pligge, M. A. (1997–1998). Comparing quantities. In Wisconsin Center for Education Research & Freudenthal Institute (Eds.), *Mathematics in context: A connected curriculum for grade 5–8*. Chicago, IL: Encyclopedia Britannica.

Martínez Pérez, M. L., da Valle, N., Zolkower, B., & Bressan, A. (2002). La relevancia del contexto en la resolución de problemas de matemática: Una experiencia para docentes y alumnos [The relevance of context in mathematics problem solving: An experience with teachers and students]. *Paradigma, 23*(1), 59–94.

O'Halloran, K. (2000). Classroom discourse in mathematics: A multi-semiotic analysis. *Linguistics and Education, 10*(3), 359–388.

Pérez, S. (2004). Un ejemplo del sentido didáctico de una evaluación de fracciones en 5° grado [Fractions in Grade 5: A sample didactic assesment]. *Premisa, 6*(20), 3–14.

Pérez, S. (2007). Midiendo... ¡¿líquenes?! [Measuring ... lichens ?!]. http://gpdmatematica.org.ar/wp-content/uploads/2015/09/liquenes.pdf.

Pérez, S., Bressan, A., & Zolkower, B. (2001). ¿Es cierto eso, señorita? [Is that true, miss?] *Novedades Educativas, 13*(131/132), 21–23 and 22–24.

Pérez, S., Bressan, A., & Zolkower, B. (2006). Las imágenes y las preguntas en la escuela [Images and questions in school]. *Novedades Educativas, 182,* 22–26.

Pérez, S., Zolkower, B., & Bressan, A. (2014). Cadenas de cálculo: Un recurso para fortalecer el sentido del número y las operaciones [Mental math strings: A resource for strengthening number sense]. *Novedades Educativas, 26*(280), 50–57.

Rabino, A., Bressan, A., & Zolkower, B. (2001). El aprendizaje de números racionales. Valor de los problemas en contextos con sentido para los alumnos [Teaching-learning rational number: Value of meaningful context problems]. *Novedades Educativas, 13*(129), 16–20.

Roodhardt, A., Abels, M., Clarke, D., Spence, M. S., Shew, J., & Brinker, L. (1997–1998). Triangles and patchwork. In Wisconsin Center for Education Research & Freudenthal Institute (Eds.), *Mathematics in context: A connected curriculum for grade 5–8.* Chicago, IL: Encyclopedia Britannica.

Shreyar, S., Zolkower, B., & Pérez, S. (2010). Thinking aloud together: A 6th grade teacher's mediation of a whole-class conversation about percents. *Educational Studies in Mathematics, 73,* 21–53.

Streefland, L. (1985). Wiskunde als activiteit en de realiteit als bron [Mathematics as activity and reality as a source], *Nieuwe Wiskrant, 5*(1), 60–67.

Streefland, L. (Ed.). (1991a). *Realistic Mathematics Education in primary school.* Utrecht, the Netherlands: CD-β Press, Utrecht University, Freudenthal Institute.

Streefland, L. (1991b). *Fractions in Realistic Mathematics Education: A paradigm of developmental research.* Dordrecht, the Netherlands: Springer.

Treffers, A. (1991). Didactical background of a mathematics program for primary school. In L. Streefland (Ed.), *Realistic Mathematics Education in primary school* (pp. 21–56). Utrecht, the Netherlands: CD-β Press, Utrecht University, Freudenthal Institute.

Van den Brink, J. (1991). Realistic mathematics education for young children. In L. Streefland (Ed.), *Realistic Mathematics Education in primary school* (pp. 77–92). Utrecht, the Netherlands: CD-β Press, Utrecht University, Freudenthal Institute.

Van den Heuvel-Panhuizen, M. (1996). *Assessment and Realistic Mathematics Education.* Utrecht, the Netherlands: CD-β Press, Freudenthal Institute, Utrecht University.

Van den Heuvel-Panhuizen, M. (2003). The didactical use of models in Realistic Mathematics Education: An example from a longitudinal trajectory on percentage. *Educational Studies in Mathematics, 54*(1), 9–35.

Van den Heuvel-Panhuizen, M. (2005a). Mathematics standards and curricula in the Netherlands. *Zentralblatt for Didaktik der Mathematik, 37*(4), 287–307.

Van den Heuvel-Panhuizen, M. (2005b). The role of contexts in assessment problems in mathematics. *For the Learning of Mathematics, 25*(2), 2–9, 23.

Van den Heuvel-Panhuizen, M. (Ed.). (2008). *Children learn mathematics: A learning-teaching trajectory with intermediate attainment targets for calculation with whole numbers in primary school.* Rotterdam, Taipei: Sense Publishers.

Van den Heuvel-Panhuizen, M. (Ed.). (2010). *Los ninos aprenden mathematicas* [Children learn mathematics] (M. F. Gallego & B. Zolkower, Trans.). Cd. Brisa, Naucalpan, México: Correo del Maestro.

Van den Heuvel-Panhuizen, M., & Buys, K. (Eds.). (2008). *Young children learn measurement and geometry. A learning-teaching trajectory with intermediate attainment targets for the lower grades in primary school.* Rotterdam, Taipei: Sense Publishers.

Van den Heuvel-Panhuizen, M., & Buys, K. (Eds.). (2012). *Los niños pequeños aprenden medida y geometría* [Young children learn measurement and geometry] (M. F. Gallego & N. da Valle, Trans.). Cd. Brisa, Naucalpán, México: Correo del Maestro.

Van Galen, F., Wijers, M., Burrill, G., & Spence, M. S. (1997–1998). Some of the parts. In Wisconsin Center for Education Research & Freudenthal Institute (Eds.), *Mathematics in context: A connected curriculum for grade 5–8*. Chicago, IL: Encyclopedia Britannica.

Wisconsin Center for Education Research & Freudenthal Institute (Eds.). (1997–1998). *Mathematics in context: A connected curriculum for grade 5–8*. Chicago, IL: Encyclopedia Britannica.

Zolkower, B. (2009). *From the bottom-up: The function of contexts, situations, tools, and texts in progressive mathematizing*. Presentation at the Second Realistic Mathematics Education Conference. Boulder, Colorado.

Zolkower, B., & Bressan, A. (2012). Educación matemática realista [Realistic mathematics education]. In M. Pochulu & M. Rodríguez (Eds.), *Educación Matemática: Aportes a la formación docente desde distintos enfoques teóricos*. Buenos Aires, Argentina: Editorial Universitaria Villa María, Universidad de General Sarmiento.

Zolkower, B., & de Freitas, E. (2012). Mathematical meaning making in whole-class conversation: Functional grammatical analysis of a paradigmatic text. *Language and Dialogue, 1*(3), 60–79.

Zolkower, B., & Pérez, S. (2007). *Pensando juntos en voz alta: El papel de una docente de matemática en el manejo de una situación de interacción de toda la clase* [Thinking aloud together: The role of a mathematics teacher in conducting a whole-class conversation]. Presentation at Winter Institute of Specialized Didactics. Buenos Aires, Argentina: University of San Martín.

Zolkower, B., & Pérez, S. (2012). *Contribuciones de la gramática sistémico-funcional al análisis de la conversación en el aula de matemática* [Contributions of systemic functional grammar to the analysis of conversations in mathematics classrooms]. Presentation at Reunión de Educación Matemática. Argentina: Universidad Nacional de Córdoba. August 6–8, 2012.

Zolkower, B., & Rubel, L. (2015). Not 'just another brick in the wall'. *Mathematics Teaching in the Middle School, 21*(2), 84–89.

Zolkower, B., & Shreyar, S. (2007). A teacher's mediation of a thinking aloud discussion in a 6th grade mathematics classroom. *Educational Studies in Mathematics, 65*, 177–202.

Zolkower, B., Shreyar, S., & Pérez, S. (2015). Teacher guidance of algebraic formula building: Functional-grammatical analysis of a whole-class conversation. Special issue on scaffolding and dialogic teaching in mathematics education. *ZDM Mathematics Education, 47*(1), 1323–1336.

Chapter 10
Realistic Mathematics Education in the Chinese Context—Some Personal Reflections

Xiaotian Sun and Wei He

Abstract In this chapter, we start with a historical review of how Professor Hans Freudenthal and Realistic Mathematics Education (RME) became known in China, and how the academic exchange between Chinese scholars in the field of mathematics education and researchers at the Freudenthal Institute initiated and continued later. Then we discuss the positive impact of RME. Specifically, we cite some living examples for how the theoretical and empirical research substances related to RME-influenced mathematics curriculum development in China. These examples include the fields of curricular policy making, textbook design and classroom teaching.

Keywords Hans Freudenthal · Freudenthal Institute · Realistic Mathematics Education · Curricular policy · Textbook design · China

10.1 Historical Review

10.1.1 Hans Freudenthal's Visit to China

Before 1985, there were no connections between mathematics education in China and the Netherlands. Chinese scholars and educators in mathematics education had little knowledge about Professor Hans Freudenthal, the Freudenthal Institute, and Realistic Mathematics Education (RME). However, all things began to change after 1985. Professor Zehan Jiang, a famous Chinese mathematician and a member of the Chinese Academy of Sciences worked at Peking University, read Freudenthal's (1973) book *Mathematics as an Educational Task* during his visit abroad, which gave him a new perspective on understanding mathematics education. Instead of just

X. Sun (✉) · W. He
Minzu University of China, Beijing, China
e-mail: sunxt0761@sina.com

W. He
e-mail: cunhw@sina.com

© The Author(s) 2020
M. van den Heuvel-Panhuizen (ed.), *International Reflections on the Netherlands Didactics of Mathematics*, ICME-13 Monographs,
https://doi.org/10.1007/978-3-030-20223-1_10

appreciating this book, Jiang introduced it to one of his former student Changpei Wang, whose main research interest was in mathematics education. At that time, Professor Wang was the Dean of the Faculty of Mathematics of the Beijing Institute of Education and the main goal of this faculty was doing research in mathematics education to improve teachers' practice. In this way, Freudenthal and his book were introduced in the field of mathematics education in China. It can be considered as the first time that mathematics education in China and RME in the Netherlands met.

Wang had taught mathematics in primary and secondary education for about 17 years. Compared to his colleagues, he had been making a greater effort to learn English. His strong interests and perseverance in learning English made it possible for him to read the English version of the book *Mathematics as an Educational Task*. Wang was deeply attracted by the ideas in that book and he was extremely eager to meet the author. As the reform and openness policy in China increased, scholars were encouraged more to go abroad to learn from the world. Therefore, the supportive political environment became an important factor in making Wang's wish come true. Finally, at the CIEAEM (International Commission for the Study and Improvement of Mathematics Teaching) conference in London in 1986, Wang got the opportunity to meet and talk with Freudenthal face-to-face. It was this meeting that started a new era of exchange in mathematics education between China and the Netherlands.

A direct result of the meeting was that Wang arranged a short visit to the Netherlands. In that week, by having more in-depth discussions and conversions with Freudenthal, Wang gained a preliminary understanding of how to put the ideas of RME into practice. During Wang's first visit to Freudenthal and their continuous discussion by exchange of letters afterwards, another plan was proposed: Wang sincerely invited Professor Hans Freudenthal to give lectures in China. After careful preparation, Freudenthal visited China in 1988, when he was 82 years old. He went to Shanghai and Beijing, and gave three separate but interrelated lectures on the themes of research in mathematics education, research in mathematics curriculum, and the future and development of mathematics education. The lectures were given at East Normal University, Beijing Normal University and the People's Education Press. By giving these lively presentations, Freudenthal elaborated the fundamental ideas and important principles described in his books to his Chinese audiences in a beautiful prose tone.

The Chinese educational authorities paid great attention to Freudenthal's visit. Mr. Bin Liu, the Vice-Minister of Education at that time, had a meeting with Freudenthal and hosted a dinner party to welcome this knowledgeable and insightful researcher in mathematics education. All this did not only show the Chinese authorities' respect for Professor Hans Freudenthal, but also demonstrated their great interest in his work and RME. After Freudenthal's visit, Professor Ruifen Tang from East China Normal University further continued the introduction of Freudenthal and his work based on Freudenthal's lectures and by publishing a series of three papers titled "Professor Hans Freudenthal's Answers to the Questions in Mathematics Education" in the journal named *Mathematics Teaching*. As these three papers were widely circulated and read, scholars, researchers, educators in mathematics education, teachers and even some students began to become familiar with the name of Hans Freudenthal and RME, as a new theory in mathematics education which is almost totally different from how mathematics is taught in China, but equally effective in guiding teaching and learning. Another important result of this visit is that the book *Mathematics as an Educational Task* was translated into Chinese and published. Since then, references have been made to this book very often. In the China National Knowledge Infrastructure (CNKI) database it has been cited more than 2000 times in journal papers, master's and doctoral theses, and conference papers and other publications. Also, our experience is that it has been widely spread among mathematics teachers in primary and secondary schools.

In addition, it is worth noting that a number of young researchers, who had just graduated from university, listened to the lectures given by Freudenthal in Shanghai and Beijing; some of them even took their courage to enter into Freudental's room in the hotel to have a face-to-face conversation. One of those young researchers was Jian Liu. He was only in his twenties at that time. Now he is the Director of the China Educational Research Centre for Creativity and one of the chief designers of the mathematics curriculum standards for compulsory education of China. According to Professor Liu, he could remember vividly the details of the conversation in Freudenthal's room: Professor Hans Freudenthal, with his grey hairs, took out his handwritten poster used in the lecture, put it on the floor, and explained it carefully. Due to the language barrier, Liu could only understand a small part of what Freudenthal tried to explain. However, how this world-renowned mathematician and mathematics educator discussed with them friendly and equally was stamped in his heart. Even until now, Liu feels full of respect when he is talking about this scene.

The book *Revisiting Mathematics Education*, with a subtitle *China Lectures* (Freudenthal, 1991) was published in 1991, one year after Freudenthal passed away. In the lectures given in China, Freudenthal summarised his lifelong thoughts and experiences. To some extent, visiting China became a perfect curtain-call performance in his career. For China, his visit was of paramount importance. It provided an irreplaceable impetus to the future development of mathematics education in China.

10.1.2   Chinese Scholars' Visits to the Freudenthal Institute

Freudenthal's visit brought new idea of teaching and learning mathematics. However, in the early 1990s, the discussion about RME in China remained at a theoretical level; no connection between RME theory and Chinese classroom practice occurred. In other words, Chinese researchers' interests in RME had not turned into the practice of using RME to guide or change teachers' daily practice in mathematics education. The reason is that there was a long tradition of mechanistic teaching in China. To be more specific, teaching procedures were the main part of the curriculum; teaching-to-the-test was the goal; in class, students learned what the teachers taught, listened to what the teachers said and did what the teacher asked them to do; and training how to solve particular problems correctly and quickly was the basic approach for enhancing students' achievement. During that period, the development of labour intensive industry was the primary goal of society in China. Therefore, to some extent, it was reasonable that mechanistic teaching was taking the leading role in mathematics education. In such societal and educational situations, it was hard to use RME in China. Another reason why Freudenthal did not become 'hot' in China at that time was that a short visit was not enough for people in China to have a thorough understanding of RME. Therefore, a bridge which could lead to more and deeper exchange in mathematics education between China and the Netherlands needed to be built.

It was under this background that a young researcher from Minzu University of China, Xiaotian Sun, got a scholarship from the Chinese government to visit the Mathematics Institute at Utrecht University in 1992. Xiaotian Sun had keen interests in doing research in mathematics education and a dream of conducting a reform in this field. In 1990, Sun published a paper titled "The Change of the Mathematics Textbooks", in which he called for changing mechanistic teaching and carrying out reform in the mathematics curriculum.

Before Sun travelled to the Netherlands, he visited Xiaoda Zhang, the Director of the Mathematics Research Group on Secondary Education of the People's Education Press. Zhang was responsible for Freudenthal's visit in Beijing in 1988 and the person who accomplished the meeting between Freudenthal and Mr. Bin Liu. When Zhang knew that Sun was going to study in the Netherlands, he was very happy. Then Zhang found an edition of the newspaper *Reference News* from his piles of documents that contained an introduction about the best ten secondary schools in the world and one of them was in Zeist in the Netherlands. By showing this piece of newspaper, Zhang explained Sun the worldwide influence of mathematics education in the Netherlands. He suggested Sun to create the opportunity to study at the Freudenthal Institute, because this could be more than helpful for the coming mathematics curriculum reform in China. When Sun arrived in the Netherlands, he started with learning graph theory at the Mathematics Institute according to his visit plan. Later on, he tried to get into contact with the Freudenthal Institute, and could study at both institutes. Shortly after that, he decided to focus all his effort on learning the theory and application of RME at the Freudenthal Institute.

In 1994, Sun invited Professor Jan de Lange, at that time the director of the Freudenthal Institute, to visit China. De Lange is one of Freudenthal's students; in his thesis *Mathematics, Insight and Meaning*, De Lange (1987) illustrated how RME was used in mathematics textbooks in senior high school. Together with Freudenthal's work that mainly focuses on the application of RME in primary education and junior high school, the research done at the Freudenthal Institute had covered all basic education phases in the Netherlands. In addition, researchers at the Freudenthal Institute were also involved in the development of the textbook series *Mathematics in Context* (Wisconsin Center for Education Research & Freudenthal Institute, 1997–1998) that was in line with the mathematics curriculum standards of the NCTM. This textbook series was chosen to be used in many places in the United States of America.

When Sun's first stay at the Freudenthal Institute was finished, he felt that it was not long enough, and with support from the Chinese government he had a second chance to visit Freudenthal Institute in 1999. Then, he worked very intensively with Marja van den Heuvel-Panhuizen, who at that time was involved in a large project funded by the Dutch Ministry of Education to develop teaching-learning trajectories for primary school mathematics.

With his two stays at the Freudenthal Institute and the accompanying learning experiences, Professor Xiaotian Sun systematically introduced what he learnt about RME to his Chinese audience. Through 15 papers and some book chapters, Sun explained in detail what main message Freudenthal tried to deliver and what RME is. Based on his observations in Dutch schools, Sun also gave a detailed explanation of some concepts which were difficult to be understood in the Chinese education context, such as context problems and mathematisation. In this way, Sun re-introduced RME in China from more different perspectives. In addition, Sun introduced the Dutch standards and curricula in primary and basic secondary education and the syllabus in senior high school. He analysed the Dutch mathematics textbooks which were designed under the guidance of RME. To make clear how statements in books are related to teachers' practice, he observed many classes in primary and secondary schools. Without audio or video equipment, Sun made substantial observation notes about what happens in real Dutch classrooms. All his work and reports aroused the attention of Chinese researchers and mathematics teachers for RME once again.

More importantly, as a result of the advent of the information era, modern information technology has become an indispensable part of social and personal life. How to prepare students for the society, especially how to foster creativity, became urgent questions to be answered. The government and educational society in China realised that reform was necessary. However, having clear goals for a needed reform is not enough. Most difficult is to have the theoretical power on which one can rely to guide concrete practice towards these goals. Since such educational theory was not generated in China, we needed to find the answer in the rest of the world. Therefore, Sun's knowledge about RME and the experiences accumulated by him during his stay at the Freudenthal Institute became a very important resource for the curriculum design group that was responsible for the trial version of the curriculum reform outline of basic education. Sun was one of three people who coordinated the work of the national design group and who were responsible for the design. In this way, the Chinese mathematics curriculum reform was inspired by RME principles such as letting students become the owner of their own learning, using mathematics to understand and reflect on reality, and making the learning of today the foundation of the creativity tomorrow.

Instead of visiting the Freudenthal Institute individually, Professor Wei He and two young researchers from Minzu University of China formed a research group to take part in a summer school organised by the Freudenthal Institute in 2014. It was the first time that researchers from a university in China visited the Freudenthal Institute in a group. During the summer school, they got a better understanding of how RME is put into practice in different educational stages. Especially they got more insights in how RME is concretised in textbook design and classroom instruction. Under the guidance of lecturers from the Freudenthal Institute, they experienced the process of how mathematisation happens in real instruction. This brand-new way of learning made the Chinese research group feel that mathematisation, as a theoretical word in their mind, became more practical. In this way, they deepened their understanding of RME.

Besides the researchers from China mentioned above, Xiaoyan Zhao, a Chinese student who obtained her master's at Nanjing Normal University got a grant from the China Scholarship Council, supported by the Chinese government, and did a PhD study[1] at the Freudenthal Institute. Under supervision of Professor Marja van den Heuvel-Panhuizen and Doctor Michiel Veldhuis she worked on a project on Chinese teachers' classroom assessment which was an extension of a project on Dutch teachers carried out in the Netherlands. The Chinese part of the project started with a literature review about how Chinese mathematics teachers in primary school used classroom assessment as reported in papers written by them. Also, a question-naire survey was carried out about teachers' classroom assessment practice. Later, an explorative pilot study was done around the use of particular classroom assess-ment techniques. Finally, in a larger quasi-experiment it was investigated whether the teachers, through using these techniques, gained new insights in their students' learning.

10.1.3   Two Forums on the Theory and Practice of RME Held in China

The first forum took place in 2000. Then, two important researchers from the Freuden-thal Institute: Doctor Marja van den Heuvel-Panhuizen and Doctorandus Martin Kindt, were invited to give a series of lectures at Forum on the Theory and Prac-tice of Realistic Mathematics Education. This first forum was held in two places: in Beijing and in Changchun. Different from the lectures given by Freudenthal, who focused more on the theoretical parts of RME, Van den Heuvel-Panhuizen's and Kindt's presentations mainly emphasised the application of RME in mathematics curriculum and classroom teaching, for example, they addressed how to teach and learn arithmetic in primary education and geometry in secondary education. Another difference with the lectures given by Freudenthal was the audience. In 1988 a small number of scholars and researchers from universities and research institutes attended the lectures, while in the forums held in 2000, hundreds of educators and in-service mathematics teachers were able to participate. In addition, instead of mainly focusing on lecturing such as Freudenthal did, Van den Heuvel-Panhuizen and Kindt adopted another way of communicating with their audience. They saved sufficient time and provided many opportunities for the audience to ask questions freely. The people in the audience asked what they wanted to know most and the speakers answered the questions by illustrating what happens in Dutch classrooms. Both the content in the presentations and the ways in which it was presented highly inspired the audience. The mathematics teachers, particularly, showed great interests in the the-

---

[1]On March 7, 2018, Xiaoyan Zhao successfully defended her PhD thesis at Utrecht University.

ory and application of RME. This forum also reflected that the curriculum reform in mathematics education in China began to step forwards to another stage: from involving researchers and scholars and focusing on the theoretical part of RME to paying more attention to mathematics teachers' understanding and the application of RME. Although, generally speaking, it is widely accepted that there is a gap between research results and teachers' practice and that it can be very difficult for researchers and teachers to be on the same wavelength, in this forum, both groups agreed with the ideas of RME and showed common interests and attention.

From then on, the academic exchanges in RME between China and the Netherlands were not only limited to the researchers' level, but extended their impact to teachers by evoking them to reflect on mathematics education and change their classroom practice. More and more mathematics teachers in primary and secondary education began to read the book *Mathematics as an Educational Task*. During the same period, the book *Revisiting Mathematics Education: China Lectures* was translated into Chinese and published. The two books, together with the first Forum on the Theory and Practice of Realistic Mathematics Education, helped people in China get a better understanding of RME and pushed the cooperation and exchange in mathematics education between China and the Netherlands to a peak in that year.

The second Forum on the Theory and Practice of Realistic Mathematics Education was held in 2013 in Beijing. Professor Marja van den Heuvel-Panhuizen and Doctor Michiel Doorman were invited to give lectures in Beijing, Chengdu and Jinan. Van den Heuvel-Panhuizen started working at the Freudenthal Institute in 1987 and made a great contribution to the development of RME in the post-Hans Freudenthal time. In the second forum, she gave three speeches in which she addressed the principles of RME, recent research in mathematics education from an RME perspective, and research on RME textbooks used in the Netherlands. The Chinese audience, after more than 10 years, got a second chance to gain more insight in RME and receive an update of the research done at the Freudenthal Institute. While Van den Heuvel-Panhuizen was explaining the principles of RME, the Chinese audience noticed that 'free productions', which was one of the key features of RME about 20 years ago, was not mentioned this time. Instead, the 'mathematisation under the guidance of the teacher' was introduced. In fact, the idea of 'free productions' was hard to be understood or put into practice in the Chinese educational context. Whereas 'mathematisation under the guidance of the teacher' was closer to the situation in China, because it not only affirms students' primary role of learning mathematics—mathematisation is considered to be the starting point of mathematics learning and teaching—but also emphasises the importance of teacher' guidance during the process of mathematisation. As a result, this idea was quickly accepted and supported by the Chinese audience.

While looking back at the process of evolvement of RME—one of the most important theory systems in mathematics education—it is clear that RME is not a finished or closed system, but is continuously open to new developments and innovations according to the ever-changing society and accumulated experiences of people. Just as a famous Chinese saying goes, it keeps pace with the times. Only when a theory can move along with the latest changes in the environment that it is generated from and serves to, it can have lasting vitality and the power to extend without limit in both theoretical and applicable aspects. Van den Heuvel-Panhuizen's interpretation of such characteristic of RME deepened our understanding of RME, which made us feel more respectful to this theory.

Doorman had been doing research in RME and its application in secondary mathematics education for nearly 20 years. In this second forum, he introduced the curriculum design and teaching practice of calculus under the guidance of RME, which aroused great interest in the audience. It is almost 30 years since calculus was included in the mathematics curriculum in secondary education in China. But there was not really a clear teaching trajectory for calculus. The main problem was that the distinction between the educational goals of learning calculus in secondary school and in tertiary education was not clear. It seemed that what students have learned in secondary school was repeated in tertiary education. For example, the teaching trajectory of calculus in secondary school starts with introducing the slope of the tangent of a graph, the average velocity and the instantaneous velocity. The same path is also taken for teaching calculus in tertiary education. Doorman pointed out the educational value of learning calculus in secondary school from the perspective of mathematisation. This means helping students to understand and analyse the relationship between finity and infinity by using various and rich contexts. It also means facilitating them to quantify the relationship rather than simply remembering the definition of the derivative, calculating it and using it to solve problems without context. In his lecture Doorman first showed in a trace graph how a hurricane approached the mainland. Then, the next step of teaching was asking students to explain how the trace graphs changed by studying the points of tangency and the slopes of the tangent. In this way, together with other contexts, the definition of limit is introduced step by step. Along these lines, it was clearly illustrated how to use RME to guide the teaching in secondary education.

Organising forums on the theory and practice of RME in China means building a platform for more researchers and mathematics teachers in China to meet and discuss with the successors of Freudenthal and gain insight in RME as a theory system in mathematics education, its application in the curriculum and in teaching, and the relation to how teachers and students perform in practice. Such forums are held every few years in China with the purpose of updating the knowledge of RME. This continuous attention to and regular updating of knowledge regarding RME reveal that there is a special interest in RME in China, especially in the context of the mathematics curriculum reform. These forums in which Chinese participants are informed about RME in the Netherlands, are not common for the cooperation in the field of mathematics education between China and other countries. Therefore, these forums reveal that there is a special interest in RME in China; in particular this is the case in the context of the mathematics curriculum reform in China.

10.2 The Influence of RME in the Chinese Context

It has been 30 years since the academic communication in mathematics education between China and the Netherlands started in 1985. In the years since then, RME research done by Freudenthal and other researchers at the Freudenthal Institute have provided rich and precious experience, which is considered an important resource by Chinese scholars and educators for developing mathematics education in China. Particularly, RME exerted an effect on the latest curriculum reform in mathematics education in China in terms of policy making, new textbook design and change in classroom teaching.

10.2.1 The Influence of RME on Curricular Policy Making

In China, the curricular policy is embodied in the publication of curriculum standards by the Ministry of Education of the People's Republic of China (MOE). There is no doubt that these standards, being the only applicable document formulated according to the intention of the educational policy, is of great importance. Scholars and researchers are largely responsible for establishing them. After being proved by an evaluation team organised by governmental authorities, the curriculum standards released by MOE had a statutory status.

In the publication *Mathematics Curriculum Standards for Full-time Obligatory Education*[2] (MOE, 2001), one can find detailed information about (1) fundamental ideas about mathematics and mathematics education, (2) the objectives of mathematics education, (3) mathematical content, and (4) suggestions for instruction, assessment, and the design of mathematics textbooks and other materials. From all these descriptions in the Curriculum Standards, it is evident that its design was obviously influenced by RME, because many keywords and expressions which echo the basic characteristics of RME had never appeared in similar official documents before 2001. Several examples are provided in the following.

> Mathematics is the process that people understand and describe the external world qualitatively and quantitatively, progressively conceptualise and generalise rules or theory, and put them into practice. (MOE, 2001, p. 1)

Here, mathematics is defined as a process, as a process of human's activities. It is consistent to how mathematics and mathematisation are interpreted in RME. In Curriculum Standards it is also stated:

> Students are the owner of their mathematics learning [and]
>
> mathematics teaching has to be built on students' cognition development and the experience they have already got. (MOE, 2001, p. 2)

---

[2]Hereafter referred to as 'Curriculum Standards'.

Such expressions put students in the central place in all teaching activities and empha-sise students' existing knowledge and experience as the starting point of teaching activities. These ideas are different from the traditional view of mathematics as a discipline and the traditional teacher-centred educational style, but more related to the connotation of 'realistic' in RME.

> The content learned in mathematics is realistic, [...], should be potential to let students be actively involved in observation, doing experiment, conjecture, proving, reasoning, commu-nication and other mathematics activities. (MOE, 2001, p. 2)

This sentence outlines the relationship between mathematics learned in school and the realistic external world around students. In this way, the sentence answers to the fundamental question that where the mathematics learned in school is from and what it serves for. This point is highly relevant to one of the basic characteristics of RME that mathematics is a human activity.

Another significant feature of RME, which does not belong to the classical teach-ing philosophy in China with its emphasis on teachers and teaching, but which is reflected in Curriculum Standards, is that

> practical activity, initiative and independent exploration, cooperation and communication are all important approaches of learning mathematics [...] (MOE, 2001, p. 2)

Although, Bloom's taxonomy was the basic requirement of mathematics teaching in China for a long time, in the new Curriculum Standards, in addition to 'knowing', 'understanding', 'remembering', and 'applying', three new requirements are added, namely 'undergoing', 'experiencing', and 'exploring'. Clearly, these three words are all associated with mathematisation. Therefore, we can conclude that many elements in the Curriculum Standards are interrelated with RME.

10.2.2   The Influence of RME on Textbook Design

Figure 10.1 shows a page from the Chinese textbook *The Primary Mathematics for the New Century* (Liu, 2014). The pictures at this page refer to the theme that is addressed here. Such a picture is called a 'context picture'. Based on the information provided in this picture, especially information related to numbers and shapes, a series of questions are posed one by one, and the last question of the series is intended to be answered by an explicit conclusion about the concept that is at issue.

In contrast to what is shown in Fig. 10.1, where one context is used, generally two or three contexts around one mathematics theme and their corresponding ques-tions series are used. In this way, the core of what has to be learned is approached from different perspectives. This example makes clear that Chinese textbook design-ers acknowledge the importance of context and mathematisation. Although there is still much room for improving the choice and design of rich context problems, and providing opportunity to students to explore problem situations by themselves, the

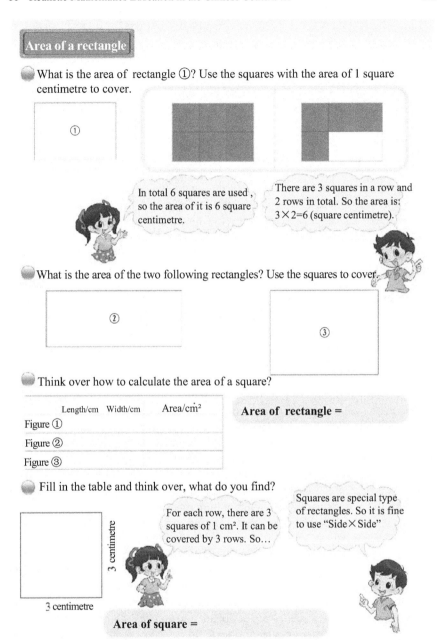

Fig. 10.1   Page from the textbook *The Primary Mathematics for the New Century* (Liu, 2014); the page is meant for Grade 3 and illustrates the structure used in such a textbook: starting with a context problem followed by a series of questions

recently designed textbook series pay much attention to students' mental and cognitive development, which is totally different from the traditional textbooks that start from definition and examples.

Generally speaking, starting with a context problem, followed by a series of questions to lead students to what they are supposed to learn, is the basic style in most textbooks series used in primary and secondary mathematics education after the curriculum reform. Until the 21st century, this way of structuring textbooks did not exist in the history of mathematics textbook design in China. To a great extent, this change was inspired by the RME idea of using context problems and mathematisation. In addition, mathematics textbooks designed within the RME approach were other important resources for the textbook design in China. For example, the textbook *Mathematics in Context* (Wisconsin Center for Education Research & Freudenthal Institute, 1997–1998) served as a model for Chinese reformed textbooks.

The style of a context followed by series of question series is not only adopted in textbooks designed for primary education, but also in textbooks for secondary education, see Fig. 10.2.

As well as in the style of structuring textbooks, the influence of RME on textbook design can be found in the aspect of content. Like in RME, in Chinese textbooks attention is paid to connecting mathematics to reality. For example, besides knowing and understanding the number system, students should also develop knowledge about daily life numbers, see Fig. 10.3.

Another clear example of adapting the content can be found in the domain of geometry. The content of geometry in traditional primary school textbooks in China involves mainly measurement, including the definition of area and volume with the main focus on calculation. So, for a long time, the concept of space which is so important for students was not included in the mathematics textbooks. However, after the curriculum reform, there was a big change in this approach. In the newly designed textbooks the concept of space was added, which is illustrated by pages from primary school textbooks shown in Figs. 10.4, 10.5, 10.6 and 10.7. From these textbook pages, one can see the impact of RME. In Fig. 10.8 this influence can also be recognised in a textbook used in junior high schools.

In China, the focus in mathematics teaching and learning has been always on problem-solving. However, what were considered as problems here were mainly bare number problems and simple word problems. Moreover, such problems were grouped into certain types of problems. Therefore, a textbook starts with a sample problem which represents a type of problems. By reflecting and generalising the way of solving this sample problem, students are expected to know how to solve that type of problems. Then, exercises aimed at enhancing students' ability to solve particular types of problems are provided in textbooks. Since exercises in textbook are always considered to be not enough, more exercises and learning material follow. The result is that Chinese students generally become the most hard-working students. The fixed procedure of grouping problems into types and solving these types of problems is effective in getting a good result in examination. However, in this approach to mathematics education not enough attention is given to prepare students for daily life and their future professional career. The question of what students can

Exploration of the Pythagorean theorem

In Fig 1-1, the upper part of a telegraph pole needs to be connected to the ground by a steel rope.

If the upper part of the pole is 8 m away from the ground and the touching point of the steel rope on the ground is 6 m away from the pole, how many metres the steel rope needs to be.

In a rectangular triangle, if two arbitrary sides are determined, the third side is also determined. Between the three sides, there is a certain relationship. In fact, people in ancient time have already found there is a particular relationship between the square of each side. Let us go to explore together!

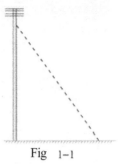

Fig   1-1

(1) Draw a rectangular triangle on the grid paper and measure its three sides. See what the relationship between the square of the three sides is, and discuss what you find with your classmates.

(2) In Fig 1-2, what are the square of the three sides? Is it fit to the rule you just discussed? How do you calculate? Discuss with your classmates. How about the rectangular triangles in Fig 1-3?

(3) If the legs of a rectangular triangle are 1.6 and 2.4 unit respectively, do you think the rule still apply? Give your reason.

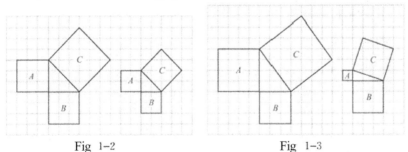

Fig 1-2   Fig 1-3

Fig. 10.2 Page from the textbook *Mathematics* (Ma, 2013) designed for junior high school; the page is meant for Grade 8 and illustrates the structure of starting with a context which is followed by a series of questions

1 Learn bigger numbers

Count

Count and learn

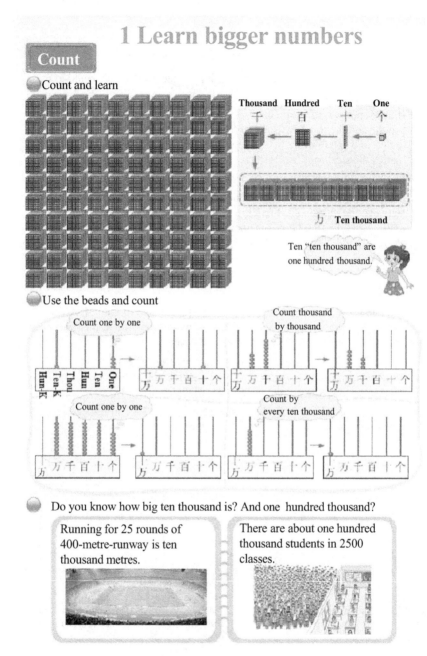

Use the beads and count

Do you know how big ten thousand is? And one hundred thousand?

Running for 25 rounds of 400-metre-runway is ten thousand metres.

There are about one hundred thousand students in 2500 classes.

Fig. 10.3 Page from the textbook *The Primary Mathematics for the New Century* (Liu, 2014) meant for primary school Grade 4; in this page, the students have to learn bigger numbers

2 Observing Object

Observation (1)

◉ Observe from different perspectives. What do you see?

> I see a ear of the rabbit…

> I see a beautiful flower on the rabbit's head…

Xiaoyu

Xiaoxia

> Have a look from a different perspective, and tell others what you see.

◉ What does Xiaoxia see?   (Draw "✓")

◉ Observe and discuss what you see with your classmates in groups.

Fig. 10.4 Page from the textbook *The Primary Mathematics for the New Century* (Liu, 2014); the page is meant for Grade 1; the students have to observe objects from different perspectives

Fold and Unfold

Cut a cubic box along its edges in order to get its net.

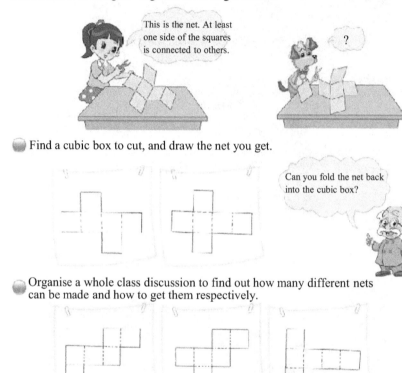

● Find a cubic box to cut, and draw the net you get.

● Organise a whole class discussion to find out how many different nets can be made and how to get them respectively.

● Cooperate with your classmates to fold each net into a cubic box again.

● What followed are the nets of a cuboid and a cube. Please find what the faces are parallel to Face 1, 2 and 3 respectively. Think over first and then fold by using the paper in appendix 1

Fig. 10.5 Page from the textbook *The Primary Mathematics for the New Century* (Liu, 2014); the page is meant for Grade 5 and addresses the content of cubic figures and their nets

2 Orientation and location

East, South, West and North

Every day, the sun rises in the east.

Go to the playground, and discern east, south, west and north. Make a note of what you see in which direction in Fig 1 in appendix 1.

The opposite of east is…

In the north of play ground, there is…

Go back to the classroom, attach your notes on the blackboard, observe and discuss.

```
          S                                                      N
        Gate                     E: Billboards                Classroom
                                                                 ↑
E  Billboards← PlayGround  → Sandpit  W    N: Classroom ← PlayGround → S: Gate    W  Sandpit ← PlayGround →Billboards  E
                                                                 ↓
      Classroom                   W: Sandpit                    Gate
          N                                                      S
```

Someone puts south on top, the others…

Fill in the blacks

In map, it is usually put north on top, south underneath, west in left and east in right.

```
      ┌──────────┐
      │          │
      └──────────┘
           ↑
┌──────┐        ┌──────────┐
│      │←Play Ground→│          │── East
└──────┘   North └──────────┘
           ↓
      ┌──────────┐
      │          │
      └──────────┘
```

Fig. 10.6   Page from the textbook *The Primary Mathematics for the New Century* (Liu, 2014) meant for Grade 2; the page addresses the content of orientation and location

I speak and you build

Xiaoxiao builds a solid figure. Taoqi builds the same solid figure according to Xiaoxiao's instruction. Have a look and give a try.

Taoqi uses the three cubes to build another solid figure. You see ☐☐ from the front, so where can you put the third cube?

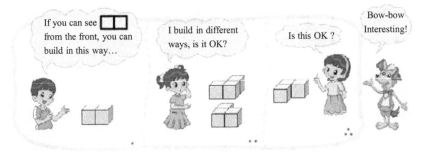

Fig. 10.7 Page from the textbook *The Primary Mathematics for the New Century* (Liu, 2014) meant for Grade 4; the page addresses the content of simple spatial reasoning

④ Observe objects from three directions

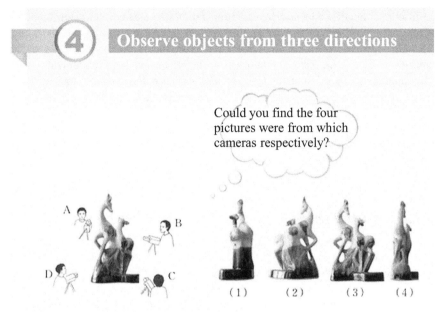

Could you find the four pictures were from which cameras respectively?

When we observe a object from different perspectives, normally what we see are different.

In mathematics lesson in primary school, we have learned to discern different images of a object from the front, the left and the top. For example, in Fig 1-18 the cubic figure is composed of some cubes. Its images from the front, the left and the top are shown in Fig 1-19 respectively.

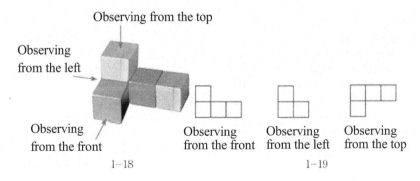

Fig. 10.8 Page from the textbook *Mathematics* (Ma, 2013) meant for junior high school Grade 7; in this page students have to observe objects from different perspectives

get from mathematics education except preparation for an examination has bothered us for a long time, even when facing the great performance of Shanghai students in PISA (Programme for International Student Assessment). At the beginning of the curriculum reform, we realised that it was needed to change both fundamental ideas of mathematics education at the level of educational policy making, and textbook design with respect to the structure of the textbooks, their content, and their connected materials. However, at a moment that the focus of teaching and learning was on solving types of problems for having high scores in tests, it was not easy to find the right direction to change mathematics education. At that moment, RME from the Netherlands provided a good example for us.

10.2.3   The Influence of RME on Classroom Teaching

Based on the principle of considering students as the owner of their mathematics learning, Chinese mathematics teachers are gradually shifting from a role as authority in class to a role as organiser, facilitator, and co-operator in students' mathematics learning. The proportion of instruction is reducing; while the proportion of students' exploration, communication, and cooperation is increasing. There is no doubt that it is a huge challenge for Chinese teachers, especially considering the deep-rooted Confucian culture in China that highly values the dignity and authority of the teacher.

From Hans Freudenthal, to Jan de Lange, to Marja van den Heuvel-Panhuizen, to Martin Kindt, and to Michiel Doorman, all the researchers at the Freudenthal Institute had put the emphasis in their lectures on students' active involvement in the learning process rather than on teachers' teaching in the sense of demonstrating what the students have to do. Especially, they underlined that teachers can reduce their unnecessary interventions by providing appropriate context problems which offer students opportunity for mathematisation. Many examples mentioned in these lectures have become classical cases used in China for mathematics teachers' professional development. By analysing and reflecting these cases, many Chinese mathematics teachers get a better understanding of RME, and try to change their former teaching practice of direct transmission. The two books written by Freudenthal are very popular among mathematics teachers in primary and secondary schools in China. Moreover, the book chapter written by Xiaotian Sun (2003) published in the book *The Development of Mathematics Curriculum from an International Perspective*, in which he vividly illustrated how RME by Dutch teachers is implemented in real classrooms, also became a resource for Chinese teachers to think over and learn from during the process of putting ideas of curriculum reform into practice.

Nowadays, students have become active learners in their mathematics class rather than learning passively. Instead of immersing themselves into exercise individually, students are given more change to voice their thought and to discuss with and learn from each other. Communication and exchange between teachers and students, between students and their peers are now mainstream in mathematics classes in China. It is delighting that Chinese students' ability of expressing themselves has been largely improved. The ability of articulating one's understanding is an important external indicator of the ability of thinking. Students' improvement in this aspect has been considered as one of the main achievements of the curriculum reform, which echoes the previously formulated expectation of the curriculum reform. Of course, this achievement is the result of multiple endeavours. One of them obviously is the contribution made by researchers from the Freudenthal Institute to bring RME from the Netherlands to China.

For a long time, China has put herself in the position of a student in the international class of mathematics education. Although Chinese students perform very well in PISA, there is still a long way to go for us as a student to learn from other countries. The improvement in curriculum reform in China is definitely related to the advanced international experience of mathematics reform worldwide. Scholars and researchers in China have done many studies on curriculum standards, textbooks and teaching practice in tens of countries, which provide important nutrition to improve curriculum reform in China. In this paper, we focus on reflecting the profound influence of RME, Hans Freudenthal and other researchers at the Freudenthal Institute in the Netherlands on the development of mathematics education in China. In our view, RME from the Netherlands has provided great power for the growth of the mathematics curriculum in China. At the same time, the application of RME in China also provides evidence of RME's power beyond the boundary of its cultural context.

Acknowledgements The authors of this chapter are very grateful to Xiaoyan Zhao for helping to translate their manuscript into English.

References

De Lange, J. (1987). *Mathematics, insight and meaning*. Utrecht, the Netherlands: OW&OC.
Freudenthal, H. (1973). *Mathematics as an educational task*. Dordrecht, the Netherlands: Reidel.
Freudenthal, H. (1991). *Revisiting mathematics education—China lectures*. Dordrecht, the Netherlands: Kluwer Academic Publishers.
Liu, J. (Ed.). (2014). *The primary mathematics for the new century [a mathematics textbook for Grade 1-6]*. Beijing, China: Beijing Normal University Press (in Chinese).
Ma, F. (Ed.). (2013). *The mathematics [a mathematics textbook for Grade 7–9]*. Beijing, China: Beijing Normal University Press (in Chinese).
Ministry of Education of the People's Republic of China (MOE). (2001). *Mathematics curriculum standards for full-time obligatory education*. Beijing, China: Beijing Normal University Press.
Sun, X. (2003). The education and mathematics education of the Netherlands. In X. Sun (Ed.), *The development of mathematics curriculum from an international perspective* (pp. 149–159). Beijing, China: Higher Education Press (in Chinese).
Wisconsin Center for Education Research & Freudenthal Institute (Eds.). (1997–1998). *Mathematics in context: A connected curriculum for Grade 5–8*. Chicago, IL: Encyclopedia Britannica.

Chapter 11
The Enrichment of Belgian Secondary School Mathematics with Elements of the Dutch Model of Realistic Mathematics Education Since the 1980s

Dirk De Bock, Johan Deprez and Dirk Janssens

Abstract In search for alternatives for the failed New Math movement of the 1960s and 1970s, Belgian mathematics educators looked with great interest to the Dutch model of Realistic Mathematics Education (RME), developed by Hans Freudenthal (1905–1990) and his team at the University of Utrecht. In this chapter, we primarily focus on how, from the mid 1980s until the mid 1990s, valuable elements of that model were integrated in Belgian secondary school mathematics. At that time, the influence of Dutch mathematics education on Belgian curricula was quite substantial, but some form of collaboration between the communities of mathematics teachers in both countries already existed since the early 1950s. However, from the 1950s until the 1970s, school mathematics in both countries evolved largely independent of each other. In Belgium, the structural New Math approach, with Georges Papy (1920–2011) as the main figurehead, became dominant in school mathematics, while the modernisation of school mathematics in the Netherlands was strongly inspired by Freudenthal's RME model emphasising the role of applications and modelling.

Keywords Georges Papy · Hans Freudenthal · Modelling and applications · New math · Realistic mathematics education · Uitwiskeling

D. De Bock (✉)
Faculty of Economics and Business, KU Leuven, Leuven, Belgium
e-mail: dirk.debock@kuleuven.be

J. Deprez · D. Janssens
Department of Mathematics, KU Leuven, Leuven, Belgium
e-mail: johan.deprez@kuleuven.be

D. Janssens
e-mail: dirk.janssens1@kuleuven.be

© The Author(s) 2020
M. van den Heuvel-Panhuizen (ed.), *International Reflections on the Netherlands Didactics of Mathematics*, ICME-13 Monographs,
https://doi.org/10.1007/978-3-030-20223-1_11

11.1   Papy and Freudenthal: Opposite Views
on Mathematics Education in Neighbouring Countries

With the creation of the International Commission for the Study and Improvement of Mathematics Teaching (CIEAEM) in the early 1950s, international, or at least Western European, collaboration in mathematics education was launched. According to Caleb Gattegno (1911–1988), the founder of the CIEAEM, national organisations of mathematics teachers had to take a leading role in international exchange. Gattegno stimulated the creation of such organisations and set a good example by creating the Association for Teaching Aids in Mathematics, now the Association of Teachers of Mathematics (ATM) in the United Kingdom in 1952. Following Gattegno's call, the Société Belge de Professeurs de Mathématiques (SBPM)/Belgische Vereniging van Wiskundeleraren (BVW) was founded in 1953 and Willy Servais (1913–1979), one of the main CIEAEM personalities of the time, became its first president (Miewis, 2003; Vanpaemel, De Bock, & Verschaffel, 2012). The SBPM/BVW brought together a few hundred mathematics teachers from both linguistic communities (Dutch and French) and from all school networks (state schools and Catholic schools). It started its own (also bilingual) professional journal *Mathematica & Paedagogia* (*M&P*) and in his first editorial, Servais held a strong plea for international openness and exchange. He wrote: "Mathematics as a truly universal language has, by its nature, an international vocation; we will open the columns of our journal to colleagues in other countries" (Servais, 1953, p. 4).[1] Servais' plea was received favourably by the international mathematics and mathematics education communities of the time. Several famous authors, most of them members of the CIEAEM, submitted contributions to *M&P*. The Belgian journal rapidly became a forum for national and international exchange in mathematics education (De Bock & Vanpaemel, 2015b).

This spirit of internationalisation was also present in the articles of the SBPM/BVW, in which the establishment of relationships with foreign associations of mathematics teachers and other international organisations sharing similar goals, was included as an important objective. In *M&P* 1, Servais presented the international network of the SBPM/BVW, including professional organisations of mathematics teachers in France, United Kingdom, Switzerland, Italy and Germany. Later, as communicated in *M&P* 5, this network was expanded through collaboration with the National Council of Teachers of Mathematics in the United States and with LIWENAGEL and WIMECOS, two associations of mathematics teachers in the Netherlands at the time (see, e.g., Maassen, 2000). The collaboration with the Dutch was realised in three ways: the associations exchanged and reviewed each other's journals and entrance exams (for future students of civil and military engineering), board meetings were mutually attended and mathematics educators of both countries gave lectures at conferences of the fellow associations. We do not claim there was a real interaction or mutual influence between Belgian and Dutch mathematics education at that time, but at the professional organisations' level, both communities

---

[1] In this chapter, all translations into English are by the authors.

of mathematics teachers were regularly informed about what happened in the other country. During the 1950s, several leading mathematics educators from the Netherlands (Freudenthal, Van Hiele, Vredenduin, …) contributed to *M&P*. Of particular interest was a contribution by Luke N. H. Bunt (1905–1984) who wrote about an interesting development in the Netherlands. Bunt was invited at the SBPM/BVW conference of 1959 to report about an introductory course on probability and statistics he had developed with a team of six mathematics teachers and with which he had experimented in the alpha streams of Dutch secondary schools (Bunt, 1959). Statistics was a blind spot in Belgian mathematics education at that time and Bunt's main target group, future students in economics, psychology and other social sciences, was mostly neglected. Bunt presented a pragmatic approach, which was also in contrast with the more systematic and rigorous approaches that were generally applied in Belgium. He deliberately started with provisional definitions, definitions that are incomplete from a scientific point of view. For example, he first defined the probability of an event as the ratio between the number of favourable and the total number of outcomes in the case of equally likely events. Based on that definition, he proved the main calculation rules for probabilities. Later on in his course, when the need arose to cover more situations, Bunt presented a new definition, based on the limit of relative frequencies and without further explanation, he stated that "for probabilities based on this new definition, the previously proven calculation rules remain valid" (Bunt, 1959, p. 38). As a consequence of his pragmatism, Bunt was able to arrive at the basic ideas of hypotheses testing in a limited number of lessons.

By the end of the 1950s and in the 1960s, Belgian school mathematics was gripped by New Math or 'modern mathematics', a structural approach to mathematics teaching that was officially launched at the Royaumont Seminar (1959) and then spread worldwide (De Bock & Vanpaemel, 2015a). One of the main objectives was narrowing the gap between school mathematics and mathematics as a scientific discipline. New Math not only led to new mathematical content—sets, relations, logic, mathematical structures (groups, rings, …), linear algebra and topology—but also to a modernisation of teaching aids, for example, the use of Venn diagrams, arrow-graphs and colour conventions. Proper notations and symbols, the use of the right jargon and theory development received a lot of attention. Barriers between mathematical subdomains (algebra, geometry, trigonometry, …) were largely eliminated and geometry education was redirected towards transformation and vector geometry. The main architect and uncontested leader of Belgian New Math was Georges Papy, professor of mathematics at the Université libre de Bruxelles, who was, at that time, also influential at the international level, for example, as president of the CIEAEM in the 1960s (Bernet & Jaquet, 1998). After some years of experimentation (Fig. 11.1), coordinated by the Centre Belge de Pédagogie de la Mathématique/Belgisch Centrum voor Methodiek van de Wiskunde, from 1968 on, New Math became compulsory in the first year of all secondary schools in Belgium (and from then on gradually in the subsequent years). It was one of the most drastic educational reforms that Belgium had ever seen. A few years later, New Math was also introduced at the primary level. For

about 20 years New Math was the dominant paradigm for the teaching and learning of mathematics in Belgium.

Also in the Netherlands, some mathematics educators fell for the charms of New Math, among them the logician and Royaumont participant Piet Vredenduin (1909–1996), who positively reported about Papy's experiments in *Euclides*, the journal of the Dutch associations of mathematics teachers (Vredenduin, 1967). But from the outset, New Math was also strongly criticised. Freudenthal summarised his critique in two words: "anti-didactic inversion" (Freudenthal, 1973, p. 103), expressing that an end product of mathematical activity, the most recently composed structure of mathematics, is taken as a starting point for mathematics teaching (Fig. 11.2). Although Freudenthal could not prevent that also in the Netherlands, a New Math inspired curriculum for the secondary level was introduced in 1968, the implementation was less radical and New Math only lasted for a few years. New Math was never introduced in Dutch primary schools. In 1971, the IOWO (Institute for the Development of Mathematics Education) was founded with Freudenthal as its first director. With a staff of 37 people, Freudenthal put into practice his ideas about mathematics education which resulted in Realistic Mathematics Education (RME), the Dutch answer to New Math and to traditional, mechanistic approaches, both for the primary and secondary level (La Bastide-van Gemert, 2015). The features of RME include the use of rich contexts and realistic situations, that is, problem situations which students can imagine, in order to develop mathematics, the use of students' own productions as well as researched activities encouraging students to move from informal to formal representations, less emphasis on algorithms and more on sense-making and the use of guided reinvention.

Fig. 11.2 Papy and Freudenthal (caricatures by Léon Jesmanowicz, 1971)

11.2 Critique on New Math in Belgium and Search for Alternatives

In 1974, the SBPM/BVW was restructured on a linguistic basis into the SBPMef (Société Belge des Professeurs de Mathématiques d'expression française) and the VVWL (Vlaamse Vereniging Wiskundeleraars), with respective journals *Mathématique et Pédagogie* and *Wiskunde en Onderwijs*. The SBPMef did not continue some form of cooperation with the community of Dutch mathematics teachers, but instead started some networking with the French and later also with French speaking mathematics teachers in Switzerland. Hence, at least at the level of professional organisations, cooperation and even exchange of information between the French speaking Belgian community and the Dutch stopped. For the purpose of this chapter, we will further focus on the evolutions in Flanders.

Although at that time and until the late 1980s, the VVWL had become a fortress of New Math proponents (including, e.g., De Bruyn, De Munter, Holvoet, Laforce, Verhulst, Vermandel, Warrinnier), cooperation with the Dutch continued formally and Vredenduin became the main contact (Holvoet, 1996). Except for a number of articles by Vredenduin himself, mostly about logical issues, *Wiskunde en Onderwijs* at that time rarely published articles by Dutch authors or contributions informing its readership about ongoing evolutions in the Netherlands. The work of Freudenthal and his team was ignored by the official association of mathematics teachers in Flanders.

The stable position of New Math in Belgium during the late 1960s and 1970s and the absence of critique in official fora, does not imply that the whole mathematics education community in Belgium was unconditionally in favour of Papy's approach. Instead, Papy's method and its implementation at school had divided this community into two camps, the so-called 'Papy'ists' and 'anti-Papy'ists' (Colot, 1969), but that latter group was not in power at that time and remained relatively silent in public fora. This silence was broken on March 11, 1980, when Albert Pirard and Paul Godfrind, professors at respectively the Université de Liège and the École Royale Militaire, published an opinion article in *La Libre Belgique*, a main newspaper of the French speaking Belgian community. The title of the article, "The Disasters of Modern Mathematics", set the tone. Among other things, the authors stated: "We now see in the entrance exam [for future students of engineering, *added by the authors*] candidates who have almost never practiced geometry" (Pirard & Godfrind, 1980, p. 15). They heckled the tough and abstract approach to geometry in the third year of secondary school in which, for example, the length of a segment was defined as the class of all congruent segments and an angle was briefly described as "a rotation that has lost its centre" (ibid.). They further argued that modern mathematics is absolutely useless and that a total aversion prevailed among students and science teachers. They advised "urgently to leave the abstract language and aberrations of modern mathematics and to return to a realistic, concrete and basic teaching of mathematics" (ibid.). However, as far as we know, the impact of Pirard and Godfrind's article in Flanders was limited.

In Flanders, the public debate opened only a few years later, in 1982, when the pedagogue and teacher educator Raf Feys published a virulent pamphlet "Moderne Wiskunde: Een Vlag op een Modderschuit" (Feys, 1982), in which he firmly criticised the fundamental principles of New Math and the way it was introduced at the primary level. In his close contacts with schools, Feys did not see the appearance of the promised fascinating world, but "artificial results in a fake reality" (ibid., p. 3) and also little enthusiasm in children, but "more disgust, disorientation and desperation" (ibid., p. 3). Feys not only criticised New Math, he also suggested how mathematics education at the primary level should evolve and the model he had in mind was the Dutch RME. Instead of taking the structure of mathematics as a starting point, mathematics education should start from and gradually develop, the intuitive, informal and real-world knowledge and skills of the children. Feys' pamphlet focused on primary education and had most impact at that level, but thanks to media attention, it also echoed at the secondary level.

A follow-up event and important step towards a broad and open societal debate in Flanders was initiated by the Foundation Lodewijk de Raet, which on April 30, 1983 organised a colloquium in Brussels titled What Kind of Mathematics for 5–15 Year Olds? (Stichting-Lodewijk de Raet, 1983). Nearly 150 people participated, including representatives of mathematics education from primary to university level, teacher educators, members of the Inspectorate of Education and of mathematics curriculum committees. In a lecture by Freudenthal, participants were confronted with developments abroad (including the decision of some German states to prohibit by law set theory at school because "it made children mentally ill" (Stichting-Lodewijk de Raet, 1983, p. 4) and they learned about the Dutch alternative, illustrated by plenty of IOWO materials. On the opposite side, Roger Holvoet (1938–1998), professor of mathematics at the University of Leuven and fervent Papy-ist, minimised elementary school students' difficulties with typical New Math elements and confirmed his confidence in the current update and innovation of mathematics education for the primary level. Another speaker at the colloquium, Jan Vermeylen, mathematics teacher at a Flemish secondary school and board member of the VVWL, showed himself more critical of the ongoing modernisation: "Little has been realised from the beautiful dream, finding an easy way to learn mathematics" (Stichting-Lodewijk de Raet, 1983, p. 12). He argued that, in most study streams, we should teach mathematics being as useful as possible, based on students' experiences and interests. He further stated that, for this purpose, set theory is not strictly prohibited, but in most cases, unnecessary and even harmful. Clearly, the colloquium revealed diverging points of view. But more importantly, it definitely made it clear that an adjustment of New Math had to take place and that "the learning materials of the IOWO and the new Dutch textbooks inspired by the RME approach, could no longer be neglected" (Stichting-Lodewijk de Raet, 1983, p. 2).

At the secondary level in Flanders, another development took place. In 1983, Dirk Janssens, recently appointed as professor in mathematics education at the University of Leuven, launched the idea to start a new journal for mathematics teachers. A group of his former students and newly started mathematics teachers (Deprez, Eggermont, Gyssels, Kesselaers, Remels, Roelens and Roels) responded positively and started the journal entitled *Uitwiskeling* (Fig. 11.3), with the first issue being published in 1984. *Uitwiskeling* is an untranslatable neologism connecting 'wiskunde' (the Dutch word for mathematics) with 'uitwisselen' (the Dutch word for 'to exchange'). The name of the journal refers to the idea of creating a forum where mathematics teachers can exchange ideas and discuss questions related to the practice of mathematics education. So, the action of *Uitwiskeling* was basically a constructive one: not directly criticising New Math, but searching for and sharing teaching resources that motivate pupils and stimulate their active participation in the learning process. *Uitwiskeling* had some fixed columns, the most important ones being "Cobweb", intended for questions and answers, hints, ideas, suggestions, reports of lessons and other short contributions from the readership; "Under the Magnifying Glass", a larger article in which members of the editorial board scrutinised and elaborated a part of the curriculum or an aspect of mathematics education; and "Guide to the Library", in which articles and books (in most cases from abroad) that were considered useful for classroom practice were identified, summarised and discussed. Soon, *Uitwiskeling* reached a large audience of Flemish mathematics teachers and became a channel through which these teachers learned about the new developments in mathematics education in other countries. Special attention was paid to developments in the Netherlands, Germany, and the French speaking part of Belgium, in which at that time Nicolas Rouche (1925–2008), professor of mathematics education at the Université catholique de Louvain and his Groupe d'Enseignement Mathématique (GEM), founded in 1978, became very influential. The journal *Uitwiskeling* still exists (www.uitwiskeling.be)—currently, that is, 2019, the 35th volume is running—and the angle of incidence remained unchanged: the practice of mathematics education and the confrontation of that practice with new ideas from didactics of mathematics.

11.3 How During the Middle 1980s and 1990s New Developments in Neighbouring Countries Reached the Community of Flemish Mathematics Teachers

11.3.1 Rounding off the Rough Edges of New Math

During the middle 1980s, the call for change became ever louder in Flanders and an official response was therefore inevitable. A first modification of the curricula for the secondary level started in 1983 and lasted until 1988. It was a modest reform that mainly rounded off the rough edges of New Math (Roels, 1995). We briefly describe some new accents in the programmes for the catholic schools (which is the largest network of schools in Flanders). Changes in the other networks ran more or less in parallel. For the first two years, a more intuitive approach to arithmetic was proposed: the different types of numbers and number operations were no longer defined in a set-theoretic environment and many proofs were eliminated. So, it became permitted again to introduce negative numbers with reference to temperatures below zero or to profit and loss and, for the rational numbers, teachers were allowed again to refer to the fractions that pupils had learned at the primary level. The time saved on theoretical issues was spent on practicing the operations and on solving equations and word problems. The plane geometry of the first two years, which was affine, remained unchanged, but the curriculum committee chose a radically different approach for metric plane geometry, which is part of the programme from the third year on. The length of a segment and the measure of an angle were accepted as primitive concepts (such as, e.g., points or straight lines) in combination with a few intuitively

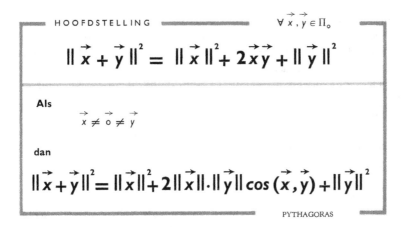

Fig. 11.4 Papy's (1967) version of the Pythagorean theorem ('Hoofdstelling' = Main theorem; 'Als' = If; 'dan' = then)

accessible axioms, and thus the need to define them fell away. Partly because of that, the extensive study of isometries (reflections, translations, rotations, ...) was shortened so that more time and attention could be spent on the classical plane figures (triangles, quadrilaterals, circles, ...) and their properties. The Pythagorean theorem, reduced to a special case of the formula for the norm of a sum of vectors during the New Math period (Papy, 1967) (Fig. 11.4), regained its central position of the past. Finally, in analytic geometry, the equation of a straight line could again be introduced without relying on vector spaces. The introduction of this new geometry programme for the third year was accompanied by a large-scale action of in-service teacher education (Janssens & Roels, 1985).

At the upper secondary level, the curriculum change was more radical. In solid geometry, in Flanders a topic traditionally reserved for study streams with a strong mathematics package (6 to 8 h per week), the synthetic perspective was revalued. The curriculum stated that solid geometry should be seen as an extension of plane geometry and no longer as a part or application of linear algebra. The synthetic approach, meant for developing students' spatial skills, had to precede the analytic treatment. Special attention had to go to the sketching and understanding of planar representations of spatial situations. It was further recommended to also include problems about area and volume of solids. But a new curriculum cannot succeed without new and appropriate teaching materials. An attempt to provide such materials was undertaken by *Uitwiskeling* (Deprez, Roelens, & Roels, 1987b) and developed in more detail in an in-service teacher education course (Deprez, Eggermont, Janssens, & Roelens, 1987a). One of the sources of inspiration was the work of the Dutch HEWET team (led by De Lange and Kindt) who had developed teaching materials, in line with the RME philosophy, on various mathematical topics for pre-university education (for an overview, see, e.g., De Lange, 1987). This work was realised under the umbrella of OW&OC (Mathematics Education Research and Educational Computer

Centre), the successor of the IOWO since 1981. *Uitwiskeling* was also influenced by publications of the GEM (Groupe d'Enseignement Mathématique) and of the French IREMs (Instituts de Recherche sur l'Enseignement des Mathématiques). A pragmatic-eclectic approach to solid geometry was presented, starting intuitively with a phase of exploration and investigation. In that phase, it was suggested, students had to work in groups on problems that are challenging, but easy to understand and imagine, such as, for example, "What types of plane figures can occur when one intersects a cube and a plane?" This phase should then result in a series of statements about possible mutual positions of straight lines and planes, of which students have to check the correctness. Next, the correct statements could be accepted as starting points—axioms—for the further development of solid geometry. Later on, based on the results of that synthetic phase and on what students have learned in the fourth year in their lessons on plane geometry (e.g., about the scalar product), space coordinates and vectors could be introduced and analytic descriptions of straight lines and planes could be deduced. Finally, a number of richer problems about solids should be investigated, using both synthetic and analytic tools.

Another important change at the upper secondary level related to the approach of analysis (calculus) in study streams with 2–4 hours of mathematics per week. This new approach was not a mere weakening of the corresponding curriculum part for study streams with 6–8 hours of mathematics per week, but tried to meet the specific needs of students who had, for some reason, chosen a limited package of mathematics in their final years of secondary school. The idea was to opt for a less formal approach by skipping the topological foundation and by introducing the concepts of continuity and limit in an intuitive-graphical way. The time saved had to be spent to derivatives and integrals and to applications of these basic concepts of calculus. Because the meaning(s) of these latter concepts was central, calculation techniques were limited to polynomial and rational functions. Another novelty was a change in the order of integral calculus for these study streams: to allow a more insightful and motivating approach, the definite integral was introduced first, as the (oriented) area under the graph of a function, before the concept of primitive function (or indefinite integral). Initially, for this important curriculum change, little or no didactical support was provided for the teachers involved, but quite soon, *Uitwiskeling* spent an issue on this new approach (Deprez, Gyssels, & Roels, 1985) and later, this was further developed in an in-service educational course for teachers (De Bock et al., 1986). This course presented a quite radical interpretation of the new curriculum: the authors immediately started with derivatives, continuity was omitted and limits were, to some extent, integrated into the section on derivatives. That section on derivatives was largely inspired by two Dutch HEWET cahiers (Kindt & De Lange, 1984, 1985) in which the derivative was distilled from different real-world contexts in which (rate of) change had to be measured. The idea of 'conceptual mathematisation', that is, mathematisation as a way to introduce mathematical concepts (De Lange, 1987), was quite innovative in Flanders at that time.

11.3.2 A Second Wave of Changes

The curriculum changes of the middle 1980s were positively welcomed by most of the Flemish mathematics teachers. The conviction grew that priority in school mathematics should be shifted from mathematics as a static, rigorous deductive system to a meaningful and useful activity related to the broader world and society. Of course, parts of the curriculum that had remained unchanged in the first curricular modification were now assessed more critically by the teachers. Therefore, a second adjustment became inevitable. The introduction of a new structure for Flemish secondary education in 1989 provided the opportunity for this second wave of curriculum changes. In terms of content, changes were in line with the foregoing: typical New Math elements, such as sets and relations, were further reduced, mathematical structures were no longer explicitly addressed and the ambition to set up a global deductive system was abandoned. The treatment of geometry in the early years of secondary school became metric from the start and the notion of area and corresponding calculations were no longer neglected. Another important innovation was the extension of combinatorics and probability to statistics, now also including descriptive statistics (data analysis) and the testing of hypotheses as a preview of the application of statistics in practice (Carbonez & Veraverbeke, 1994; Kesselaers & Roelens, 1992). Finally, the modernisation of analysis that had started with the first curricular modification in study streams with a limited package of mathematics was now added to the study streams with a strong mathematical component. The idea was to start with sequences as a basis for a mathematically rigorous, but at the same time more intuitive and dynamic approach to the concepts of continuity and limit (De Bock et al., 1992). In these study streams the time spent on continuity and limits was also diminished: derivatives and integrals were considered the core concepts of secondary school analysis and had to receive maximum attention.

This second wave of programme changes was not limited to the content of secondary school mathematics, but also brought a number of didactical innovations. First, and perhaps most importantly, there was the role given to modelling and applications. In contrast with the previous period in which mathematics was basically taught as an autonomous discipline, the applicability of mathematics in other domains was now strongly emphasised. These domains did not only include the traditional areas of application (such as physics), but also biology, economics and other social sciences. Once again, inspiration was found in the Dutch RME materials, in particular in the HEWET cahiers. In contrast to the classical role of applications in mathematics education (i.e., applying a pre-designed mathematical method in another domain), also the idea of conceptual mathematisation (as explained above) enjoyed increasing attention in Flanders: mathematical ideas that are developed from diverse contexts, get a richer meaning and may subsequently be applied more easily in new domains (De Lange, 1987). Emphasising the applied side of mathematics also fitted with the belief that it is motivating for students to realise that mathematics is closely related to their own living environment. Second, more attention was given to (guided) self-discovery and active learning processes in the teaching and learning of mathematics. Contemporary research in educational psychology had shown that effective learning is based on constructive processes, mediated and guided by adequate and supportive intervention strategies (De Corte, 1996). Applied to mathematics education, it means that students should not only be confronted with 'end products' of mathematical activity (i.e., 'finished' mathematical texts), but should also have the opportunity to go through the process of mathematical discovery and to authentically (re-)build pieces of mathematics themselves. Third, the growing importance of graphing calculators and computers was recognised, not only as powerful calculation tools, but also as means for authentic mathematical exploration, discovery and simulation (Cleve, De Bock, & Roelens, 1993). These new technological tools made a more graphical approach to mathematics—and even an approach based on multiple representations—achievable in mathematics classrooms at the secondary level.

The above-mentioned curricular innovations were again supported by the large-scale action of in-service teacher education Mathematics Taught By Applications (De Bock, Janssens, Roelens, & Roels, 1994; Janssens, 1993; Roels et al., 1990). The idea was to integrate the modelling perspective into the study of elementary functions, matrices, derivatives and integrals. In line with the objective to activate pupils during the mathematics classes, an active involvement of the participants was promoted and therefore, the sessions were perceived as real working sessions. During these sessions, groups of upper secondary mathematics teachers were confronted with real, and hence rather complex, modelling problems. In order to find appropriate solutions, they had to go through the whole modelling cycle (see, e.g., Verschaffel, Greer, & De Corte, 2000). An interesting case concerned the journey of the drilling rig called 'Yatzy' on the river Scheldt near Antwerp. The passage of the Yatzy under a high-voltage cable, taking into account the tides of the river, created considerable tension—both on board the platform, and among the teachers who participated! This authentic and large-scale modelling exercise, in which several mathematical models were integrated, also caught the attention of Dutch colleagues: the case was published in *Nieuwe Wiskrant* (De Bock & Roelens, 1990) (Fig. 11.5), the mathematics education journal published by OW&OC, which in 1991 was renamed as Freudenthal Institute after its founder. By that time, Flemish mathematics educators had become very familiar with the design principles of Dutch realistic mathematics education, and therefore exchange was no longer one-way traffic!

11.3.3   Consolidation

History continued and soon a new development took place. In 1989, the Flemish Government became responsible for educational matters. To promote and control the quality of education, it was decided to develop attainment targets for mainstream education at the primary and secondary level. The targets were designed as minimal objectives, which the government considered necessary and attainable for school children at these levels. These objectives referred either to knowledge, to skills or to attitudes. The attainment targets were approved by the Flemish Parliament and

Fig. 11.5 Cover *Nieuwe Wiskrant* with the *Yatzy*, 1990

gradually implemented as parts of the curricula of the different educational networks (of Catholic and publicly run schools) from 1997 on; and they are still valid now. In this third wave of curriculum changes, the innovations of the previous phases, such as, e.g., the role of modelling and applications, the importance of a constructivist vision on learning and a meaningful implementation of ICT tools, were consolidated and continued. Remarkably, modern mathematics was no longer an issue and even elementary set theory was definitively removed from the new curricula: none of the attainment targets still referred to these icons of New Math! More importantly, a number of vertical learning trajectories were identified in the attainment targets. We briefly exemplify three such trajectories throughout students' secondary school careers.

A first vertical learning trajectory refers to statistics (Deprez, Roels, & Roelens, 1992). Nowadays, statistics starts in the first two years of secondary school with the analysis, representation and interpretation of real data and with some basic elements of probability related to fractions. Hence, a bridge with what students had learned at the primary level is made. In the middle two years of secondary education, the attainment targets state that students have to be able to select by themselves representations that are most appropriate in a given situation and should learn about different measures for the central tendency and the spread of a set of data. In addition, students learn to use probability trees to solve more complex probability problems. In the final two years, all students study the normal distribution, and students in a study stream with a strong mathematical component are introduced to confidence intervals or the testing of hypotheses, with a strong emphasis on conceptual understanding over technical fluency (see above). This development is in line with those in many countries, especially in the Netherlands, which played a pioneering role in statistics education since the 1950s and which has served as a model for Flanders (Bunt, 1959; Garst, 1990; Zwaneveld, 2000).

A second vertical learning trajectory refers to functions (Eggermont & Roels, 1997). While in the New Math period, this topic immediately started with an abstract and technically advanced definition ('a special type of subset of the Cartesian product of two sets') in the first year in secondary school, now students first encounter tables, graphs and formulas as representations of various types of meaningful relationships (e.g., proportional and inverse proportional relationships). Gradually, more functional skills are developed (e.g., transforming the graph of a function), the level of abstraction is raised and several classes of functional relationships are studied, leading to the notion of a 'real function of a real variable'. A more general and abstract definition of the concept of function, treated as an independent mathematical object, only occurs in the final years of secondary education. That way, students of different ages learn about and work with different aspects of functions that are adapted to their situation. This approach was closely related to the Dutch 'TGF analysis' (tables, graphs, formulas), promoted from the late 1980s on by the HAWEX team (led by Kindt, Roodhardt, Van der Kooij and Van Reeuwijk), but also to contemporary developments in the United States (National Council of Teachers of Mathematics, 1989).

A third vertical learning trajectory refers to solid geometry (Deprez & Roels, 2000; Op de Beeck, Deprez, & Roels, 1997; Thaels, Eggermont, & Janssens, 2001). The emphasis came to lie on gaining insight into spatial objects and their planar representations. During the New Math period, this component of geometrical thinking was completely absent in the first four years of secondary education because it did not fit with an axiomatic approach at these levels. Now in primary school, pupils learn about solids by seeing and doing, most often in realistic contexts. They gain insight in such objects on the basis of three-dimensional models or on the basis of planar representations. This learning trajectory is continued in the first years of secondary school. At that level, the (re)construction of situations in space starting from a planar representation is developed further and some attention is already paid to argumentation related to properties of solids. Area and volume of elementary solids (cubes, cuboids and cylinders) are also part of the curriculum. In the middle years of secondary school, students learn to build more precise arguments about straight lines and planes in space, but this argumentation is always embedded in concrete problem situations, for example, about planar sections of solids. In the final two years of secondary school, for those students following a study stream with a strong mathematical component, a more structured—analytical—approach to solid geometry is developed. The development has a sound mathematical basis using a modern axiom system based on points and vectors. But the system works only at the background and can eventually be discussed at the end of the course. For some students, this gives the opportunity to sketch the way to 4-dimensional geometry (Deprez et al., 1987a, b). In the new view on solid geometry for the first four years of secondary school, the influence from scholars of the Freudenthal Institute (see, e.g., the HAWEX and HEWET materials) and from Nicolas Rouche and his team is also very prominent.

11.4 Some Topics that Underwent a True Metamorphosis

In this section, we describe in some detail a number of topics that, compared to New Math, have been drastically changed and in which the influence of the RME approach is particularly clear. The first topic relates to exponential and logarithmic functions. The treatment of exponential and logarithmic functions during the 1960s and 1970s in Belgium was a textbook example of Freudenthal's (1973) notion of 'anti-didactical inversion'. In the sixth year of secondary education, first, the natural logarithmic function was defined as an integral function of $1/x$. Next, logarithmic functions with other bases were introduced as multiples of the natural logarithmic function and finally, the exponential functions were defined as the inverses of these logarithmic functions with arbitrary base. At the end, an aha experience was evoked: for rational exponents, the 'new' exponents coincide with the ones students had previously met in the fourth year. Needless to argue that this approach, although mathematically logical, had many educational disadvantages. The RME alternative is to start with exponential functions as models for exponential (or cumulative) growth, a context that gives a concrete meaning to the exponent (time) and proved to be very useful to understand various problems situations related to this class of functions (De Lange & Kindt, 1984a, 1986). The functions $x \rightarrow 2^x$ and $x \rightarrow 0.5^x$ (a model for negative growth) serve as prototypes of, respectively, increasing and decreasing exponential functions, and logarithmic functions are introduced as their inverses (and thus no longer vice versa). The transition from rational to real exponents is handled intuitively. The context of growth also proves to be very helpful for reasoning about logarithms and their properties (e.g., the fundamental theorem of logarithms was clarified as "time needed for doubling + time needed for tripling = time needed for multiplication by six"). Furthermore, it is 'proved' that the slope function of an exponential function is proportional to itself and the natural exponential function (and the number e) is introduced as the exponential function for which the proportionality factor equals 1 (hence, as the function that is equal to its derivative). A lot of additional applications are given (logarithmic scales, drawing log-log graphs, the Carbon 14 dating method, ...).

A second topic that underwent a thorough metamorphosis was trigonometry. In fact, classical trigonometry was not so much influenced by New Math—those reformers generally showed little interest for this type of 'applied mathematics'—and was still taught in a rather mechanistic (pre-New Math) way, focusing on trigonometric formulas and the (technical) solution of trigonometric equations and inequalities. The new curricula separate the geometric part about angles and the solution of triangles, taught in the third and fourth year, from the functional part—in which the arguments of sine and cosine are real numbers—that is part of the fifth and sixth year curriculum. In the functional part, trigonometric functions are seen as models for periodic phenomena, such as, for example, tides (De Lange & Kindt, 1984c, 1985). The 'sine model' and its main characteristics (amplitude, period, and horizontal and vertical translation) receive ample attention. These model characteristics are systematically explained and graphs of generalised sine functions are drawn using a grid frame. This system not only allows to approach some more complex modelling problems, but also provide a framework for the graphical solution of trigonometric equations and equalities.

Matrices are a third example. In the New Math period, this topic was part of a linear algebra course. After some practicing of computational techniques, matrices were studied in a very abstract way, with much emphasis on aspects related to properties of operations leading to the identification of underlying algebraic structures. Also, here, the HEWET materials provided an alternative for a more concrete point of view, connecting matrices to graphs and different types of contexts, such as distance and connectivity, population dynamics, consumer behaviour ... (De Lange & Kindt, 1984b). In this vision, much attention is paid to the contextual interpretation of a matrix, its square and its product with another matrix. The widespread availability of ICT tools makes it also possible to perform calculations with big matrices that arose from real contexts. That way, matrices become a powerful tool for modelling various application problems in which blocks of numbers are involved. These problems originate from different disciplines (biology, economics, other social sciences, ...) and proved to be a better introduction to abstract algebra than an immediate start with abstract structures.

We conclude this section with the fourth example: the new approach to differential and integral calculus. In this domain, the versatility in meanings of the concept of derivative and (definite) integral, that one cannot possibly understand based only on a definition, was given a central place. Meaning depends on the context in which these concepts occur, or, as Freudenthal (1973, p. 513) wrote: "What the differential quotient and the integral of a function mean depends on what the function means, and this can be many different things." Basically, the derivative is meant for measuring change (Kindt & De Lange, 1984, 1985). To arrive at a solid understanding of the concept of derivative, conceptual mathematisation was promoted. On the basis of different contexts in which change occurs and has slightly different meanings (speed of an animal, population growth, marginal cost, ...), the notions of average and instantaneous change are explored and interpreted graphically as, respectively an average slope (slope of a secant) and the slope in a point (slope of the tangent). The transition from average to instantaneous change can be clarified on the basis of an intuitive concept of limit. This pre-formal phase is meant to equip the derivative with a rich and flexible meaning, and only at a later moment, a formal-analytical quantification is presented (as, respectively, a difference quotient and a differential quotient or derivative). In line with Poincaré's (1908, p. 83) words that "mathematics is the art of giving the same name to different things", the derivative appears as a common name for rate of change. The didactical track continues with the differentiation rules, first deduced for polynomial functions, but gradually expanded when other classes of functions are involved, and ending with various new applications, e.g., problems related to optimisation, in which, thanks to the rich pre-formal phase, the derivative is now recognised and applied more easily.

Unfortunately, directly usable HEWET or other RME materials for the teaching of integral calculus were not available, but it proved possible to design a course in the same spirit, that is, giving a central place to the versatility of meaning of the concept of (definite) integral (De Bock, 1990; De Bock et al., 1994; Roelens, Roels, & Deprez, 1990). Inspiration was, among other sources, found in the work of German mathematics educators (see, e.g., Kirsch, 1976). Although integrals are defined geometrically—directly as the (oriented) area under the graph of a function or by means of lower and/or upper sums—their meaning in different contexts and, hence, the type of problems that can be solved using integrals, is emphasised. Three types of such problems are identified. A first type is labelled 'reconstruction problems': starting from the rate of change of a variable, the variable itself can be reconstructed. So, for example, the area under a graph of flow rate of a river, velocity or marginal costs enables to reconstruct, respectively, water volume passing, distance travelled or total costs. A second type relates to summation. Integrals are not only approximated by sums (the idea of 'numerical integration'), but also vice versa: sums of a large number of terms can be approximated or idealised by integrals. Sometimes, it is also helpful to perceive a magnitude (e.g., a volume, a surface area or the length of an arc) as a sum to discover how that magnitude can be calculated as the integral of some function. Third, integral problems are also related to averaging continuously changing magnitudes. Definite integrals with variable upper limit lead to the concepts of integral function and anti-derivative or indefinite integral. Finally, the link between the concepts of (anti-)derivative and (definite) integral is established (leading to the so-called 'fundamental theorem of calculus').

11.5 Conclusion

The Dutch RME model enriched Flemish mathematics education in secondary schools during the 1980s and 1990s and its positive influence is generally recognised. However, this does not mean that mathematics education in Flanders nowadays is a copy of that Dutch RME model (as embodied in, e.g., the HEWET and HAWEX materials). Elements of the more traditional approach, focusing on calculation drill and algebraic techniques, as well as more structural elements, focusing on a logical organisation of content and on proof and argumentation, are still essential parts of Flemish mathematics curricula and of classroom practice, although their importance has decreased. In our view, this has resulted in a more or less balanced approach to mathematics education in Flanders. This specificity of Flemish mathematics education, which was the result of multiple influences, is probably one of the reasons why an orthodox version of the RME model could never be implemented. For example, a project in the late 1980s in which some of the HEWET cahiers were 'translated' to the Flemish context, proved to be unsuccessful, likely because Flemish teachers missed a clear structure, the provided modelling problems were sometimes too open and computational skills received insufficient attention. It may also be one of the reasons why the Math Wars, that originated in the 1990s in the United States, have had very limited impact in Flanders (while they have been an important educational-political issue in the Netherlands).

References

Bernet, T., & Jaquet, F. (1998). *La CIEAEM au travers de ses 50 premières rencontres* [The CIEAEM through its first 50 meetings]. Neuchâtel, Switzerland: CIEAEM.

Bunt, L. N. H. (1959). L'enseignement de la statistique dans les écoles secondaires des Pays-Bas [The teaching of statistics in Dutch secondary schools]. *Mathematica & Paedagogia, 17,* 35–48.

Carbonez, A., & Veraverbeke, N. (1994). *Eindige kansmodellen en toetsen van hypothesen* [Finite probability models and testing of hypotheses]. Leuven/Amersfoort, Belgium/the Netherlands: Acco.

Cleve, M., De Bock, D., & Roelens, M. (1993). Onder de loep genomen: De grafische rekenmachine in de wiskundeles [Under the magnifying glass: The graphing calculator in the mathematics lesson]. *Uitwiskeling, 9*(4), 15–50.

Colot, L. (1969). Lettre d'un professeur de mathématique à un collègue [Letter of a mathematics teacher to a colleague]. *Mathematica & Paedagogia, 38,* 34–40.

De Bock, D. (1990). Een driesporige benadering van het integraalbegrip [A three-track approach to the concept of integral]. *Wiskunde & Onderwijs, 62,* 141–159.

De Bock, D., Deprez, J., Eggermont, H., Janssens, D., Kesselaers, G., Op de Beeck, R., et al. (1992). Onder de loep genomen: Analyse [Under the magnifying glass: Analysis]. *Uitwiskeling, 8*(4), 15–53.

De Bock, D., Deprez, J., Gyssels, S., Eggermont, H., Janssens, D., Kesselaers, G., et al. (1986). *Analyse: Een intuïtieve kennismaking* [Analysis: An intuitive introduction]. Leuven, Belgium: Acco.

De Bock, D., Janssens, D., Roelens, M., & Roels, J. (1994). *Afgeleiden en integralen* [Derivatives and integrals]. Leuven, Belgium: Acco.

De Bock, D., & Roelens, M. (1990). De reis van de Yatzy [The journey of the Yatzy]. *Nieuwe Wiskrant, 10*(2), 21–26.

De Bock, D., & Vanpaemel, G. (2015a). Modern mathematics at the 1959 OEEC Seminar at Royaumont. In K. Bjarnadóttir, F. Furinghetti, J. Prytz, & G. Schubring (Eds.), *"Dig where you stand" 3. Proceedings of the Third International Conference on the History of Mathematics Education* (pp. 151–168). Uppsala, Sweden: Uppsala University, Department of Education.

De Bock, D., & Vanpaemel, G. (2015b). The Belgian journal *Mathematica & Paedagogia* (1953–1974): A forum for the national and international scene in mathematics education. In E. Barbin, U. T. Jankvist, & T. H. Kjeldsen (Eds.), *Proceedings of the Seventh European Summer University on the History and Epistemology in Mathematics Education* (pp. 723–734). Copenhagen, Denmark: Aarhus University, Danish School of Education.

De Corte, E. (1996). Actief leren binnen krachtige onderwijsleeromgevingen [Active learning in powerful teaching-learning environments]. *Impuls, 26,* 145–156.

De Lange, J. (1987). *Mathematics, insight and meaning.* Utrecht, the Netherlands: OW&OC.

De Lange, J., & Kindt, M. (1984a). *Exponenten en logaritmen* [Exponents and logarithms]. Culemborg, the Netherlands: Educaboek.

De Lange, J., & Kindt, M. (1984b). *Matrices* [Matrices]. Culemborg, the Netherlands: Educaboek.

De Lange, J., & Kindt, M. (1984c). *Sinus* [Sine]. Culemborg, the Netherlands: Educaboek.

De Lange, J., & Kindt, M. (1985). *Periodieke functions* [Periodic functions]. Culemborg, the Netherlands: Educaboek.

De Lange, J., & Kindt, M. (1986). *Groei* [Growth]. Culemborg, the Netherlands: Educaboek.

Deprez, J., Eggermont, H., Janssens, D., & Roelens, M. (1987a). *Ruimtemeetkunde* [Solid geometry]. Leuven, Belgium: Acco.

Deprez, J., Gyssels, S., & Roels, J. (1985). Onder de loep genomen: Analyse [Under the magnifying glass: Analysis]. *Uitwiskeling, 2*(1), 16–47.

Deprez, J., Roelens, M., & Roels, J. (1987b). Onder de loep genomen: Ruimtemeetkunde [Under the magnifying glass: Solid geometry]. *Uitwiskeling, 3*(3), 10–40.

Deprez, J., & Roels, J. (2000). Onder de loep genomen: Ruimtemeetkunde in de tweede graad [Under the magnifying glass: Solid geometry in the second grade]. *Uitwiskeling, 16*(4), 12–38.

Deprez, J., Roels, J., & Roelens, M. (1992). Onder de loep genomen: Kansen van 1 tot 6 [Under the magnifying glass: Probabilities from 1 to 6]. *Uitwiskeling, 8*(2), 20–58.

Eggermont, H., & Roels, J. (1997). Onder de loep genomen: Het functiebegrip [Under the magnifying glass: The concept of function]. *Uitwiskeling, 14*(1), 11–33.

Feys, R. (1982). Moderne wiskunde: een vlag op een modderschuit [Modern mathematics: a flag on a mud barge]. *Onderwijskrant, 24*, 3–37.

Freudenthal, H. (1973). *Mathematics as an educational task*. Dordrecht, the Netherlands: Reidel.

Garst, S. (1990). Wiskunde en onderwijs in Nederland IV: Statistiek en kansrekening [Mathematics and education in the Netherlands IV: Statistics and probability]. *Wiskunde en Onderwijs, 62*, 241–244.

Holvoet, R. (1996). Piet Vredenduin (1909–1996), geziene gast in Vlaanderen [Piet Vredenduin, respected guest in Flanders]. *Wiskunde en Onderwijs, 87*, 374–376.

Janssens, D. (1993). Implementation of teaching of mathematics by applications. In J. de Lange, C. Keitel, I. Huntley, & M. Niss (Eds.), *Innovation in maths education by modelling and applications* (pp. 203–210). New York, NY: Ellis Horwood.

Janssens, D., & Roels, G. (1985). *Meetkunde voor het derde jaar secundair onderwijs* [Geometry for the third year of secondary education]. Leuven, Belgium: Acco.

Kesselaers, G., & Roelens, M. (1992). Onder de loep genomen: Stochastiek [Under the magnifying glass: Statistics]. *Uitwiskeling, 9*(1), 9–55.

Kindt, M., & De Lange, J. (1984). *Differentiëren 1* [To differentiate 1]. Culemborg, the Netherlands: Educaboek.

Kindt, M., & De Lange, J. (1985). *Differentiëren 2* [To differentiate 2]. Culemborg, the Netherlands: Educaboek.

Kirsch, A. (1976). Eine "intellektuell ehrliche" Einführung des Integralbegriffs in Grundkursen [An "intellectually honest" introduction to the concept of integral in basic courses]. *Didaktik der Mathematik, 4*, 87–105.

La Bastide-van Gemert, S. (2015). *All positive action starts with criticism. Hans Freudenthal and the didactics of mathematics*. New York, NY: Springer.

Maassen, J. (2000). De vereniging en het tijdschrift [The society and the journal]. In F. Goffree, M. van Hoorn, & B. Zwaneveld (Eds.), *Honderd jaar wiskundeonderwijs* [Hundred years of mathematics teaching] (pp. 43–56). Leusden, the Netherlands: Nederlandse Vereniging van Wiskundeleraren.

Miewis, J. (2003). Mathematica et Paedagogia... 1953–1974. *Mathématique et Pédagogie, 142*, 5–22.

National Council of Teachers of Mathematics. (1989). *Curriculum and evaluation standards for school mathematics*. Reston, VA: National Council of Teachers of Mathematics.

Op de Beeck, R., Deprez, J., & Roels, J. (1997). Onder de loep genomen: Meetkunde in de eerste graad, ook in de ruimte [Under the magnifying glass: Geometry in the first grade, also in space]. *Uitwiskeling, 13*(2), 18–49.

Papy, G. (1967). *Mathématique moderne 3. Voici Euclide* [Modern mathematics 3. Euclid now]. Bruxelles: Didier.

Pirard, A., & Godfrind, P. (1980, March 11). Les désastres de la mathématique moderne [The disasters of modern mathematics]. *La Libre Belgique*, p. 15.

Poincaré, H. (1908). *The future of mathematics* [English version translated from *Revue Générale des Sciences Pures et Appliquées, 19th Year, No. 23*, Paris]. Available at: https://archive.org/stream/monist09instgoog#page/n86/mode/2up.

Roelens, M., Roels, J., & Deprez, J. (1990). Onder de loep genomen: Integralen [Under the magnifying glass: Integrals]. *Uitwiskeling, 6*(4), 9–54.

Roels, G. (1995). Tien jaar evolutie van het wiskundeonderwijs in Vlaanderen. Een schets uit de praktijk [Ten year of evolution in mathematics education in Flandres. A sketch from practice]. *Uitwiskeling, 11*(3), 2–13.

Roels, J., De Bock, D., Deprez, J., Janssens, D., Kesselaers, G., Op de Beeck, R., et al. (1990). *Wiskunde vanuit toepassingen* [Mathematics taught by applications]. Leuven, Belgium: Aggregatie HSO Wiskunde – K.U. Leuven.

Servais, W. (1953). Éditorial [Editorial]. *Mathematica & Paedagogia, 1,* 2–4.

Stichting-Lodewijk de Raet. (1983). Verslagboek van het colloquium "Welke Wiskunde voor 5- tot 15-Jarigen?" [Proceedings of the colloquium "What Kind of Mathematics for 5 to 15 Year Olds?"]. *Onderwijskrant, 32,* 2–30.

Thaels, K., Eggermont, H., & Janssens, D. (2001). *Van ruimtelijk inzicht naar ruimtemeekunde* [From insight in space to solid geometry]. Deurne, Belgium: Wolters Plantyn.

Vanpaemel, G., De Bock, D., & Verschaffel, L. (2012). Defining modern mathematics: Willy Servais (1913–1979) and mathematical curriculum reform in Belgium. In K. Bjarnadóttir, F. Furinghetti, J. Matos, & G. Schubring (Eds.), *"Dig where you stand" 2. Proceedings of the Second International Conference on the History of Mathematics Education* (pp. 485–505). Lisbon, Portugal: New University of Lisbon.

Verschaffel, L., Greer, B., & De Corte, E. (2000). *Making sense of word problems.* Lisse, the Netherlands: Swets and Zeitlinger.

Vredenduin, P. J. G. (1967). Het experiment Papy [The experiment Papy]. *Euclides, 42*(6), 167–172.

Zwaneveld, B. (2000). Kansrekening en statistiek [Probability and statistics]. In F. Goffree, M. van Hoorn, & B. Zwaneveld (Eds.), *Honderd jaar wiskundeonderwijs* [Hundred years of mathematics teaching] (pp. 239–251). Leusden, the Netherlands: Nederlandse Vereniging van Wiskundeleraren.

Chapter 12
Echoes and Influences of Realistic Mathematics Education in Portugal

João Pedro da Ponte and Joana Brocardo

Abstract This chapter traces the connections between Realistic Mathematics Education (RME) and Portuguese developments in mathematics education in terms of research studies and curriculum development. The basis for this work is a literature review of papers and other documents, with special attention to the period 2005–2015, and research studies organised by mathematical topic. Although there is no research group in Portugal that is perfectly aligned with RME principles and curriculum materials, noticeable influences may be seen in the frequent references made in some research groups to key RME ideas, notably the importance of students working from tasks in meaningful contexts, the role of representations and models to support students' thinking, and the levels of students' mathematical activity. This is most noticeable in conceptual frameworks for developmental research studies in the area of number and in the use of realistic contexts in task design, and it is also apparent in the official 2007 Portuguese curriculum document.

Keywords Tasks · Representations · Numbers · Algebra · Geometry

12.1 Introduction

Realistic Mathematics Education (RME) has a clear influence in Portugal, both in research and in curriculum development. Portuguese mathematics educators began to know about RME ideas from reading Freudenthal (1973) and from their participation in two international meetings, that of PME (International Group for the Psychology of Mathematics Education) and of CIEAEM (International Commission for the Study and Improvement of Mathematics Teaching), which both took place in

J. P. da Ponte (✉)
Instituto de Educação, Universidade de Lisboa, Lisboa, Portugal
e-mail: jpponte@ie.ulisboa.pt

J. Brocardo
Escola Superior de Educação, Instituto Politécnico de Setúbal, Setúbal, Portugal
e-mail: joana.brocardo@ese.ips.pt

© The Author(s) 2020
M. van den Heuvel-Panhuizen (ed.), *International Reflections on the Netherlands Didactics of Mathematics*, ICME-13 Monographs, https://doi.org/10.1007/978-3-030-20223-1_12

the Netherlands in 1985. Since then, contacts have been frequent, in other international meetings, in study visits made by Portuguese researchers to the Freudenthal Institute (FI) in Utrecht, and also through the visits made by researchers of the FI to Portugal to attend mathematics education conferences,[1] to participate in activities of research and evaluation projects, and to deliver seminars to doctoral students.[2]

Research in mathematics education in Portugal began its development from the 1980s, with several doctoral degrees obtained abroad (in the United States and the United Kingdom), but only in the 2000s did it become more intensive, with doctoral degrees offered at several Portuguese universities (mainly in Lisbon, Aveiro, and Braga). It was around these doctoral programmes that the most important research groups developed, with the association of several schools for higher education (such as those in Lisbon, Setúbal, and Viana do Castelo).

In this chapter, we give an account of the main influences of RME in Portugal, with special attention for the last 10 years (2005–2015). The chapter is constructed from a revision of doctoral theses, edited books, articles published in mathematics education national and international scientific journals (*Quadrante, BOLEMA, Relime, Uni-Pluri/Versidad*), articles published in the teacher journal *Educação e Matemática* of APM (Associação de Professores de Matemática[3]) and communications in proceedings of the national mathematics education research meetings SIEM (Seminário de Investigação em Educação Matemática) and EIEM (Encontro de Investigação em Educação Matemática). The chapter contains two main sections, one concerning research studies (subdivided in mathematical topics) and another concerning curriculum development. In each section, the studies and documents are highlighted in which the influence of RME ideas appears to be stronger, seeking to identify the main contributions to theory and practice of mathematics education as well as the aspects in which this influence may be traced. The chapter concludes with a summary of RME influence in our country.

12.2   Influences on Research Studies

12.2.1   Whole Numbers and Operations

The notion of number sense inspired several researchers of the Developing Number Sense (DNS) project to develop an alternative approach to teaching whole numbers and operations that includes certain central RME ideas. This project is a central reference in the mathematical domain of number in Portugal. Here the fundamental

---

[1] Koeno Gravemeijer has been at EIEM in 1997 (Castelo de Vide), Marja van den Heuvel-Panhuizen at CIEAEM in 1997 (Setúbal), Rijkje Dekker, Koeno Gravemeijer and Jean-Marie Kraemer at 'Mathematics Education: Paths and Crossroads in Memory of Paulo Abrantes' in 2005 (Lisbon), and Henk van der Kooij at EIEM in 2006 (Monte Gordo).

[2] Especially Koeno Gravemeijer and Jean-Marie Kraemer.

[3] Association of Mathematics Teachers.

influences can be identified related to the role of counting, place value and standard algorithms, the role of the context of tasks and the use of models in mathematics learning.

Also in this perspective, in a book published by the Portuguese Ministry of Education to support the activity of infant education teachers, Castro and Rodrigues (2008) indicated that children may use counting to compute. From a sequence of tasks, they exemplified how the activity of counting may evolve from one to one counting to the re-invention of informal mental strategies based on counting, one of the RME big ideas (Beishuizen & Anghileri, 1998). Still in the same vein, Rodrigues (2010), in a study addressing the development of number sense in children from three infant schools, concluded that it is from the numerical sequence and from counting competences that children develop other numeral competences. The children that she studied used counting as an informal strategy that, based in diversified experiences in meaningful numerical contexts, was progressively structured, discovering counting in patterns and jumps.

12.2.1.1   Place Value and Standard Algorithms

The tradition of focussing numerical learning in the early use of place value aiming at the quick construction of standard algorithms was strongly questioned by several RME authors. Brocardo, Serrazina and Kraemer (2003), following this trend and basing their argumentation on authors such as Gravemeijer (1991) and Fosnot and Dolk (2001a) highlighted the need to link structurally the development of computation methods and techniques to the construction of numbers, their organisation and structure. In order to achieve this, all these authors argued that it is necessary to delay the learning of algorithms the early introduction of which they viewed as hindering an adequate development of number sense. Brocardo and Serrazina (2008), reflecting on the work carried out by the DNS project, strongly influenced by Gravemeijer (1991, 1994, 2005), Treffers (1987, 1991) and Buys (2008) on the teaching and learning of numbers and operations, suggested that the algorithms must not be the central focus of the curriculum, and that students must learn them in a long journey based in developing number sense.

Two teaching experiments carried out as doctoral theses underscore this perspective. In the first, carried out in a Grade 2 class, Ferreira (2012) was strongly inspired by the notion of landscape of learning of Fosnot and Dolk (2001a, b) in which students were invited to construct their ideas and strategies based on the analysis and manipulation of numbers as a whole. As proposed by RME, this teaching experiment did not include explicit references to place value and emphasised a holistic approach to number, with the development of 'horizontal' written calculation strategies. The author concluded that the four students studied managed to solve the proposed addition and subtraction problems without using the standard algorithm. Instead, they began to reason arithmetically, using familiar relations between numbers and between addition and subtraction, as indicated by Blöte, Van der Burg, and Klein (2001) and Gravemeijer (2005).

In another teaching experiment, in a Grade 3 class, Mendes (2012) got support on the theoretical ideas of Fosnot and Dolk (2001b) related to multiplication. The big ideas that Mendes assumed in her work included unitizing (numbers are used to count not only objects but also groups), the distributive property (realising that 7×5 can be solved by adding 5×5 and 2×5, or any combination of groups that add up to seven groups), the associative property ($2 \times \{5 \times 9\} = \{2 \times 5\} \times 9$) and the commutative property ($52 \times 2 = 2 \times 52$).

12.2.1.2 The Role of the Context of Tasks and the Use of Models and Manipulative Materials

The influence of RME ideas regarding the context of tasks inspired the production of classroom materials in the DNS project (Brocardo et al., 2005; Brocardo & Serrazina, 2008) and of research studies (such as Delgado, 2013; Mendes, 2012; Rodrigues, 2010). In these studies, the context of tasks was carefully planned as a starting point and source for modelling. Attention was paid to the clarity of the written text, to the accompanying images that should not be simple illustrations, and to how the task might arouse students' curiosity. Explaining the way the project team thought about the context of tasks, Brocardo and Delgado (2009) underlined the idea of Freudenthal (1968) that mathematics must be learned as a process of mathematising reality and, if possible, in the process of mathematising mathematics itself. They also indicated the important characteristics of the context of tasks so that it would become a situation that lends itself to mathematising, as Fosnot and Dolk (2001b) suggested—to allow the use of models, to make sense for students, to create surprise and arouse questions.

The tasks with contexts that appeal to models are one of the RME influences that it is possible to identify in many research studies carried out in Portugal (such as Delgado, 2013; Ferreira, 2012; Mendes, 2012). An example is the 'Drinks machine' task (Brocardo et al., 2005), inspired by a task developed by Kraemer and Paardekooper (1998) in which cans with drinks of different flavours are put in a machine with a maximum capacity of twenty cans for each variety. There are horizontal limits that organise the stacks of cans in groups of five, allowing for connections with the string of beads and the empty number line model structured from five in five (Fig. 12.1).

The exploration of contexts such as fruit boxes or tile tessellations are paradigmatic examples of contexts associated with the rectangular model widely used to structure multiplication. Another example was provided by Rocha and Menino (2009) who presented a task chain inspired by Fosnot and Dolk (2001b) with an underlying progression aimed at using the rectangular model in successive phases of abstraction. To achieve that, the context used began by allowing a counting of the objects that are all visible (fruits shown on a box), then allowing to count all the objects of a half of a rectangular array (two equal curtains in which one has all patterns visible and the other does not), and, finally, situations in which counting was discouraged by covering part of the rectangular patterns with objects or people leading students to think in terms of lines and columns and begin to use the rectangular model, thus leaving addition and using multiplication.

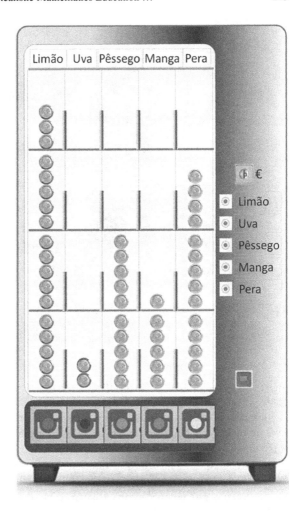

Fig. 12.1 The drinks machine (Brocardo et al., 2005)

Mendes (2012) used this type of contexts in her research focussed on learning of multiplication, and in the design of the sequence of tasks, she sought that the numbers involved, carefully framed from task to task, would appeal to multiplicative numerical relationships, as suggested by Treffers and Buys (2008) (Fig. 12.2).

The results of this research indicated that the chosen context for the multiplication tasks contributed to consolidating the use of multiplicative procedures. She also concluded that students who established connections among the contexts and the numbers of sequential tasks constructed procedures based on that relationship, and there were multiplicative procedures used by students (such as the use of relationships involving doubling) that were induced by the numbers used in the tasks. In her study, focussed on the practices of two teachers, Delgado (2013) concluded that in an initial phase of the study the teachers mainly valued contexts of tasks that were close to

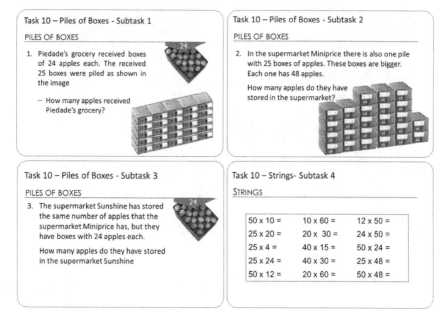

Fig. 12.2 Example of one multiplicative context used by Mendes (2012)

students' daily life situations, to motivate them and lead them to engage in solving the tasks. As the study progressed, the teachers also began to recognise the importance of contexts in developing meaning for the numbers and operations associated with them, as underlined by Fosnot and Dolk (2001b) when referring to the characteristics of the contexts of tasks that foster the development of number sense.

In Portugal, there is not a strong tradition of using manipulative materials, despite the fact that all official curricula since 1975 refer to the importance of manipulating objects and using structured materials such as MAB or the abacus. RME influenced a reflection on the use of such materials, in contrast with the use of models, in particular the empty number line. Brocardo et al. (2005) made a detailed analysis of the potential of the empty number line, and followed RME perspectives in reflecting on the potential and limitations of MAB. They argued that usual materials for learning computation with whole numbers are often difficult for many students, provide few opportunities for the use of informal strategies, and do not promote the evolution of mental computation strategies. Brocardo and Serrazina (2008) referred to the comparison that Beishuizen (2001) made between the use of the one hundred square and the empty number line, highlighting the importance that the model must lead the students to think in the strategy that they use and the computations that they do. Therefore, they criticised the use of the one hundred square because it is possible to calculate using mechanical procedures such as "add 10 is to come down one line and read the number" or "take away 5 is to move 5 numbers backwards and see where we stop" that allows to arrive at a result doing no thinking at all. Several tasks produced in the DNS project discuss the advantages of the empty number line, indicating that its use enables children to have an image of jumping forwards and backwards keeping the multiples of ten as landmarks and thinking in numbers and their relations, calculating with the head. Use of the empty number line began to spread since 2005 and was recommended for the first time in an official curriculum of the Ministry of Education (Ministério da Educação, ME, 2007). In later research studies focussed on teaching and learning numbers and operations (such as Delgado, 2013; Ferreira, 2012) and in some textbooks, the use of the empty number line model became usual.

12.2.2 Mental Calculation

The concept of mental arithmetic referred to by Buys (2008) and widely used in the Netherlands gained certain acceptance in Portugal. Brocardo and Serrazina (2008) indicated that for the DNS project mental calculation implied dealing with number values (not with digits), using elementary calculation properties and number relationships, and allowing for the possible use of suitable intermediate written notes. This notion aligns well with that of Buys and is adopted by many other Portuguese researchers. Several booklets edited by the Portuguese Ministry of Education to support the implementation of the 2007 Portuguese mathematics curriculum adopted this concept of mental calculation and exemplified it with appropriate tasks for how it can be developed.

Several studies were undertaken in the last decade focussing on the development of mental calculation. These studies emphasised the development of mental calculation strategies supported by a careful articulation of sequences of tasks (for example, Delgado, 2013; Ferreira, 2012; Mendes, 2012; Pinto, 2011). Following RME perspectives, these authors considered the written methods as specific developments of the mental strategies that children learn, which should be organised in a continuous progression. To ensure that this development happens, it is important that students learn to use mental calculation strategies in a flexible way. These strategies may be organised in three big groups: (i) stringing strategies, in which the operations are movements along the counting row, (ii) splitting strategies, in which operations are performed by splitting and processing the numbers based on the ten's structure; and (iii) varying strategies, based on arithmetic properties.

The teaching experiment conducted by Mendes (2012) included several mini lessons with mental mathematics strings (as suggested by Fosnot & Dolk, 2001a, b). This researcher concluded that the articulation between the numbers used in the problems and the numbers used in the mental mathematics strings was important since students were able to adapt from each other the procedures that they used. She also concluded that the numbers used in the mental mathematics strings and the way they were constructed enabled students to use numerical relationships based on multiplication properties. The studies of Pinto (2011), Ferreira (2012), Mendes (2012) and Delgado (2013) provided evidence that an approach to mental calculation that articulates the knowledge of number facts and strategic methods has big potential to develop students' numerical competences. In fact, the students studied evolved in a significant way, using adequate strategies, and in many cases flexibly adapted to contexts and numbers.

Brocardo (2011) proposed the setting up of goals for mental calculation to attain at the end of each school cycle based on the distinction of three categories of mental calculation proposed by Buys (2008). Referring to ideas of the TAL team,[4] she indicated that this distinction demystifies the idea that such calculation cannot include written notes, and clarified that mental calculation is not just automatic calculation. She also presented a proposal for the development of mental calculation that included several RME ideas. Underlining that mental calculation work must be systematic and intentional, she exemplified that mental mathematics strings (Fosnot & Dolk, 2001a, b) may contribute to constructing basic numerical knowledge important for the development of mental calculation strategies from Grades 6 to 12. Brocardo (2011) proposed exploring open tasks, in which students discover interesting numerical patterns that may lead to efficient calculation techniques that students get for their use. She also suggested that systematic work in constructing a web of relationships, as recommended by Kraemer and Van Benthem (2011). Such a web is based on the idea of beginning from a known fact such as 4×5 is 20 and constructing all multiplicative relations connected to it. In her proposal, Brocardo (2011) emphasised that the teacher has a key role in selecting tasks that arouse students' curiosity and leading them to develop mental calculation, in distinguishing situations in which it is appropriate to use the calculator from those in which that does not make any sense and in assuring that students use mental calculation always when appropriate.

12.2.3   Rational Numbers

Teaching and learning rational numbers has attracted significant attention from Portuguese researchers in mathematics education, with two particularly noticeable influences—from the Rational Number Project (Behr, Harel, Post, & Lesh, 1992) and from RME. We analyse here the influence of RME.

12.2.3.1   Mapping Students' Difficulties

In a literature review on teaching and learning rational numbers that has been an important reference for research on this topic in Portugal, Monteiro and Pinto (2006) discussed students' difficulties in working with fractions and their strategies in solving problems. The presense of RME ideas is particularly noticeable in the point

---

[4]The TAL team was responsible for developing a teaching-learning trajectory for calculation with whole numbers in primary school (Van den Heuvel-Panhuizen, 2008). Kees Buys was one of the members of this TAL team.

on students' strategies, as the authors underlined the idea that mathematics must be reinvented by students in a progressive process of generalisation and formalisation (De Lange, 1996; Gravemeijer, 1991, 1997; Streefland, 1986, 1991; Treffers, 1991). Monteiro and Pinto (2006) indicated that, in the perspective of RME, students' learning is based on informal strategies for solving tasks, from which they develop concepts and connections among concepts, in a mathematising process. They also referred to horizontal mathematising and to modelling of real situations through the use of symbols as well as to vertical mathematising as a path internal to mathematics (Gravemeijer, 1997). Monteiro and Pinto (2006) presented the ideas of Keijzer (2003) regarding mathematising processes (modelling, symbolisation, generalisation, formalisation and abstraction). They pointed out that, to bridge the gap between concrete and abstract, students need tools such as visual models, schemas, and diagrams that work for them as supports for thinking (Streefland, 1993). They also indicated that symbols may become objects of thinking, constituting images for more abstract levels of understanding (Streefland, 1991).

Monteiro and Pinto (2006) recalled the ideas of Streefland (1986) about the algebraic structure of rational numbers being the support for the most common view on the teaching of fractions. In their perspective, that explains why operations appear in the Portuguese curricula in a given order and why the algorithms to compare, add and multiply fractions have so much weight. They considered that it is the role of the teacher to provide students with opportunities to reinvent mathematics, instead of seeking to make accessible to them 'ready-made' mathematics.

12.2.3.2 Use of Representations and Models

Based on a teaching experiment, Ponte and Quaresma (2011) studied the development of Grade 5 students' understanding of the notion of rational number, ordering and comparing rational numbers, and equivalence of fractions. In this study, a fundamental idea was the simultaneous use of different representations, as well as of different meanings, kinds of magnitudes, and kinds of task. The authors referred to the 'iceberg model' of representations of Boswinkel (see Webb, Boswinkel, & Dekker, 2008) that suggests that students need a large amount of experience with different informal and preformal representations as a basis to construct a meaning for formal mathematical representations. In this way, the students used pictorial representations as a support for their work with the more formal representations of decimal numerals, fractions, percentages, and mixed numerals. Based on ideas from Streefland (1991), who underlined that the work on fractions must be done based on their names, such as 'a half', 'a third', 'a quarter', and so on, the authors considered that verbal representation, which is sometimes neglected in research, fulfils a fundamental role in the work with rational numbers, notably in oral communication. In addition, echoing ideas from Gravemeijer (2005), through all the teaching unit, as a starting point for constructing concepts, they valued the students' intuitive and informal strategies as well as their prior knowledge. In their results, they pointed out that students tend to begin by using simultaneously verbal and pictorial representations that enable the interpretation of the information in the statement of the task and support the reasoning to get to the solution.

The study of Ventura (2014), carried out with Grade 5 students, aimed to understand their evolution in learning the concept of rational number, based on a teaching experiment that was based essentially on the use of the numerical bar and the numerical line, and at the same time to ascertain the potential of this approach. In this study, the notion of model (based on Van den Heuvel-Panhuizen, 2003), fulfilled a key role as a representation of a problematic situation that reflects essential aspects of the mathematical concepts and that, therefore, constitutes a tool for solving problems. Ventura concluded that the students evolved in their learning of the concept of rational number, and indicated that, as a problem-solving strategy, many of them began to use the numerical bar as a 'model of', and later used it as a 'model to' reason (Gravemeijer, 2005; Streefland, 2003).

Guerreiro and Serrazina (2014) also studied students' strategies in solving problems involving rational numbers, but in this case in Grade 3. They based themselves on the perspectives of Fosnot and Dolk (2002) that indicate that students must understand important ideas and progressively refine their strategies in order to make them more efficient. Guerreiro and Serrazina assumed as central the notion of mathematical model, regarded as a tool for problem solving, and referred to examples such as "ratio tables, double numerical lines, clocks, grids and percent bars" (Fosnot & Dolk, 2002, p. 83). In the perspective of Guerreiro and Serrazina, these models may support students in generalising, going beyond what is specific in each situation. Building on ideas of Fosnot and Dolk (2002) and Gravemeijer (2005), Guerreiro and Serrazina considered that models emerge from situations experienced by students that evolve towards mathematical models of numerical relationships, becoming mathematical tools.

In other studies involving teaching and learning rational numbers in several grade levels, Ponte and Quaresma (2011, 2014b), Quaresma and Ponte (2012) and Guerreiro and Serrazina (2015), also based themselves on the model of different levels of mathematical activity of Gravemeijer (2005) and on the iceberg model of Boswinkel (Webb et al., 2008) to indicate the need for working from contexts meaningful for students and to assume that, in a first phase, an emphasis must be placed on informal representations that students already know, in order to introduce then, gradually, more formal new representations and working processes with rational numbers.

12.2.3.3 Learning Multiplication and Division

The study of Pinto (2011) analysed the development of the multiplication and division sense in Grade 6 students in working with rational numbers through a teaching unit. This unit involves the exploration of multiplication and division of rational numbers in meaningful contexts, based on RME principles. The unit values solving problems with contexts meaningful for students, their written productions, the development of models of the situations, the mathematical connections, the interactions in the classroom, and formative and regulatory evaluation. Underlying this unit is a hypothetical learning trajectory for multiplication and division of rational numbers that emphasises the development of multiplicative reasoning and operation sense in an integrated way. Building on RME researchers (such as Fosnot & Dolk, 2002; Freudenthal, 1973, 1983, 1991; Treffers, 1987, 1991; Treffers & Goffree, 1985), Pinto assumed that the study of rational numbers in school must begin based on fair sharing contexts related to students' reality and be oriented towards a constructive mathematising process. She also valued ratio problems (quoting Streefland, 1991, 1993) and suggested ratio tables as models for comparing fractions, especially in the case of fractions that are difficult to compare without applying rules. She noted, however, that students need to work with the other meanings of fractions (ratio, part-whole, measure and operator). In her analysis, she also assumed an important role for the notion of model as a learning support in moving from concrete to abstract knowledge (Van den Heuvel-Panhuizen, 1996, 1998; Van den Heuvel-Panhuizen & Wijers, 2005). The results of the study indicated that the students develop a sense for the multiplication and division of rational numbers, showing familiarity with different meanings and contexts of operations, flexibility in the use of proprieties of operations, critical ability in the analysis of processes and results, and capacity to use symbols and formal mathematical language with meaning.

12.2.4 Algebra

In the last ten years, algebra has attracted much attention in mathematical education research in Portugal. This investigation is mainly influenced by the ideas of Carpenter, Kaput, Kieran and Radford concerning the development of algebraic thinking. Nevertheless, influences deriving from RME have also been noted. For example, in an article for mathematic teachers, Ponte, Branco, and Matos (2008) analysed the role played by symbols in the development of students' algebraic thinking. The authors presented the perspective of Freudenthal (1983) concerning the teaching of algebra, indicating that "the symbols must mean something, at least initially, by analogy to what happened in the historical development of algebra" (Ponte et al., 2008, p. 90). They underline the importance of the process of progressive formalisation and also presented Freudenthal's perspective concerning algebraic language as a system framed by syntactic rules, which allow for the development of certain actions and highlights that the complexity of the algebraic language may originate incorrect interpretations from students.

In their study, Pereira and Saraiva (2013), proposed a learning and teaching model based on the notion of the parameter of a function to structure the mathematical reasoning of secondary school students in Grade 11. This model analyses the students' concepts, concerning relevance, cohesion and algebraic coherence, with teaching organised in three levels: reference operational, informal operational, and structural operational. For the authors, the concepts are structured at each level, representing contexts that promote the creation of meanings in a hierarchical logic. This work showed the influence of Gravemeijer's perspective of levels of students' mathematical activity (2005) in the construction of tasks in a teaching experiment, with the reference operational level matching the 'model of' level, the informal operational level matching the 'model to' level, and the structural operational level matching the formal level. According to Pereira and Saraiva, the results of their study suggest that this model is useful to structure tasks to promote students' thinking and to develop students' reasoning with mathematical concepts.

In an investigation carried out with Grade 4 students, intended to understand how to promote their relational thinking, Mestre and Oliveira (2013) focussed on the issue of the context and its connection to representations. They gave special attention to the way the teacher orchestrates the whole class discussion of a mathematical task and guides the systematisation of learning. For the authors, the tasks have an important role, with special emphasis on their contexts that must be significant to promote the development of students' relational thinking. Supported by Gravemeijer and Doorman (1999), the authors considered that contextualised problems constitute a source for mathematical activity, allowing the transition from informal to formal strategies. They also indicated that as students experiment with the process of reinventing mathematics through solving contextualised problems, they develop their mathematical knowledge and broaden their understanding of the real world. On this matter, the authors underlined the reflexive relation between the utilisation of contextualised problems and the apprehension of reality, arguing that these problems have roots in this reality and their solution helps students to broaden their own notion of reality. They concluded that the students used several representations, successfully presenting the values of the variables in the algebraic symbolic form.

The development of students' mathematical reasoning is an issue that has been studied in Portugal, mainly in studies related to the learning of algebra and also of rational numbers. Ponte, Mata-Pereira, and Henriques (2012), Mata-Pereira and Ponte (2013) and Ponte and Quaresma (2014a) regarded mathematical reasoning as the process of formulating inferences in a justified way, considering that this involves deductive, inductive and abductive aspects. In their view, justification is the central process of deductive thinking and generalisation is the central aspect of inductive and abductive reasoning. One of the main ideas of these studies is that reasoning is strictly connected to the representations used, which may assume a more formal or informal nature. In a study carried out with Grade 5 students, Ponte and Quaresma (2014a) presented a model that distinguishes between formal reasoning with and without understanding, where formal reasoning with understanding is based on informal reasoning, in a back and forth process, while formal reasoning without understanding relies essentially on memorised learning. This perspective on mathematical reasoning assumes that the big problem in teaching this subject is knowing how to make the progressive articulation between formal and informal reasoning processes and is supported by Gravemeijer's (2005) model of levels of mathematical activity.

In other research reports involving the teaching and learning of algebra, the influence of the RME authors is also visible. For example, Ponte (2005), in an article discussing the approach to algebra in the school curriculum, pointed to the role of 'real situations' in learning, making reference to the work of De Lange (1993). Pimenta and Saraiva (2013), in research aimed at the development of the algebraic thinking of Grade 4 and 5 students, referred to Freudenthal's notion of vertical mathematising (1973). And Silvestre and Ponte (2012), in a study of the development of the proportional reasoning of Grade 6 students, mentioned Gravemeijer's (2005) model of levels mathematical activity.

12.2.5 Geometry

In contrast to numbers and algebra, geometry is a mathematical topic that has attracted less attention from Portuguese mathematics education research. At an early stage, in the 1980s, the model of Van Hiele's (1984) levels of geometrical reasoning played an important role, especially in the work of Matos (1984), who studied the geometric thinking ability of prospective early-years teachers. However, in recent years, there is no record of references based on this model of geometric thinking. In today's Portuguese work on geometry the most visible influences are those of American authors such as Battista and Clements. However, there are also echoes of RME ideas, especially with regard to general perspectives on the teaching of geometry.

Pinheiro and Carreira (2013) discussed the development of geometric reasoning in the context of the use of Geogebra in a teaching experiment with Grade 7 students in order to know how they develop their understanding of the properties and relationships of geometric figures in studying triangles and quadrilaterals. In formulating their educational perspective, Pinheiro and Carreira presented the ideas of Freudenthal (1971, 1991) on the role of geometry in the school curriculum and on the teaching of geometry. Hence, the authors emphasised the role of geometry, given its importance to understand and organise spatial phenomena and they assumed that teaching should focus on the construction of conceptual models. They also valued the importance of manipulating physical materials in specific situations. Furthermore, they found that deductive reasoning should be promoted in accordance with students' maturity and that the most suitable way to learn geometry is "to allow the pupil to gradually become aware of their intuitive understanding of space" (Pinheiro & Carreira, 2013, p. 148). The results of this study showed that the sequence of tasks built and the way that the tasks were solved in the classroom helped to promote students' understanding of the mathematical concepts involved. They also found that the use of the dynamic geometry environment contributed to the development of students' spatial reasoning ability, and therefore of their geometric reasoning.

In another study, Mestrinho and Oliveira (2012) analysed how the use of the tangram may support understanding of the area concept in prospective early-years teachers, as part of a teacher education experiment in the second year of the programme. The authors referred to the idea of Freudenthal (1983), according to which the concept of area is much more complex than the concept of length, since the definition of an equivalence relation and of an order relation as well as the creation of a composition operation are much more complex for area. They also showed three perspectives on the concept of area referred to by Freudenthal (1983), namely 'equitable distribution' (situations in which it is necessary to divide a figure into equivalent parts), 'comparison and reproduction' (situations that involve the comparison of two parts of a surface or the reproduction of a certain amount of area with a different shape), and 'measurement' (situations involving filling a part of a surface with congruent figures, decomposition and recomposition operations or the use of general geometric relationships). The authors found that the use of the tangram as a resource promotes the development of basic ideas for understanding of area measurement, and allows to explore different approaches to this concept.

12.3   Influences on Curriculum Documents

Abrantes (1994) studied how an innovative curriculum developed by the project MAT$_{789}$[5] influenced the ability and disposition of students to tackle problems involving relationships of mathematics with reality and the way they saw mathematics and mathematics learning. In this experimental curriculum, there are two clear influences of RME: the perspectives about how to conduct curriculum development and how to frame evaluation processes. On a small scale the work of Abrantes is similar to the Dutch approach to curriculum development through projects such as carried out at OW&OC,[6] the predecessor of the Freudenthal Institute, or the curriculum development that was done in collaboration with SLO, Netherlands Institute for Curriculum Development. Characteristics of this curriculum development was that successive versions of materials were trialled, evaluated, and modified before being generalised. Abrantes (1994) referenced that regarding evaluation, the major influence came from the HEWET[7] project (De Lange, 1987)—in which teaching materials were developed on various mathematical topics for pre-university education—and highlighted the concern that evaluation must generate learning situations, be consistent with aims and methodologies, have a positive nature, and occur in a climate of trust and clarity.

At the national level, the mathematics curriculum for basic education (ME, 2007) shows a clear influence of RME ideas, notably in the topic of numbers and operations. An important methodological guideline is the informal use of counting that evolves through replay and repetition to become structured knowledge. For example, the mathematics curriculum for basic education indicates that

> the exploration of counting processes used by students associated with different possibilities to structure and relate numbers, contributes to the understanding of the first numerical relationships. These relationships are fundamental to understand the arithmetic operations and, besides, are a foundation for the development of number sense. (ME, 2007, p. 14)

---

[5] A project that developed and tested an innovative curriculum for students aged 12 to 15 years carried out by Paulo Abrantes, Eduardo Veloso, Leonor Santos, Paula Teixeira, and Margarida Silva.

[6] Onderzoek Wiskundeonderwijs en Onderwijs Computercentrum (Mathematics Education Reasearch and Educational Computer Centre).

[7] Herverkaveling Wiskunde I en II (Re-allotment Mathematics I and II); the HEWET project resulted in Mathematics A and Mathematics B, a new mathematics curriculum for the upper grades (age 16–18) of VWO, the pre-university level of secondary education.

This curriculum does not integrate the RME approach to written calculation in number operations, but it recognises the importance of delaying the introduction of the standard algorithms and stresses the idea that it is important to progressively develop more high-level abbreviated strategies. This document also recommends the use of the empty number line as a model that can be used alongside others. In addition, for teaching all topics, this curriculum stresses the importance of working from tasks posed in meaningful contexts, highlighting the importance of contexts that may engage students in asking questions, notice patterns, and lead them to use mathematical models and adequate representations.

12.4   Conclusion

As indicated in this chapter, many RME authors have influenced Portuguese mathematics education. The most salient are, in a first phase, Freudenthal, Treffers and Streefland, and, in more recent times, Gravemeijer, Van den Heuvel-Panhuizen, Fosnot and Dolk and Buys. Such influences can be seen in many mathematical fields, from numbers and operations to algebra and geometry, often mixed with influences from other mathematics education research programmes. The influences concern RME general ideas such as the perspective about representations and the notion of model and the levels of mathematical activity with attention to the progressive refinement of students' strategies from informal towards formal levels. There are also frequent references to the processes of vertical and horizontal mathematising and to the use of experientially real situations as a basis for learning.

The importance of carefully formulating the contexts of tasks as well as the articulation among them stands in studies related to numbers and operations. Tasks and the work that is done based on them in the classroom must favour the transformation of students' reasoning and mental calculation processes, from informal towards progressively more formal levels, and support the development of mathematical concepts. The importance of algebraic language as well as the process of progressive formalisation stands in studies regarding the teaching and learning of algebra. In the case of geometry, RME influences concern the importance of this topic in the curriculum and the didactical approach, underlining the role of the manipulation of materials, as well as the phenomenological analysis of concepts. There are several other fields in which Portuguese research comes close to RME ideas, such as the use of technology as a support for students' learning, organising teacher education with a strong connection to practice, and framing studies as design-based research; however, in these cases, the most quoted authors are usually from other approaches.

In several crosscutting topics, we also see RME influences. The mathematical tasks used in most recent research studies in Portugal strive to be framed in interesting contexts and to allow for a wide variety of students' solutions. The sequences of tasks constructed in these studies indicate possible learning routes, supporting a process of progressive mathematising, an important RME principle. Didactical phenomenology, another important RME idea, is also present in several research studies, in which a given mathematical topic is explored in depth, with great attention to everyday situations in which it can be traced. At another level, we may say that the pragmatic spirit of RME, and its concern for improving mathematics education by working in close connection with teachers and schools is also present in studies undertaken in our country. Globally, the work developed by Portuguese researchers using RME notions and tools has proven to be fruitful and underscores the value of the results and ideas of RME perspectives. In addition, these perspectives have been an important support for the development of research in mathematics education in Portugal, with positive effects on teachers' professional practices and, we believe, on students' learning.

References

Abrantes, P. (1994). *O trabalho de projecto e a relação dos alunos com a Matemática: A experiência do projecto MAT 789* [Project work and the relation of students with mathematics: The experience of the project MAT789] (Doctoral thesis). Lisbon, Portugal: University of Lisbon.

Behr, M., Harel, G., Post, T., & Lesh, R. (1992). Rational number, ratio and proportion. In D. Grouws (Ed.), *Handbook of research on mathematics teaching and learning* (pp. 296–333). New York, NY: Macmillan.

Beishuizen, M. (2001). Different approaches to master mental calculation strategies. In J. Anghileri (Ed.), *Principles and practices in arithmetic teaching* (pp. 119–130). Buckingham, UK: Open University Press.

Beishuizen, M., & Anghileri, J. (1998). Which mental strategies in the early number curriculum? A comparison of the British ideas and Dutch views. *British Educational Research Journal, 24*(5), 519–538.

Blöte, A. W., Van der Burg, E., & Klein, A. S. (2001). Pupils' flexibility in solving two-digit addition and subtraction problems: Instruction effects. *Journal of Educational Psychology, 93*, 627–638.

Brocardo, J. (2011). Uma linha de desenvolvimento do cálculo mental: Começando no 1.º ano e continuando até ao 12.º ano [A line of development of mental computation: Beginning at grade 1 and going on up to grade 12]. In *Atas do ProfMat 2011*. Lisbon, Portugal: APM.

Brocardo, J., & Delgado, C. (2009). Desafios e complexidades na concepção e exploração de tarefas para o desenvolvimento do sentido do número [Challenges and complexity in the conception and exploration of tasks for the development of number sense]. In C. Costa, E. Mamede, & F. Guimarães (Eds.), *Actas do XIX EIEM*. Secção de Educação Matemática da Sociedade Portuguesa de Ciências da Educação: Vila Real.

Brocardo, J., Delgado, C., Mendes, F., Rocha, I., Castro, J., Serrazina, L., & Rodrigues, M. (2005). Desenvolvendo o sentido do número [Developing number sense]. In Equipa do projecto DSN (Eds.), *Desenvolvendo o sentido do número: Perspetivas e exigências curriculares* (pp. 7–27). Lisbon, Portugal: APM.

Brocardo, J., & Serrazina, L. (2008). O sentido do número no currículo de Matemática [Number sense in the mathematics curriculum]. *O sentido do número: Reflexões que entrecruzam teoria e prática* (pp. 97–115). Lisbon, Portugal: Escolar Editora.

Brocardo, J., Serrazina, L., & Kraemer, J.-M. (2003). Algoritmos e sentido do número [Algorithms and number sense]. *Educação e Matemática, 75*, 11–15.

Buys, K. (2008). Mental arithmetic. In M. van den Heuvel-Panhuizen (Ed.), *Children learn mathematics: A learning-teaching trajectory with intermediate attainment targets for calculation with whole numbers in primary school* (pp. 121–145). Rotterdam, the Netherlands: Sense.

Castro, J., & Rodrigues, M. (2008). *Sentido de número e organização de dados* [Number sense and data organisation]. Lisbon, Portugal: DGIDC.

De Lange, J. (1987). *Mathematics, insight and meaning*. Utrecht, the Netherlands: OW&OC, Utrecht University.

De Lange, J. (1993). Innovation in mathematics education using applications: Progress and problems. In J. de Lange, C. Keitel, I. Huntley, & M. Niss (Eds.), *Innovation in maths education by modelling and applications* (pp. 3–18). New York, NY: Ellis Horwood.

De Lange, J. (1996). Using and applying mathematics in education. In A. J. Bishop, K. Clements, C. Keitel, J. Kilpatrick, & C. Laborde (Eds.), *International handbook of mathematics education* (Vol. 1, pp. 49–98). Dordrecht, the Netherlands: Kluwer.

Delgado, C. (2013). As *práticas do professor e o desenvolvimento do sentido de número: Um estudo no 1.º ciclo* [Teacher practices and the development of number sense] (Doctoral thesis). Lisbon, Portugal: University of Lisbon.

Ferreira, E. (2012). *O desenvolvimento do sentido de número no âmbito da resolução de problemas de adição e subtração no 2.º ano de escolaridade* [The development of number sense in solving addition and subtraction problems at grade 2] (Doctoral thesis). Lisbon, Portugal: University of Lisbon.

Fosnot, C. T., & Dolk, M. (2001a). *Young mathematics at work: Constructing number sense, addition and subtraction*. Portsmouth, NH: Heinemann.

Fosnot, C. T., & Dolk, M. (2001b). *Young mathematics at work: Constructing multiplication and division*. Portsmouth NH: Heinemann.

Fosnot, C. T., & Dolk, M. (2002). *Young mathematicians at work: Constructing fractions and percents*. Portsmouth, NH: Heinemann.

Freudenthal, H. (1968). Why to teach mathematics so as to be useful? *Educational Studies in Mathematics, 1*, 3–8.

Freudenthal, H. (1971). Geometry between the devil and the deep sea. *Educational Studies in Mathematics, 3*, 413–435.

Freudenthal, H. (1973). *Mathematics as an educational task*. Dordrecht, the Netherlands: Reidel.

Freudenthal, H. (1983). *Didactical phenomenology of mathematical structures*. Dordrecht, the Netherlands: Kluwer.

Freudenthal, H. (1991). *Revisiting mathematics education: China lectures*. Dordrecht, the Netherlands: Kluwer.

Gravemeijer, K. P. E. (1991). An instruction-theoretical reflection on the use of manipulatives. In L. Streefland (Ed.), *Realistic mathematics education in primary school* (pp. 57–76). Utrecht, the Netherlands: Freudenthal Institute.

Gravemeijer, K. P. E. (1994). *Developing realistic mathematics education*. Utrecht, the Netherlands: CD-β Press/Freudenthal Institute, Utrecht University.

Gravemeijer, K. P. E. (1997). Mediating between concrete and abstract. In T. Nunes & P. Bryant (Eds.), *Learning and teaching mathematics: An international perspective*. Hove, UK: Psychology Press.

Gravemeijer, K. P. E. (2005). What makes mathematics so difficult, and what can we do about it? In L. Santos, A. P. Canavarro, & J. Brocardo (Eds.), *Educação matemática: Caminhos e encruzilhadas* (pp. 83–101). Lisbon, Portugal: Associação de Professores de Matemática (APM).

Gravemeijer, K. P. E., & Doorman, M. (1999). Context problems in realistic mathematics education: A calculus course as an example. *Educational Studies in Mathematics, 39*, 111–129.

Guerreiro, H. G., & Serrazina, L. (2014). Contributos de um projeto de turma para o design de tarefas [Contributions of a class project for the design of tasks]. In J. Brocardo, A. M. Boavida, C. Delgado, E. Santos, F. Mendes, J. Duarte, M. Baía, & M. Figueiredo (Eds.), *Tarefas matemáticas: Livro de Atas do Encontro de Investigação em Educação Matemática (EIEM2014)* (pp. 81–93). Lisbon, Portugal: SPIEM.

Guerreiro, H. G., & Serrazina, L. (2015). A construção do conceito de número racional através de múltiplas representações [The construction of the concept of rational number through multiple representations]. In L. Santos, M. V. Pires, R. T. Ferreira, A. Domingos, C. Martins, H. Martinho, I. Vale, N. Amado, S. Carreira, & T. Pimentel (Eds.), *Investigação em educação matemática: Representações matemáticas* (pp. 99–113). Lisbon, Portugal: SPIEM.

Keijzer, R. (2003). *Teaching formal mathematics in primary education: Fraction learning as a mathematising process*. Utrecht, the Netherlands: CD-β Press/Freudenthal Institute, Utrecht University.

Kraemer, J., & Paardekooper, E. (1998). Développement des connaissance et compétences des élèves et des professeurs dans un contexte de soutien des apprentissages [Development of knowledge and competences of teachers in a context of supporting learning]. In P. Abrantes, J. Porfírio, & M. Baía (Eds.), *The interactions in the mathematics classroom. Proceedings of the CIEAEM 49* (pp. 63–75). Setubal, Portugal: Escola superior de Educacao de Setubal.

Kraemer, J. M., & van Benthem, M. (2011). *Diagnosticeren en plannen in de bovenbouw [Diagnosing and planing in teaching]*. Arnhem, the Netherlands: Cito.

Mata-Pereira, J., & Ponte, J. P. (2013). Desenvolvendo o raciocínio matemático: Generalização e justificação no estudo das inequações [Developing mathematical reasoning: Generalisation and justification in the study of inequalities]. *Boletim GEPEM, 62,* 17–31.

Matos, J. M. L. (1984). *Van Hiele levels of preservice primary teachers in Portugal*. Master's dissertation University of Boston.

Mendes, F. (2012). *A aprendizagem da multiplicação numa perspetiva de desenvolvimento do sentido de número: Um estudo com alunos do 1.º ciclo* [Learning multiplication in a perspective of developing number sense: A study with grade 1 students] (Doctoral thesis). Lisbon, Portugal: University of Lisbon.

Mestre, C., & Oliveira, H. (2013). Um percurso na generalização matemática: Uma experiência de ensino no 4.º ano [A journey in mathematical generalisation: A teaching experiment at grade 4]. In L. Santos, A. Domingos, I. Vale, M. J. Saraiva, M. Rodrigues, M. C. Costa, & R. A. T. Ferreira (Eds.), *Investigação em Educação Matemática 2013: Raciocínio Matemático* (pp. 254–276). Lisbon, Portugal: SPIEM.

Mestrinho, N., & Oliveira, H. (2012). A integração do tangram na aula de geometria: Uma primeira abordagem ao conceito de área na formação inicial de professores dos primeiros anos [The integration of the tangram in the geometry classroom: A first study of the concept of area in elementary school teachers' initial education]. In A. P. Canavarro, L. Santos, A. M. Boavida, H. Oliveira, L. Menezes, & S. Carreira (Eds.), *Práticas de ensino da Matemática: Atas do Encontro de Investigação em Educação Matemática* (pp. 529–540). Lisbon, Portugal: SPIEM.

Ministério da Educação (ME). (2007). *Programa de matemática do ensino básico (Mathematics curriculum of basic education)*. Lisbon, Portugal: DGIDC.

Monteiro, C., & Pinto, H. (2006). A aprendizagem dos números racionais [Learning rational numbers]. *Quadrante, 14*(1), 89–108.

Pereira, M., & Saraiva, M. J. (2013). Um modelo de ensino-aprendizagem de parâmetros em funções: Um estudo com alunos do ensino secundário [A model of teaching and learning parameters in functions: A study with secondary school students]. In L. Santos, A. Domingos, I. Vale, M. J. Saraiva, M. Rodrigues, M. C. Costa, & R. A. T. Ferreira (Eds.), *Investigação em Educação Matemática 2013: Raciocínio Matemático* (pp. 297–317). Lisbon, Portugal: SPIEM.

Pimenta, C., & Saraiva, M. J. (2013). O desenvolvimento do pensamento algébrico nos primeiros anos do ensino básico [The development of algebraic thinking at the first years of basic education]. In L. Santos, A. Domingos, I. Vale, M. J. Saraiva, M. Rodrigues, M. C. Costa, & R. A. T. Ferreira (Eds.), *Investigação em Educação Matemática 2013: Raciocínio Matemático* (pp. 318–341). Lisbon, Portugal: SPIEM.

Pinheiro, A., & Carreira, S. (2013). O desenvolvimento do raciocínio geométrico no tópico triângulos e quadriláteros [The development of geometrical reasoning in the topic of triangles and quadrilaterals]. In L. Santos, A. Domingos, I. Vale, M. J. Saraiva, M. Rodrigues, M. C. Costa, & R. A. T. Ferreira (Eds.), *Investigação em Educação Matemática 2013: Raciocínio Matemático* (pp. 146–169). Lisbon, Portugal: SPIEM.

Pinto, H. (2011). *O desenvolvimento do sentido da multiplicação e da divisão de números racionais* [The development of multiplication and division sense of rational numbers] (Doctoral thesis). Lisbon, Portugal: University of Lisbon.

Ponte, J. P. (2005). Álgebra no currículo escolar [Algebra in the school curriculum]. *Educação e Matemática, 85*, 36–42.

Ponte, J. P., & Quaresma, M. (2011). Abordagem exploratória com representações múltiplas na aprendizagem dos números racionais: Um estudo de desenvolvimento curricular [Exploratory approach with multiple representations in learning rational numbers: A curriculum development study]. *Quadrante, 20*(1), 53–81.

Ponte, J. P., & Quaresma, M. (2014a). Representações e processos de raciocínio na comparação e ordenação de números racionais numa abordagem exploratória [Representations and reasoning processes in comparting and ordering rational numbers in an exploratory approach]. *BOLEMA, 28*(50), 1464–1484.

Ponte, J. P., & Quaresma, M. (2014b). Representações e raciocínio matemático dos alunos na resolução de tarefas envolvendo números racionais numa abordagem exploratória [Representations and mathematical reasoning in solving tasks involving rational numbers in an exploratory approach]. *Uni-Pluri/Versidad, 14*(2), 102–114.

Ponte, J. P., Branco, N., & Matos, A. (2008). O simbolismo e o desenvolvimento do pensamento algébrico dos alunos [Simbolism and development of students' algebraic thinking]. *Educação e Matemática, 100*, 89–95.

Ponte, J. P., Mata-Pereira, J., & Henriques, A. (2012). O raciocínio matemático nos alunos do ensino básico e do ensino superior [Mathematical reasoning in basic and higher education students]. *Praxis Educativa, 7*(2), 355–377.

Quaresma, M., & Ponte, J. P. (2012). Compreensão dos números racionais, comparação e ordenação: O caso de Leonor [Understanding rational numbers, comparing and ordering]. *Interacções, 20*, 37–69.

Rocha, I., & Menino, H. (2009). Desenvolvimento do sentido do número na multiplicação. Um estudo de caso com crianças de 7/8 anos [Development of number sense in multiplication: A case study with 7/8 years old children]. *Relime, 12*(1), 103–134.

Rodrigues, M. (2010). *El sentido del número: Una experiencia de aprendizaje y desarrollo en educación infantile* [Number sense: A learning and development experience in infant education] (Doctoral thesis). Universidad de Extremadura, Spain.

Silvestre, A. I., & Ponte, J. P. (2012). Proporcionalidade directa no 6.º ano de escolaridade: Uma abordagem exploratória [Direct proportion at grade 6: An exploratory approach]. *Interacções, 20*, 137–158.

Streefland, L. (1986). Rational analysis of realistic mathematics education as a theoretical source for psychology: Fractions as a paradigm. *European Journal of Psychology of Education, 1*(2), 67–82.

Streefland, L. (1991). Fractions an integrated perspective. In L. Streefland (Ed.), *Realistic mathematics education in primary school* (pp. 93–118). Utrecht, the Netherlands: CD-ß Press/Freudenthal Institute, Utrecht University.

Streefland, L. (1993). Fractions: A realistic approach. In T. Carpenter, E. Fennema, & T. Romberg (Eds.), *Rational numbers, an integration for research* (pp. 289–327). Mahwah, NJ: Laurence Erlbaum.

Streefland, L. (2003). Learning from history for teaching in the future. *Educational Studies in Mathematics, 54*, 37–62.

Treffers, A. (1987). *Three dimensions. A model of goal and theory description in mathematics instruction—The Wiskobas project.* Dordrecht, the Netherlands: D. Reidel.

Treffers, A. (1991). Didactical background of a mathematics program for primary education. In L. Streefland (Ed.), *Realistic mathematics education in primary school* (pp. 21–56). Utrecht, the Netherlands: CD-ß Press/Freudenthal Institute, Utrecht University.

Treffers, A., & Buys, K. (2008). Grade 2 (and 3)—Calculation up to 100. In M. van den Heuvel-Panhuizen (Ed.), *Children learn mathematics. A learning-teaching trajectory with intermediate attainment targets for calculation with whole numbers in primary school* (pp. 61–88). Rotterdam, the Netherlands: Sense.

Treffers, A., & Goffree, F. (1985). Rational analysis of realistic mathematics education: The Wiskobas program. In L. Streefland (Ed.), *Proceedings of the Ninth International Conference for the Psychology of Mathematics Education* (pp. 97–122). Utrecht, the Netherlands: OW&OC, Utrecht University.

Van den Heuvel-Panhuizen, M. (1996). *Assessment and realistic mathematics education.* Utrecht, the Netherlands: CD-β Press/Freudenthal Institute, Utrecht University.

Van den Heuvel-Panhuizen, M. (1998). Realistic mathematics education: Work in progress. In T. Breiteig & G. Brekke (Eds.), *Theory into practice in mathematics education. Proceedings of Norma98, Second Nordic Conference on Mathematics Education.* Kristiansand, Norway: Agder College, Research Series No. 13.

Van den Heuvel-Panhuizen, M. (2003). The didactical use of models in realistic mathematics education: An example from a longitudinal trajectory on percentage. *Educational Studies in Mathematics, 54*(1), 9–35.

Van den Heuvel-Panhuizen, M. (Ed.) (2008). *Children learn mathematics: A learning-teaching trajectory with intermediate attainment targets for calculation with whole numbers in primary school.* Rotterdam, the Netherlands: Sense.

Van den Heuvel-Panhuizen, M., & Wijers, M. M. (2005). Mathematics standards and curricula in the Netherlands. *Zentralblatt fur Didaktik der Mathematik, 37*(4), 287–307.

Van Hiele, P. M. (1984). A child's thought and geometry. In D. Fuys, D. Geddes, & R. Tischler (Eds.), *English translation of selected writings of Dina van Hiele-Geldof and Pierre M. van Hiele* (pp. 243–252). New York, NY: Brooklyn College School of Education.

Ventura, H. (2014). *A aprendizagem dos números racionais através das conexões entre as suas representações: Uma experiência de ensino no 2.º ciclo do ensino básico* [Learning rational numbers through the connections among their representations: An experience at 2nd cycle of basic education] (Doctoral thesis). Lisbon, Portugal: University of Lisbon.

Webb, D., Boswinkel, N., & Dekker, T. (2008). Beneath the tip of the iceberg: Using representations to support pupil understanding. *Mathematics Teaching in the Middle School, 14*(2), 110–113.

Chapter 13
Supporting Mathematical Learning Processes by Means of Mathematics Conferences and Mathematics Language Tools

Christoph Selter and Daniel Walter

Abstract In recent decades, the instructional theory of Realistic Mathematics Education has exerted a powerful influence on mathematics education around the world. The idea of progressive mathematisation has gained international acceptance. In this chapter, we will illustrate the way in which we benefited from the idea of organising the teaching and learning of mathematics in keeping with this guiding principle. After some personal memories of the first author, we start by describing what we consider to be the central elements of the principle of progressive mathematisation. This is followed by a description of two methods, the mathematics conferences and mathematics language tools, for rendering the learning and teaching concepts entailed by the principle of progressive mathematisation—especially its vertical component—even more expedient and fruitful. The contribution concludes with an explanation of how we understand the term 'realistic' in Realistic Mathematics Education.

Keywords Progressive schematisation · Mathematics conferences · Language and mathematics · Individual learning processes · Co-operative learning · Mathematics language tools

13.1 The Santa Claus Problem

It must have been at the end of 1983 that the first author—at the time studying to become a primary school teacher—became aware of Adri Treffers' paper "Fortschreitende Schematisierung – ein natürlicher Weg zur schriftlichen Multiplikation und Division im 3. und 4. Schuljahr" (Treffers, 1983). Taking the multiplication of large

C. Selter (✉)
Faculty for Mathematics/IEEM, TU Dortmund, Dortmund, Germany
e-mail: christoph.selter@math.tu-dortmund.de

D. Walter
Faculty for Mathematics, Münster University, Münster, Germany
e-mail: daniel.walter@uni-muenster.de

© The Author(s) 2020   229
M. van den Heuvel-Panhuizen (ed.), *International Reflections*
on the Netherlands Didactics of Mathematics, ICME-13 Monographs,
https://doi.org/10.1007/978-3-030-20223-1_13

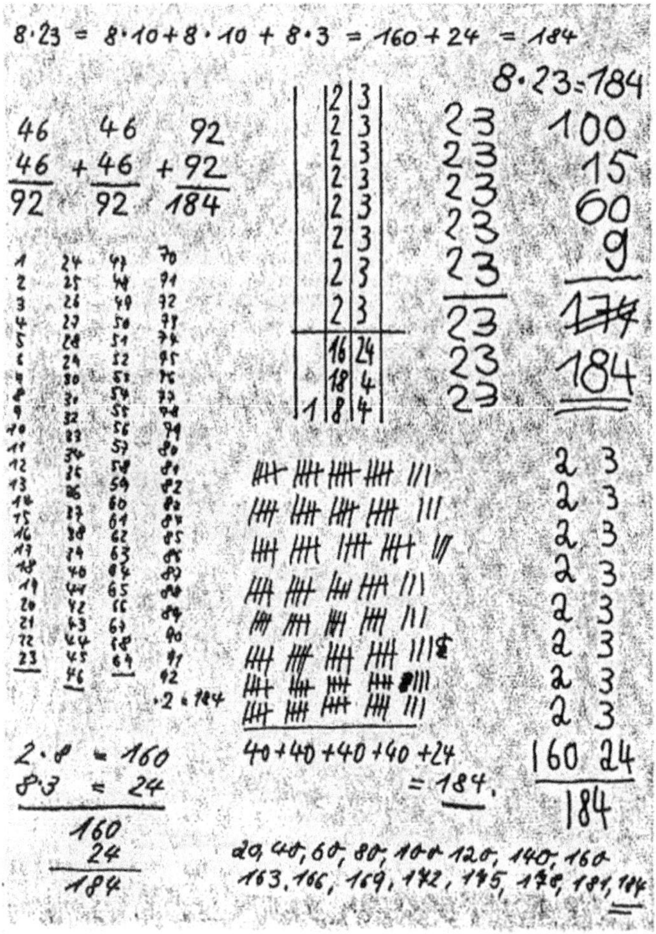

Fig. 13.1 Solutions to the Santa Claus problem

numbers as an example, this paper describes how students can be motivated to apply their individual approaches and develop them further in a purposeful manner. The starting question in the paper is: "Santa Claus has his gifts distributed in the village by eight helpers. Each has 23 parcels. How many parcels do they have altogether?"

Treffers' paper describes how eight-year-old students solved this problem using strategies they had individually developed in various ways (Fig. 13.1). The strategies naturally differed in terms of elegance and efficiency (Treffers, 1993), and therewith either represent the stages observable in the development of a single child or the heterogeneity noticeable within a learning group of students. The 'Santa Claus' problem serves as a representative example for illustrating a possible starting point of the so-called 'principle of progressive mathematisation'.

Starting from problems like this one, the various solution strategies of the students are discussed, explained, and elaborated in interactions between the students or between the teacher and the students. The students can see how other students work and thereby assess the advantages and disadvantages of different strategies (Treffers, 1991). An individual student's (mental) actions are as vitally important as his or her interaction with other students. The illustrations included in the paper are taken from a lesson where the students were not shown how to solve this type of problem based on the principles of isolating difficulties and increasing complication—as was still widespread in use in the classrooms of that time—but instead by encouraging them to develop their own approaches and then also develop them further. To put it briefly: from inventions to conventions.

Reading Treffers' paper was a key event for the first author because he realised that the principle of progressive schematisation—or progressive mathematisation, as it should preferably be called—is by no means only important for learning written calculation algorithms, but could also be considered a comprehensive, generally applicable principle for the organisation of mathematical learning or teaching processes. In the German speaking countries, within the didactics of mathematics for primary schools, progressive mathematisation is nowadays considered a guiding principle (Krauthausen & Scherer, 2007).

The principle of progressive mathematisation has naturally also undergone specific adaptations and further developments in Germany. This chapter is meant to report on them. To do this, it starts in Sect. 13.2 with a description of what the central elements of the principle of progressive mathematisation are in our opinion. Then we describe methods for making teaching/learning processes that follow the principle of progressive mathematisation even more expedient and productive.

As conversations amongst students are often not automatically task-specific and efficient, it is an important task for the teacher to stimulate and organise exchanges amongst the learners that will promote learning. In this respect, we describe the method of so-called 'mathematics conferences' in Sect. 13.3. As students occasionally find it difficult to verbalise the description and justification of mathematical facts and contexts, it is also necessary to provide them with tools for further developing their ability to express themselves in words. In this context, Sect. 13.4 describes the so-called 'mathematics language tools'. Our chapter concludes with comments on how we understand the term 'realistic' in Realistic Mathematics Education (RME).

13.2   The Guiding Principle of Progressive Mathematisation

Mathematics classes and the didactical research and development dedicated to them around the world have been inspired by the conception of RME for over four decades. This development arose from the dissatisfaction with the understanding of teaching and learning predominant in the 1960s. In the Netherlands (and not only there), mathematics was reduced to its formal character in an atomised manner, leading to an overemphasis on its structuralist aspects. Teachers taught the procedures demonstratively step-by-step, whereupon the students exhibited inflexible and reproduction-based knowledge (Van den Heuvel-Panhuizen & Drijvers, 2014).

The efforts revolving around RME and its influence on an international level laid one of the cornerstones of the constructivistic informed understanding of teaching and learning mathematics established nowadays internationally (see, e.g., Verschaffel, Greer, & De Corte, 2007; Wittmann, 2005).

Starting from Freudenthal's (1968) claim that mathematics is a human activity, the core principle of RME is that formal mathematical knowledge can be derived from students' thinking (Treffers, 1993). Learners should learn to mathematise, that is "the organising and structuring activity during which acquired knowledge and abilities are called upon in order to discover still unknown regularities, connections, structures" (Treffers, 1987, p. 247). The core principle of RME is that mathematics can be developed from personal reality. That means that formal knowledge can be developed from students' thinking (Treffers, 1993). This process should be natural and the students should contribute to the teaching/learning process as much as possible. To this end, five basic keystones have been formulated for the principle of progressive mathematisation (see, e.g., Streefland, 1990):

– Learning is a (re)constructive activity stimulated by concreteness; teaching involves the use of problems that can be realised by students (thus 'realistic' does not necessarily mean real-life).
– Learning is a long-term process moving from concreteness to abstraction; teaching involves globally guiding students from their informal, context-bound strategies to formal mathematics.
– Learning is facilitated by reflection on one's own thought processes and those of others; teaching involves encouraging students to look back and to reflect on the teaching/learning process.
– Learning is always embedded in a socio-cultural context; thus, teaching involves opportunities for communication and cooperation as in small group work or whole-class discussion.
– Learning is the construction of knowledge and skills to a structured entity; teaching involves intertwining different learning strands.

Besides these five overarching characteristics, the principle of progressive mathematisation has two interlocking components, that is, vertical and horizontal mathematisation: "In the horizontal component the way towards mathematics is paved via model formation, schematising, symbolising. The vertical sketch is concerned with mathematical processing and level raising in the structuring of the problem field under consideration" (Treffers, 1987, p. 247).

Horizontal mathematisation is hence described as a bridge from the real world to formal symbolic mathematics, while vertical mathematisation concerns activities *within* the formal symbolic realm. It is meanwhile of decisive importance that a student will only be enabled to reach a higher level of mathematics (Gravemeijer & Doorman, 1999) by way of vertical mathematisation which, amongst other aspects, includes activities devoted to reorganising, economizing and linking numerical structures (see Van den Heuvel-Panhuizen, 2002).

The distinction between horizontal and vertical mathematisation, also known as "two-way mathematisation" (Van den Heuvel-Panhuizen, 2010, p. 3), fundamentally contributes to our understanding of the RME concept while also distinguishing it from other learning and teaching approaches (see, e.g., Streefland, 1991; Treffers, 1987; Van den Heuvel-Panhuizen, 2010). There should nevertheless be no sharp distinction between horizontal and vertical mathematisation activities. That horizontal and vertical mathematisation processes can dovetail is part and parcel of the RME theory (Treffers, 1993). "The distinction between horizontal and vertical mathematizing depends on the specific situation, the person involved and his environment" (Freudenthal, 1991, p. 42).

Although RME hence attaches great value to the theoretical equality of horizontal and vertical mathematisation, there have also been phases in the development of RME where there was a tendency to focus on engaging with questions of horizontal mathematisation (see Treffers 1993; Van den Heuvel-Panhuizen, 2002). Even today, the research into vertical mathematisation appears to be paid less attention in international mathematical didactics than is the case with horizontal mathematisation (see Glade & Prediger, 2017). Therefore, the focus in this chapter will be on aspects of vertical mathematisation.

Nevertheless, it should be emphasised that the principle of progressive mathematisation in its horizontal and vertical component is paid a great deal of attention in Germany, as mentioned above. Progressive mathematisation is repeatedly referred to in research and development papers published by staff of the Institute for Development and Research in Mathematics Education in Dortmund (IEEM) (Akinwunmi, 2012; Glade, 2016; Link, 2012), and also in projects such as PIKAS[1] and KIRA,[2] which contribute to the professionalisation of teachers. This is also where further developments and adaptations to German education take place. In this chapter, we report about two adaptations of vertical mathematisation: mathematics conferences and mathematics language tools. The examples have been taken from the PIKAS project.

13.3 Using Mathematics Conferences

13.3.1 Learning to Subtract in the Number Domain up to 1000

Based on Sundermann and Selter (2012) and as a further development of Selter (1998), a concrete implementation for subtraction in the domain up to 1000 is to be described first. The third graders involved in the PIKAS project were, from their experiences in the previous school year, already familiar with various ways of calcu-

---

[1] pikas.dzlm.de (website in German).

[2] kira.dzlm.de (website in German).

Table 13.1 Possible calculation strategies

Pair of problems	Standard calculation	A clever calculation could be
$68 - 25$ and $568 - 325$	$68 - 25$ $68 - 20 - 5$ Jump strategy or $60 - 20 = 40$ $8 - 5 = 3$ $40 + 3 = 43$ Split strategy	$568 - 325$ $500 - 300 = 200$, so 243 Analogy strategy
$72 - 46$ and $872 - 546$ $95 - 32$ and $795 - 432$	Jump strategy or Split strategy	Analogy strategy
$61 - 26$ and $761 - 226$	Jump strategy or Split strategy	$60 - 25$ or $760 - 225$ Adjustment strategy
$71 - 68$ and $471 - 468$ $92 - 87$ and $792 - 587$	Jump strategy or Split strategy	$68 + \_ = 71$ or $587 + \_ = 592, +200$ Determining the difference
$142 - 99$ and $642 - 299$ $171 - 98$ and $871 - 398$	Jump strategy or Split strategy	$142 - 100 + 1$ or $871 - 400 + 2$ Auxiliary problem

lating in the domain up to 100. Now they were challenged in three activities of each several teaching hours to expand the number domain to 1000.

In the first activity, "This is how I calculate!—How do you calculate?", the students were asked to document how they calculate specific problems. To this end, the students were provided with various problems which, at least from the perspective of experienced calculators, each suggested one particular calculation strategy, based on the numbers involved (Table 13.1).[3]

The task given was: "Calculate as cleverly as possible! Write down your calculation strategies so that other children can understand them." The students were furthermore encouraged to explain their calculation strategy and justify why they had done it this way. Finally, they were asked to give their calculation strategy a name, because this would raise their awareness of how different the various calculation strategies are, and ease their communication about the various strategies.

Ronja's work (Fig. 13.2) shows that she recognised that the tens and ones of the minuend and subtrahend are close together. She calculated all the problems by turning the minuend into a round number using subtraction, then she performed the subtraction that is now easier for her to do, and finally she applied a compensation operation by adding the ones of the minuend again. At the top section of the worksheet (Fig. 13.3) the students were asked to initially think about a possible calculation strategy. Ronja noticed that in the case of $71 - 68$, the minuend is close to a ten.

The students initially worked on the task on their own, with the teacher providing individual support. Then they were encouraged to form mathematics conferences,

---

[3]For more information on the various calculation strategies, see kira.dzlm.de/062.

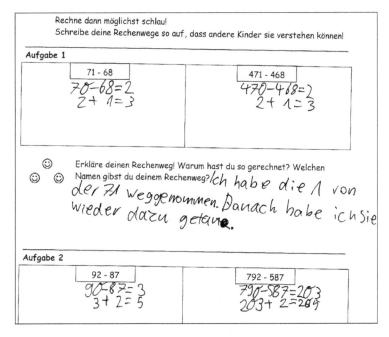

Fig. 13.2 Ronja's work (Translation: try to calculate as cleverly as possible! Write down your way of calculation so that other children can understand it!; Explain your way of calculation! Why did you calculate like that? What name do you give your way of calculation? Ronja: "I took away 1 from the 71. Subsequently I added it again.")

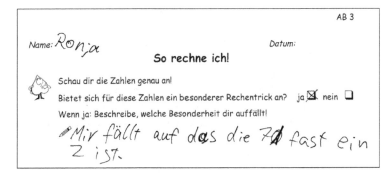

Fig. 13.3 Top section of the work sheet (Translation: take a close look at the numbers. Does a particular calculation trick suggest itself for these numbers? If yes, please describe the special thing that you notice. Ronja: "I notice that 71 is almost a ten.")

Table 13.2 Problems for Activity 3

Problem	Standard calculation	A clever calculation could be
864 − 243	864 − 200 − 40 − 3 Jump strategy or 800 − 200 = 600 60 − 40 = 20 4 − 3 = 1 600 + 20 + 1 Split strategy	–
546 − 198	Jump strategy or Split strategy	546 − 200 + 2 Auxiliary problem
917 − 458	Jump strategy or Split strategy	–
672 − 668	Jump strategy or Split strategy	668 + _ = 672 Determining the difference

a method we will describe in greater detail below, for communicating about their calculation strategies. The results of these conferences were finally presented to the entire class, attended by a discussion of why certain strategies can be cleverer than others, depending on the numerical values.

The second activity, titled "We calculate the way other children calculated", was aimed at sensitizing the students to the variety of possible calculation strategies. First, the students were involved in actively applying the various clever strategies of other students, and then they were asked to rate the strategies. The goal of the activity was not that children master all strategies. However, they should have the opportunity to encounter each of them.

Figure 13.4 again shows Ronja's work, who initially copied the strategy (a jump strategy with the help of the empty number line) applied by her classmate Jenny and then rated it as very clever. In the end, the special characteristics of the individual calculation strategies were reflected upon with the students, while also highlighting in which cases each strategy might be particularly clever. The exchange stimulated justifications why particular strategies suggested themselves for the particular problems (dependent on the numbers involved) and gave students the opportunity to identify and name less clever calculation strategies.

The third activity, titled "We calculate as cleverly as possible!", was focused on the independent grading and assessing of students' own strategies and those of others in terms of efficiency. Thanks to the various numbers used in the problems, each problem suggested a specific calculation strategy (Table 13.2).

The students were also allowed to follow their own preferences here again (if possible, with giving a reason for this). The worksheets below illustrate that the students were sensitised to the variety of possible calculation strategies by trying them out, and they were also increasingly better able to name them (Fig. 13.5).

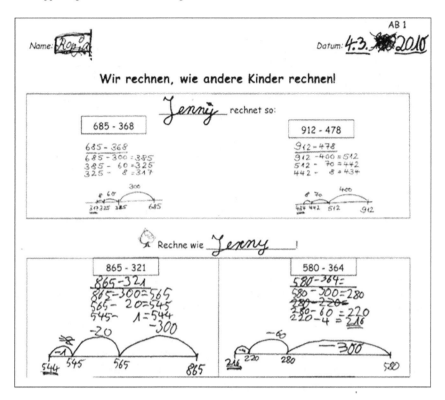

Fig. 13.4 Ronja's work (Translation: We calculate the way other children calculate. Jenny calculated in this way. Calculate like Jenny.)

The students initially worked on their own. Lara-Maria described her approach with the help of Dienes blocks. She also confirmed the statement that for $864 - 243$ a particular calculation strategy suggested itself. She justified this as follows:

> All the numbers (i.e., digits) of the first number are greater than those of the second number, which is why one can easily subtract the hundreds from the hundreds, the tens from the tens and the ones from the ones.

For the second problem she noted:

> The one number is very close to the next hundred, which is why one can very easily apply the change-trick.

She indicated with arrows how she converted the $546 - 198$ problem into $548 - 200$.

Afterwards, the students were asked to communicate in mathematics conferences with their classmates about their calculation strategies and give reasons why they thought their calculation strategy was clever. In the end, the students wrote for one or several problems a note about a so-called 'particularly clever strategy'. This note

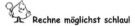

Rechne möglichst schlau!

Schau dir die Zahlen genau an! Bietet sich für diese Zahlen ein besonderer Rechentrick an? Rechne dann möglichst schlau!
Erkläre deine Rechenwege so, dass andere Kinder sie verstehen können!

864 - 243 = 521 (handwritten figures)	Bietet sich für diese Zahlen ein besonderer Rechentrick an? ja ☒ nein ☐ Erkläre deinen Rechenweg! *Weil Bei der ersten Zahl sind alle Zahlen größer als bei der zweiten Zahl deswegen kann mann gut Hunderter minus Hunderter Zehner Minus Zehner und einer Minus einer rechnen*
546 - 198 = 348 $546 - 198 =$ $548 - 200 = 348$	Bietet sich für diese Zahlen ein besonderer Rechentrick an? ja ☒ nein ☐ Erkläre deinen Rechenweg! *Die eine Zahl ist sehr nah an dem nächsten Hunderter deswegen kann mann sehr gut den verändern gleich trick machen nemehn*

Fig. 13.5 Lara-Maria's work (Translation of the instruction: Look at the numbers! Does a particular calculation trick come into your mind for these numbers? Then, calculate as cleverly as possible! Write down your calculation strategies so that other children can understand them.)

was meant to be discussed in class in the reflection phase. In this phase, individual students or group of students could visualise, explain and justify their results by putting their notes on the board underneath the corresponding problem.

13.3.2 Task-Related Exchange with the Help of Mathematics Conferences

In the activity previously described, the task-related discussion between the students in mathematics conferences acted as a central activity for joint learning (see also, Anders & Oerter, 2009; Götze, 2007; Sundermann, 1999). A mathematics conference is understood as a meeting of students in which in small (heterogenic) groups individual solution strategies of students are presented and reflected on (see Sundermann & Selter, 1995). However, this does not mean that all teamwork can immediately be called a mathematics conference. Important is that the students are challenged to describe and justify their approach to solving a problem, to explain their discoveries, and to follow the thought processes of the other students.

This task-related exchange benefits all students, so the mathematics conference has a dual function. On the one hand the students who act as an author (author-student) benefit by verbalising their own thought processes and attempting to present them understandably. On the other hand, students who are the listeners (listener-student), are simultaneously actively involved as well by being asked to trace and compare the approaches of the students who describe their strategies. In this way, they can provide the author-students criteria-led feedback.

In contrast to having only a reflection phase in a whole-class setting, this form of cooperation in small groups steps up the verbal involvement (and engagement with the posed problem) of the individual student and also offers weaker and less communicative students a chance to speak. Of course, organising mathematics conferences will not render the reflection phase in the whole-class setting superfluous. Discussions in whole-class remain important. The mathematics conferences with the small groups can be a particularly good preparation for them. By having the backing of their small group quieter students will possibly be encouraged to articulate their thoughts here as well.

Mathematics conferences can already be introduced from the first year of school. The essential requirement for making this method successful is the quality of the problem that is used. The problem needs to be demanding enough and should permit various ways of thinking and solving it, so that an exchange is also meaningful from the perspective of the students.

13.3.3 Tools for Organising Mathematics Conferences

The ability to take part in mathematics conferences, which means being able to explain your own results and approaches, and to understand the ideas and solution strategies of others, will not come about in the students all by itself. Like any other method, a mathematics conference also needs to be introduced to become a common method in class. Providing students with an overview poster, titled "Solving mathematics problems together" (see Fig. 13.6) can help them to become familiar with this method. The guideline makes a distinction in three phases.

In Phase 1 (the I-phase) the students have enough time for their individual work and for describing their own solution strategy, so that they will be able to engage in an exchange about their approach afterwards. They write down their thoughts about solving the problem and then try to present them in a manner that the other students can understand. When a student has completely solved and understandably explained the given problem from his or her perspective or possibly wants to have support from the other students, he or she registers for the mathematics conference by writing down his or her name in a list that is displayed in the classroom on paper or on the blackboard. As soon as three students—as a rule—have registered, they convene for a mathematics conference. The exchange can begin as soon as the group has come together in a quiet place.

In Phase 2 (the You-phase) a joint elaboration of guiding questions is recommended in order to prevent mathematics conferences from ending up in an unstructured stringing together of information or to avoid that students get lost in details. The structuring can be provided by the poster titled "Tips for the mathematics conference" (Fig. 13.7) available to the students. The tips subdivide the progress of

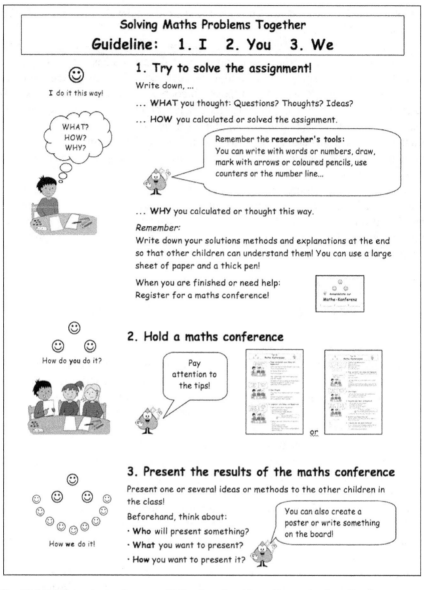

Fig. 13.6 Mathematics conference guideline (translated from German by the authors)

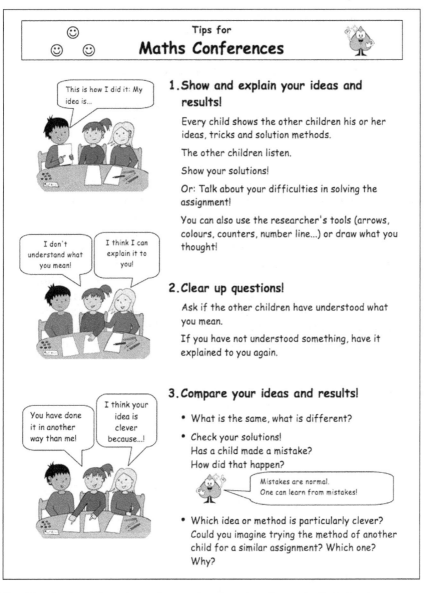

Fig. 13.7 Tips for mathematics conferences (translated from German by the authors)

the mathematics conference into several sections and thus furnish the students with orientation aids and examples for possible guiding questions:

– How has the author-student solved the problem?
– Why did he or she proceed in this way?
– Is the attempt at explanation by the author-student understandable?

– Is the selected approach clever?
– Who has chosen another route? What is different about it?
– ....

If asking these kinds of guiding questions has become a natural habit of the students, this habit can contribute to structuring the conversation and hence to students' learning from each other. The questions can deliberately direct the students' attention from their individual approaches to other ways of looking at things, and can stimulate a critical and constructive questioning of the solution strategies amongst the students.

Although the responsibility for a mathematics conference is largely in the hands of the students, adequate support by the teacher is nonetheless of vital importance. The teacher, in the role of moderator, can keep the conversation going and cognitively activate the students by way of targeted interventions. In this way, the teacher contributes to the constructive progress of the mathematics conference.

If the students are not yet used to discuss their solution strategies in mathematics conferences, it can be helpful for students to reflect upon this method with other students at a meta level. An advantageous way to do this is the so-called 'fishbowl'. This means that a group of volunteers who were just about to start a mathematics conference moves to the centre of a circle of chairs. In addition to the chairs provided for the three students, there is also another empty chair with three smileys, ☺ ☺ ☹, lying on it. These can be used after the conference by the observing students in the outer circle to indicate constructive (method-related or content-related) feedback ("I liked that everyone was allowed to finalise his/her speaking" or "I find that your solution strategy is not so clever because....") and/or for giving tips ("If you also used arrows or colours in the description of your discovery packages, the other students could probably understand that better"). To ensure that discussion rules are complied, the student providing feedback is going to sit down on the empty chair.

In Phase 3 (the We-phase) the evaluation of the process and the reflection upon the results of the discussion can be finally presented in the whole-class setting. The questions formulated in the overview poster (see Fig. 13.6) about the organisation of this presentation will urge the students to prepare it in a as structured and target-oriented manner as possible.

13.4 Learning to Describe and Explain by Using Mathematics Language Tools

This section is dedicated to describing a second adaptation of the RME approach, the so-called 'mathematics language tools'. Before starting this description, we should make clear the importance that mathematics language has in German mathematics teaching as reflected in the German mathematics curricula. In the nation-wide education standards of the Standing Conference of Ministers of Education and Cultural Affairs (KMK, 2004), start from the assumption that learning mathematics involves

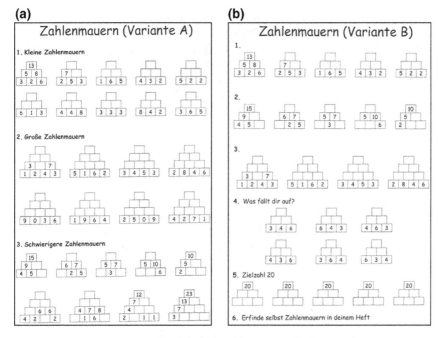

Fig. 13.8 Work sheets for number pyramids (**a** Translation worksheet on the left: Number pyramid (Variant A); 1. Small number pyramids; 2. Large number pyramids; 3. Difficult number pyramids; **b** Translation worksheet on the right: number pyramid (Variant B); 4. What do you notice?; 5. Target number 20; 6. Make your own number pyramids in your notebook)

more than the acquisition of knowledge, such as knowing multiplication tables by heart, and skills, such as completely mastering the standard way of written addition.

13.4.1 Mathematics, More Than Calculating

Besides such content-related competences, German mathematics lessons are always also meant to promote process-related competences such as arguing and presenting. The added value can be illustrated by comparing two work sheets for the so-called 'number pyramids' (see Fig. 13.8). In these number pyramids, numbers are first entered into their bottom row of bricks and then the bricks above are each filled with the sum of the bricks below. Variant A only poses problems of the same type. Hence, the focus here is on practicing addition and subtraction.

The first three tasks of Variant B are also included in Variant A, but Variant B focuses on more. In Task 4 of this worksheet, the students are asked to examine the impact of the different arrangements of 3, 4 and 6 on the other numbers in the pyramid. In Task 5, they are asked to create pyramids with the target number of 20.

And in Task 6, they are finally invited to freely invent number pyramids. This touches upon content-related as well as process-related competences.

The development of process-related competences is hence a central objective in mathematics education. It is, however, also observable that some students, for example, found it difficult to discover interdependencies between the bricks of a pyramid, describe these interdependencies or give reasons why the bricks are interdependent.

Based on these considerations, it is in our opinion essential for the design and selection of learning environments aimed at promoting process-competences as well as content-related competences that particular attention is paid to the following.

– A learning environment should be characterised by a challenging yet easily understandable problem definition(s) to ideally render the assignments accessible for every student.
– The challenging problem should lend itself to various ways of solving it (i.e., not only by means of a single approach) so that students at different levels of learning can address it in keeping with their individual skills and capabilities.
– The students should be supported to be able to adequately present their discoveries orally and in writing.

13.4.2 Sums of Consecutive Natural Numbers

How these principles can be implemented can be illustrated by the sample lesson titled "Sums of consecutive natural numbers" (see Schwätzer & Selter, 1998), which core idea is to make additions of consecutive natural numbers to reach at a particular target number—a type of problem that poses challenging difficulties for students in various grades and where the five cornerstones of the principle of progressive mathematisation (see above, Streefland, 1990) are also fulfilled because

– the assignment can be realised by students
– the assignment enables learning processes moving from concreteness to abstraction
– the students are continuously stimulated to reflect on their own thought processes and those of others
– opportunities are created for communication and cooperation in small groups or whole-class discussions, and
– the assignment supports the construction of knowledge and skills into a structured entity.

An assignment that is used in 4th grade is about finding all numbers up to 25 which can be written as the sum of consecutive natural numbers (see Schwätzer & Selter, 1998, 2000; kira.dzlm.de/171; see Table 13.3).

These numbers can be found in various ways. However, it must be noted here that the required time may vary, that not all students will be able to identify all the possible additions, and that students will initially often notate the found additions

Table 13.3 Numbers up to 25 that can be written as the sum of consecutive natural numbers

Sum	Addition with				
	2 summands	3 summands	4 summands	5 summands	6 summands
1					
2					
3	$1 + 2$				
4					
5	$2 + 3$				
6		$1 + 2 + 3$			
7	$3 + 4$				
8					
9	$4 + 5$	$2 + 3 + 4$			
10			$1 + 2 + 3 + 4$		
11	$5 + 6$				
12		$3 + 4 + 5$			
13	$6 + 7$				
14			$2 + 3 + 4 + 5$		
15	$7 + 8$	$4 + 5 + 6$		$1 + 2 + 3 + 4 + 5$	
16					
17	$8 + 9$				
18		$5 + 6 + 7$	$3 + 4 + 5 + 6$		
19	$9 + 10$				
20				$2 + 3 + 4 + 5 + 6$	
21	$10 + 11$	$6 + 7 + 8$			$1 + 2 + 3 + 4 + 5 + 6$
22			$4 + 5 + 6 + 7$		
23	$11 + 12$				
24		$7 + 8 + 9$			
25	$12 + 13$			$3 + 4 + 5 + 6 + 7$	

in an unsystematic and spontaneous manner. Experience has shown that students proceed in ever more systematic ways, and meanwhile develop various strategies, in the course of their progressive engagement with the assignment. Table 13.4 shows the repertory of strategies observed in the students (adapted from Schwätzer & Selter, 1998).

After finding numbers up to 25 which can be written as the sum of consecutive natural numbers, the objective now resides in checking and establishing

Table 13.4 Strategies for finding numbers that can be written as the sum of consecutive natural numbers

Strategy	Description	Example
1. Extension at the end	The addition is extended by the consecutive summand	$3 + 4 + 5 \rightarrow 3 + 4 + 5 + \mathbf{6}$
2. Extension at the front	The addition is extended by the previous summand	$3 + 4 + 5 \rightarrow \mathbf{2} + 3 + 4 + 5$
3. Reduction at the end	The last summand is left out	$3 + 4 + 5 \rightarrow 3 + 4$
4. Reduction at the front	The first summand is left out	$3 + 4 + 5 \rightarrow 4 + 5$
5. Increasing all	All summands are increased by one	$3 + 4 + 5 \rightarrow 4 + 5 + 6$
6. Decreasing all	All summands are decreased by one	$3 + 4 + 5 \rightarrow 2 + 3 + 4$
7. Starting with the next natural number	The first summand is the consecutive natural number of the last summand from the previous addition	$2 + 3 + 4 \rightarrow$ e.g., $5 + 6 + 7$
8. Starting with the precursor	The last summand of the new addition is the 'precursor' of the previous addition	$\mathbf{7} + 8 + 9 \rightarrow 2 + 3 + 4 + 5 + \mathbf{6}$
9. Starting with the last summand	The first summand is same as the last summand of the previous addition	$3 + 4 + 5 \rightarrow$ e.g., $5 + 6$
10. Starting with the addition	The first summand is the sum of the previous addition	$3 + 4 + 5 \rightarrow$ e.g., $12 + 13$
11. Analysing the first summands	Looking for which number has not been used as the first summand	$3 + 4 + 5 = 12$, e.g., $2 + 3 + 4 = 9$ $5 + 6 + 7 = 18$
12. Combinations of different strategies	Consecutively use of (different or equal) strategies, e.g., "extension at the end" and afterwards "reduction at the front"		$3 +$	$4 + 5$	
		$\rightarrow$	$3 +$	$4 + 5 + 6$
		$\rightarrow$		$4 + 5 + 6$

the completeness. Three approaches are generally observable for this. The first and most systematic strategy is starting with checking the first summand and followed by the possible number of summands $[1 + 2]$, $[1 + 2 + 3]$, $[1 + 2 + 3 + 4, \ldots]$, $[2 + 3]$, $[2 + 3 + 4]$, etcetera). The second strategy is when students primarily focus on the number of summands and only later take into account the variable of the first summand $(1 + 2, 2 + 3, 3 + 4, \ldots, 1 + 2 + 3, \ldots)$. In this way, the focus is first on all additions with two summands, then on those featuring three, four and finally five summands. The summands can then be presented in an ascending manner (see Fig. 13.9). In the third strategy, the focus is on the results of the additions. In this strategy, the

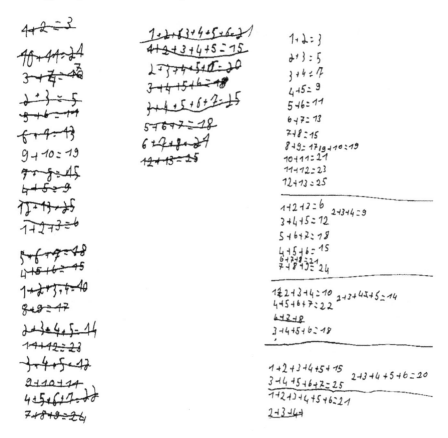

Fig. 13.9 Establishing completeness, sorted by the number of summands

students check whether each sum is reached by comparing the additions they found with the results shown in Table 13.3. This latter strategy may be effective, but cannot be considered as desirable, because the students only compare results and do not invent a systematic procedure for checking the results.

13.4.3 Mathematics Language Tools

A number of students will need support for describing how to find numbers that can be written as the sum of consecutive numbers and giving reason to be sure that they found them all. Even if the students are able to find all the additions and can develop a systematic approach for finding them all, this does not necessarily mean that they can always express their way of working and their 'proof' in a manner which is comprehensible to their classmates and the teacher.

> # Consecutive natural numbers
>
> ## 1 + 2 + 3 = 6
>
> 1st summand   2nd summand   3rd summand   Sum of three

Fig. 13.10 Lexical store for working with consecutive natural numbers (translated from German by the authors)

These difficulties are normal and can, among other things, be traced back to the fact that students resort to the language they primarily use in everyday life. Just as most students will not learn multiplication tables or standard algorithms without any further support, they will also not automatically acquire competences in describing strategies and giving reasons why using this results in all possible additions.

In our opinion, it is therefore helpful to offer the students language structures in agreement with the so-called 'scaffold' approach (see for more information, Gibbons, 2002, 2006), which can serve to support the description of things they noticed (Götze, 2015). The promotion of a specific technical language can be approached at two levels. Besides the communication in the teaching situation (micro-scaffolding) is essential, elements for advancing the technical language are in the planning of the lessons (macro-scaffolding) are vital as well. The possibilities of macro-scaffolding will be addressed below by way of the sample lesson, titled "Sums of consecutive natural numbers".

Agreement on a common language is already decisive in the introductory stage. What suggests itself for this is the creation of so-called 'lexical stores' which include frequently used terms that can then be applied when working on an assignment. This is in no way meant to prescribe a normatively defined use of language to the students. The objective rather implies establishing a consensus for mutual communication that both is based on the students' previous language skills and also is technically adequate.

It is advisable for an initial orientation to name the assignments' central mathematical objects with corresponding technical terms in a joint effort with the students. Naming the objects as specifically as possible is particularly important for this. In the example shown in Fig. 13.10, simply calling the numbers to be added "1st, 2nd and 3rd number" was deliberately not used, because the use of "1st, 2nd and 3rd summand" directly creates a closeness to the addition which is of relevance for this assignment. The same should also be considered for the sum of the addition. In line with the deliberations above, this could for example be labelled as a 'sum of three' (in German this is called 'Dreiersumme').

In building up to the terms of mathematical objects, it can also be helpful to integrate the names and anchor examples of the individual strategies step-by-step, along with formulation aids (see Fig. 13.11).

These words can help you:

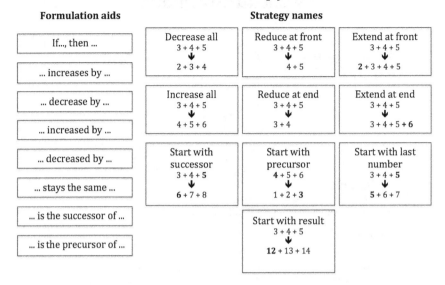

Fig. 13.11 Formulation aids and anchor examples of strategies for sums of consecutive natural numbers (translated from German by the authors)

These formulation aids can be used to support students when they describe their discoveries and the causal relationships in technical terms. It is, for example, conceivable that a student who repeatedly applies the increase-all strategy in the addition of consecutive natural numbers with three summands initially discovers changes in the sum, and will then base his or her description on the offered mathematics language tools. This could help to establish a reason like "If all three summands are increased by 1 each, the sum of them will increase by 3." Applying the decrease-all strategy could conversely enable the statement: "The sum is decreased by 3 if every summand is decreased by 1."

A further variant for promoting technical language in mathematics instruction can consist of analysing series of assignments concerning adding consecutive natural numbers and having predefined descriptions rated by the students. The example in Fig. 13.12 shows the mathematical terms required by students for being able to provide a suitable assessment.

Another option is having the students creating descriptions by their own for a series of assignments that they analyse in partner work. Further ideas for the creation and embedding of mathematics language tools can be found on the website of the PIKAS project.[4] One can say in summary that the creation of a lexical store can on the one hand be helpful because the students are provided with an optional orientation for description and argumentation when working on assignments concerning the sum

---

[4]See pikas.dzlm.de/304 (website in German).

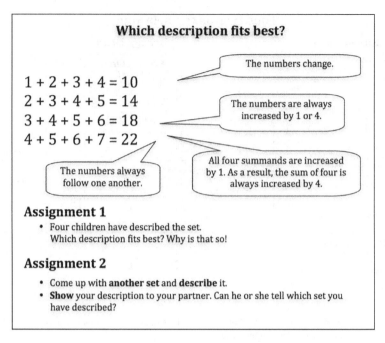

Fig. 13.12 Assigning descriptions to sums of consecutive natural numbers (translated from German by the authors)

of consecutive natural numbers. And on the other, it can also support the communication amongst the students, as well as the dialogue with the teacher. Advancing the ability to express oneself can productively stimulate the task-related exchange in the classroom.

13.5   Numbers Can Be Realistic Too

It may appear surprising at first glance that a book about Realistic Mathematics Education features a detailed description of two sample activities that in any way fail to refer to the real environment. A contradiction? Not at all. The reason that this is possible in Realistic Mathematics Education becomes apparent as soon as the Dutch meaning of 'realistic' is analysed. In Dutch, to realise also means 'zich realiseren' which refers to any process that can be realised in the mind (see Van den Heuvel-Panhuizen, 2002). Thus, the term does not necessarily refer to a reality in the objective sense. Instead, everything that can appear concrete and meaningful to a student is understood as realistic (see Streefland & Treffers, 1990).

> Therefore, in RME, problems presented to students can come from the real world but also from the fantasy world of fairy tales, or the formal world of mathematics, as long as the prob-

lems are experientially real in the student's mind. (Van den Heuvel-Panhuizen & Drijvers, 2014, p. 521)

The equal status of real-life and formal problems is also repeatedly underscored in the RME literature (see, e.g., Freudenthal 1991; Van den Heuvel-Panhuizen & Drijvers 2014). RME is nonetheless occasionally accused of attaching greater (or a too great) value to references to real life, which means that the ideas of RME's inventors are not always adequately understood (see Van den Heuvel-Panhuizen, 2002; Wittmann, 2005).

A search for possible reasons why RME is often reduced to approximations of real contexts could rely on various explanation patterns. The name alone suggests a proximity to real-life issues in various languages, as described above. The German translation of the term 'realistic' also tends to be more signified by a relation with real life than it is the case in the Dutch language.

The mechanistic and structuralistic teaching and learning concepts so rightly criticised by RME will, at best, place references to contexts at the end of the learning process, in order to apply the structures that have been formally learned before. RME attaches a different value to the role of contexts. References to contexts are additionally characterised as starting points for the process of learning mathematics. The initially acquired 'real' models serve to support the mastery of mathematical problems on a formal and symbolic level (see Gravemeijer & Doorman, 1999; Treffers & De Moor, 1996; Van den Heuvel-Panhuizen 2008). To distinguish itself from traditional teaching and learning concepts, RME has attached very great importance to the doubtlessly essential meaning of references to daily life.

But the Wiskobas[5] Bulletins, surely one of the sources of RME, or the publications of the TAL[6] project, for example, not only show that the vertical component is absolutely present, but also that mathematics (with no relation to reality) is regarded as a context of its own, as we tried to show in our contribution. RME could possibly highlight this aspect even more strongly.

As mentioned earlier on, what counts for students is the existence of a context that makes sense. The context does not have to be a real-life one. Pure numerical contexts can also be quite meaningful for students (e.g., Steinweg, 2001), or, to put it differently, 'numbers can be realistic, too!'

References

Akinwunmi, K. (2012). *Zur Entwicklung von Variablenkonzepten beim Verallgemeinern mathematischer Muster [On the development of variable concepts in the generalisation of mathematical patterns]*. Wiesbaden, Germany: Springer.

---

[5]Wiskunde op de Basisschool (Mathematics in Primary School). Wiskobas Bulletin is the journal published by the Wiskobas project from 1971 to 1981.

[6]Tussendoelen Annex Leerlijnen (Intermediate Attainment Targets and Learning Lines). In the TAL project, the so-called 'teaching-learning trajectories' for primary mathematics education have been developed (see, e.g., Van den Heuvel-Panhuizen, 2008).

Anders, K., & Oerter, A. (2009). *Forscherhefte und Mathematikkonferenzen in der Grundschule, 3 + 4 [Explorer books and mathematics conferences in primary school]*. Seelze, Germany: Kallmeyer.

Freudenthal, H. (1968). Why to teach mathematics so as to be useful? *Educational Studies in Mathematics, 1,* 3–8.

Freudenthal, H. (1991). *Revisiting mathematics education. China lectures.* Dordrecht, the Netherlands: Kluwer Academic Publishers.

Gibbons, P. (2002). *Scaffolding language, scaffolding learning. Teaching second language learners in the mainstream classroom.* Portsmouth, NH: Heinemann.

Gibbons, P. (2006). Unterrichtsgespräch und das Erlernen neuer Register in der Zweitsprache [Teaching conversation and learning new registers in the second language]. In P. Mecheril & Th. Quehl (Eds.), *Die Macht der Sprachen. Englische Perspektiven auf die mehrsprachige Schule* (pp. 10–35). Münster, Germany: Waxmann.

Glade, M. (2016). *Individuelle Prozesse der fortschreitenden Schematisierung – Empirische Rekonstruktionen zum Anteil vom Anteil [Individual processes of progressive schematisation—Empirical reconstructions to proportion of proportion].* Wiesbaden, Germany: Springer.

Glade, M., & Prediger, S. (2017). Students' individual schematization pathways—Empirical reconstructions for the case of part-of-part determination for fractions. *Educational Studies in Mathematics, 94*(2), 185–203.

Götze, D. (2007). *Mathematische Gespräche unter Kindern. Zum Einfluss sozialer Interaktion von Grundschulkindern beim Lösen komplexer Aufgaben [Mathematical talks among children. On the influence of social interaction of primary school children in solving complex tasks].* Hildesheim, Germany: Franzbecker.

Götze, D. (2015). *Sprachförderung im Mathematikunterricht [Fostering mathematical language in mathematics teaching].* Berlin, Germany: Cornelsen.

Gravemeijer, K., & Doorman, M. (1999). Context problems in Realistic Mathematics Education: A calculus course as an example. *Educational Studies in Mathematics, 39,* 111–129.

KMK. (2004). *Bildungsstandards für das Fach Mathematik im Primarbereich [Educational standards for primary mathematics].* München, Germany: Wolters-Kluwer, Luchterhand Verlag.

Krauthausen, G., & Scherer, P. (2007). *Einführung in die Mathematikdidaktik [Introduction to didactics of mathematics].* Heidelberg, Germany: Spektrum Akademischer Verlag.

Link, M. (2012). *Grundschulkinder beschreiben operative Zahlenmuster [Primary school children describe operative number patterns].* Wiesbaden, Germany: Springer Spektrum.

Schwätzer, U., & Selter, Ch. (1998). Summen von Reihenfolgezahlen - Vorgehensweisen von Viertklässlern bei einer arithmetisch substantiellen Aufgabenstellung [Sums of consecutive natural numbers—Approaches of fourth graders with an arithmetically substantive task]. *Journal für Mathematikdidaktik, 98*(2/3), 123–148.

Schwätzer, U., & Selter, Ch. (2000). Plusaufgaben mit Reihenfolgezahlen – Eine Unterrichtsreihe für das 4. bis 6. Schuljahr [Addition problems with consecutive natural numbers—A series of lessons for the 4th to 6th school year]. *Mathemathische Unterrichtspraxis, 2,* 28–37.

Selter, C. (1998). Building on children's mathematics—A teaching experiment in grade 3. *Educational Studies in Mathematics, 36,* 1–27.

Steinweg, A. S. (2001). *Zur Entwicklung des Zahlenmusterverständnisses bei Kindern [On the development of children's concept of number patterns].* Münster, Germany: LIT Verlag.

Streefland, L. (1990). Free productions in teaching and learning mathematics. In K. Gravemeijer, M. van den Heuvel-Panhuizen, & L. Streefland (Eds.), *Contexts, free productions, tests and geometry in Realistic Mathematics Education* (pp. 33–52). Utrecht, the Netherlands: OW&OC, Utrecht University.

Streefland, L. (1991). *Fractions in Realistic Mathematics Education.* Dordrecht, the Netherlands: Kluwer Academics Publishers.

Streefland, L., & Treffers, A. (1990). Produktiver Rechen-Mathematik-Unterricht [Productive mathematics teaching]. *Journal für Mathematikdidaktik, 90*(4), 297–322.

Sundermann, B. (1999). Rechentagebücher und Rechenkonferenzen. Für Strukturen im offenen Unterricht [Math diaries and math conferences. For structures in open learning]. *Grundschule, 1,* 48–50.

Sundermann, B., & Selter, C. (1995). Halbschriftliches Rechnen auf eigenen Wegen [Informal addition and subtraction on own ways]. In G. N. Müller & E Ch. Wittmann (Eds.), *Mit Kindern rechnen* (pp. 165–178). Frankfurt, Germany: Arbeitskreis Grundschule.

Sundermann, B., & Selter, Ch. (2012). Halbschriftliches Subtrahieren auf eigenen Wegen [Informal subtraction on own ways]. In G. N. Müller, Ch. Selter, & E Ch. Wittmann (Eds.), *Zahlen, Muster und Strukturen – Spielräume für aktives Lernen und Üben* (pp. 201–208). Leipzig, Germany: Klett.

Treffers, A. (1983). Fortschreitende Schematisierung. Ein natürlicher Weg zur schriftlichen Multiplikation und Division im 3. und 4. Schuljahr [Progressive schematisation. A natural way to written multiplication and division in grade 3 and 4]. *Mathematik lehren, 1,* 16–20.

Treffers, A. (1987). *Three dimensions. A model of goal and theory description in mathematics instruction—The Wiskobas project.* Dordrecht, the Netherlands: D. Reidel Publishing Company.

Treffers, A. (1991). Didactical background of a mathematics program for primary education. In L. Streefland (Ed.), *Realistic Mathematics Education in primary school – On the occasion of the opening of the Freudenthal Institute* (pp. 21–56). Utrecht, the Netherlands: CD-ß Press/Freudenthal Institute, Utrecht University.

Treffers, A. (1993). Wiskobas and Freudenthal – Realistic Mathematics Education. *Educational Studies in Mathematics, 25,* 89–108.

Treffers, A., & De Moor, E. (1996). Realistischer Mathematikunterricht in den Niederlanden [Realistic mathematics education in the Netherlands]. *Grundschulunterricht, 43*(6), 16–19.

Van den Heuvel-Panhuizen, M. (2002). Realistic Mathematics Education as work in progress. In F.-L. Lin (Ed.), *Common sense in mathematics education. Proceedings of 2001 The Netherlands and Taiwan Conference on Mathematics Education, Taipei, Taiwan* (pp. 1-42). Taipei, Taiwan: National Taiwan Normal University.

Van den Heuvel-Panhuizen, M. (Ed.). (2008). *Children learn mathematics. A learning-teaching trajectory with intermediate attainment targets for calculation with whole numbers in primary school.* Rotterdam, the Netherlands/Taipei: Sense Publishers.

Van den Heuvel-Panhuizen, M. (2010). Reform under attack – Forty years of working on better mathematics education thrown on the scrapheap? No way! In L. Sparrow, B. Kissane & C. Hurst (Eds.), *Proceedings of the 33rd Annual Conference of the Mathematics Education Research Group of Australasia* (pp. 1–25). Fremantle, Australia: MERGA.

Van den Heuvel-Panhuizen, M., & Drijvers, P. (2014). Realistic Mathematics Education. In S. Lerman (Ed.), *Encyclopedia of mathematics education* (pp. 521–525). Dordrecht, the Netherlands: Springer.

Verschaffel, L., Greer, B., & De Corte, E. (2007). Whole number concepts and operations. In F. K. Lester (Ed.), *Second handbook of research on mathematics teaching and learning* (pp. 557–629). Charlotte, NC: Information Age Publishing.

Wittmann, E Ch. (2005). Realistic Mathematics Education, past and present. *Nieuw Archief voor Wiskunde, 5/6*(4), 294–296.

Chapter 14
Reinventing Realistic Mathematics Education at Berkeley—Emergence and Development of a Course for Pre-service Teachers

Dor Abrahamson, Betina Zolkower and Elisa Stone

Abstract A central principle of Realistic Mathematics Education (RME) is that learners experience guided opportunities to reconstruct cultural practices and artefacts in the course of attempting to solve engaging problems using emerging resources as structuring tools. The same principle plays out at the meta level, across ages, geography, and functions, where instructors experience opportunities to reinvent RME as they adapt its principles to satisfy specific design constraints and local needs. This chapter recounts a collaborative effort to create at the Graduate School of Education, University of California, Berkeley, graduate and undergraduate courses for pre-service mathematics teachers that incorporates tenets of RME, while accommodating to prescribed and emerging constraints of local contexts, such as stipulation of federal funding, as well as the collective histories and prior schooling experiences of pre-service teachers, most of whom are encountering this didactical approach for the first time.

Keywords Course development · Mathematics education · Pre-service teachers · Problem solving · Undergraduate

D. Abrahamson (✉)
Graduate School of Education, University of California, Berkeley, USA
e-mail: dor@berkeley.edu

B. Zolkower
Secondary Education, Brooklyn College, City University of New York, New York, USA
e-mail: zolkowerbetina@gmail.com

E. Stone
Cal Teach Program, University of California, Berkeley, USA
e-mail: emstone@berkeley.edu

© The Author(s) 2020
M. van den Heuvel-Panhuizen (ed.), *International Reflections on the Netherlands Didactics of Mathematics*, ICME-13 Monographs,
https://doi.org/10.1007/978-3-030-20223-1_14

255

14.1 Reinventing Realistic Mathematics Education at Tel Aviv University: Dor's Story

The story begins in the fall of 1992 when I, Dor Abrahamson enrolled as a graduate student in the cognitive psychology master's programme at Tel Aviv University. Having served as a 'big brother' in Jerusalem, taught enrichment classes in the periphery, and enjoyed some circumscribed adventures in designing instructional devices, I arrived with a deep humanistic conviction that children's prospects could be greater than what educational systems offer. I was astonished by the epistemic abyss between students' natural perceptual sensitivities to the phenomenal world and their confusion over mathematical propositions that model the very same phenomena.

Mathematics learning, I believed, should always begin from situated sensorimotor experiences. There should be some engaging activity that gives rise to a surprising problem; and through tackling this problem with available resources, the student should arrive at new insights. Throughout, the teacher facilitates this activity by highlighting relevant elements of the situation, providing these resources that productively problematise the child's judgments, shaping the child's reflection on the experience, and supporting a formulation of the insight in cultural structures that mediate mathematical practices.

During the second year of my studies, I chose to focus my thesis on the early development of multiplicative concepts. In particular, I was looking to evaluate empirically an activity I had previously created for students to ground the concept of fractions in proportional judgement of geometrically similar images. The activity involved an elongated wooden contraption with a stretchable rubber ruler that enabled students to measure the heights of vertically oriented parallel elements in pictures they had judged as 'the same.' For example, by stretching the ruler we find that Danny and Snowman standing side by side are 2 and 3 units tall, respectively, whether in the small, middle-sised, or large prints (see Fig. 14.1).

Yet, if we do not stretch the ruler and keep the small units from the small picture on the left to measure the heights in the other pictures, then the heights of the three pictures would measure at 2 and 3, 4 and 6, and 6 and 9. In particular, the difference between Danny and Snowman's heights then measures as 1, 2, and 3 units, respectively. I was interested in understanding whether or not children's tacit perceptual expectations ('same difference') might cause cognitive conflict with the normative quantification routines ('different differences'!) and if, somehow, resolving this conflict may support students' articulated understanding of proportional equivalence as an entry into the multiplicative conceptual field.

My case studies had suggested that, indeed, children naturally expect pictorial identity to imply uniform measures: "If it is the same picture, then the heights should be the same, too." They were invariably befuddled when I pointed out that the absolute differences between these measured heights are different across the images: "If these are the same pictures, then how can the difference be different?" And yet, then they would reason: "The bigger the picture, the bigger the difference!" This insight, which much later I would learn to theorize either as a hypostatic abstraction,

Fig. 14.1 A 'photograph' of Danny and Snowman is printed in three different sizes; they always measure as 2 and 3 units tall, respectively, but the absolute size of the measure unit changes across the prints

reflective abstraction, or abductive inference…, would then impel the children to further experimentation with larger pictures and finally to validation, to their great gratification as well as to mine (Abrahamson, 2002, 2012).

Still back in the 1990s at Tel Aviv University, I sought to develop my thesis by grounding my observations in the literature of the discipline. And yet that did not prove to be too simple. The epistemic climate of cognitive psychology, at least the climate of the leading experimental journals that populated our library, appeared uninviting of a perspective on mathematics learning grounded in tacit perceptual capacity. My quest brought me to the pinnacle of Tel Aviv University—the Education Library that resided on the very top floor of the Sackler Faculty of Medicine. There, amid stunning Mediterranean sunsets, I found it: a paper by Van den Brink and Streefland (1979) that was about to change everything.

Van den Brink and Streefland discuss a conversation between Coen (8;0) and his father about a poster showing a man and a whale. The child realised something was wrong with the ratio between the man and the whale that had been exaggerated for effect. Coen reasoned about this error by citing an image he had seen elsewhere. That child was taken very seriously by the authors of the paper. It is precisely these didactical materials and these forms of reasoning, they argued, that we should be recruiting so as to promote and support meaningful mathematical learning. Finally, I had found my 'sensei' in Realistic Mathematics Education (RME).

Fast-forward a decade or so, this chapter recounts the story of an international effort, a mixed relay to carry the RME torch from Utrecht across the Atlantic, by way of Brooklyn, to the University of California Berkeley (UC Berkeley). Along the way, this torch was carried by different athletes and took many forms, and yet we have all been attempting to keep the essential flame alive. We describe how, at each station westward, local objectives and contingencies shaped the specific materialisations of the RME didactics. In particular, we discuss the development of courses for preparing pre-service mathematics teachers to design and facilitate problem-based instruction inspired by RME. In the next section, Betina Zolkower, the second author, will narrate her ongoing life-long investment in RME dissemination by way of Southern Argentina, the Netherlands, and Brooklyn, New York. A chance meeting with Abrahamson, the first author, instigated the appropriation of Zolkower's methods for teaching mathematics in middle school courses to Berkeley, where it framed a graduate-level course on cognition catering to pre-service mathematics teachers. At the behest of Stone, the third author, and again with Zolkower's support, this course was re-redesigned into an undergraduate course for pre-service mathematics teachers, part of Berkeley's Cal Teach initiative. A successful staple of Cal Teach, since then this course is taught annually by Abrahamson in collaboration with doctoral students from the Graduate School of Education.

This chapter is not offered as a theoretical piece, neither should it count remotely as experimental. Instead, we present a brief case study—a biography of sorts—with a modest scope of generalisation, with the hope that this story might encourage our fellow practitioners that Realistic Mathematics Education can and should be reinvented in diverse guises. Fiat lux!

14.2 Meanwhile, in New York City: Betina's Story

14.2.1 At the Graduate Center of City University of New York

In 1987, I, Betina Zolkower, enrolled in the PhD Sociology Program at the Graduate Center of City University of New York. As a graduate student in that programme I acquired analytical tools for inquiring into the mechanisms through which, notwithstanding cycles or reforms and counter-reforms, mathematics education continues to perpetuate social inequality by providing uneven opportunities to different socioeconomic status groups to acquire that form of academic capital that constitutes successful performance in school mathematics. My thesis included fieldwork in 4th and 5th grade classrooms in Spanish Harlem attended by recently migrated, Spanish-speaking children, many of them from Mexico. There I witnessed first-hand the effects of camouflaging the ubiquitous, stereotypical word problems into supposedly culturally relevant story problems. Rather than contributing meaning and purpose to classroom activities, these micro-narratives added an extra layer of noise to students' efforts at deciphering the underlying mathematical structure of those problems.

14.2.2 Mathematics in the City: Learning and Practicing Realistic Mathematics Education

> Word problems are rather unappealing, dressed up problems in which the context is merely window dressing for the mathematics put in there. One context can be changed for another without substantially altering the problem [...]. The aim of RME, by contrast, is to place oneself in the context and learn to think within it [...]. (Van den Heuvel-Panhuizen, 1996, p. 20)

The experience of witnessing first-hand the negative effects of story and word problems on English language learners directed me towards RME, an approach premised on the view of mathematics as a human activity that consists of mathematising subject matter from reality, including mathematics itself (Freudenthal, 1991), with the aims of searching for generality, certainty, exactness, and brevity (Gravemeijer & Terwel, 2000), and mathematics teaching/learning as guided reinvention: mathematics is best learned when students are guided to reinvent mathematising by organising or structuring problematic situations embedded in realistic contexts and situations using mathematical tools (Freudenthal, 1991). In other words, as they organise mathematically those situations, students are guided to reconstruct their initial, situated material/mental activity, by verbalising, symbolising, and diagramming the relationships found therein. In Dutch, 'zich realiseren' means to imagine; thus, in this broader sense, a situation is realistic insofar as it appears to the learner as reasonable or imaginable (Freudenthal, 1991; Van den Heuvel-Panhuizen, 1996).

During the final stages of my doctoral studies, I joined Mathematics in the City, a teacher enhancement project funded by the National Science Foundation and directed by Catherine T. Fosnot in collaboration with two faculty members from the Freudenthal Institute, Willem Uittenbogaard and Maarten Dolk. Participation in this project apprenticed me into mathematics learning, teaching, and teacher education from the perspective of RME. In 1996, I visited the Freudenthal Institute to attend a summer institute on the textbook series (in preparation) *Mathematics in Context* (National Center for Research in Mathematical Sciences Education [NCRMSE] & Freudenthal Institute, 1997–1998). This experience as well as the ongoing mentorship of Uittenbogaard, with whom we collaborated in co-teaching lessons and co-facilitating workshops and seminars, helped me appropriate Freudenthal's ideas. I learned how to plan and enact mini-lessons to strengthen students' mental arithmetic skills; acquired an eye for finding mathematisable matter in the world and using it as raw material for instructional design; developed flexibility in using a variety of structuring models (e.g., open and double number line, ratio table, bar model, notebook notation, combination charts); and appreciated the value of models as level-raising tools, the central role of students' constructions and productions in teaching/learning processes, and the paramount function of teacher-guided interaction in expanding students' potential for making and exchanging mathematical meanings.

14.2.3 At Brooklyn College

Since the fall of 2000, as a Brooklyn College faculty member, I have been teaching initial and advanced methods courses as well as the capstone action-research course for graduate students in the 5–9 Grade and 7–12 Grade programmes. In the capstone course, my students, many of them beginning teachers, formulate researchable questions related to the teaching and learning of a specific mathematics topic, analyse relevant units of the textbook series *Mathematics in Context* (National Center for Research in Mathematical Sciences Education [NCRMSE] & Freudenthal Institute, 1997–1998), review literature on that topic (including seminal work by RME specialists) and, in light of all of the above, design and carry out a teaching experiment to address those questions. Among the master's theses I have directed are:

– Mathematising and didactising dissection puzzles
– Connecting geometry, measurement, estimation, and ratio and proportion through problems involving large numbers
– Exploring whole-class share and discussion formats that maximise opportunities for students to exchange mathematical ideas
– Teaching students to use diagrams as tools for solving non-routine problems
– The number line as a tool for solving linear equations
– Using geometric contexts to teach algebra.

All of the above show evidence of my students' creative appropriation of RME ideas.

A central principle of RME is the pivotal function of interaction in guiding students to reinvent mathematical objects, ideas, tools, and strategies, hence the need to prepare teachers to guide such exchanges in manners that support reinvention. With that in mind, my courses include activities that focus on the multiple intersections between language and mathematics. Worth highlighting among those is the interpretative analysis of whole-group conversations conducted by highly experienced and effective teachers. Treating the transcribed conversations as multi-semiotic texts (Halliday, 1994; O'Halloran, 2000), our interpretative analysis centres on the teachers' choices of grammar and vocabulary and the effect of these choices on expanding students' mathematical meaning potential. Among the problems we studied, which found their way into the Berkeley courses, are 'What do you mean by relationship? (de Freitas & Zolkower, 2009), 'Chunking necklaces' (Zolkower & de Freitas, 2010), 'Numbers on a triangle' (Zolkower & Shreyar, 2007), 'Ways to go' (Zolkower & de Freitas, 2012), and 'Marching ants' (Zolkower, Shreyar, & Pérez, 2015).

14.3   Reinventing Algebra Brick by Brick: A Graduate Level Pre-service Mathematics Teaching Course

In May of 2008, following a chance meeting at a Spencer reception during the annual meeting of the American Educational Research Association in New York City, Zolkower and Abrahamson began collaborating on an RME-inspired research project, Paradigmatic Didactical–Mathematical Problematic Situations. In this section, we will revisit the construct of these situations, which evolved as our means for importing Zolkower's RME course from Brooklyn College to University of California Berkeley. We will introduce the 'Brick pyramid' problem as well as our graduate students' work on it to exemplify its mathematical and didactical–mathematical potential.

14.3.1   Paradigmatic Didactical–Mathematical Problematic Situations

The project involved co-designing and evaluating a course in mathematical cognition, learning, and teaching. As we define them, paradigmatic didactical–mathematical problematic situations are activities evoked as contexts for collaborative inquiry into the practices of mathematics, mathematics learning, and mathematics teaching. Our experimental course builds upon and contributes to a body of work on rich problems as contexts for teaching and learning to teach mathematics. Included in this growing domain are: realistic modelling problems (Verschaffel & De Corte, 1997); emergent modelling problems (Gravemeijer, 1999; Van den Heuvel-Panhuizen, 2003); problems that yield multiple solutions (Silver, Ghousseini, Gosen, Charamboulous, & Font Strawhun, 2005; Zolkower & Shreyar 2007); model-eliciting tasks (Lesh, Middleton, Caylor, & Gupta, 2008); substantial learning environments (Wittmann, 1995, 2002); open-ended problems (Cifarelli & Cai, 2005); spiral tasks (Fried & Amit, 2005); and example-generating problems (Watson & Mason, 2005).

Our common interest in paradigmatic didactical–mathematical problematic situations sparked from noticing the potential of these activities, which we both had been using independently, sporadically, and anecdotally, to engage classroom practitioners as well as researchers-in-training in reflective inquiry into a panoply of cognitive, social, technological, and other aspects of mathematics teaching and learning. Consequently, we designed and implemented a semester-long course based on guided study and classroom try-outs of paradigmatic didactical–mathematical problematic situations. Our experimental course is entirely organised and driven by them. Paraphrasing Turkle and Papert's (1991, p. 117) proverbial call to "put logic on tap, not on top," we place mathematics instruction theories on tap rather than on top. That is, our problematic situations serve as scenarios for the targeted mathematical–didactical ideas to emerge out of participants' guided engagement in those situations.

Abrahamson first taught the course in the Fall Semester of 2008. Our research consisted of investigating the effect of this course on participants' mathematical understandings and didactical-mathematical abilities and disposition. Our data included rich documentation from both the college sessions and the field-placement classrooms, where student–teachers tried out the same or similar problems (Zolkower & Abrahamson, 2009). Central to the paper is a particular RME-style problem, the 'Brick Pyramid' problem, which we introduce and discuss below.

14.3.2 The 'Brick Pyramid' Problem

Figure 14.2 shows the 'Brick Pyramid' problem. Students are first presented a picture of bricks configured in the shape of a triangle. The bricks' numerical contents are bound to each other by the following rule: in each brick triad, the number within the top brick is the sum of the numbers in the two contiguous bricks directly below it. The task is to solve the puzzle-like problem by filling in the missing numbers. The brick pyramid discloses the top number and three more, thus creating an implicit system of constraints that emerges as determining a single solution for each additional input inserted, resulting in a structure with surprising mathematical relationships. The instruction given to the students is: "Fill in the brick pyramid. How many solutions did you find? Could there be more? Explain."

Although this problem can be solved using formal algebraic tools, non-algebraic and proto-algebraic (informal) methods can be used as well. Working with positive integers and 0, one possible algebraic treatment begins by assigning to the bottom-leftmost brick the variable x and then stepping upwards, sideways, and downwards, abiding with the addition rule for each triad, until all the bricks have been filled (see Fig. 14.3).

This process indicates that the range of possible values for x is 0–6 (see in Fig. 14.3 the expression "$6 - x$" for the bottom-rightmost brick), thereby giving seven solutions with integers. Interestingly enough, the rightmost brick on the second row is the only one where x cancels out, resulting in the constant value of 24, which is a puzzling phenomenon that may merit an investigation of its own. For example, several

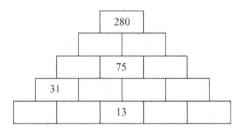

Fig. 14.2 'Brick Pyramid' problem

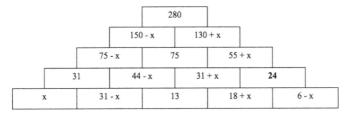

Fig. 14.3 Algebraic treatment of the brick pyramid as a space shaped by numerical constraints

questions can come up: Why 24? How is this number, 24, related to the four given constraints (280, 75, 31, and 13) and their respective locations on the pyramid?

Four graduate students (all names are pseudonyms) participated in the study: Justin, Emily, and Nora, who are all three in their first year in a master's programme, and Zoran, who is in his second year in a doctoral programme. Zolkower, the designer of this course, assisted Abrahamson, remotely, in facilitating this course. Occasionally, Zolkower participated through video-conferencing. The focus lesson took place during the fifth week of instruction of a Fall Semester. During the fifth week, course participants were just beginning to become involved in school placement observations and other fieldwork-related assignments.

14.3.3 Reinventing Algebra by Thinking Aloud Together About the Brick Pyramid and Beyond

In the subsection below, we analyse and discuss selected excerpts from a whole-group conversation about the brick pyramid in the course. This text, made up of 432 turns (changes of speaker), consists of a series of exchanges whereby participants engaged in thinking aloud together (Shreyar, Zolkower, & Pérez, 2010; Zolkower & Shreyar, 2007; Zolkower, Shreyar, & Pérez, 2015) about the problem at hand. Borrowing from Christie (2002), we parsed the conversation into episodes. These are:

I. Opening: framing the problem
II. Solving the problem: thinking aloud together, scribbling, speaking, diagramming, and gesturing
III. Comparing and contrasting approaches and moving forwards to 'more algebraic' approaches
IV. Reflecting back on the experience as reinventing algebra while moving forwards towards algebraisation of the situation
V. Closure: considering the problem as a potential classroom activity while also discussing it from the point of view of instructional design (for this latter part readers are referred to Zolkower & Abrahamson, 2009).

Fig. 14.4 Coding system for labelling the cells

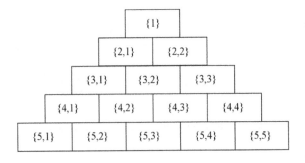

Below we describe the overt activities in this text, that is, what a non-omniscient 'fly-on-the-wall' observer, who is engaged in the solution process, would witness. We begin with Episode II, when students began to think aloud together. In the interest of brevity and clarity, we shall use the following coding system to refer to each of the fifteen cells in the brick pyramid (see Fig. 14.4).

14.3.3.1   Episode II: Solving the Problem

Emily sets off the discussion by going up to the board and presenting her solution procedure (see Fig. 14.5).

Explaining her work, Emily says the following:

> ...What I decided to do was, pick a value, put it somewhere in here [indicates bottom row], build off of that. And I figured I'd pick a value that was under one of these given, permanent numbers. So, I put a number here that's less than 31. [indicates {5,2}] Any number I wanted. [enters 17 into {5,2}] And I went with 17 because... I don't know why....

In order to begin familiarizing herself with the problem, Emily inserts a value, 17, which she selects somewhat arbitrarily, into an empty cell in the bottom row {5,2}, and then works that value so as to fill the entire pyramid according to the addition rule. As it turns out, assigning that particular value to that cell-variable is not permissible in this system. Yet, due to an arithmetic error, $45 - 13 = 22$, this violation appears to go unnoticed.

Next, Justin replaces Emily at the board and presents his solution (see Fig. 14.6). Justin, possibly building off Emily's work, is already more systematic than her, in that he orients toward searching for the range of the solutions, and so his choices of input numbers are governed by an attempt to determine one limit of this range.

As he solves, he articulates emergent insights:

> Okay, so, 75 here, 31 here, 13 here, 280 here, oops, right. [enters values as he utters them] And so, <what> I did was, I looked at each box and thought, what are the limits bounding the number in each box? [emphasises boxes with given values] So, I guess I kind of like started up at the top, and I was like, well these have to be 75 or more, [indicates {2,1}, {2,2}] right, and then.... [Nora points to the 'less than' constraints in Justin's approach].

Fig. 14.5 Emily uses numbers and moves from the bottom up; note diagonal lines connecting between cells to express algebraic relations

Dor highlights the double-using issue, which affects the way one distributes the values throughout the pyramid. Namely, Justin begins to realise that the pyramid can be viewed as a system, rather than a collection of local overlapping three-cell triadic structures; because each sum is constituted by addends below it, recursively, there appears to be some overall systematic set of relations governing the distribution of addends. However, Justin does not yet specify the nature of this system of relations.

Nora, commenting on Justin's work, adds that in order to determine the range of values, one would need to find the other limit, too. Dor comments on embodied constructions of addition that, he believes, may be implicitly biasing the solution procedure. First, he suggests a view of addition as 'adding *up*,' for example, a privileging of an upward-adding construction of the problem, at the expense of attending to the equally important downward constraints. Second, he portrays addition as 'using up

Fig. 14.6 Justin uses 'numbers +' or 'greater than' constraints and moves from the top down

resources'—once a value is used in one sum, e.g., in conjunction with the cell to the right, it must be used again for the cell on the left, and this re-use might be violating the grounding multi-modal dynamical images that tacitly underlie the sense of addition. Emily responds that, indeed, the sum of the numbers on the bottom row is not equal to the number up top, so that her implicit model of the situation seems to have shifted.

Nora thinks aloud:

> So, if we did it in this square [indicates {5,4}], we would end up, maybe we would only have to do, like, a fourth of 72, or something. Because then, by the time it gets up to the top, then you'll have the full 72 that you want. But then I don't know if that takes into consideration… I don't know exactly how this ** but I think <it would fit it> somehow if you did some fraction of 72, then, you know, it's gonna be multiplied here, there's gonna be… two of them up here, and then that'll count as one, and that'll count as two, so that's three. [indicates boxes above {5,4}] If we had some number here, then we'd have that number, then twice that number, then three times that number, and then…
>
> …
>
> If we had some number here [enters a into {5,2}], then… [draws next row] okay, well, kind of ignoring the numbers that are already in there, once you go up here, so, well, it's like what you were saying, we feel like okay, if the a is here, then it's already taken care of, we don't need to worry about it again, but actually it's gonna – you have to count it again in this box and in this box. [enters a into {4,1}, {4,2}] And then, when you come to the next level…

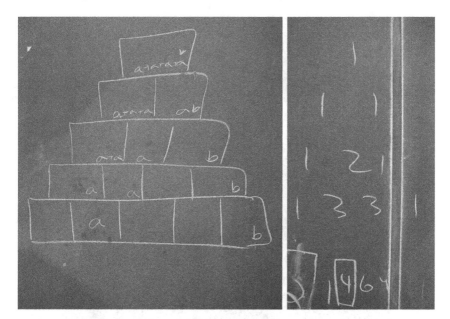

Fig. 14.7   Nora enters *a*, then *b*; this links to Pascal's triangle

Nora thus explores how—given the repeated use of addends—a sum that is written fairly high in the pyramid could be viewed as constituted by the addends below it. She recognises that the relation is not a direct distribution of the sum into equal parts, but initially she cannot explain just how this distribution works or could be represented to support this inquiry. A significant move forwards in the group's collective inquiry is when Nora uses algebraic symbols to explain how a numerical value on the bottom 'ripples' up (see Fig. 14.7). She distinguishes between values in the centre of the bottom row (a) and those on the extremities (b), in terms of how much they contribute to the upward accumulating sums.

Up to this point, participants have each made unique contributions to the collaborative problem-solving process. One can discern a progression from Emily's first hesitant exploration of a single solution through Justin's analysis of the pyramid as an emerging system of constraints to Nora's introduction of algebraic symbols in an attempt to spell out the spread of upward addend contributions of a single number on the bottom row, depending on whether it is in a central or extreme brick, and how two such 'deltas' (the spreading contribution tributaries) mingle in an addend confluence. The instructor's insistence that the work be done up at the board had two related results. On the one hand, students were initially diffident to share half-baked ideas. On the other hand, these ideas, like Nora's *a* and *b* addends, appear to have spread and mingled upwards, receiving at each level the input and reformulation of additional minds on tap.

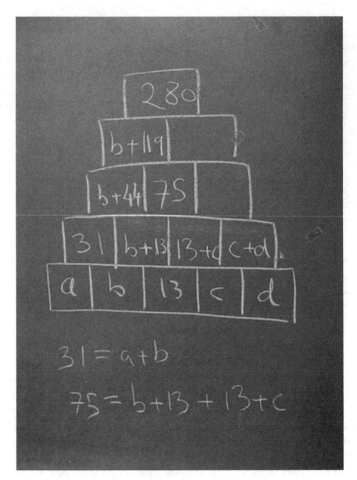

Fig. 14.8 Zoran's brick pyramid; he enters *a*, *b*, *c*, and *d*

14.3.3.2 Episode III: Comparing and Contrasting

Zoran elaborates on the work of Emily, Justin, Nora, and Dor, and he, too, recognises the inadequacy of trial-and-error techniques to cope with the load of arithmetical constraints imposed by the pyramid system. He acknowledges the value of the algebraic system introduced by Nora, to support this inquiry. Zoran introduces additional variables (*a* through *d*), in order to articulate general relations among the fifteen cells of this particular pyramid (see Fig. 14.8).

Zoran continues discussing the distribution issue, talking in terms of 'sets': "With this we have this set here, and this set here… this set is only going up to 31…." Zoran concludes that it would be unreasonable to attempt the problem "purely arithmetically," thereby calling for an algebraic approach.

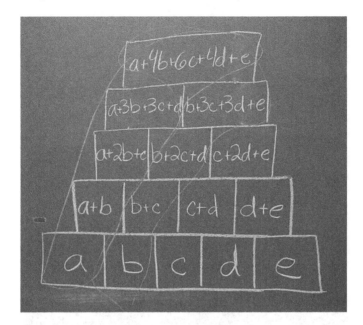

Fig. 14.9 Emily again enters a, b, c, d, e in the bottom row, and the group notes an unexpected association with Pascal's triangle, albeit in inverted form

Emily, possibly building on Nora and Zoran's suggestion, expands the number of symbols to five (a through e) and uses these 'variables' to demonstrate attributes of the pyramid family, regardless of the given numbers. In particular, Emily develops the idea that Pascal's triangle can be viewed as lodged upside-down in the pyramid (Fig. 14.9).

Emily says:

Say you just have your numbers down here: a, b, c, d, e. [enters letters, as she utters them, into the bottom row, in that order] Okay, there's one of each of those, I'm just saying they're… distinct, or they could be <one> , I don't know, um, they're variables. So, to get here, you do $a + b$, and this is $b + c$…

…. this is sort of becoming the, uh, Pascal's triangle in reverse. And this one would be $b + 2c + d$. [enters value into {3,2}] This would be $c + 2d + e$. [enters value into {3,3}] And up here, I need to start making the bricks bigger. And now, we have $a + 3b + 3c + d$, I think. [enters sum into {2,1}] Someone correct me if I'm wrong. And then $b + 3c + 3d + e$. [enters sum into {2,2}] And for the last one… Make it a little bigger…! [expands first box borders] Okay. $a + 4b + 6c + 4d + e$. [enters sum into {1}] And then, <see> you have 1, 4, 6, 4, 1, just like this guy. [Indicates Pascal's triangle fragment on the board] And this is just like coefficients.

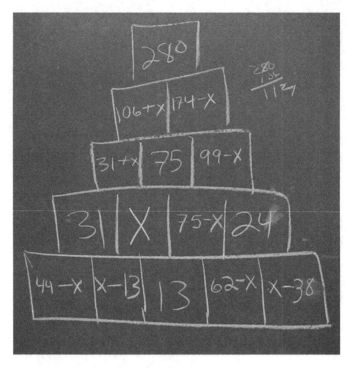

Fig. 14.10 Nora again, now working with a single variable

14.3.3.3 Episode IV: Reflecting

The instructor introduces the following constructs, as they apply to the joint mathematising effort under way: 'sprouting' of algebraic notation from speech and gesture (Radford, 2003); 'distributed cognition' (Hutchins, 1995); 'cognitive artefacts' that amplify reasoning (Norman, 1991); 'working memory' (Baddeley & Hitch, 1974); and 'hypostatic abstraction' (Peirce, 1931–1958). This mini lecture may or may not have had any direct impact on the collaborative solution process. In any case, Nora—possibly also inspired by Emily and Zoran's attempts—then suggests working with a single variable x and expresses all of the numerical values using this variable (see Fig. 14.10).

Nora explains:

> So, I picked this box right here. Just because it was touching so many other things, I figured I could get a lot of information out of it. [places x in {4, 2}] So this one is $31+x$, and then this is $106+x$, and then this is $75-x$, and this is, let's see, $x-13$, and then….

As we have shown in the section above, the brick pyramid allows prospective (and in-service) teachers to encounter central issues in the learning and teaching of algebra, including: (1) symbol sense, informal sense-making, and formal algebra (Arcavi, 1994); (2) the relationship between language proficiency and algebraic learning

(MacGregor & Price, 1999); (3) the role of realistic situations in developing algebra tools (Van Reeuwijk, 1995; Van Reeuwijk & Wijers, 1997); (4) the challenges in guiding the transition from informal to formal algebra (Nathan & Koellner, 2007; Stacey & MacGregor, 2000; Swafford & Langrall, 2000); and (5) the complex interplay among algebraic thinking, algebraic generalisation, and algebraic symbolisation (Linchevski, 1995; Radford, 2003, 2006; Van Ameron, 2003; Zazkis & Liljedahl, 2002).

In what sense is the Brick Pyramid is a paradigmatic problematic situation? In his homage commentary on the life of Hans Freudenthal, Goffree (1993) likens paradigmatic mathematical problems to scientific benchmark discoveries, following which the scientists' extant paradigm shifts and the world is forever seen in a new way. Participants in our graduate course are mathematically literate adults, according to normative standards, such that the algebraic machinery is quite at their fingertips, ready for application. The question is whether, when, and how this application is triggered. This paradigmatic didactical–mathematical problematic situation presents a scenario that calls for mathematising but does not cue or furnish, in an explicit manner, a specific toolbox, let alone a particular tool. Implicit in this principle is the belief that didactical approaches that deny students the opportunity to search for appropriate tools to structure or organise problematic situations have limited effects in developing in them a genuine disposition towards mathematising. The Brick Pyramid is not just a problem-solving tool. It is also and primarily a thinking device (Lotman, 1988). Lyrically speaking, the brick pyramid—once a curious inscribed structure on a worksheet—becomes colourful, animated, mobilised, and enmeshed in multiple intersecting dimensions of mathematical thinking, thereby functioning as a model for thinking about the very meaning and purpose of algebra as a situated human activity.

One might comment that developing paradigmatic didactical–mathematical problematic situations was little more than reinventing RME. We would proudly concede. Our goal of building a graduate-level practicum on mathematics education posed for us the problem of designing sets of interconnected vehicles and experiences around them as means for facilitating encounters between prospective mathematics teachers and Freudenthal's didactical vision. In the course of seeking such architecture, the paradigmatic didactical–mathematical problematic situations emerged in our discourse—first as 'models of,' then as our 'models for'—specifying what we view as opportunities for teachers' productive engagement in thinking about students' thinking. Examining the *Standards for Mathematics Education* (Goffree & Dolk, 1995) published by the Netherlands Institute for Curriculum Development (SLO) and the Freudenthal Institute, we are both heartened to find correlates with our own insights and awed to learn how far we have yet to go. In that volume, eighteen standards are framed as spotlights: "When all eighteen spotlights are 'on,' the entire educational process becomes brightly illuminated" (Goffree & Dolk, 1995, p. 11).

Moving forwards, new problems of practice emerged for us. In particular, we were commissioned to develop an undergraduate course for pre-service mathematics teachers. The next section describes the Education 130 course (hereafter called EDUC 130)—its constitution and credo as well as a set of didactical heuristics that have evolved as our means of cultivating college cohorts of RME disciples from graduates of the mainstream schooling in the United States.

14.4 An Undergraduate Course for Pre-service Mathematics Teachers

University courses are complex cultural phenomena. They are born at the nexus of institutional needs and individual convictions, evolve in negotiation with emerging constraints from multiple and shifting stakeholders, and become blueprints for communities of practice—emblems of departmental ethos and praxis. Semester after semester, courses, like rivers, function as structures and schemes that host and shape the trajectory of their contained water, and in turn are shaped by these waters. Similar to the Heraclitean river, you can never quite step twice into the same course. In this section, we explain the origins and tributaries of the EDUC 130 course, its credo as it appears in the course syllabus, and the didactical heuristics that evolved over time.

The EDUC 130 course Knowing & Learning at UC Berkeley was designed and implemented as part of Cal Teach, a new undergraduate teacher education programme set within the College of Letters & Sciences, aimed at addressing the critical shortage of mathematics and science teachers in California. In creating EDUC 130, faculty members of the Graduate School of Education were attempting to build a new form of community—a haven safe from what we viewed as less productive aspects of mainstream education, a space where pre-service mathematics teachers could experience what it might be like to centre classroom instruction around guided collaborative activities of framing and solving rich, accessible, open-ended problems. We were attempting to forge a new form of identity for pre-service mathematics teachers as activist careerists—reflective practitioners, intuitive action researchers, keen observers who keep experimenting with their resources and process. In creating EDUC 130 we were thus asking what it might take to administer a course where such a person could grow who would become our ideal teacher: inquisitive, reflective, and knowledgeable of both subject matter and its didactics.

Regardless of the particularities in one's image for the ideal teacher, this image becomes the 'product' that the course should 'deliver.' As such, the process of building EDUC 130 was akin to that of solving a design problem. The question was: What should pre-service mathematics teachers' experience in our course be so that they become our ideal teachers? We therefore created a 'course credo' that specifies our views on why and how teachers should become, in addition to educators, also designers, researchers, and 'hackers' (fluent in current technological developments). We placed the credo in our course syllabus.

Surely, though, we never expected this credo to effect any change. Such an expectation would defeat the very assertion within the credo itself that hermetic definitions rarely suffice as a form of instruction. We posted the text in our syllabus and let it be. At the time, we had our course resources and a collective, unarticulated professional know-how for making these resources work in our course. With time, this unarticulated know-how would become articulated in the form of a set of didactical heuristics, as we now explain. Still, the credo speaks to a vision. What we needed was a means by which to achieve this vision. Enter our 'didactical heuristics,' which speak to how we might go about realising the credo.

Didactical heuristics are classroom routines for effective participation in the course as well as in future practice as high-school teachers. These didactical heuristics capture recurring framings, emphases, imagery, and metaphors that we use so as to position and project the pre-service mathematics teachers into a new 'figured world' of reform-oriented teachers (see Ma & Singer-Gabella, 2011). We view these didactical heuristics as capturing our 'tricks of the trade,' design solutions for introducing pre-service mathematics teachers to RME.

In developing EDUC 130, we never intended to develop a set of didactical heuristics. Rather, these notions, which instantiate much of the course credo, sprouted into our practice as useful means of explicating our instructional philosophy and methodology, first to ourselves, then to each other, and finally to our colleagues. The didactical heuristics are structures that emerged as our invented means of solving a problem. The set of heuristics constitute EDUC 130's collective models for solving a problem of practice faced by college instructors, that is, the problem of bootstrapping a community of practice (see Visintainer, Little, & Abrahamson, 2011).

We submit that these didactical heuristics constituted our emergent structures for enabling and enhancing the solving of situated problems of practice. They were our 'models of' teaching a RME course for pre-service mathematics teachers. They were models that we were hence able to carry forth, document, and propagate as 'models for,' just as we are doing in this chapter.

14.5 Reflection: Reinventing Reinvention

> Mathematics is said to have, for example, disciplinary value in habituating the pupil to accuracy of statement and closeness of reasoning; it has utilitarian value in giving command of the arts of calculation involved in trade and the arts; culture value in its enlargement of the imagination in dealing with the most general relations of things; even religious value in its concept of the infinite and allied ideas. But clearly mathematics does not accomplish such results, because it is endowed with miraculous potencies called values; it has these values if and when it accomplishes these results, and not otherwise. (Dewey, 1944, p. 245)

The proverbial human capacity to solve problems—a vital skill that is apparently so desirable yet so rare these days that it has been rebranded in the U.S. educational reform discourse as a 21st century skill—has been the vision of Realistic Mathematics Education from its very incipience. Freudenthal makes the following bold statement that connects the teaching of mathematics to youth ethos, mores, identity, and agency in extra-mathematical realms of life.

> Our cultural assets are too dangerous to be offered the youth as ready-made material. The instruction we provide should create the opportunity for youth to acquire the cultural heritage

by their own activity. They should learn that the self-reliance they claim elsewhere extends
to their own role in the learning process. (Freudenthal, 1971, p. 415)

What a vision! Mathematics education could fulfil the virtuous role of fostering youth
independence and empowerment. To make this vision a reality, college instructors
must cultivate a generation of pre-service mathematics teachers who are prepared
to offer high-school students experiences by which they can recognise their own
capacity to reason deeply as a means of solving problems. A teacher education
course guided by RME principles could thus possibly prepare high school students
for life.

We have described the evolution of our EDUC 130 course for pre-service mathematics teachers. The course is founded on the idea of preparing pre-service mathematics teachers by running them through the same problem-solving experiences
their own prospective high-school students will undergo. Once they become teachers, EDUC 130 course participants are then to emulate our classroom practices 'one
step down,' with them now as instructors and their high-school students solving and
reflecting on engaging problems.

Building a course is certainly a form of problem solving. And yet how does one
know whether and when the problem has been solved? We cannot quite look up the
correct answers at the end of the book! Still, a set of guiding principles may serve
as a book of sorts by which to evaluate our progress. It is in this sense that RME
has served us as a standard by which to evaluate the course design, its implementation, and its effects. And in so doing we have developed our own set of principles,
the didactical heuristics, that evolved as our practical means of apprenticing pre-
service mathematics teachers into RME. Yet we do not offer these cultural assets as
ready-made materials. Rather, we steer our college students to reinvent the didactical heuristics through guided reflection on their problem-solving experiences. In a
sense, the didactical heuristics constitute the emergent structures we have cultivated
through and for our own guided reinvention of RME at Berkeley.

In designing and promoting this course, we are conscious of valuing depth of
experiencing over breadth in coverage. When a college course is planned so as to
cover an entire methodology textbook, with its complementary readings, it seems
rather certain that one would get through the syllabus by the end of the course. However, when mathematical content, didactical subject matter knowledge, and assigned
readings are positioned as ancillary to the 'actual' learning, one may not be as certain to cover it all (and perhaps, even more troublesome, the course is unlikely
to be instructor-proof so as to enable standardisation). Yet, as a trade-off, there is
the perceived opportunity that participants would have rich experiences of learning
'what really matters.' And what is it that matters, really? Learning to teach mathematics involves reflective back-and-forth movements between classroom practice
and instructional theory; mathematical content and didactical form; observing one's
learning processes and observing those of others (Freudenthal, 1991). Our RME-
inspired course materials, activities, credo, and heuristics, in synergic unison with
our grounding of college-classroom discussions in actual school-classroom experiences, engage future teachers and mathematics education researchers in working on

and thinking through mathematics problems and mathematics learning and teaching problems and, in so doing, contribute to the all-cherished goal of making mathematics meaningful, relevant, and accessible for every student in every classroom.

References

Abrahamson, D. (2002). When "the same" is the same as different differences: Aliya reconciles her perceptual judgment of proportional equivalence with her additive computation skills. In D. Mewborn, P. Sztajn, E. White, H. Wiegel, R. Bryant, & K. Nooney (Eds.), *Proceedings of the Twenty Fourth Annual Meeting of the North American Chapter of the International Group for the Psychology of Mathematics Education* (Vol. 4, pp. 1658–1661). Columbus, OH: Eric Clearinghouse for Science, Mathematics, and Environmental Education.

Abrahamson, D. (2012). Discovery reconceived: Product before process. *For the Learning of Mathematics, 32*(1), 8–15.

Arcavi, A. (1994). Informal sense-making in formal mathematics. *For the Learning of Mathematics, 14*(3), 24–35.

Baddeley, A. D., & Hitch, G. J. L. (1974). Working memory. In G. A. Bower (Ed.), *The psychology of learning and motivation: Advances in research and theory* (Vol. 8, pp. 47–89). New York, NY: Academic Press.

Cifarelli, V., & Cai, J. (2005). The evolution of mathematical explorations in open-ended problem solving situations. *Journal of Mathematical Behavior, 24*(3), 302–324.

Christie, F. (2002). *Classroom discourse analysis: A functional perspective*. New York, NY: Continuum.

de Freitas, E., & Zolkower, B. (2009). Using social semiotics to prepare mathematics teachers to teach for social justice. *Journal of Mathematics Teacher Education, 12*(3), 187–203.

Dewey, J. (1944). *Democracy and education*. New York, NY: The Free Press (Originally published 1916).

Freudenthal, H. (1971). Geometry between the devil and the deep sea. *Educational Studies in Mathematics, 3*(3–4), 413–435.

Freudenthal, H. (1991). *Revisiting Mathematics Education. China lectures*. Dordrecht, the Netherlands: Kluwer.

Fried, M., & Amit, M. (2005). A spiral task as a model for in-service teacher education. *Journal of Mathematics Teacher Education, 8*(5), 419–436.

Goffree, F. (1993). HF: Working on mathematics education. *Educational Studies in Mathematics, 25*(1–2), 21–49.

Goffree, F., & Dolk, M. (1995). *Standards for primary mathematics teacher education*. Utrecht, the Netherlands: Freudenthal Institute.

Gravemeijer, K. P. E. (1999). How emergent models may foster the constitution of formal mathematics. *Mathematical Thinking and Learning, 1*(2), 155–177.

Gravemeijer, K., & Terwel, J. (2000). Hans Freudenthal: A mathematician on didactics and curriculum theory. *Journal of Curriculum Studies, 32*(6), 777–796.

Halliday, M. A. K. (1994). *An introduction to functional grammar* (2nd ed.). London, UK: Arnold.

Hutchins, E. (1995). *Cognition in the wild*. Cambridge, MA: M.I.T. Press.

Lesh, R., Middleton, J. A., Caylor, E., & Gupta, S. (2008). A science need: Designing tasks to engage students in modeling complex data. *Educational Studies in Mathematics, 68*(2), 113–130.

Linchevski, L. (1995). Algebra with numbers and arithmetic with letters: A definition of pre-algebra. *Journal of Mathematical Behavior, 14*(1), 113–120.

Lotman, Y. (1988). Text within a text. *Soviet Psychology, 24*(3), 32–51.

Ma, J. Y., & Singer-Gabella, M. (2011). Learning to teach in the figured world of reform mathematics: Negotiating new models of identity. *Journal of Teacher Education, 62*(1), 8–22.

MacGregor, M., & Price, E. (1999). An exploration of aspects of language proficiency in algebra learning. *Journal for Research in Mathematics Education, 30*(4), 449–467.

Nathan, M. J., & Koellner, K. (2007). A framework for understanding and cultivating the transition from arithmetic to algebraic reasoning. *Mathematical Thinking and Learning, 9*(3), 179–192.

National Center for Research in Mathematical Sciences Education (NCRMSE) & Freudenthal Institute (1997–1998). *Mathematics in context: A connected curriculum for grades 5–8.* Chicago, IL: Encyclopaedia Britannica Educational Corporation.

Norman, D. A. (1991). Cognitive artifacts. In J. M. Carroll (Ed.), *Designing interaction: Psychology at the human-computer interface* (pp. 17–38). New York, NY: Cambridge University Press.

O'Halloran, K. L. (2000). Classroom discourse in mathematics: A multisemiotic analysis. *Linguistics and Education, 10*(3), 359–388.

Peirce, C. S. (1931–1958). *Collected papers of Charles Sanders Peirce.* In C. Hartshorne & P. Weiss (Eds.), Cambridge, MA: Harvard University Press.

Radford, L. (2003). Gestures, speech, and the sprouting of signs: A semiotic-cultural approach to students' types of generalization. *Mathematical Thinking and Learning, 5*(1), 37–70.

Radford, L. (2006). Algebraic thinking and the generalization of patterns: A semiotic perspective. In J. Novotná, H. Moraová, M. Krátká, & N. Stehlíková (Eds.), *Proceedings of the 30th Conference of the International Group for the Psychology of Mathematics Education* (Vol. 1, pp. 2–21). Prague, Czech Republic: PME.

Shreyar, S., Zolkower, B., & Pérez, S. (2010). Thinking aloud together: A teacher's semiotic mediation of a whole-class conversation about percents. *Educational Studies in Mathematics, 73*(1), 21–53.

Silver, E. A., Ghousseini, H., Gosen, D., Charamboulous, Ch., & Font Strawhun, B. T. (2005). Moving from rhetoric to praxis: Issues faced by teachers in having students consider multiple solutions for problems in the mathematics classroom. *Journal of Mathematical Behavior, 24*(3–4), 287–301.

Stacey, K., & MacGregor, M. (2000). Learning the algebraic method of solving problems. *Journal of Mathematical Behavior, 18*(2), 149–167.

Swafford, J. O., & Langrall, C. W. (2000). Grade 6 students' pre-instructional use of equations to describe and represent problem situations. *Educational Studies in Mathematics, 31,* 89–112.

Turkle, S., & Papert, S. (1991). Epistemological pluralism and the revaluation of the concrete. In I. Harel & S. Papert (Eds.), *Constructionism* (pp. 161–192). Norwood, NJ: Ablex Publishing.

Van Ameron, B. (2003). Focusing on informal strategies when linking arithmetic to early algebra. *Educational Studies in Mathematics, 54*(1), 63–75.

Van den Brink, J., & Streefland, L. (1979). Young children (6–8): Ratio and proportion. *Educational Studies in Mathematics, 10*(4), 403–420.

Van den Heuvel-Panhuizen, M. (1996). *Assessment and Realistic Mathematics Education.* Utrecht, the Netherlands: CD-ß Press/Freudenthal Institute, Utrecht University.

Van den Heuvel-Panhuizen, M. H. A. M. (2003). The didactical use of models in realistic mathematics education: An example from a longitudinal trajectory on percentage. *Educational Studies in Mathematics, 54*(1), 9–35.

Van Reeuwijk, M. (1995). *The role of realistic situations in developing tools for solving systems of equations.* Utrecht, the Netherlands: Freudenthal Institute, Utrecht University.

Van Reeuwijk, M., & Wijers, M. (1997). Students' construction of formulas in context. *Mathematics Teacher in the Middle School, 2*(4), 230–236.

Verschaffel, L., & de Corte, E. (1997). Teaching realistic mathematical modeling in the elementary school: A teaching experiment with fifth graders. *Journal for Research in Mathematics Education, 28*(5), 577–601.

Visintainer, T., Little, A., & Abrahamson, D. (2011). *Pedagogical heuristics for teacher preparation: Reflections from Cal Teach.* Paper presented at the annual UTeach Institute/NIMSI conference, Austin, TX, May 24–26.

Watson, A., & Mason, J. (2005). *Mathematics as a constructive activity. Learners generating examples.* Mahwah, NJ: Lawrence Erlbaum Associates.

Wittmann, E. (1995). Mathematics education as a 'design science'. *Educational Studies in Mathematics, 29*(4), 355–374.

Wittmann, E. (2002). Developing mathematics education in a systemic process. *Educational Studies in Mathematics, 48*(1), 1–20.

Zazkis, R., & Liljedahl, P. (2002). Generalization of patterns: The tension between algebraic thinking and algebraic notation. *Educational Studies in Mathematics, 49*(3), 379–402.

Zolkower, B., & Abrahamson, D. (2009). *Studying paradigmatic didactical-mathematical situations: Design and implementation of an experimental graduate level course for pre-service mathematics teachers and doctoral students.* Paper presented at the Annual Meeting of the American Educational Research Association, San Diego, April 13–17.

Zolkower, B., & de Freitas, E. (2010). What's in a text: Engaging mathematics teachers in the study of whole-class conversations. In U. Gellert, E. Jablonka, & C. Morgan (Eds.), *Proceedings of the 6th Mathematics Education and Society Conference* (MES) (Vol. II, pp. 508–518). Berlin, Germany: Freie Universität Berlin.

Zolkower, B., & de Freitas, E. (2012). Mathematical meaning-making in whole class conversation: Functional-grammatical analysis of a paradigmatic text. *Language and Dialogue, 2*(1), 60–79.

Zolkower, B., & Shreyar, S. (2007). A teacher's mediation of a thinking aloud discussion in a 6th grade mathematics classroom. *Educational Studies in Mathematics, 65*(2), 177–202.

Zolkower, B., Shreyar, S., & Pérez, S. (2015). Teacher guidance of algebraic formula building: Functional-grammatical analysis of a whole-class conversation. *ZDM Mathematics Education, 73*(1), 21–53.

Chapter 15
Korean Mathematics Education Meets Dutch Didactics

Kyeong-Hwa Lee, YeongOk Chong, GwiSoo Na and JinHyeong Park

Abstract Dutch didactics—in Korean mathematics education society often referred to as Realistic Mathematics Education (RME)—has become one of the major perspectives on mathematics education which have been widely discussed and applied by Korean mathematics educators and mathematics teachers to reform Korean mathematics education over the past 35 years. This chapter briefly depicts how RME has been introduced in both theoretical and practical viewpoints through doctoral and master's theses as well as through journal articles and curriculum documents in Korea. It turns out that RME has provided integral and meaningful issues to be constantly discussed among Korean mathematics educators since its introduction in the 1980s. In conclusion, RME has contributed largely to activating and reshaping Korean mathematics education in multiple ways although several barriers to overcome or perspectives to modify have emerged due to Korea's different social and educational backgrounds. Parts of these barriers as well as recognised benefits come to the fore through feedback and reflections from the teachers and students who experienced RME in Korean contexts, as described at the end of this chapter.

Keywords Realistic Mathematics Education (RME) · Dutch didactics in Korean context · Mathematics curriculum · Mathematics textbooks · RME-based mathematics class

K.-H. Lee (✉)
Seoul National University, Seoul, Korea
e-mail: khmath@snu.ac.kr

Y. Chong
Gyeongin National University of Education, Anyang, Korea
e-mail: yochong@ginue.ac.kr

G. Na
Cheongju National University of Education, Cheongju-si, Korea
e-mail: gsna21@cje.ac.kr

J. Park
Gongju National University of Education, Gongju, Korea
e-mail: demxas@gjue.ac.kr

© The Author(s) 2020
M. van den Heuvel-Panhuizen (ed.), *International Reflections
on the Netherlands Didactics of Mathematics*, ICME-13 Monographs,
https://doi.org/10.1007/978-3-030-20223-1_15

15.1   Introduction

There is a long history, like in other countries, in which Korean mathematics educators have struggled with many serious issues in practice such as students' low understanding of mathematical concepts and blind memorisation of mathematical rules and procedures, poor connection between school mathematics and out-of-school mathematics, and teacher-centred mathematics teaching. Dutch didactics, in Korean mathematics education society often referred to as Realistic Mathematics Education (RME), has been considered one of the major perspectives by which Korean mathematics educators and mathematics teachers handle the aforementioned issues in Korean mathematics education practice. This article traces the efforts of the Korean mathematics educators who have tried to introduce RME to Korea's mathematics education society over the past 35 years. Section 15.2 describes how and by whom the RME perspective was introduced to Korea and how it has been interpreted, applied, and integrated into Korean mathematics education and its practice. Section 15.3 covers the influences of the RME perspective on the Korean mathematics curriculum, textbooks, and assessments. Section 15.4 discusses the recognitions and reflections of the teachers and students who experienced mathematics teaching-learning based on the RME perspective. Section 15.5 summarises the discussions and suggests conclusions.

15.2   The Research History of RME in Korea

In his paper published in 1980, Woo referenced RME for the first time in Korea. After that, Woo continually discussed RME in theoretical views (Woo, 1980, 1986, 1994, 1998), which has made significant contributions to the influence of RME on the research and practice of Korean mathematics education. In particular, Woo supervised his students to didactically analyse mathematical themes such as function, rational number, probability, variable, and calculus at elementary and secondary school levels for their doctoral theses (Han, 1997; Kim, 1997; Lee, 1996; Park, 1992; Yu, 1995), leading to broad evaluations on the RME perspective. These studies show how the RME perspective has influenced the research bases of Korean mathematics education, or how the mathematics educators have understood the RME perspective compared with other contemporary research perspectives affecting Korean mathematics education.

The RME perspective has been an important key to understand and reform the Korean mathematics curriculum, textbook, and education practices. The aforementioned doctoral theses focused on understanding RME in general and from a theoretical standpoint. At the same time, various papers published in the mathematics education research journals in Korea employed the RME perspective as a frame and reference of analysis to discuss Korean mathematics curriculum, textbook, and education practices. The studies show the influence of the RME perspective on reflecting about and improving Korean mathematics education.

The next section will cover the understandings and discussions about RME in Korean mathematics education society, followed by its interpretations and applications in the Korean context.

15.2.1 Understanding and Discussions About RME in the Korean Context

The first discussion about RME in Korea was Woo's paper in 1980 titled "A Criticism about Anti-Piaget's Theories on the Mathematics Educational Point of View". In this paper, Woo refuted Freudenthal and Van Hiele who criticised Piaget and supported Piaget's viewpoint. However, in the paper published in 1986, titled "Some Remarks on the Van Hiele's Level Theory of Mathematical Learning", Woo (1986) recognised the significance of Freudenthal's approach. Then, he was talking about "a reasonable justification about honest confidence of a mathematics teacher in class based on a practical theory that is developed by an insight about the nature of mathematical thinking" (Woo, 1986, p. 91). Furthermore, at the end of this paper, Woo suggested mathematics teachers in Korea should focus more on mathematical thinking rather than on the content itself.

In 1992, the first doctoral thesis on mathematics education in Korea was published by Park under the supervision of Woo. In the thesis, Park criticised traditional teaching practice of function in Korea and suggested to introduce the perspective of Freudenthal's didactical phenomenology.

> It [the traditional teaching practice in Korea] repeats a traditional deductive approach that exposes the essential of function to the students as it is, which should have been organized by the students themselves, and neglects most of the organization process of function. (Park, 1992, p. 159)

In the doctoral theses that followed, RME took an important role as a reference perspective to critically understand and to draw directions from for reform of Korean mathematics education. Chong's (1997) thesis, titled *A Study on Freudenthal's Mathematization Instruction Theory*, extracted didactical principles and its assessment principles based on mathematising, and suggested a direction for teaching function through progressive mathematisation. In Ko's (2005) thesis, titled *A Study on Active Construction of Number Concept at the Beginning of School Age* an active approach was suggested to instruct various aspects of the concepts of natural number in the early school ages, referencing Freudenthal's discussion about the organisation and instruction of the concept of natural number through activities. Also, Lee (2007) developed a learning model for mathematising activities in geometry and reported its results in his thesis, titled *A Study on the Development and the Effect of Realistic Mathematization Learning Model*, which was based on the RME theory of Freudenthal and the textbook series *Mathematics in Context* (MiC) (NCRMSE & Freudenthal

Institute, 1997–1998) developed at the University of Wisconsin in collaboration with the Freudenthal Institute at Utrecht University.

Among those mentioned above, the thesis of Chong compared the viewpoint of Freudenthal in mathematics education with those of Bruner and Dewey. These viewpoints were compared and discussed as follows.

> Dewey regarded learning as a growth of experiences, while Freudenthal recognized it as an expansion process of mathematized reality. In fact, the meaning of 'experience' by Dewey and that of 'reality' by Freudenthal were used in a similar context. [...] 'Experience' used by Dewey, however, focused on its applications to more direct and concrete daily situations, while 'reality' by Freudenthal emphasized the world to be mathematized in addition. (Chong, 1997, p. 116)

In the same manner, Chong compared RME with Bruner's theory and discussed how the RME perspective supplemented that of Bruner.

Comparative studies similar to Chong's, which analyse the theories of other scholars with respect to the RME theory, are still one of the branches of Korean mathematics education research. This is attributed mainly to Woo, who introduced RME and has continued the supervision of doctoral theses about it. Also, the popularity of RME was due to its appropriateness to reveal the problems deeply rooted in the tradition of Korean mathematics education.

15.2.2 The Interpretation and Applications of the RME in the Korean Context

As mentioned above, Woo initially criticised the theory when he introduced RME. However, he did pay attention to its positive aspects and highlighted it as a potential perspective that would improve and compliment Korean mathematics education. This was mainly due to the fact that RME focused on the discussion about the education curriculum and didactics, as it provided specific directions and arguments that could be used to reorganise Korean mathematics textbooks and reform the mathematics curriculum. In particular, the two books by Freudenthal, *Mathematics as an Educational Task* published in 1973, and *Didactical Phenomenology of Mathematical Structures* published in 1983, had much influence on this trend.

For example, Kim and Na (2008) claimed that the context for the instruction of ratios and rates in the elementary school textbook was inappropriate and sequences of lessons of instruction should be changed. The basis of this claim can be found in the following discussion, which is related to Freudenthal (1983) and Streefland (1985).

> From the perspective of 'looking into our daily life,' the context included in the current textbook for the introduction of ratios is very artificial. [...] A relation of ratio is not implied in the two given quantities, that is three boys and five girls. [...] In the current textbook, the definition of rates is given after the introduction of the value of ratios, and the instruction focuses on the value of ratios and not on rates. Although rates are a mathematical mean to compare the relative magnitude of various quantities, the textbook failed to provide the

experiences to students to learn the natural meaning of rates because of the intentional emphasis on the value of ratio rather than on rates in the meaning-rich context. (Kim & Na, 2008, pp. 314–316)

Kim and Na gave lessons using a version of the textbook that was reorganised according to the RME perspective, and they had very positive results. When adapting the textbook, they experienced that it was necessary to pay extra attention to contexts which contain cultural differences such as the currency unit.

Kang and Kang (2008) analysed the chapter on probability in the Korean textbook, and tried to reorganise it. The study pointed out that the instruction of probability in Korea focused on algorithms rather than on the concept. They suggested a four-step instruction reflecting the reinvention method of Freudenthal instead; that is a method containing (i) introducing a realistic context, (ii) devising informal solutions by the students, (iii) applying the devised solutions in various realistic contexts, and (iv) using progressive condensation and formalisation when the students are prepared for this. Kang and Kang suggested improvements in six directions in the Korean textbook. First, ample realistic contexts should be given to the students to learn the concept of probability in various contexts. Second, various concepts of probability should be taught that can be experienced in daily activities. Third, qualitative comparisons of probability as a measurement should precede quantitative comparisons. Fourth, various representations for probability should be taught. Fifth, the concept of probability should be followed by the concept of the number of cases. Sixth, formalisation should be placed in the last section of the course (Kang & Kang, 2008, pp. 85–86).

Lee and Lee (2006) introduced the RME perspective to improve the instruction method of irrational numbers. Based on the Korean mathematics textbook, irrational number is taught by defining the square root and rapidly formalising irrational number based on its definition. The students, therefore, have not had a chance to learn the concept of irrational number, which is considered to result in failure of understanding irrational number operation. In the study, Lee and Lee (2006, p. 299) hypothesised that "the instructional viewpoint of irrational number starts from rich contexts that stimulate reflective thinking about rational number, and acquires the essence of irrational number through progressive mathematization." According to this viewpoint, the historic-genetic background of irrational number was investigated, from which the context to reveal the existence and necessity of irrational number was developed. After that, they suggested activities that promote relating students' existing knowledge of rational numbers to irrational number. Unlike the then current Korean curriculum that introduced the Pythagorean theory after irrational number, the suggested new approach was teaching irrational number based on the intuitive level of understanding of the Pythagorean theory. Finally, the students understood the characteristics of irrational number by themselves through exploring the decimal expression of irrational number using a calculator (Lee & Lee, 2006, p. 310). The results from the instructional materials developed in the research were satisfactory and meaningful. The students recognised the necessity of the concept of irrational number and its existence, and found a suitable way to represent it.

To implement the suggestion of Freudenthal that 'defining' should be taught instead of 'definition', Cho and Park (2011) designed lesson plans that introduced the monster-barring approach as shown by Lakatos (1976) in *Proofs and Refutations*. The study showed examples and non-examples of prisms, and made the students experience 'defining' through the activities of defining and refining the definition of a prism. The instruction was designed in six steps. The first step was to find various properties from examples of prisms. The second step was to draft a definition of a prism from the properties found. The third step was to refine the definition to not include a non-example shown by the teacher. From this process, a second definition was made. From the fourth to sixth steps, an additional non-example was shown for each step to refine the definition. After the sixth step, the students refined their definitions to exclude the four non-examples. This study suggests that a definition can be acquired by an activity that transforms a naive definition to a sophisticated one by refining, rather than by a sudden creation. The results showed that the students felt difficulties in how to define a prism as they focused more on subsidiary properties than essential ones that were necessary for the definition. The initial definitions made by students were often too naive to be used as a definition, which necessitated the intervention of the teacher.

15.3   Mathematics Teaching-Learning in Korea and the RME

15.3.1   Mathematics Curriculum

The mathematics curriculum in Korea specifies the standards for students and the relevant teaching-learning methods. The contents of the mathematics textbooks are composed to comply with the curriculum guideline. Therefore, the mathematics curriculum in Korea has exercised great influence on the introduction of a certain mathematical content and its teaching-learning methods.

RME theory and the MiC textbook series have influenced the mathematics curriculum and the textbook development in implicit as well as explicit ways. Since the early 1980s, Korean mathematics educators have conducted research on the RME theory and on didactical phenomenology. In the studies which attempted a didactical phenomenological analysis on mathematical concepts such as function, negative number, and proportion, the researchers reflected the problems underlying the instruction methods of such concepts so far in Korea and proposed desirable instruction methods at a theoretical level. Those research results have exercised a concrete influence on the standards and the teaching-learning methods of mathematics since 2000.

Here the concept of function is chosen as a representative example of changes in the instruction method through a didactical phenomenological analysis. Research into didactical phenomenological analysis on the concept of function and its teaching-learning method for mathematisation based on the RME theory has been conducted in Korea since the 1990s (Chong, 1997; Park, 1992). In particular, Chong (1997) analysed the research of Freudenthal (1983), Van Hiele (1986), Verstappen (1982), and Janvier (1980), and suggested an instruction method of function through activities aimed at progressive mathematisation, an approach that was introduced in RME by Treffers (1987). Regarding the instruction on function in Korea, Chong (1997) pointed out that the bottom level activities, which preceded formal instruction in the concept of function, such as the study of dependency relations as a mean for the organisation of phenomena, the study of patterns as a mean of the organisation of dependency relations, and the formation of a mental image about the concept of function, have been insufficient.

Those studies contributed to the 2007 *Mathematics Curriculum* (Ministry of Education and Human Resource Development, 2007), which has reset the achievement standard in order to teach the concept of function through progressive mathematisation. Before introducing the formal definition of function, the concept of function is introduced in an intuitive manner using "a correspondence relation of two quantities where one quantity is determined as the other changes" (Ministry of Education and Human Resource Development, 2007, p. 31). This helped the students to experience various phenomena that make the concept of function work as a mean for organisation and to form a mental object of the concept.

The teaching-learning method through progressive mathematisation is still emphasised in the 2015 *Mathematics Curriculum* (Ministry of Education, 2015b). This mathematics curriculum is changed so that the concept of function is introduced formally in the 8th grade, which is preceded by sufficient interpretations and explanations about the given graphs from various realistic situations in the 7th grade. This is to make the students experience various phenomena that show the properties of function and to express the changes through means such as linguistic expressions, qualitative graphs, and diagrams, which is followed by the formal introduction of the concept of function. The changes in the mathematics curriculum released in 2015 were intended to implement the progressive mathematisation of the concept of function in an active manner.

15.3.2 Mathematics Textbook

While the mathematical achievement of Korean students in the cognitive area is very high, their attitude towards mathematics is very negative (Kim et al., 2008, 2010). In this situation, Korean mathematics educators have tried various methods to increase students' interest in and positive attitudes to mathematics. One of the methods is to improve mathematics textbooks.

Korean mathematics educators have tried to develop a textbook which not only helps the students to have an interest in and positive attitudes to mathematics, but also sufficiently covers mathematical concepts, principles, and laws that need to be learned by the students. During the course of the textbook development, textbooks from other countries have been investigated as benchmarks to reflect their advantages while keeping the strengths of the Korean textbook.

The MiC textbook is one of the textbooks from other countries which has inspired mathematics textbook developers in Korea since the 1990s. The mathematics textbook developers have studied the rich contexts that the MiC textbook contains, and tried to find suitable contexts that fit Korean students. Through the contexts, the students were expected to experience the fact that mathematics is a human activity existing near to them, to learn the principles and concepts of mathematics naturally through the activities, and to improve their interest in and positive attitude towards mathematics.

In the following it will be explained how Korean researchers have tried to improve students' learning of operating with integers by introducing various contexts and activities into the mathematics textbook, which shows direct or indirect influences by MiC textbook. As widely known, operating with integers is one of the subjects with which students have much difficulty. In particular, the operation that includes negative integers is very difficult for students to understand.

Figure 15.1 is extracted from the Korean mathematics textbook as an example in relation to the instruction of addition of positive and negative integers using multiple models that is one of the key features of the MiC textbook (Lee et al., 2008, p. 60). The figure shows that in the Korean textbook, a red and a blue ball are introduced to represent '+1' and '−1', respectively, to be used for the instruction of the operation method and its principle through the activity. Also, to go to the 'right' and the 'left' are introduced to represent '+' and '−', respectively, in order to help students to understand the addition operation of integers and the use of the number line.

15.3.3 Assessment of Mathematics Learning

The direction of RME for the assessment of mathematical literacy has influenced the method of evaluating students' mathematical achievement in Korea. This section describes the contents of the unit on assessment included in the teacher guidebook for teaching mathematic in elementary school in Korea provided by the Ministry of Education (2015a).

The teacher guidebook gives the following five principles for the assessment of mathematics learning:

- To assess what the students know and think in mathematics
- To integrate the assessment into teaching
- To assess the overall viewpoint of mathematics and focus on broad mathematical tasks
- To design the problem situations that require applications of various concepts
- To employ various assessment tools including not only paper-and-pencil tests but also oral tests and performance tests etcetera. (Ministry of Education, 2015a, pp. 30–33).

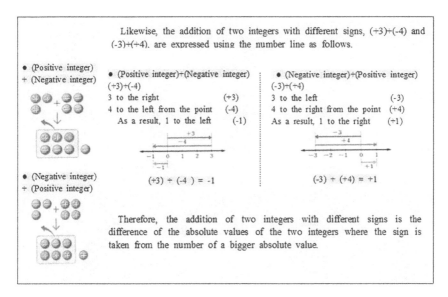

Likewise, the addition of two integers with different signs, (+3)+(-4) and (-3)+(+4), are expressed using the number line as follows.

Fig. 15.1 Part of explanations on how to add two integers in a Korean mathematics textbook (Lee et al., 2008, p. 60)

A unit assessment is one of the summative evaluations, which is provided to the students after finishing a unit in the textbook. In the frame of the unit assessment as included in the teacher guidebook and shown in Fig. 15.2, number and operations, shape, measurement, pattern, and probability and statistics fall into the mathematical content domain suggested by the mathematics curriculum in Korea, while communication, problem solving, and reasoning fall into the mathematical process domain. This frame of the unit assessment has been organised based on the pyramid model of De Lange (2003).

The frame of the unit assessment is intended to provide the students with well-balanced assessment items and to realise the assessment principle of mathematics learning as mentioned above in a concrete manner by considering various assessment factors such as mathematical content, mathematical process, the level of understanding, and the problem context connected to daily life. In addition, the Korean researchers have tried to develop the tasks and problems in the unit assessments in reference with Van den Heuvel-Panhuizen's (1996, pp. 140–153) suggestions to make paper-and-pencil tasks more informative.

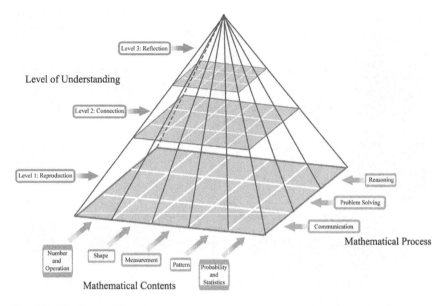

Fig. 15.2 The frame of the unit assessment

15.4 Voices from Korean Teachers and Students on RME

15.4.1 Voices from Teachers Regarding RME

Teachers in Korea who are interested in RME have tried to reflect the didactics of RME by practicing mathematics classes and mathematical activities based on RME through research meetings of either a school level or at an individual level. This section presents some teacher voices from a middle school and a research group.

15.4.1.1 Voices from Teachers in Middle School IW

Although the application of the RME-based mathematics classes faces many difficulties as the traditional Korean mathematics teaching is very different from that based on RME, Middle School IW, an alternative school established in September 2003, has practised RME-based mathematics classes in the 7th and 8th grades using MiC textbooks translated into Korean since its opening.

The teachers in Middle School IW have studied the theories related with RME and shared their ideas and experiences so that the mathematics classes based on RME fit into the Korean education environments, and tried to extract and instruct the essence of the MiC textbook without distorting its overall composition (Park et al., 2010, pp. 71–73).

In such environments, students have drawn up various strategies of their own through investigation of the context, learned how to communicate in their own words that they fully understood instead of using only formal mathematical terms, and participated in the classes more actively. Teacher B testified the impressions he got from one of the classes based on RME as follows:

> Who can be silent when he witnesses these various problem solving strategies? I was thrilled when the students presented their strategies. (Baek, 2004, p. 672)

Though they were often tempted to stop the mathematics classes based on RME due to the energy demanded for class preparations, such as continuous care and observations on the students and the arrangement of each class in the overall curriculum, and the pressure that the students should face in usual mathematics classes in the next grades, the teachers in Middle School IW have been encouraged by the changes to students and alumni. Teacher K testified about the impression on the mathematics class based on RME as follows:

> The efforts and the changes that the students make and the fact that they create their own mathematics make me happy. (Park et al., 2010, p. 78)

> Though it had been so difficult to go on, I have been encouraged by the alumni when they said: "Sir! We want you to keep going no matter what others say." (from a telephone interview in June 2015)

15.4.1.2 Voices from the Teachers of Research Group G

A voluntary group of teachers, Research group G, has tried to apply the mathematics classes based on RME. It is a small group of middle school teachers in Gwangju, formed by Teacher J, who knew about RME when he joined the Korean Society of Teachers of Mathematics. The teachers in the group have become aware of RME through trainings, lectures at university, teacher's associations, and colleagues. Having reorganised the class contents through the process of instructional design, instruction implementation, and instruction analysis based on the MiC textbooks since 2010, they have been implementing the RME-based mathematics classes and providing the RME-based after-school activities to the students. They have continued discussions and reflections about their instruction designs on whether the designs were in line with RME as they had not studied the theory in detail.

A survey involving 21 teachers of Research group G in which these teachers were asked about the strengths and weaknesses of the RME-based mathematics classes (see Table 15.1) revealed that overall, the number of teachers responding positively was much larger than the number of teachers responding negatively.

The survey suggested that the RME-based mathematics instruction has a need for a course rearrangement that shortens the progressive mathematisation process to fit into the Korean education environment, and a need for explicit expressions of the principles and concepts, and the exercises for review. At the same time, the instruction should provide the atmosphere for the students to think by themselves and share their ideas, while keeping the strengths of the mathematics classes based

Table 15.1 Teachers' opinions about strengths and weaknesses of RME-based mathematics classes

Strengths of RME-based mathematics classes	Weaknesses of RME-based mathematics classes
It is connected to daily life	The book is too verbose
It helps to get to know mathematics through situations	The flow is too slow to make a progress
It helps to improve the ability to think mathematically	The structure is not organised well
	There are not enough exercises
It provides ample chances for mathematical inquiry and reasoning	The expressions are too diverse and informal
	Though interesting, the context is not well aligned with the concept and the principle
It provides natural motivations to learn mathematics	It does not look like a mathematics textbooks
The situation is natural and interesting	The objective of each lesson is not obvious
Mathematical communication is natural and active	
Many activities are presented	
It exposes various thoughts and experiences of the students	

on RME, that is, its various contexts that are likely to happen in daily life and the emphasis on mathematical thinking, communication, and practical activities.

In addition to what the teachers themselves thought about the strengths and weaknesses of the RME-based mathematics classes they were also asked to describe positive and negative impacts on student learning (see Table 15.2).

15.4.2 Voices from the Students Themselves Regarding RME

15.4.2.1 Voices from the Students in Elementary School J

Under the supervision of Professor C, Teacher H of Elementary School J conducted the mathematics classes utilising the Korean version of the MiC textbook in a sixth-grade class during the Creative Extracurricular Courses for about eight months from April to December 2004. After the courses finished, the students were interviewed to understand how the characteristics of the course influenced them, which is shown in their reactions.

From the interview with Student Y:

The course presented many stories and examples. It was good to improve mathematical reasoning as well as writing skills. But, I have to understand and calculate at the end, and the Korean instruction method was also necessary because it emphasised calculation. The course content was similar to what we have really done in daily activities. It was tough because the course needed more thinking than the Korean instruction method and it focused on principles and understanding. But it was worth doing after all. It was useful to apply the contents to daily activities because the examples in the book were more relevant to daily life.

From the interview with Student G:

Table 15.2 Teachers' opinions about positive and negative impacts on student learning in the RME-based mathematics classes

Positive impacts on student learning	Negative impacts on student learning
Students learned that mathematics was relevant to daily life	Students were uncomfortable because they had to think too much
Students liked that they could know various ways other students thought and found	Students felt difficulty to express what they thought
Students knew that mathematics was not only about formulas	Students who were poor at mathematics showed less satisfaction
Students found interests in mathematics	The instant effect seemed poor compared to the time and effort
Students liked to be actively involved in the class	More exercises were needed to understand
Students gained confidence during the course to solve challenging problems	Students were unfamiliar with multiple correct answers
Students liked that they could think more than just calculating only	Students were reluctant to expose their thought to other students
Students liked that they could learn a single subject in great detail	Students were not accustomed to understanding mathematics by context unlike the conventional instruction that teaches explicit principles and concepts
	Students were bothered by too much participation being demanded
	Students felt difficulty to find solutions by themselves
	Students were not familiar with the instruction style

The solution for a question in the Korean mathematics class is always determined. I mean about how to solve it. However, the Creative Extracurricular Courses did not make it determined, and allowed a second way. All the things were different from the Korean course, and the Creative Extracurricular Courses encouraged thinking and understanding while the Korean course taught the principle for calculation only. It was more comfortable and easy to understand and draw a result, because it dealt with common senses that we have already known without relying on tough calculations.

Student Y, whose academic achievement was mediocre, described that the RME-based instruction provided a chance to take pride in himself when he solved difficult problems, helped to improve the skills for mathematical thinking as well as for communication due to its diverse stories and examples presented, and was applicable to daily life because of its contexts linked with real situations. Student G, whose academic achievement was also mediocre, told that the instruction was easy and interesting because it focused on understanding by thinking and emphasised the diversity in thinking so that he could use his common senses.

After the course finished, students did show changes in their attitudes and viewpoints regarding mathematics, which is clearly shown in the following reactions.

From the interview with Student K:

> Beforehand, I had thought calculation was all of mathematics. Now I have started to try various methods for a question and compared with others. It would be good if Korean textbooks present various methods.

From the interview with Student L:

> Before I took the Creative Extracurricular Courses, I thought mathematics was to calculate according to formulas. But now I solve by my own methods that I create, and mathematics is interesting to me. Often, I think I find new aspects of mathematics when I try with a different method.

Student K, whose academic achievement was high, developed his viewpoint on mathematics that requires reasoning and provides chances to communicate with others, and hoped Korean mathematics textbooks would present various methods and reasons. Student L, whose academic achievement was low, said that he found new aspects of mathematics as he knew he could use his own methods, while he had thought mathematics was to apply given formulas to calculate before.

In summary, the students described the characteristics of the mathematics instruction as an instruction of mathematics that deals with situations and stories relevant to daily activities, encourages reasoning over calculation, suggests various methods over formulas, provides creative activities, is applicable to daily activities, and is fun.

15.4.2.2 Voices from the Students in Elementary School G

The teachers in Elementary School G conducted mathematics classes using Korean version of the MiC textbook for all Grade 4 students from September to December 2005, and studied the effects of RME-based mathematics instruction on the students' view on mathematics- related issues by comparing the results in this experimental group with Grade 4 students in a control group in which the students were taught in a regular way. Although the MiC textbook was developed for Grade 5–8, the teachers considered it appropriate for Grade 4 students because the students are relatively high achieving and they have learned necessary mathematical concepts such as angle (Shin, Park, Chong, & Chang, 2006).

The students were asked about professions that require mathematical competences and what they think about problem solving. Table 15.3 shows that the experimental group recognised more professions that need mathematical competence than the control group did and also showed more fluency in recognising these occupations. In addition, the experimental group was more positive about the process of reasoning for problem solving. The results support that RME-based mathematics instruction with the Korean MiC textbook is more effective to improve the recognition of mathematical competence required in professions and a positive attitude towards mathematical reasoning than the traditional mathematical instruction.

Table 15.3 Students' view in the experimental and the control group on professions that need mathematical competence and on problem solving (Shin et al., 2006, p. 40)

Students' view	Experimental group			Control group			t	p
	n	M	SD	n	M	SD		
Fluency on recognition of professions that require mathematical competence	210	3.80	2.68	122	2.50	1.65	4.82	0.00
Diversity in recognition of professions that require mathematical competence	210	2.36	1.68	122	1.77	1.28	3.34	0.00
Originality in recognition of professions that require mathematical competence	210	0.55	0.91	122	0.33	0.69	2.36	0.02
Negative attitude to reasoning for problem solving	210	0.17	0.40	122	0.31	0.56	2.74	0.01

15.5 Concluding Remarks

Many research groups for mathematics education in Korea have paid attention to RME over 30 years. In Sect. 15.2, it was reported that RME has been actively discussed from both theoretical and practical viewpoints through doctoral and master theses as well as journals. As a result, RME has greatly influenced the research and practices of Korean mathematics education. In particular, it has been one of the useful perspectives and references that helped to identify and revise many issues in Korean mathematics education. However, the introduction of the RME perspectives to Korean mathematics education has been discussed very carefully because of its very different, and often contrary, aspects from what has been emphasised traditionally in Korean mathematics education.

In Sect. 15.3, the influences of RME and the MiC textbook on mathematics teaching-learning in Korea have been discussed, which focused on the curriculum, the textbook, and the assessments. In the adjustments on the standards of mathematics curriculum, the RME theory and its didactical phenomenological analysis influenced adopting progressive mathematisation. Regarding the textbook, the RME theory and the MiC textbook have inspired mathematics educators in Korea to find and develop appropriate contexts that improve the negative attitudes of Korean students to mathematics and help to experience mathematics as a human activity. The pyramid model of De Lange (2003) has played a critical role to reorganise the frame of unit assessments of the Korean mathematics textbook in elementary school. In addition, the suggestions of Van den Heuvel-Panhuizen (1996) to make paper-and-pencil tasks more informative have influenced the development of tasks and problems in the unit assessments of the elementary school mathematics textbook in Korea.

Section 15.4 reported the voices from teachers and students in Korea about RME. Both teachers and students told that mathematics instruction based on RME could change the recognition of mathematics to a positive stance, because it provided natural situations and activities that encouraged students to actively participate through diverse thoughts and communications. However, they added that it should be considered to shorten the process of mathematisation and to have repetitive exercises that fit the Korean education environment. Meanwhile, a study of the influence of RME-based mathematics instruction on the attitudes of students showed that the instruction improved recognition of the mathematical competence required in professions and attitude on mathematical reasoning. In order to extend the efforts done at the school level so far in relation with RME-based instruction, communication between the teachers and the researchers will be essential, which leads to sharing of perspectives on adapting the RME theory to Korean mathematics education.

References

Baek, H. B. (2004). Case study about teaching mathematics using textbook series of 'Mathematics in Context' in Iwoo Middle School. In Y. Chong, J. Hong, D. Seo, S. Kwon, & J. Pang (Eds.), *Proceedings of the 26th Conference on the Mathematics Education* (pp. 665–676). Seoul, South Korea: The Korea Society of Educational Studies in Mathematics.

Cho, Y. M., & Park, H. N. (2011). A scheme of the instruction of prism definition for 5th grade students. *Journal of Elementary Mathematics Education in Korea, 15*(2), 317–332.

Chong, Y. O. (1997). *Study on Freudenthal's mathematising instruction theory.* Unpublished doctoral dissertation. Seoul, South Korea: Seoul National University.

De Lange, J. (2003). *The great assessment picture book.* http://www.fi.uu.nl/catch/products/GAP_book/intro.html.

Freudenthal, H. (1973). *Mathematics as an educational task.* Dordrecht, the Netherlands: D. Reidel Publishing Company.

Freudenthal, H. (1983). *Didactical phenomenology of mathematical structures.* Dordrecht, the Netherlands: D. Reidel Publishing Company.

Han, D. H. (1997). *A study on the genetic approaches to calculus.* Unpublished master dissertation. Seoul, South Korea: Seoul National University.

Janvier, C. (1980). Translation processes in mathematics education. In R. Karplus (Ed.), *Proceedings of the Fourth International Conference for the Psychology of Mathematics Education* (pp. 237–242). Berkeley, CA: International Group for the Psychology of Mathematics Education.

Kang, H. J., & Kang, H. K. (2008). A reconstruction of probability unit of elementary mathematics textbook based on Freudenthal's reinvention method. *Journal of Elementary Mathematics Education in Korea, 12*(1), 79–100.

Kim, N. H. (1997). *Didactical analysis of variable concept and search for the direction of its learning-teaching.* Unpublished doctoral dissertation. Seoul, South Korea: Seoul National University.

Kim, S. H., & Na, G. S. (2008). Teaching the concept of rate and ratio—Focused on using the reconstructed textbook. *The Journal of Educational Research in Mathematics, 18*(3), 309–333.

Kim, K., Kim, S., Kim, N., Park, S., Park, H., & Jung, S. (2008). *Findings from trends in international mathematics and science study for Korea: TIMSS 2007 international report in Korea.* Seoul, South Korea: Korea Institute of Curriculum & Evaluation.

Kim, K., Kim, M., Ok, H., Rim, H., Kim, S., Jung, S., et al. (2010). *The programme for international students assessment (PISA 2009) results.* Seoul, South Korea: Korea Institute of Curriculum & Evaluation.

Ko, J. H. (2005). *A study on activistic construction of number concept at the beginning of school age.* Unpublished doctoral dissertation. Seoul, South Korea: Seoul National University.

Lakatos, I. (1976). *Proofs and refutations.* Cambridge, UK: Cambridge University Press.

Lee, H. R. (2007). *A study on the development and the effect of realistic mathematization learning model*. Unpublished doctoral dissertation. Seoul, South Korea: Hongik University.

Lee, J. Y., Choi, B., Kim, D. J., Song, Y. J., Yoon, S. H., Hwang, S. M., et al. (2008). *Middle school Math 1*. Seoul, South Korea: Chunjae Education.

Lee, K.-H. (1996). *A study on the didactic transposition of the concept of probability*. Unpublished doctoral dissertation. Seoul, South Korea: Seoul National University.

Lee, Y. R., & Lee, K.-H. (2006). A case study on the introducing method of irrational numbers based on the Freudenthal's mathematising instruction theory. *The Journal of Educational Research in Mathematics, 16*(4), 297–312.

Ministry of Education and Human Resources Development (2007). *Mathematics curriculum. [Supplement 8]*. Statute Notice of Ministry of Education & Human Resources Development (No. 2007-79). Seoul, South Korea: Ministry of Education and Human Resources Development.

Ministry of Education. (2015a). *Teacher guidebook for mathematics 6-1*. Seoul, South Korea: Chunjae Education.

Ministry of Education (2015b). *Mathematics curriculum. [Supplement 8]*. Statute Notice of Ministry of Education (No. 2015-74). Seoul, South Korea: Ministry of Education.

National Center for Research in Mathematical Sciences Education (NCRMSE) & Freudenthal Institute (1997–1998). *Mathematics in context: A connected curriculum for grades 5–8*. Chicago, IL: Encyclopaedia Britannica Educational Corporation.

Park, K.-S. (1992). *The didactically phenomenological approach in instruction of function concept*. Unpublished doctoral dissertation. Seoul, South Korea: Seoul National University.

Park, K., Chong, Y., Kim, H., Kim, D., Choi, S., & Choi, J. (2010). *A research on the developmental plan for mathematics education in elementary and secondary school* (Report No. 2010-20). Seoul, South Korea: Ministry of Educational Science and Technology & Korea Foundation for the Advancement of Science & Creativity.

Shin, J., Park, Y., Chong, Y., & Chang, S. (2006). *The effects of MiC program on learner's problem solving ability and attitudes*. Seoul, South Korea: Association of Research on Cognitive Learning in College of Education of Seoul National University.

Streefland, L. (1985). Search for the roots of ratio: Some thoughts on the long term learning process (towards a theory) part II: The outline of the long term learning process. *Educational Studies in Mathematics, 16,* 75–94.

Treffers, A. (1987). *Three dimensions. A model of goal and theory description in mathematics instruction—The Wiskobas project*. Dordrecht, the Netherlands: Reidel.

Van den Heuvel-Panhuizen, M. (1996). *Assessment and Realistic Mathematics Education*. Utrecht, the Netherlands: CD-ß Press/Freudenthal Institute, Utrecht University.

Van Hiele, P. M. (1986). *Structure and insight: A theory of mathematics education*. Orlando, FL: Academic Press.

Verstappen, P. (1982). Some reflections on the introduction of relations and functions. In G. van Barneveld & H. Krabbendam (Eds.), *Proceedings of Conference on Functions* (pp. 166–184). Enschede, the Netherlands: National Institute for Curriculum Development.

Woo, J. H. (1980). A criticism about anti-Piaget's theories about the mathematics educational point of view. *The Research of Mathematics and Science Education, 7,* 15–29.

Woo, J. H. (1986). Some remarks on the van Hiele's level theory of mathematical learning. *Education Research and Practice, 33,* 85–103.

Woo, J. H. (1994). A study on the H. Freudenthal's phenomenological theory of mathematics education. *The Journal of Educational Research in Mathematics, 4*(2), 93–128.

Woo, J. H. (1998). *Educational foundations of school mathematics*. Seoul, South Korea: Seoul National University Press.

Yu, H. J. (1995). *Didactical-phenomenological analysis of rational number concept and the direction of its learning-teaching*. Unpublished doctoral dissertation. Seoul, South Korea: Seoul National University.

Chapter 16
The Influence of Realistic Mathematics Education Outside the Netherlands—The Case of Puerto Rico

Omar Hernández-Rodríguez, Jorge López-Fernández,
Ana Helvia Quintero-Rivera and Aileen Velázquez-Estrella

Abstract In this chapter, we describe the genesis and evolution of Realistic Mathematics Education (RME) in Puerto Rico, and analyse the aspects that allowed or deferred its influence on local mathematics education. RME was introduced in Puerto Rico thanks to a group of mathematics professors at the University of Puerto Rico, Río Piedras Campus, who collaborated, first with staff from Wisconsin University and later more closely with a team of designers from the Freudenthal Institute. This was the beginning of a collaboration that lasted several years and accounted for the design and development of quality educational materials adapted to the Puerto Rican reality. The initial goal was to develop a curriculum for the elementary level, but it soon developed into a more comprehensive project *Las Matemáticas en Contexto en Puerto Rico* (MeC-PR) that included training for teachers and developers, implementation efforts, and research initiatives. RME in Puerto Rico went through interconnected, and sometimes overlapping, stages of design, training, implementation, and research. All of them left their mark in different areas such as educational practices, official documents, and research practices.

Keywords Realistic Mathematics Education · Mathematics in context · Puerto Rico

O. Hernández-Rodríguez (✉)
Department of Graduate Studies, School of Education, University of Puerto Rico, Río Piedras, Puerto Rico
e-mail: omar.hernandez4@upr.edu

J. López-Fernández · A. H. Quintero-Rivera
Department of Mathematics, University of Puerto Rico, Río Piedras, Puerto Rico
e-mail: jorgemar.lopez@gmail.com

A. H. Quintero-Rivera
e-mail: aquinter_2000@yahoo.com

A. Velázquez-Estrella
Carmen D. Ortiz School, Aguas Buenas, Puerto Rico
e-mail: aileen.velazquez@gmail.com

© The Author(s) 2020
M. van den Heuvel-Panhuizen (ed.), *International Reflections
on the Netherlands Didactics of Mathematics*, ICME-13 Monographs,
https://doi.org/10.1007/978-3-030-20223-1_16

297

16.1   Introduction

This chapter is divided into five sections that describe: (1) the beginnings of Realistic Mathematics Education (RME) in Puerto Rico; (2) the efforts for the development of educational materials based on RME principles and adapted to Puerto Rican culture; (3) the training of teachers for the implementation of the materials in their class-rooms; (4) the incorporation of some elements of RME into the official documents of the Puerto Rican Department of Education (PRDE), the official government cus-todian of public mathematics education in Puerto Rico; (5) and the research efforts based on RME. The advances consider the significant developments experienced in RME in Puerto Rico, largely possible thanks to a collaborative effort between the Department of Graduate Studies of the College of Education and the Department of Mathematics at the University of Puerto Rico, Río Piedras Campus (UPR-RP). Finally, some concluding remarks are given to set the most likely directions for future endeavours. The authors took into consideration the contributions of many people related to RME: the people that brought the idea to Puerto Rico, the principals of the Regional Training Centres on Mathematical Instruction (CRAIM) that shaped and made possible training workshops for teachers, the people who promoted the inclusion of RME in official PRDE documents, the school teachers and university professors who participated in the design and development of the materials, and the teachers that later on used the materials in their classrooms, thus making a notable contribution to the validation of the materials, and, in doing so, giving an eloquent example of the effectiveness of the principles of RME when applied to mathematics teaching and learning.

16.2   The First Steps

RME was introduced in Puerto Rico in 1992 when Thomas A. Romberg, then director of the National Center for Research in Mathematical Sciences Education (NCRMSE) and professor of Curriculum and Instruction at the University of Wisconsin in Madi-son, visited Puerto Rico as an evaluator of the National Science Foundation for the Puerto Rico Statewide Systemic Initiative project. On that occasion, Romberg con-tacted Jorge López-Fernández to propose collaboration with him and Jan de Lange, director of the Freudenthal Institute (FI) at Utrecht University in the Netherlands, for the development of Spanish versions of the materials of the textbook series *Mathe-matics in Context* (MiC) (NCRMSE & Freudenthal Institute, 1997–1998), meant for the U.S. middle school (Grades 5–8), being developed at the University of Wisconsin-Madison together with the Freudenthal Institute. Romberg had become familiar with the RME approach developed at the FI at Utrecht University, and considered that it was consistent with the vision of the emerging standards recently developed and published by the National Council of Teachers of Mathematics (NCTM) and that it could serve as a model for the middle grades curriculum for the United States (Webb & Meyer, 2007).

By that time, Jorge López-Fernández, a mathematician by training, was the director of the CRAIM, one of the few centres responsible for giving training in mathematics to Puerto Rican in-service teachers. By then, trainings given by CRAIM were focused mainly on the improvement of the mathematical content knowledge of teachers. Initially, most trainers were university professors in mathematics from different campuses of the University of Puerto Rico.

From that initial contact, Jorge López-Fernández and Professor Víctor García-Muñiz were engaged in the translation to Spanish and cultural adaptation of the MiC units and the corresponding teacher guides developed at NCRMSE. The first materials for middle school (Grades 5–8) in Spanish based on RME principles were developed. In this effort, several people from different campuses of the University of Puerto Rico were integrated into the CRAIM team.[1] As part of the Puerto Rican participation in the development of the MiC units, CRAIM got special permission to use the materials for teacher training seminars and workshops as long as there was no commercial version available. This access to using the experimental materials with teachers gave a significant boost to RME in Puerto Rico.

From the beginning, it became clear that the units developed at the FI were of exceptional quality. This led the CRAIM principals to implement the teaching of these units at various schools in Puerto Rico and investigate their effect on students. In 1995, with financial and logistical support from the Encyclopaedia Britannica Educational Corporation, a CRAIM team piloted some of the recently created materials with students from a second unit[2] school in a rural area of the municipality of Yabucoa. Participants in the experimental group were disadvantaged students and surprisingly outperformed their peers in the regular stream. This led Jorge López-Fernández to consider establishing a direct partnership with the people who developed the materials for MiC.

16.3 A Productive Collaboration

After the MiC project with Romberg, around 1995 a second collaboration ensued between the FI and CRAIM, with the purpose of developing a curriculum for elementary school. In fact, it was desirable to co-develop instructional materials with the FI to incorporate RME's philosophic views to the design of mathematics materials fitting Puerto Rican culture. The public policy of the time supported the solution of problems as a strategy to teach mathematics, however, teachers had difficulties implementing it. Most of the teachers required for the didactical material to be full

---

[1] Among these, Ana Helvia Quintero-Rivera and René Hernández-Toledo, mathematics professors at respectively the UPR Río Piedras and Cayey campuses, stood out.

[2] Locally, the term 'second unit' is used to describe schools with all grades from elementary to intermediate (Grades K–9).

of interesting and concise contexts avoiding general and open-ended tasks. In addition, findings from previous pilot testing show MiC material requires students to do extensive reading, an obvious deterrent to its use. A more piecemeal approach became the goal, and it was achieved thanks to the collaboration between the FI and CRAIM, which lasted several years. Eventually the Mathematics Program of the PRDE became interested in the project and decided to give financial support.

The project was then called Las Matemáticas en Contexto en Puerto Rico[3] (MeC-PR) and its goal was to develop a curriculum for the elementary level (Grades K–6), based on the principles of RME, to meet the needs of the Puerto Rican school system. The plan to undertake the task was two-fold: to create a collaborative development team with developers from the FI and CRAIM, and to train Puerto Rican teachers, developers and researchers on RME. Koeno Gravemeijer led the Dutch team and Jorge López-Fernández the Puerto Rican team that participated in the design of the curriculum materials. The Puerto Rican team consisted of mathematics professors and teachers from public schools.

The purpose of the initial stage was to form a critical mass of developers able to undertake a series of projects to create materials based on Gravemeijer's textbook series *Rekenen & Wiskunde*, but taking into consideration the normative documents of PRDE mathematics education and the very particular contexts suitable for Puerto Rican students. CRAIM's staff encountered many problems that had to be overcome. For example, the materials as well as the teacher guides were in Dutch. Non-specialised translators were contracted to translate some of the students' materials; in fact, they were Puerto Rican students that learned the language while holding internships in Dutch universities. In addition, the Dutch team developed executive summaries in English that served as guides to start the development of the units. However, the most difficult and important issue was the need to transform the paradigms of Puerto Rican educators, given that the RME principles and design methods were different from the ones used in the development of the Puerto Rican curriculum. It was a slow process that took several years. The first production of the Puerto Rican team was the creation of the principles of MeC-PR to be used as reference for the design and development of the materials, and also for the training of teachers who would implement the materials in their classrooms later on. Ana Helvia Quintero-Rivera and Jorge López-Fernández developed five learning principles and five teaching principles based on those exposed by Treffers (1991).

The general principles, succinctly presented in Table 16.1, were stated in *Los Principios Generales del Aprendizaje y de la Enseñanza* (López-Fernández & Quintero-Rivera, 1995), a document widely used to promote the MeC-PR goals and philosophy. In the document, these principles are explained and illustrated with examples on how to use them in training workshops for teachers, and for the design and development of curriculum materials.

After the initial statement of principles and goal, several years of intense labour followed under the guidance of Koeno Gravemeijer, who was instrumental in overcoming the many difficulties that this project encountered. A lot of time was invested

---

[3]Mathematics in Context in Puerto Rico.

Table 16.1 Learning and teaching principles as stated in the document *Los Principios Generales del Aprendizaje y de la Enseñanza* (López-Fernández & Quintero-Rivera, 1995)

Learning principles	Teaching principles
Learning is a constructive process, that is, learning is built. Students learn by building their own knowledge, that is, relating new ideas and concepts to the body of knowledge they already have	Teaching must come from students (exploring their informal or prior mathematical knowledge) and must originate in the consideration of specific situations that arise in contexts of interest to students. Overall teaching should follow the outline concrete, pre-formal, formal stages
Knowledge is achieved over long periods of time and across levels of abstraction that become progressively higher	Education should be planned to provide the circumstances for the student to develop their mathematical knowledge through progressively higher levels of abstraction. It must be specifically designed to 'integrate' vertically the elements of mathematics education in order to provide opportunities for the introduction of models, notations, conceptual schemes, symbols, etc., that promote the transition from lower to higher levels of knowledge
The students' reflection about their own and others' reasoning promotes the learning of mathematics and elevates the levels of abstraction of the knowledge acquired	The mathematics curriculum should provide students with multiple opportunities to reflect on the learning of mathematics and to anticipate the mathematical development that still lies ahead. Teachers should make use of challenging situations and conflicting problems to make the students reflect on the nature and the consequences of the mathematical knowledge acquired. Student productions that result from such reflections allow the teacher to determine with more certainty the development reached by the students
Rather than an individually based activity, learning is an activity of social nature. The social and cultural contexts stimulate and guide learning	Education should have an interactive character that promotes the exchange of ideas between students with each other, and between students and the teacher
Learning must be structured and schematic. Learning requires the structuring of data and mathematics skills in a coherent whole. Learners should be able to connect between different areas of the curriculum	Teachers should provide environments that allow students to discover and build relationships between different areas of study of the curriculum. Such linkage should promote the development of connections between the normative documents of mathematics education and individual students. The integration of knowledge must be based on the consideration of actual or contextual situations taken from the everyday world of students, which empower them to use informal strategies in the search for mathematical connections

in educating CRAIM's staff in the theoretical aspects of RME and studying, in seminars and special meetings, different features of RME and the ways in which to apply it to Puerto Rico. CRAIM principals were convinced that RME offered realistic possibilities to develop and execute a solid curriculum.

One example of such difficulties was related to the fact that in Puerto Rico it is expected that students learn the digit-based algorithms (known in Puerto Rico as 'column algorithms') for addition and subtraction of natural numbers very early in elementary school. This expectation remains, even though mathematics education research shows that direct exposure to these algorithms fosters serious conceptual errors related to order of magnitude and the decimal representations of numbers. In contrast, students who precede the study of these algorithms with activities based on informal arithmetic and counting strategies, such as rounding to the nearest multiple of five or ten, counting by doubles, among others, end up understanding the digit-based algorithms for addition and subtraction better and faster (Cobb et al., 1991).

To solve the situation, an RME context was adapted at the suggestion of the Dutch team: the cookie factory. At the factory, cookies are sold individually, in packages of ten, in boxes of 10 packages of 10 cookies, and so on. Children had to pack or unpack boxes to solve contextual problems. Horizontal and vertical mathematisation were present in the situations proposed to students (López-Fernández & Velázquez-Estrella, 2007, 2011). The metaphor made it to the textbook materials and research was carried out afterwards to ascertain the possible cognitive advantages related to the discussion and solution of problems that arise in the context of the cookie factory, which naturally led to the digit-based addition and subtraction algorithms. This is exemplary in at least one way; RME incorporates the use of familiar contexts (which could be and most likely are culturally dependent) with the ideas of modelling (descriptive and prospective) as a vehicle for applying Freudenthal's principles to present coherent mathematics education units. In practice, educational systems where innovations are proposed have their own views, judgments and prejudices. For example, in Puerto Rico, if the column algorithms are not present in the arithmetic lessons for the second grade, teachers and the official educational system will not accept such lessons as adequate for teaching. We opted to follow the expected presense of these algorithms, but formulated them in robust MeC-PR units that made their teaching more meaningful and improved significantly student understanding of the algorithms as follow-up research has shown.

The collaboration between the FI and the CRAIM staff finally gave results. The first MeC-PR products for students were thirteen textbooks, two for each elementary Grade 1–6 and one for kindergarten, all including their corresponding teacher guides. The RME materials were designed to minimise printing costs for the production of the student units. All materials can be accessed online and can be made available for students in the form of low cost pamphlets. Furthermore, the MeC-PR materials admit the possibility of continuing renewal and improvement by allowing for the creation of new contexts of current interest. The possibilities for improvement are truly amazing.

It should be appended that in the development of the materials for kindergarten, collaboration was sought by the CRAIM team from the Autonomous University of Barcelona at Bellaterra, led by Joseph Maria Fortuny Aymeni. Traditionally (in Puerto Rico as well as in the Netherlands), kindergarten materials are usually in the hands of both mathematics educators and early childhood experts. The Dutch materials of interest to the CRAIM principals, at the time, did not include kindergarten topics. Monserrat Torra Bitlloch, from the Barcelona Team, worked with Puerto Rican kindergarten teachers to develop the materials for that grade. A by-product of this partnership was the design of a master's degree in the area of elementary mathematics in context for schoolteachers. The entire curriculum was designed and some of the intended virtual courses were prepared.

A few years later, the units went through two stages of revisions. Due to official requirements, the materials had to be aligned to the PRDE mathematics standards released in 2000 and 2007. This represented a problem since in some instances there were huge cultural differences between our mathematics education traditions (influenced mostly by the U.S. Department of Education) and those of the Dutch. On these revisions, materials were edited to a form that made it easier for them to be used as handbooks; the teacher's guides were also revised. These efforts represent an honest way to gain a hold and take possession of the intense and deep didactical tradition of the Netherlands. The textbooks were converted to 'stations', a kind of workbooks with more focalised topics and few objectives. Twenty-eight stations were developed for grades from kindergarten to third grade. All the stations had a teacher's guide with explanations on the use of the models and its connection to MeC-PR principles of learning. Testing and assessment tools were also developed for these stations. Figure 16.1 shows the cover for Station 25 for third grade, and Fig. 16.2 the translation to English of an example of the use of ratio tables to solve problems related to the farm context presented in the station (Centros Regionales de Adiestramiento e Instruccion Matematica, 2011, p. 15).

The Dutch experience had other important effects. Through the influence of Martin Kindt of the FI, it inspired the production of educational materials for talented students. A series titled *Tesoros de la Matemática* (Centros Regionales de Adiestramiento e Instruccion Matematica, 2008) as produced with around fifteen titles. The authors of the series units were renowned local mathematicians from different universities in Puerto Rico. These didactical materials made an honest attempt to keep the mathematical formalities at a distance while conveying the mathematical ideas and intuitions to the young minds interested in finding out about the frontline discoveries of this discipline. They were inspired by Hilbert's old dictum that affirms that a mathematical theory is not to be considered complete until you have made it so clear that you can explain it to the first man whom you meet on the street.

Along with these productions, there were the accompanying trainings of teachers who were to implement the materials in their classrooms. There were also teams of people interested in showing the positive effects of the materials in student learning.

As part of the outreach activities of CRAIM, some of the Grade 1–3 materials were translated into Haitian Creole to be used in teacher training and subsequently with students in Haiti. Also, all of the materials for Grade K–3 have been translated into English to be eventually used with the population of bilingual students in Puerto

Fig. 16.1 Cover of Station
25 (Centros Regionales de
Adiestramiento e Instruccion
Matematica, 2011)

Rico, who typically come to the island having completed part of their studies in the mainland United States.

16.4 Training of Local Staff and Teacher Leaders

Training started right from the beginning of the collaboration with the FI. Jan de Lange, Martin Kindt, Els Feijs, Marja van den Heuvel-Panhuizen, Nisa Figueiredo, Jaap den Hertog, and Koeno Gravemijer were members of the FI team. Some of them came to Puerto Rico to lead workshops on RME principles and methodologies useful in the design of teaching materials. Simultaneously, members of the CRAIM team visited the FI at Utrecht University. Gradually selected teachers from different geographical areas of Puerto Rico were invited to participate in the training sessions. The first effort was to form a team of teacher leaders that would, at a later stage, help the CRAIM staff to develop and pilot the materials. Many materials were locally developed to be used as guides for the training of workshops leaders. The book *Children Learn Mathematics* (Van den Heuvel-Panhuizen, 2001) based on the Dutch TAL project that developed teaching-learning trajectories for primary school and was led by Marja van den Heuvel-Panhuizen, was translated to Spanish[4] and used to train workshop leaders.

An important result of this effort was that a team of workshop leaders was formed to provide training to other teachers. Initially, the focus was on strategies for using

---

[4]Later Spanish versions of these teaching-learning trajectories were also published by Correo del Maestro (see Van den Heuvel-Panhuizen, 2010; Van den Heuvel-Panhuizen & Buys, 2012).

3. How much milk does the dairy farm sell?

a. Don Julio, a farmer, has 40 cows.
If one cow produces 15 liters of milk a day, how many liters in total does he get from his 40 cows?

b. The milk industry pays $75.00 for every 100 liters of milk. How much money does Don Julio recieve daily from his milk?

Price	$75										
Liters of Milk	100										

c. Don José, another farmer, gets 750 liters of milk from milking his cows. How many cows does he have?

Cows	1										
Liters of Milk	15										

d. The milk factory pays the farmer $75.00 for every 100 liters. How much does he receive for 750 liters?

Price	$75										
Liters of Milk	100										

e. If Don Juan recieves $375 from the milk industry, how many liters did he sell?

Price	$75										
Liters of Milk	100										

Mathematics in context   15

Fig. 16.2 Sample of ratio tables used to solve problems related to the farm context (Centros Regionales de Adiestramiento e Instruccion Matematica, 2011, p. 15)

Fig. 16.3 Task that revealed teachers' mathematics shortcoming

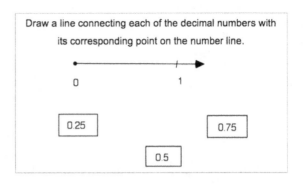

the MeC-PR materials in the school context. But soon it became clear that much more was needed. The need to have teachers participate 'as students' in working out together the details of the units was recognised immediately. Such sessions were followed by detailed discussions around the mathematics of the units and a reflection on the use of paradigmatic situations and the use of apparent areas of conflict. It was clear that these units were not the type of materials that you could place in the hands of teachers and expect them to follow (or even understand) the underlying principles of RME. During these discussions, the teachers asked the leaders to work the problems and tasks presented in the MeC-PR materials with them. As the problems and tasks were solved it became evident that some teachers did not understand some of the mathematical concepts they were supposed to teach. For example, when asked to place the numbers 0.25, 0.5 and 0.75 on the corresponding points on the positive ray of the real line, many K–3 elementary teachers did not take into consideration the decimal position and order of magnitude implied by such decimal expressions, ending this with ordering like: 0.5 < 0.25 < 0.75 (Fig. 16.3).

Surprising as this may appear, it is important to note that this is not only a problem of Puerto Rican teachers. Similar situations have been documented in several studies with teachers and pre-service teachers from other parts of the world (Humarán-Martínez, 2012; Ma, 1999; Simon, 1993; Zazkis & Campbell, 1996). Interaction with teachers revealed that mathematical learning has been dedicated to rules and algorithms, and that their conceptual knowledge was very weak.

To overcome these situations, CRAIM's staff introduced changes. Instead of focusing on the strategies to teach the MeC-PR materials, the leaders of the workshops solved the MeC-PR activities with the teachers, clarifying and building their conceptual knowledge. After working the MeC-PR material, reflection about how the strategies helped them to build their own understanding was stimulated. Teachers discussed how these strategies should be used or modified when teaching their students.

Another shift was necessary when workshop leaders visited the classroom of the teachers participating in the workshops and noticed they were only able to 'integrate' the MeC-PR materials in the mainstream of their classes in a piecemeal manner, without allowing the materials to become the centre of their lessons. As the situation was discussed between CRAIMS's principals and the workshop leaders, it was evident that integrating the MeC-PR materials in the curriculum was not an easy task. The main difficulties arose from the fact that the PRDE mathematics curriculum follows a very well established and rather monolithic approach that makes it particularly difficult to readily apply the new materials, given the need for time for repetition and revisiting the discussion of topics of the curriculum at different grades in order to allow for integration, coherence and verticalisation of seminal mathematical ideas. These experiences were used to feed the design process and introduce improvements to the materials.

The most challenging and important issue to be overcome was the change of paradigm that Puerto Rican educators had to make, given that the RME principles and design methods were different from the ones used in the development of the Puerto Rican curriculum. There was a major balancing act to be completed: promoting teachers' inventiveness on how to work the MeC-PR materials while following the official curriculum.

From 2004 to 2008 intensive training sessions were scheduled during the summer months with follow-ups in Saturday meetings during the regular academic year. Hundreds of teachers participated and some of them were selected to implement materials in their classrooms. For example, teachers from the Antonio S. Pedreira School in the San Juan School District were selected to implement the MeC-PR curriculum. All support and materials were given to help teachers in this enterprise.

In 2009, Doctor Omar Hernández-Rodríguez, from the College of Education of the University of Puerto Rico, Río Piedras Campus (UPR-RP), started to use the CRAIM materials to train K–6 teachers from the Mathematics and Science Partnerships Project (MSP) that he directed. Aileen Velázquez Estrella and María del Pilar Díaz, two of the CRAIM staff who were also public-school teachers and users of MeC-PR materials, trained a dedicated group of K–3 level teachers in the use of these materials in the classroom.

Graduate students from the College of Education were integrated into the training sessions and acted as research assistants. They interviewed some of the participant teachers, led focal groups, and visited the classrooms of the teachers using the MeC-PR materials. Several video recordings of the leaders of the workshops and the participating teachers' classrooms were completed. A new wave of research initiatives started to emerge. These will be described in more detail in the research section of this paper.

16.5 A Parallel Effort that Led to Official Recognition

By the time, in 1995, that the FI and CRAIM collaboration started, Professor Leonardo Torres Pagan, then a high school mathematics teacher, developed ten units using the RME principles. These units were part of an academic endeavour to fulfil his master's degree requirements (Torres-Pagán, 1997). Unlike the ones developed by the CRAIM team, his units were aimed at high school students, specifically tenth grade.

The units, of a contextual nature, were intended to "present new ways of working with mathematics" (Torres-Pagán, 1997, p. 45). These were adapted from the examples found by Torres-Pagán on the articles published by FI staff in international journals. Each unit presented a context, and students were required to use mathematical concepts to solve problems related to the context. For example, students were asked to submit proposals to develop the economy of a Caribbean island through ecotourism. They also had to submit statistical data to support their development plan. By 1997, Torres-Pagán came to meet Professor Gail Burrill, then collaborating with Romberg in the MiC project. Positively impressed by the quality of his activities, Burrill invited Torres to attend her lectures at the annual convention of the NCTM. Torres-Pagán also came to meet Professor Glenda Lappan who worked in the Connected Mathematics project. Burrill and Lappan gave Torres-Pagán advice on how to improve the materials he developed. It is important to mention that Gail Burrill was elected president of the NCTM and also participated in the top-level project Core-Plus Mathematics. All the projects, Mathematics in Context, Connected Mathematics, and Core-Plus Mathematics, were funded by the National Science Foundation and were intended to develop instructional materials aligned to the NCTM standards that were released in 1989 (see Hirsch, 2007).

By 2000, Torres-Pagán presented a proposal to PRDE to extend the use of his materials to a total of ten schools. The PRDE Office of Federal Affairs supported the proposal. Training was given to all participating high school teachers (Grade 10–12); the materials were reproduced and distributed to all participating schools. However, the materials did not have the expected effect. The main reasons were: the pressure on teachers regarding the issue of how to address the curricular contents in harmony with the standardised test then used for students' assessment; the little amount of contact between the director of the proposal and the participating teachers (Torres-Pagán was also a teacher and had to attend his own classroom); and, to a lesser extent, the lack of alignment with the contents of the Puerto Rican curriculum.

By 2006, Torres-Pagán became director of the PRDE's Mathematics Program office. The previous director, Professor Leida Negrón, had initiated collaboration with MeC-PR, funding the development of materials and elementary teachers' training. She also included some ideas of RME in the curriculum framework published in 2003 endorsed by the PRDE (Departamento de Educación de Puerto Rico, 2003). For example, it stated the importance of the use of contexts for mathematics learning, included the idea that the teaching/learning of mathematics is a social process, and included many references to RME authors such as Freudental and Treffers. This curriculum framework is the one currently being enforced in Puerto Rico.

When Torres-Pagán assumed the PRDE's Mathematics Program director's position, he continued the collaboration with MeC-PR and promoted the principles of RME as the theoretical framework of the PRDE Mathematics Program. For example, the use of contexts familiar to students was included in the *Circular Letter Number 1* of the academic year 2007–2008 (Departamento de Educación de Puerto Rico, 2007), which states public policy about the teaching of mathematics in public schools. From that position, Torres-Pagán also sponsored López-Fernández' proposals for the design and development of curriculum materials from kindergarten through third grade. As for the administrative aspects, he directly supervised the bureaucratic processes to ensure the contracting of services between the UPR-RP and PRDE.

From the very beginning, educational research was present in CRAIM efforts. First to establish the effect of the translated MiC materials for Grades 5–8 created at the University of Wisconsin by Romberg's and the FI team, then to establish the perceptions of teachers on the possibilities and difficulties in the implementation of RME materials, and more recently in a series of projects that try to determine the way mathematics is taught in schools and how the process can be improved using the foundation and principles of RME. The next section describes the major achievements of research.

16.6   Research as an Integral Part or RME in Puerto Rico

As previously mentioned, the quality of the work of the FI was evident from the very beginning. It was CRAIM's interest to adequately document the effectiveness of the materials. The first research effort was with the MiC units for Grades 5–8 created at the University of Wisconsin by Romberg's and the FI team and translated to Spanish by CRAIM team. This project was sponsored by Encyclopaedia Britannica Educational Corporation in 1994. All participants were fifth-grade students of the School Segunda Unidad of Yabucoa, both regular stream and Title I students. The Title I programme was then intended to provide special services to students from low-income homes showing academic deficiencies. Title I students were randomly divided into two groups. The experimental group used the MeC-PR materials, while the control group used the traditional materials associated with the official curriculum developed by PRDE. Students from the experimental group obtained the highest scores on the standardised mathematics test when compared to similar students from the same school district. All students from the experimental group obtained 85% or more on the mathematics test, and only three students had less than 90%. The following year, all Title I students of the experimental group, that is, using the MeC-PR materials, became regular stream students. The other students in the pilot project had similar scores on the standardised tests mentioned before. This results pleasantly surprised CRAIM team since, normally, students that are trained with materials designed to develop high mathematical thinking skills do not often get particularly high scores on standardised tests that measure routine skills for numerical computations (such as those used in 1995). However, participant students from the experimental group developed such an interest in mathematics that they managed to improve in all areas, including computational skills.

The quality of the MiC materials along with the results from Yabucoa's students encouraged CRAIM principals to develop a complete curriculum for elementary mathematics based on RME principles.

In a similar track, the research of Torres-Pagán had the purpose of showing the effectiveness of the RME-based educational materials. The lessons were tested with a group of fifty students from tenth grade. The students took a test before and after treatment and the averages were compared with an equivalent group receiving the same content using the curriculum from the PRDE (Torres-Pagán, 1997). The difference on the posttest between groups was statistically significant. Despite the reported success, the lessons were not well received by PRDE administrators.

Another research activity was conducted at the School Carmen D. Ortiz in Aguas Buenas, Puerto Rico. The context of the cookies factory was used with second grade students for the development of digit-based addition and subtraction in separate columns (in which every digit takes the value of the column). At the request of teachers, members of CRAIM modelled the use of the materials, and interviewed the children. The effectiveness of the strategy was evident. Even after a year, the children mentioned the context to solve addition and subtraction problems as a point of reference. Results showed that students who went through the arithmetic counting and rounding activities in contextual settings (such as the one of the cookies factory) at an early stage were more prone to learning the algorithms faster than those who jump right into the study of such algorithms. This research is based on similar investigations carried out by Koeno Gravemeijer and others regarding this topic done in the United States. A description of the contexts and results of the research was published in professional journals from Spain and the United States (López-Fernández & Velázquez-Estrella, 2007, 2011).

By 2004, Emely Fernández-Dávila, then a graduate student at the School of Education of the UPR-RP, became interested in determining the impact of the training offered by CRAIM on teachers. Specifically, she wanted to determine how teachers conceived RME as an educational tool, the needs identified to try to bring the materials to the classroom and assessing positive and negative aspects of the implementation. She gathered information by interviewing two participant teachers, the director, and the coordinator of the workshops. To triangulate the data, she analysed the evaluations of the workshops given during the summer of 2004. A complete revision of the literature was carried out, a 130-page report was composed and an executive summary of 30 pages was written. Results indicated that teachers had some doubts about how to implement RME materials in their classes. They felt that activities modelled by international designers were significantly different to those developed locally. Evidence indicated that teachers had problems understanding Freudenthal's guided-reinvention principle and how to apply it with students. The pressure to cover all the curriculum material to be evaluated in the standardised tests, and the time-consuming process to implement the new materials were deterrents to transfer the materials to the classroom. The recommendations called for increasing research projects and the importance of disseminating its findings. The importance of maintaining a link between teachers, trainers and developers was also stated.

In 2008, Jorge López-Fernández and Omar Hernández-Rodríguez met each other and their affinity allowed them to establish collaboration between the Department of Mathematics and the Department of Graduate Studies of the School of Education, both of the UPR-RP. A joint seminar to study issues related to mathematics education was established with the participation of graduate students from mathematics and mathematics education. Simultaneously, graduate students participating at the seminar became familiar with RME principles and methodologies. The main idea was, and still is, to do research to make evident the way Puerto Rican students learn, and to determine how to improve through local solutions. A new wave of efforts on research started to emerge. Some of the results have been published in *Puentes*, a journal edited by graduate students of mathematics and mathematics education, the purpose of which is to disseminate the seminar assistants' findings.

By 2010, Hernández-Rodríguez started to use the MeC-PR materials to train teachers from the Mathematics and Science Partnerships Program (MSP-San Juan) he directed. A group of teachers from the metropolitan area was selected with the purpose of being trained and to transfer RME to their classroom. Graduate students from the School of Education of the UPR-RP were integrated as research assistants to help with the collection of information to be used on further research. Interviews with the workshops leaders and the participating teachers were carried out, videos of model lessons and teachers' class sessions were recorded, and a focus group to explore teachers' perceptions were performed.

Ortiz-Fernández (2015) conducted an analysis of the recordings of the participation of teachers on the focus group and of the videos of four elementary school teachers (Grades K–3) when teaching their classes. In his analysis, he used the guidelines of Godino's onto-semiotic approach to mathematics education (Godino, Batanero, Font, 2007). Discursive and operational productions were analysed to get evidence of epistemic, cognitive, mediational, interactional and emotional elements. He found that teachers had an adequate theoretical knowledge of the discipline, which was evidenced as a holistic view of the learning process. During classes, he observed some specific practices from the MeC-PR trainings, such as the bus that picks up and drops off passengers at bus stops. The activity was conducted with concrete materials developed by the teachers themselves. The use of an environment that allows students manipulation of concrete objects was a common practice of the participant teachers. Activities to motivate students' participation and learning of mathematics were also reported. Although the document evidences, to a certain extent, the use of RME principles and methodologies, a deep analysis of students' mathematical productions was not given.

Meanwhile, Hernández-Bosch (2015) determined the knowledge about the principles and methodologies that still exists in the participants of the 2010 training sessions. He proposed deep interviews with five teachers who participated in training and are still teaching in elementary school. The purpose was to establish how they were using the strategies, models and contexts studied in RME training in their current practice.

On other dissemination efforts, Ana Helvia Quintero-Rivera published the book *Matemáticas con Sentido* (Quintero, 2010) with the purpose to describe RME principles and methodologies. The book is intended for in-service and pre-service elementary teachers and includes ample discussion of activities that promote a deep understanding of mathematics. All the work presented has its roots in the findings over the many years that Doctor Quintero-Rivera has participated on research and development on MeC-PR materials. The book was translated by World Scientific and is available to the English-speaking public under the title *Math Makes Sense! A Constructivist Approach to the Teaching and Learning of Mathematics* (Quintero & Rosario, 2016).

The authors of this chapter published a book titled *Sentido Numérico: Más Allá de Los Números* (López-Fernández, Quintero-Rivera, Hernández-Rodríguez, & Velázquez-Estrella, 2016) the purpose of which is to state the importance of the development of number sense at school level. Through a taxonomy of the current models used by the RME, readers will encounter plenty of examples to develop number sense in a comprehensive way.

16.7   Concluding Remarks

In this chapter, the authors report on the beginnings of RME in Puerto Rico; the efforts made for the development of educational materials adapted to the particular culture, resulting in MeC-PR; the training of teachers for the implementation of the materials in their classrooms; the incorporation of some elements of RME into the official documents of the Puerto Rican Department of Education (PRDE), and the research efforts based on RME. Achievements are mainly due to CRAIM; however, the efforts of others are reported.

At some point, all the elements pointed to the possibility that the MeC-PR could become the spearhead of mathematics education in Puerto Rico. Public policy existed, the educational materials were developed, training was given and there was an entire infrastructure to disseminate MeC-PR. What factors blocked the continuity of scaling up the project? A first element was the change in Puerto Rico's governing party. The PRDE is strongly associated with the governing party. So once there is a political switch, all programme directors usually change. As a result, Professor Torres ceased to be the Mathematics Program director in 2009. Piloting and implementing the MeC-PR materials required additional effort and accompaniment of specialists. Both are expensive and impossible without adequate funding. Given that the new PRDE Program of Mathematics Director was not as enthusiastic about the MeC-PR, the funds were not allocated.

Yet, the most difficult and important issue to be overcome is the change of paradigm that Puerto Rican educators had to make, given the RME principles and design methods, which are different from the ones used in the development of the Puerto Rican curriculum. Indeed, the educational community assigned too much importance to the PRDE mathematical standards, which are for their part aligned to the U.S. standards. The perceived lack of alignment with the educational materials created with the PRDE standards led teachers, supervisors and other officials to discard MeC-PR materials.

We have two major tasks in order to implement the MeC-PR materials. The first one is promoting a change in the professors and professionals that work curriculum development towards RME. Our work with the graduate students at the UPR College of Education is a first step in that direction. Yet we have to work with the professors of mathematics education in the other universities.

In the meantime, we should promote teachers' inventiveness on how to adapt the MeC-PR materials to follow the official curriculum. Indeed, the teachers' manual deals with this issue. The manual suggests ways of working the PRDE standards at the same time that the MeC-PR material is used.

Changing paradigm is not an easy task. Once seen in practice, an example of the new paradigm helps in the transformation. So, another task is to develop a school that follows the MeC-PR materials. We expect that this school will have outstanding results in the PR standard exams, as did the group of Yabucoa. We can then invite PRDE officials and professors of mathematical education to study in practice the model of the new paradigm in action. This might be a third line of action.

As can be seen, we still have an agenda for promoting RME in Puerto Rico. Advances may be possible if people from different governmental and private offices were to consolidate a collaboration project.

References

Centros Regionales de Adiestramiento e Instrucción Matemática. (2008). *Tesoros de la Matemática* [Treasures of mathematics]. San Juan, Puerto Rico: Publicaciones CRAIM.

Centros Regionales de Adiestramiento e Instrucción Matemática. (2011). *La Matemática en Contexto en Puerto Rico. Tercer Grado. Estación 25* [Mathematics in Context in Puerto Rico. Third Grade. Station Number 25]. San Juan, Puerto Rico: Publicaciones CRAIM.

Cobb, P., Wood, T., Yackel, E., Nicholls, J., Wheatley, G., Trigatti, B., et al. (1991). Assessment of a problem-centred second-grade mathematics project. *Journal for Research in Mathematics Education, 22*(1), 3–29.

Departamento de Educación de Puerto Rico. (2003). *Marco curricular del Programa de Matemáticas [Curriculum framework of the Mathematics Program]*. San Juan, Puerto Rico: Author.

Departamento de Educación de Puerto Rico. (2007). Política pública sobre la organización y la oferta curricular del Programa de Matemáticas en los niveles elemental y secundario de las escuelas públicas [Public policy on the organisation and curricular offer of the Mathematics Programme at elementary and secondary levels of public schools]. *Carta Circular Núm. 1*, 2007–08. Documento interno no publicado. San Juan, Puerto Rico: Author.

Godino, J., Batanero, C., & Font, V. (2007). The onto-semiotic approach to research in mathematics education. *ZDM Mathematics Education, 39*(1–2), 127–135.

Hernández-Bosch, J. (2015). *Transferencia de la Matemática en Contexto a los salones del nivel kinder a tercero: reflexiones ante procesos cognitivos y motivacionales* [Transfer of Mathematics in Context to classrooms from kindergarten to third level: Reflections on cognitive and motivational processes]. Unpublished doctoral dissertation Universidad de Puerto Rico.

Hirsch, C. R. (Ed.). (2007). *Perspectives on the design and development of school mathematics curricula*. Reston, VA: National Council of Teachers of Mathematics.

Humarán-Martínez, Y. T. (2012). *El entendimiento del concepto fracción que poseen los maestros en formación para el nivel elemental* [Preservice teachers understanding of the concept of fraction]. Unpublished doctoral dissertation Universidad de Puerto Rico. Disponible en ProQuest Dissertations and Theses (UMI No. 3545795).

López-Fernández, J., & Quintero-Rivera, A. H. (1995). *Los principios generales del aprendizaje y de la enseñanza* [General principles of learning and teaching]. Unpublished document. San Juan, Puerto Rico: CRAIM.

López-Fernández, J., & Velázquez-Estrella, A. (2007). Un ejemplo de la utilidad de los contextos en la matemática realista: los algoritmos de suma y resta por columnas [An example of the usefulness of contexts in Realistic Mathematics: Addition and subtraction algorithms by columns]. *Revista Uno: Didáctica de las Matemáticas, 44,* 95–103.

López-Fernández, J., & Velázquez-Estrella, A. (2011). Contexts for column addition and subtraction. *Teaching Children Mathematics, 17*(9), 540–548.

López-Fernández, J., Quintero-Rivera, A. H., Hernández-Rodríguez, O., & Velázquez-Estrella, A. (2016). *Sentido numérico: más allá de los números [Number sense: Beyond numbers].* Charleston, SC: CreateSpace.

Ma, L. (1999). *Knowing and teaching elementary mathematics: Teachers' understanding of fundamental mathematics in China and the United States.* Mahwah, NJ: Lawrence Erlbaum Associates.

National Center for Research in Mathematical Sciences Education (NCRMSE) & Freudenthal Institute. (1997–1998). *Mathematics in context: A connected curriculum for grades 5–8.* Chicago, IL: Encyclopaedia Britannica Educational Corporation.

Ortiz-Fernández, J. E. (2015). Análisis del conocimiento didáctico matemático del maestro de Matemática en Contexto a partir del enfoque ontosemiótico [Analysis of mathematical didactic knowledge of Mathematics in Context teachers from an ontosemiotic approach]. Unpublished doctoral dissertation Universidad de Puerto Rico.

Quintero, A. H. (2010). *Matemática con sentido [Math makes sense].* San Juan, Puerto Rico: Editorial de la Universidad de Puerto Rico.

Quintero, A. H., & Rosario, H. (2016). *Math makes sense! A constructivist approach to the teaching and learning of mathematics.* London, UK: Imperial College Press.

Simon, M. A. (1993). Prospective elementary teachers' knowledge of division. *Journal for Research in Mathematics Education, 24*(3), 233–254.

Torres-Pagán, L. (1997). *Matemática integrada en contexto: Un currículo realista de matemáticas para estudiantes de décimo grado* [Mathematics integrated in contex: A realistic mathematics curriculum for tenth-grade students]. Unpublished doctoral dissertation Universidad de Phoenix, Guaynabo, Puerto Rico.

Treffers, A. (1991). Realistic Mathematics Education in the Netherlands 1980–1990. In L. Streefland (Ed.), *Realistic Mathematics Education in Primary School.* Utrecht, the Netherlands: CD-ß Press/Freudenthal Institute, Utrecht University.

Van den Heuvel-Panhuizen, M. (Ed.). (2001) *Children learn mathematics.* Utrecht, the Netherlands: Freudenthal Institute, Utrecht University.

Van den Heuvel-Panhuizen, M. (Ed.). (2010). *Los niños aprenden matemáticas [Children learn mathematics].* Cd. Brisa, Naucalpan, México: Correo del Maestro.

Van den Heuvel-Panhuizen, M., & Buys, K. (Eds.). (2012). *Los niños pequeños aprenden medida y geometría [Young children learn measurement and geometry].* Cd. Brisa, Naucalpan, México: Correo del Maestro.

Webb, D. C., & Meyer, M. R. (2007). The case of Mathematics in Context. In C. R. Hirsch (Ed.), *Perspectives on the design and development of school mathematics curricula* (pp. 81–94). Reston, VA: National Council of Teachers of Mathematics.

Zazkis, R., & Campbell, S. (1996). Divisibility and multiplicative structure of natural numbers: Preservice teachers' understanding. *Journal for Research in Mathematics Education, 27*(5), 540–563.

Chapter 17
The Impact of Dutch Mathematics Education on Danish Mathematics Education

Mogens Niss

Abstract Hans Freudenthal—in his capacity as a mathematician as well as a very articulate and thoughtful mathematics educator, as an international 'politician' of mathematics education, as the founder of *Educational Studies in Mathematics*, as a prolific writer, as an organiser of meetings and conferences—exerted quite an influence on Danish mathematics education from the late 1960s onwards. The Dutch mathematics education tradition thus founded always received close attention from the Danish mathematics education community. In this chapter, I outline and discuss the nature of this influence and I attempt to provide an explanation of why this tradition has resonated so well with implicit and explicit movements in Denmark.

Keywords Freudenthal · Freudenthal Institute · Guided re-invention · Mathematical modelling · PISA · Realistic Mathematics Education

17.1 Introduction

For centuries, the relationship between the Netherlands and Denmark has been one of mutual sympathy as well as of cultural and commercial exchange. We both are small, flat and democratic countries without strong formal hierarchies. And we have never been at war with one another. Our languages are part of the same sub-Germanic family, which friendly foreigners are kind enough to label throat diseases.

When it comes to mathematics and mathematics education, historical links are not of an old age, though. However, when Hans Freudenthal (of the University of Utrecht) took office in 1967 as the President of ICMI (the International Commission on Mathematical Instruction), later (in 1969) created the ICMEs (the International Congresses of Mathematical Education), and established the journal *Educational Studies in Mathematics* in 1968, the Netherlands strongly manifested itself in the international limelight and caught the attention of Danish mathematics educators.

M. Niss (✉)
INM—Department of Science and Environment, Roskilde University, Roskilde, Denmark
e-mail: mn@ruc.dk

This interest may in some respects be seen as somewhat surprising. The reason is that the set theory based so-called 'New Math' (or 'Modern Mathematics') movement that gained momentum in some parts and quarters of the world in the years 1955–1975, officially had Denmark as an enthusiastic member, whereas Freudenthal was quite a bit of a sceptic, to put it mildly, certainly much more so than leading Danish mathematicians and mathematics educators, above all Svend Bundgaard of the University of Aarhus and Bent Christiansen of the then Royal Danish School of Education. The brief biography of Freudenthal on the home page of the Freudenthal Institute leaves no doubt of Freudenthal's viewpoint and influence when it states: "Single-handedly Freudenthal saved Dutch education from the American teaching method of New Math, which was introduced in many countries from 1960 onwards".[1] An indication of Freudenthal's scepticism can be found in an ICMI symposium on the teaching of geometry in secondary school that was hosted by the University of Aarhus in 1960, at which Freudenthal and a leading member of the Bourbaki group and New Math advocate Jean Dieudonné of France—two intellectuals who shared a weakness for polemic—engaged in no less than a quarrel.

Freudenthal (Elementærafdeling, 1960, p. 46):

> It is dangerous with too radical changes. We don't obtain anything by introducing too much too early without thinking about the psychological and pedagogical problem.

Dieudonné (Elementærafdeling, 1960, p. 46):

> There are many psychological difficulties; but we don't get anywhere if we are too cautious. There must come a change.

Freudenthal (Elementærafdeling, 1960, p. 47):

> Much harm could be done by introducing new subjects in the school if the teachers don't know these subjects. Then it is better to wait until students reach university. It is more important to abandon obsolete subjects than to introduce new ones.

Freudenthal (Elementærafdeling, 1960, p. 104):

> We cannot teach the pupils everything. There are certain psychological and pedagogical principles which must not be violated.

Dieudonné (Elementærafdeling, 1960, p. 104):

> The important thing is to teach the students some good mathematics. The psychological considerations are of secondary importance. (La psychologie, je m'en fiche).

---

[1] See www.fisme.science.nl/fisme/en/organisation/freudenthal.html. Accessed 7 March 2016 (the text can currently be found at http://www.mathunion.org/icmi/activities/awards/hans-freudenthal-award/).

Over time, Bent Christiansen developed views which came rather close to Freudenthal's, which may well be a reflection of Christiansen's involvement as an ICMI Executive Committee Member and Vice-President, during the years 1975-1986.

17.2 Mathematics as an Educational Task and the Development of Realistic Mathematics Education

To Danish mathematics educators, Dutch mathematics education was, for quite some time, synonymous with Hans Freudenthal, not the least so when he published his massive and impressive monograph *Mathematics as an Educational Task* (Freudenthal, 1973), which soon became a classic in the field and a must-read for the few people involved in research and development in mathematics education in Denmark in the 1970s and 1980s, but also for the more ambitious amongst the mathematics teacher educators in the teacher training colleges.

Freudenthal insisted on seeing mathematics not primarily as an established edifice of finished knowledge, which school may introduce and transmit to students and make them admire, but rather as a field of human activity, and not only that, also as a field of activity that is accessible to 'ordinary' students from the earliest grades. This view made a big impression on Danish mathematics education from the 1970s onwards, which was reflected in national syllabi and curriculum guidelines, in textbooks, and in actual teaching. Also, Freudenthal's emphasis on students' experiential sense-making in mathematics—by way of exploration and guided re-invention—as an essential component of learning exercised considerable and lasting influence on Danish mathematics educators.

In the context of the IOWO[2] and its subsequent 'survivor research group' OW & OC,[3] existing until the establishment in 1991 of the Freudenthal Institute after Freudenthal's death in 1990, the signature programme of Dutch mathematics education, Realistic Mathematics Education (RME), was developed by Freudenthal himself and his collaborators and successors, including internationally well-known mathematics educators such as Jan de Lange, Adri Treffers, Leen Streefland, Koeno Gravemeijer, Marja van den Heuvel-Panhuizen and several others. Many Danish mathematics educators took—and take—great interest in this programme and quite a few have paid shorter or longer visits to the Freudenthal Institute and have established links with Dutch colleagues.

Why is it that RME has resonated with Danish mathematics educators to the extent it has? Let me offer a few elements of an explanation.

---

[2]Instituut voor Ontwikkeling van het Wiskundeonderwijs (Institute for the Development of Mathematics Education); IOWO as a part of Utrecht University was established by Freudenthal in 1971 and closed by the university in 1981.

[3]Onderzoek Wiskundeonderwijs & Onderwijs Computercentrum (Mathematics Education Research and Educational Computer Centre).

First of all, the Netherlands and Denmark seem to have a somewhat liberal, individualistic, independent and anti-authoritarian view of life and approach to education in common. This means that students' individual conceptions and experiences have to be respected and taken as points of departure for teaching and learning. Students—rather than being told what is the case, what to do and how to do it—have to see things for themselves, explore their environment and the world, make experiments, try to figure out how things are related, produce independent reasoning to explain their deliberations, undertakings and findings so as to justify their work and its results. Of course, students need inspiration and stimuli by means of challenging tasks and subsequent guiding by competent teachers so as to ensure the process of guided re-invention. However, the teacher is perceived as a more experienced ally and supervisor rather than as an absolute authority. The individual student's thinking is not only to be taken seriously, but is considered interesting in its own right—as is illustrated so well in Freudenthal's accounts of his dialogues with his grandson Bastiaan.

What about the term 'realistic'? This may be a point where some divergence can be found between the Dutch and the Danish positions. In the Dutch position, 'real' and 'realistic' tend to refer to students' experiential or emotional worlds, not necessarily to reality in some domain of an objective external world. Thus, worlds of adventure, fantasy or games are considered real and realistic if they are so to the students in focus. Of course, this does not imply that objective external reality is excluded from being considered real and realistic, if only students perceive it as motivating and engaging to deal with. In contrast, the Danish position tends to emphasise the external objective reality of the surroundings in which students live, be it the surroundings constituted by family, friends, school, sports, leisure or holidays, be it in the civic or societal surroundings in the local, national or global community, or be it in other scholarly and scientific fields or areas of practice.

17.2.1 Mathematical Modelling

A related point of common interest in Dutch and Danish mathematics education—and yet another reason why RME has attracted attention in Denmark—is the notion and role of mathematical models and mathematical modelling. Once again, Freudenthal took an early initiative by involving himself in organising an international colloquium Why to Teach Mathematics as to Be Useful, held in Utrecht in 1967, by giving the opening address titled "Why to Teach Mathematics so as to Be Useful" at that symposium, and by publishing the talks of the symposium, including his own talk in the first volume of *Educational Studies in Mathematics* (Freudenthal, 1968). During the 1970s, 1980s and 1990s, both countries developed a strong interest in mathematical applications and mathematical modelling for educational purposes, especially at the upper secondary school level, and a fair amount of mutual inspiration and exchange of information, ideas and materials took place between educators from both countries.

As is well-known, the Dutch RME tradition distinguishes between two different sorts of mathematisation, horizontal and vertical mathematisation, a distinction introduced by Adri Treffers in his doctoral dissertation from 1978, later transformed into a book in English (Treffers, 1987). In horizontal mathematisation, an extra-mathematical situation or context is translated into some mathematical domain with the purpose of subjecting aspects of the situation or context to mathematical treatment and eventually inference making. This is the key process in what is usually—in the mathematical modelling literature—called mathematical modelling (see, e.g., Blum, Galbraith, Henn, & Niss, 2007). In vertical mathematisation, a mathematical entity, situation or problem under consideration is transformed into another mathematical entity, situation or problem, typically belonging to a different area than did the original, with the purpose of utilising conceptualisations and approaches of the new area to deal with the transformed entity, situation or problem so as to obtain results pertaining to the original situation. It is worth noting that initially Freudenthal was sceptical towards the usefulness of this distinction, but ended up favouring it in his *China Lectures* (Freudenthal, 1991, p. 41).

This distinction, however, never gained a foothold in Danish mathematics education, primarily because mathematical modelling, including (horizontal) mathematisation, involving some extra-mathematical domain, is perceived as categorially very different from the internal mathematical transformations and processes involved in vertical mathematisation. One might speculate that the reason why, in the Netherlands, horizontal and vertical mathematisation are seen as two sides of the same coin might be that in the RME tradition reality, experience, human minds and mathematics are perceived as constituting a continuum, whereas there is a much more pronounced distinction between reality and mathematics, and between reality and the mind, in Danish mathematics education.

A key point in RME is Koeno Gravemeijer's notion of 'emergent mathematical modelling' (Gravemeijer, 1999, 2007), in which students' attempts at coming to grips with realistic situations (in the sense as it is conceived in RME) may lead them to (re-)invent concepts and relations of formal mathematics as well as to eventually engage in more full-fledged mathematical modelling. The transition from 'models of' to 'models for' is a pivotal idea in this approach that originates with Leen Streefland (1996, 2003). Put somewhat pointedly, this approach may be condensed into a goal stated as if it were a slogan 'modelling for the sake of mathematics (learning)'. The Danish position tends to put emphasis on the reverse goal, namely 'mathematics (learning) for the sake of modelling'. This means that modelling the extra-mathematical world existing outside students' minds is a primary goal in its own right. It goes without saying that there is no contradiction whatsoever between 'modelling for the sake of mathematics (learning)' and 'mathematics (learning) for the sake of modelling'. The difference rather lies in priorities and emphases. Moreover, a given activity may well lend itself to both goals, thus leaving the distinction a bit blurred in actual practice.

One platform for students' engagement in mathematical modelling of aspects of extra-mathematical domains is the A-lympiad, which is an annual modelling contest for students in the upper levels of secondary education in the Netherlands and elsewhere, organised for many years by the Freudenthal Institute, and currently being led by Ruud Stolwijk, in collaboration with colleagues in other European countries. The 'A' stands for the application-oriented curriculum in Dutch upper secondary mathematics, a curriculum which largely grew out of RME. Also, Danish schools have students who participate in this contest.

17.2.2   Integrating Research and Development

A very significant aspect of RME in the Netherlands is that it integrates research and development work, in the sense that the implementation of developmental ideas is followed up and assessed by research and vice versa: research findings lead to further developmental ideas. It is no surprise that this approach has been generalised into one version of what might well be considered a meta research paradigm for (mathematics) education, of course a paradigm with a multitude of different ramifications, called 'design research'. Protagonists in this development are Koeno Gravemeijer, Paul Drijvers, Michiel Doorman, and others, oftentimes in close collaboration with Paul Cobb. These versions of design research have been an inspiration for several Danish mathematics educators as well.

17.2.3   Criticism

It is no secret that RME in the Netherlands has been met with criticism, sometimes fierce criticism, especially in recent years, from mathematicians and others who find the philosophy and the implementation of RME detrimental to mathematics teaching and learning, because they put too much emphasis on exploration and inductively oriented guided re-invention and too little emphasis on formal concept formation and mathematical deduction, thus tending to undermine the recruitment of students to 'serious' tertiary mathematics programmes. Presumably such criticism has also contributed to changing the structure, role and position of the Freudenthal Institute in relation to Utrecht University. Perhaps one might even speak about a sort of Math War in the Netherlands. Even if views do of course vary greatly across and within different quarters of mathematicians and mathematics educators in Denmark, we have not experienced anything like Math Wars, despite the fact that much Danish school mathematics has been markedly influenced by RME. However, in some respects similar divides may be emerging in Denmark, in particular because graphing and symbolic calculators and computers with dynamic geometry and CAS (computer algebra systems) programs tend to replace formal mathematical concept formation and reasoning as well as procedural skills, partly with (undue) reference to RME inspired views of mathematics.

17.3 PISA

It is widely known that when the Organisation for Economic Cooperation and Development (OECD) decided to launch the Programme for International Student Assessment (PISA) in the late 1990s and made mathematics one of the three domains of assessment, Jan de Lange of the Freudenthal Institute was appointed chair of the Mathematics Expert Group (MEG). The author of this chapter became one of the other members. The MEG provided the first definition ever of mathematical literacy, the crucial notion in the mathematics domain in PISA. The fact that Jan de Lange chaired the MEG was instrumental for the genesis and development of the spirit of PISA mathematics, both when it came to the design of the framework for the mathematics part of the assessment, and—perhaps even more so—when it came to the development of assessment items. This fact and the fact that one of the leading test developers throughout the years was another Dutchman, Kees Lagerwaard, left an unmistakably Dutch fingerprint on PISA mathematics from the very beginning, above all on the nature of the test items. This state of affairs was amplified by the involvement in the first PISA consortium of Cito, the Dutch national institute for educational measurement.

So, in many places around the world people tended to see PISA as dominated by a Dutch—or, to be more precise, an RME—perspective. This is evidently an important part of the truth because of the marked Dutch involvement in PISA mathematics, but it is not the whole truth, since all those involved in the MEG, myself included, were in full agreement about everything that was going on in mathematics. We saw PISA's undertakings with respect to mathematics as sound outlets of mathematical literacy at large rather than as a particularly Dutch project. As a matter of fact, a non-trivial part of the thinking and writing on PISA mathematics came from MEG members other than the chair.

Against this background, it is no surprise that PISA mathematics was well received amongst Danish mathematics educators, even though there is a general scepticism and criticism in Denmark about the very idea of international comparative studies such as PISA, and above all about the political (ab)uses of PISA country rankings. However, that scepticism pertains to the overall enterprise rather than to the mathematics component of PISA. Especially the (released) test items have generally been perceived as relevant and reasonable expressions of mathematical literacy.

17.4 Concluding Remarks

In this chapter I have tried to identify some significant points with respect to which Dutch mathematics education has—and has had—an impact on Danish mathematics education, in research and development as well as in practice. As is presumably evident, this impact is certainly non-negligible, even though there are also important differences between Dutch and Danish mathematics education. The influences identified mainly stem from Hans Freudenthal, the Freudenthal Institute and from RME. It should not go unnoticed, however, that there are also other links between Dutch and Danish mathematics education, for example, through Jan van Maanen, whose work on the role of the history of mathematics in mathematics education has inspired more than one Danish mathematics educator.

It remains to be seen whether the fundamental changes of the Freudenthal Institute will also fundamentally undermine the contributions of Dutch mathematics education to mathematics education in the world and in Denmark. We certainly hope not.

References

Blum, W., Galbraith, P. L., Henn, H.-W., & Niss, M. (Eds.). (2007). *Modelling and applications in mathematics education: The 14th ICMI Study*. Dordrecht, New York, Heidelberg: Springer.

Elementærafdeling. (1960). *Lectures on modern teaching of geometry and related topics held at the ICMI-seminar in Aarhus, May 30 to June 2, 1960*. Elementærafdeling nr. 7 AaU, Matematisk Institut. Aarhus, Denmark: Matematisk Institut.

Freudenthal, H. (1968). Why teach mathematics so as to be useful. *Educational Studies in Mathematics, 1*, 3–8.

Freudenthal, H. (1973). *Mathematics as an educational task*. Dordrecht, the Netherlands: D. Reidel Publishing Company.

Freudenthal, H. (1991). *Revisiting mathematics education—China lectures*. Dordrecht, the Netherlands: Kluwer Academic Publishers.

Gravemeijer, K. (1999). How emergent models may foster the constitution of formal mathematics. *Mathematical Thinking and Learning, 1*(2), 155–177.

Gravemeijer, K. (2007). Emergent modelling as a precursor to mathematical modelling. In W. Blum, P. L. Galbraith, H.-W. Henn, & M. Niss (Eds.), *Modelling and applications in mathematics education: The 14th ICMI Study* (pp. 37–144). Dordrecht, New York, Heidelberg: Springer.

Streefland, L. (1996). Learning from history for teaching in the future. Regular lecture held at the ICME-8 in Sevilla, Spain.

Streefland, L. (2003). Learning from history for teaching in the future. *Educational Studies in Mathematics, 54*, 37–62.

Treffers, A. (1987). *Three dimensions: A model of goals and theory description in mathematics education—The Wiskobas project*. Dordrecht, the Netherlands: Kluwer Academic Publishers.

Chapter 18
Two Decades of Realistic Mathematics Education in Indonesia

Zulkardi Zulkardi, Ratu Ilma Indra Putri and Aryadi Wijaya

Abstract In this chapter, we report on the process of adapting Realistic Mathematics Education (RME), a didactic approach founded by Freudenthal in the Netherlands, to the Indonesian context. In Indonesia, RME is called 'Pendidikan Matematika Realistik Indonesia' (PMRI). The chapter starts with describing how RME came to Indonesia. It was Sembiring from the Institut Teknologi Bandung who saw Jan de Lange, the director of the Freudenthal Institute of Utrecht University, presenting a keynote at the ICMI conference in Shanghai in 1994. Then the story continues with the decision of the Indonesian government to send six doctoral candidates to the Netherlands to learn about RME. The chapter also explains the process and results from the development and implementation of RME through a Dutch-Indonesian project Dissemination of PMRI (Do-PMRI). Moreover, the chapter describes examples of implementation strategies such as developing a master's program on RME, designing learning materials using RME theory and the development of a national contest of mathematical literacy using context-based mathematics tasks similar to those employed in the PISA test. The chapter ends with a discussion of two new initiatives at Sriwijaya University in Palembang, namely the development of a Centre of Excellence of PMRI and the establishment of a doctoral programme on PMRI.

Keywords Didactic · Realistic mathematics education · PMRI (Pendidikan Matematika Realistik Indonesia) · Impome (International Master's Programme on Mathematics Education) · PISA · Mathematical literacy · Context-based mathematics tasks

Z. Zulkardi (✉) · R. I. I. Putri
Sriwijaya University, Palembang, Indonesia
e-mail: zulkardi@unsri.ac.id

R. I. I. Putri
e-mail: ratu.ilma@yahoo.com

A. Wijaya
Yogyakarta State University, Yogyakarta, Indonesia
e-mail: a.wijaya@uny.ac.id

M. van den Heuvel-Panhuizen (ed.), *International Reflections on the Netherlands Didactics of Mathematics*, ICME-13 Monographs, https://doi.org/10.1007/978-3-030-20223-1_18

18.1   Mathematics Reform Using Realistic Mathematics Education in Indonesia

Learning from the successes in the United States and South Africa in reforming mathematics using Realistic Mathematics Education (RME), Indonesia also used and adapted RME to improve mathematics education. RME is a didactic approach or a domain-specific instruction theory for mathematics founded in the Netherlands (Van den Heuvel-Panhuizen, 2003; Van den Heuvel-Panhuizen & Drijvers, 2014). In the Indonesian context, it is called 'Pendidikan Matematika Realistik Indonesia' (PMRI). The head of the PMRI team is Professor Sembiring, a mathematician from the Institut Teknologi Bandung. From 2001 to 2010 he managed the movement of PMRI through two projects supported by the Netherlands: the project Netherlands Programme for the Institutional Strengthening of Post-Secondary Education and Training Capacity (NPT) and the project Dissemination of Pendidikan Matematika Realistik Indonesia (Do-PMRI). Reports about the development and implementation of PMRI during these projects can be found in a journal article written by Sembiring, Hadi, and Dolk (2008) and in a book titled *A Decade of PMRI in Indonesia* written by Sembiring, Hoogland, and Dolk (2010a). In this book, all activities can be found that have taken place during ten years of PMRI in which PMRI has been disseminated in about 20 out of the 33 provinces in Indonesia.

Currently, five years after the Do-PMRI Project finished, one can question the sustainability of PMRI. Further publications about PMRI are rare. Also, the National Centre of PMRI that was set up in Bandung formally ended when the Department of National Education was split into two departments from 2015 on, one for compulsory education and one for higher education. Many questions about the continuation of PMRI are coming up. Is PMRI still alive in mathematics education in Indonesia? And if yes, what are the activities or developments of PMRI currently?

All three authors know a lot about RME or PMRI. They all have a doctorate either related to RME or to PMRI. The first author learned RME in the Netherlands and was the first person who got a doctoral degree on RME. Moreover, he was involved in the PMRI team from 1998. The second author learned about PMRI while the project was running in Indonesia and got a doctoral degree based on her dissertation about PMRI. The last author learned about RME at Utrecht University, first during his master's study and later during his doctoral study of which he graduated in 2015. All our experiences with RME and PMRI, and our efforts to develop and implement PMRI have coloured this chapter.

The purpose of this chapter is to report the untold story of PMRI from the initiation of the adaptation process of RME into PMRI in Indonesia. This story covers a long period of time from the ICMI (International Commission on Mathematical Instruction) conference Shanghai 1994 to ICME (International Congress of Mathematical Education) Hamburg 2016, and is divided in three phases. The first phase focusses on the initiation of PMRI. The second phase describes the implementation and dissemination of PMRI, while the last phase focusses on how to sustain PMRI as an innovation after the project is over. In the following sections, these three phases will be presented and discussed. Hereafter, we will summarise the main merits and yields of PMRI.

18.2   The Development of PMRI

PMRI has been developed based on a joint Indonesian-Dutch project and its development can be divided in three time periods: (1) before the PMRI project (1994–2000); (2) during the PMRI project (2001–2010); and (3) after the PMRI project (2011–2015).

18.2.1   Before the PMRI Project (1994–2000): Initiation Phase

In 1994, it was Professor Sembiring from the Institut Teknologi Bandung who saw Professor Jan de Lange, the director of the Freudenthal Institute of Utrecht University presenting a keynote about RME at the ICMI conference in Shanghai. Sembiring, who represented the government of Indonesia, told Jan de Lange that Indonesia needed to reform school mathematics by changing the approach to teaching and learning school mathematics that was influenced by New Math. De Lange's presentation inspired Sembiring, and he asked De Lange to persuade the government that RME is the right approach to reforming mathematics education. Four years later, Jan de Lange agreed to help with the change, and he came to Indonesia twice, in 1998 and 2000.

In 1998, the story continued with the decision of the Indonesian government to send six doctoral candidates to the Netherlands to learn about RME. Professor Jan de Lange and Professor Tjeerd Plomp (from the University of Twente) selected six teacher educators out of about twenty applicants from teacher education institutions all over Indonesia. These doctoral candidates were Ahmad Fauzan, Dian Armanto, Ipung Yuwono, Sutarto Hadi, Turmudi and Zulkardi. As students, they learned new knowledge and skills in the area of education and RME at the University of Twente in collaboration with Utrecht University. They went to Enschede and started the 'sandwich PhD programme' of the University of Twente and Utrecht University. The programme took four years and the research was conducted in Indonesian schools. In 2002, four of the participants received a PhD in mathematics education. Others received PhDs in Australia and Indonesia and also became leaders in the field. Now, all of these candidates are professors in RME and are the backbone of the continuation of PMRI.

In 2000, Jan de Lange was a keynote speaker at the Tenth National Conference on Mathematics at the Institut Teknologi Bandung. He informed the participants about two important concepts, namely RME and its success in the United States and in the Programme for International Student Assessment (PISA). That year, the first PISA international test was administered. As the head of the PISA Expert Group on Mathematics, he showed that PISA and RME have a strong relationship with respect to the use of context and the competences that were tested. When a participant asked him what the proof is that RME is a real solution to mathematics education in Indonesia, his argumentation was clear and simple. He mentioned that after the use of RME in a particular state in the United States, the average mathematics score in this state increased significantly. Also at this conference, one of his doctoral students, Zulkardi, presented his dissertation research in a panel session. It was on how to support student teachers both by a face-to-face course and a website about RME as an innovation in mathematics education in Indonesia (Zulkardi, 2002; Zulkardi, Nieveen, Van den Akker, & De Lange, 2002a).

18.2.2   During the PMRI Project (2001–2010): Implementation and Dissemination Phase

The first project of PMRI was the NPT project (Netherlands Programme for the Institutional Strengthening of Post-Secondary Education and Training Capacity). It was funded by the Indonesian Directorate General of Higher Education (DIKTI) and supported by the Dutch Organisation for International Co-operation in Higher Education (Nuffic). The NPT project started in 2001 and ended in 2003. The first experiment of RME was at twelve primary schools with pre-service teacher education institutions at four universities. The four universities were Universitas Negeri Surabaya (UNESA) in Surabaya, Universitas Pendidikan Indonesia (UPI) in Bandung, Universitas Sanata Dharma (USD) in Yogyakarta, and Universitas Negeri Yogyakarta (Yogyakarta State University, UNY) also in Yogyakarta. Eight schools were managed by the Ministry of National Education, while four of the primary schools fell under the responsibility of the Ministry of Religious Affairs. All schools participated voluntarily. Each teacher education institution worked in close collaboration with three primary schools and became the coordinator and local centre of the reform in its region. In 2001, four of the doctoral students did research in Bandung, Yogyakarta and Surabaya. They played a significant role in helping the process of the PMRI experiment.

The second project is the Do-PMRI project (2006–2010). This project was also a joint project of Indonesia and the Netherlands. In Indonesia, DIKTI participated, and in the Netherlands, Algemeen Pedagogisch Studiecentrum (APS, national centre for school improvement) and FI. The managers of the project were Kees Hoogland, Maarten Dolk, and Sembiring. The primary development activities of this project were summarised as follows (Sembiring, Hadi, Zulkardi, & Hoogland, 2010b):

– Development of PMRI learning materials such as exemplary lesson materials as well as textbooks for primary school level, including student books and teacher guides. At the end of the project, the textbooks for Grade 1-3 were published and used in primary schools all over Indonesia.

- Developing a professional development programme or workshops on PMRI. There were two types of workshops, namely a start-up workshop and an implementation workshop. The participants were from primary schools and teacher education institutions. The implementation workshop was followed only by teachers and teacher educators who had implemented PMRI in their schools. In total, teachers and teacher educators from about twelve teacher education institutions were involved. The trainers of the workshop were about ten experts from FI and APS.
- Establishing the *Bulletin PMRI* for disseminating PMRI to student teachers, teachers, teacher educators and society. This newsletter consisted of implementation activities from all over Indonesia, such as experiences of teachers using PMRI in teaching, lesson plans and mathematics problems and it was published three times a year. Each volume was printed and disseminated by the project to PMRI schools and teacher education in all provinces in Indonesia.
- Developing centres for the development and research of PMRI, called Pusat Pengembangan dan Penelitian PMRI (P4MRI). Such centres were a place for PMRI teams to develop and do research on PMRI and were also a meeting point for teacher educators and school teachers doing activities on PMRI.
- Establishing a task force on design research. Within this task force, the guiding teacher educators and teachers in the project designed lesson materials using the PMRI approach, tried it out in classrooms and analysed their findings. Through this activity teacher educators could gain experience in doing design research by doing it themselves, which helped them in supervising their student teachers when they did design research in the final year.
- Initiation of the two-year master programme on RME at the FI. The programme was called IMPoME (International Master's Programme on Mathematics Education). This programme was followed by seven students and one of them was Aryadi Wijaya, the third author of this chapter. They went to Utrecht and were entirely funded by the Do-PMRI project and graduated in 2008.

In all activities above, the content and the didactics were based on PMRI. The overall goal of these activities was to improve the learning results in mathematics of students of primary school age in Indonesia. The learning of mathematics must be an inspiring and meaningful activity for all students, must be taught at each student's level, and must bring about that all students acquire a practical knowledge base that will help them to cope with quantitative situations in the world around them. Based on the results of the observations of the international advisory board of the PMRI project, the four-year project was a success. However, what worked in the selected pilot schools is not automatically implementable at a large scale. The international advisory board stated that the implementation and institutionalisation of PMRI in classrooms all over Indonesia was still an enormous endeavour. It can only be accomplished through the hard and enduring efforts of many: teachers, parents, principals, teacher educators, mathematicians, publishers, journalists, policy makers, politicians, and many more (Ekholm & Van den Hoven, 2010).

18.2.3   After the PMRI Project (2011–2015): Dissemination Phase

This phase elaborated on activities that were already developed and started within the PMRI project as well as activities that were initiated by the first author at the University of Sriwijaya (UNSRI) in Palembang. The activities are very important to make PMRI still alive as an innovation in Indonesian mathematics education.

18.3   PMRI Growths Beyond the Project

Over the years, PMRI resulted in a number of activities, programmes and events that were important for mathematics education in Indonesia. In the following sections we will subsequently discuss in more detail (1) the International Master's Program on Mathematics education (IMPoME); (2) the International Conference on Design Research (SEA-DR); (3) the Mathematical Literacy Contest (KLM) and the Context-Based Mathematics Tasks Indonesia (CoMTI) project; (4) the web portal on PMRI set up by the P4MRIs; (5) the Course on Realistic Mathematics Education for Junior Secondary School Mathematics Teachers in Southeast Asia (SEA-RME course), and (6) the *Journal of Mathematics Education* (JME).

18.3.1   IMPoME

The development of IMPoME was based on the master's programme that was designed by the Do-PMRI project. The success of this programme was proved by the graduation in 2007–2008 of seven master's students on the topic of RME. Then, in October 2008, a memorandum of understanding among the Sriwijaya University (UNSRI), the State University of Surabaya (UNESA) and Utrecht University was signed in Jakarta in the presense of DIKTI and Nuffic Neso Indonesia, which were responsible for the scholarships while the UNSRI and UNESA and Utrecht University were responsible for running the master's program. Also, a full curriculum was jointly developed. Good students were selected from candidates from all provinces in Indonesia, who then spent a year at UNSRI in Palembang or at UNESA in Surabaya, and a year in Utrecht.

One of the real outcomes of the Do-PMRI project was thinking about the future of PMRI in Indonesia which resulted in the design of IMPoME, the new master's programme on Realistic Mathematics Education. This legacy of PMRI was also acknowledged by the management of Nuffic, in the person of Kon Yap Tjay. According to him:

> Important spin-offs of this project are a new master's degree programme along with a master's degree scholarship programme. The scholarship programme is funded by the Indonesian

government, coupled with Nuffic-NESO Jakarta's funding of an international component for selected candidates. The new international master's degree programme in mathematics education is set up by universities in Surabaya and Palembang. (Yap, 2011, p. 90)

To begin with IMPoME, seven students were selected from all provinces in Indonesia. The selection team consisted of Maarten Dolk, Kees Hoogland, Sutarto Hadi and Zulkardi. The selection criteria were both knowledge about mathematics and mathematics education, proficiency in English, motivation to study hard and contribute, later when they would be back in Indonesia, to the dissemination of RME. The seven master's students were Ariyadi Wijaya, Al Jupri, Meliasari, Neni, Puspita, Roselyna, and Novi. All of them received their master's degree in 2009. Three of them also became a doctoral student. Ariyadi and Al Jupri got their doctorate from Utrecht University supervised by Professor Marja van den Heuvel-Panhuizen and Professor Paul Drijvers, and Roselyna graduated at the National Taiwan Normal University and was supervised by Professor Fou Lai Lin.

From 2009–2014, there was a total of 55 IMPoME students who learned about RME at Utrecht University. Their theses are published online by the FI and can be freely and fully downloaded at http://www.fisme.science.uu.nl/en/impome/.

In 2016, a new IMPoME is coming alive. This programme only involves a collaboration between UNSRI and Utrecht University. The scholarship will be supported by the Indonesian Endowment Fund for Education (LPDP), a part of the Financial Department of the Republic of Indonesia that manages the educational budget. The new programme uses the IMPoME model: students learn about RME in the Netherlands for one year, and in Indonesia for another year.

18.3.2 International Conference on Design Research

There are two things we learned and brought to Indonesia, namely RME and design research. All developments towards PMRI that have been conducted over the years used a design research method, which involved mostly starting with a preliminary study, then designing teaching material, followed by a teaching experiment and finally a retrospective analysis. The mathematical content and the didactics of the designs were based on RME. This design approach is one of the success strategies in disseminating PMRI in Indonesia.

For instance, IMPoME students had to write their theses using design research. They had to develop or design products such as lessons, assessment materials and learning media. All these were used as tools to support students learning mathematics using the PMRI approach. Two years after IMPoME started, students had to present their design and research results on PMRI in a local seminar either at UNSRI in Palembang or at UNESA in Surabaya.

In the third year, as a result of the collaboration between FI and UNSRI this seminar was extended into a national conference and an international conference for the Southeast Asian region on design research, called SEA-DR. Since 2013, this conference has taken place at UNSRI in Palembang. In 2016, the conference is held at Universitas Negeri Padang (UNP) in West Sumatera, Padang.

Some advantages of the SEA-DR conference are the following: (1) networking among researchers on PMRI; and (2) increasing the research and number of publications on PMRI in which design research is used. Up to now, each conference had about 400 researchers from all provinces in Indonesia and from Southeast Asian countries. In the future, this conference will move to other cities in- or outside Indonesia.

18.3.3 Development of Mathematical Literacy in Indonesia

Mathematical literacy has been a concern of the Indonesian government for years. In 2004, the Indonesian Ministry of National Education started implementing a competence-based curriculum, the Kurikulum Berbasis Kompetensi (KBK). In contrast to previous curricula that emphasised students' acquisition of knowledge, KBK focussed on developing students' ability to apply knowledge. Concerning mathematics education, KBK explicitly stated that mathematics education should target developing students' ability to: (1) understand the concepts of mathematics, explain the relevance of concepts, and apply the concepts or algorithms in a flexible way in problem solving; (2) solve problems that include being able to understand a problem, design and complete a mathematical model to solve it, and interpret the solution; and (3) appreciate the purpose of mathematics in life (Pusat Kurikulum, 2003). In the newly implemented curriculum of 2013, the Indonesian government also mandates that education must be relevant to the needs of life and should offer students opportunities to apply their knowledge in society. In line with these curricula, PMRI promotes mathematical literacy through the use of real-world problems in learning mathematics (Sembiring et al., 2008, 2010b).

Despite Indonesia's attention for mathematical literacy, the results of the PISA studies indicate Indonesian students' poor mathematical literacy. In the PISA 2012 study, for example, only 0.3% of Indonesian students were top performers in mathematical literacy who could solve mathematics problems requiring sophisticated mathematical modelling and well-developed reasoning skills (Organisation for Economic Cooperation and Development, OECD, 2013). In contrast, most Indonesian students, that is, 75.7% of students, did not reach Level 2, which is set as the baseline level of mathematical literacy. These students could only solve mathematics problems that use familiar contexts, have obvious questions, and present all relevant information. Furthermore, they were able to identify relevant information and carry out routine mathematical procedures only if explicit instructions were given. This poor performance of Indonesian students in PISA has prompted initiatives to improve students' mathematical literacy. In this chapter, we would like to report two attempts that have been carried out to improve Indonesian students' mathematical literacy, namely the Kontes Literasi Matematika (KLM, mathematical literacy contest) and the Context-Based Mathematics Tasks Indonesia (CoMTI) project.

18.3.3.1 Mathematical Literacy Contest

The KLM is conducted for junior high school students, that is, around 14–15 years old students. The rationale of this contest is that improving students' mathematical literacy can be done by providing them with problems addressing the application of mathematics. It is expected that KLM may raise awareness of mathematical literacy. The participants in KLM have to deal with PISA-like problems. In the first round, the participants have to solve the problems in a written format. About 20% of participants who get the highest grade will continue to the second round of the contest. In this round, the participants have to solve problems and present their solutions and solving strategies orally. The three best performers in the second round of the contest were named as the champions (for more details, see Stacey et al., 2015).

The first KLM took place in 2010 and was initiated by Professor Zulkardi of Sriwijaya University, and was therefore only conducted in Palembang (South Sumatera). In 2011, KLM was held in seven cities in seven provinces, that is, Jakarta (Jakarta), Surabaya (East Java), Yogyakarta (Yogyakarta), Medan (North Sumatera), Palembang (South Sumatera), Makassar (South Sulawesi), and Banjarmasin (South Kalimantan). After 2011 the number of participating cities increased. In 2012, five new cities joined KLM to make a total of twelve participating cities. These five new cities were Kupang (East Nusa Tenggara), Malang (East Java), Padang (West Sumatera), Semarang (Central Java), and Singaraja (Bali). In 2015, eighteen cities in seventeen provinces participated in the contest. From the second KLM in 2011 on, the contest was conducted at two levels, that is, regional (towns or areas) and the national level, with the champion from every region competing to get the national champion. At the regional level, KLM is organised by the P4MRI in the participating city. At the national level, KLM is organised by the Institute for the Development of PMRI (Institut Pengembangan PMRI or IP PMRI). In the beginning, KLM was only held by IP PMRI and P4MRIs. However, later on, P4TK Matematika[1] joined as an additional organising committee of the KLM at the national level. P4TK Matematika is a government institution under the Indonesian Ministry of Education. The involvement of P4TK Matematika in KLM indicates the government's support for developing Indonesian students' mathematical literacy.

18.3.3.2 The Context-Based Mathematics Tasks Indonesia Project

Another attempt to improve students' mathematical literacy is the Context-Based Mathematics Tasks Indonesia (CoMTI) project. CoMTI was a PhD project of Ariyadi Wijaya under the supervision of Professor Marja van den Heuvel-Panhuizen and Doctor Michiel Doorman at the Freudenthal Institute at Utrecht University. The similarity between KLM and the CoMTI project is the use of context-based tasks, that is, KLM uses PISA-like tasks and CoMTI used released PISA tasks. However,

---

[1]Pusat Pengembangan dan Pemberdayaan Pendidik dan Tenaga Kependidikan Matematika (Centre for the Development and Empowerment of Mathematics Teachers and Educational Personnel).

unlike KLM that attempts to improve mathematical literacy by using PISA-like problems as springboards for raising awareness on mathematical literacy (Widjaja, 2011), the CoMTI project took a broader perspective. The CoMTI project focussed on three interrelated issues regarding mathematical literacy in Indonesia. The first issue was Indonesian students' difficulties in solving context-based tasks. Second, the reasons for students' difficulties were examined. Lastly, based on the first and second issue, it was studied how students' performance on context-based tasks, or on mathematical literacy, could be improved.

In relation to Indonesian students' difficulties in solving context-based tasks, Wijaya, Van den Heuvel-Panhuizen, Doorman, and Robitzsch (2014) performed an analysis of students' errors. The error analysis revealed that of the errors made by the students 38% were comprehension errors, 42% were transformation errors, 17% were mathematical processing errors, and 3% were encoding errors. These results indicate that when solving context-based tasks, Indonesian students mostly experienced difficulties in comprehending what the tasks are about and in transforming them into mathematical problems. These difficulties mean the students could not identify relevant mathematics concepts or procedures required to solve a context-based task; which in fact is a key ability for mathematical literacy. To know possible reasons for students' difficulties in solving context-based tasks, the CoMTI project focussed on investigating opportunities received by students to learn to solve context-based tasks. For this purpose, two dimensions of opportunity-to-learn were considered: textbooks and teachers' teaching practices. A study by Wijaya, Van den Heuvel-Panhuizen, and Doorman (2015a) revealed that Indonesian mathematics textbooks do not provide enough opportunities for students to learn to solve context-based tasks. After analysing three Indonesian mathematics textbooks, Wijaya et al. found that only 10% of the tasks in the textbooks were context-based tasks. Of these context-based tasks, only a quarter required mathematical modelling or asked students to identify the relevant mathematics concepts or procedures. It means that only 2.5% of the tasks in Indonesian mathematics textbooks were found to address mathematical literacy. Furthermore, of the context-based tasks in the textbooks, 85% of the tasks provided only the relevant information. It indicates that the complexity of context-based tasks found in Indonesian textbooks was mostly below PISA's baseline Level 2. The second dimension of opportunity-to-learn investigated in the CoMTI project was teachers' teaching practices. For this dimension Wijaya, Van den Heuvel-Panhuizen, and Doorman (2015b) found that the way teachers taught context-based tasks also did not provide sufficient opportunities for students to learn to solve context-based tasks. The teachers tended to use a directive teaching approach in which they tell the students what a context-based task is about, translate the task into a mathematical problem, and explain what mathematical procedure to carry out. In such teaching, students are not encouraged to carry actively out and reflect on the stages of solving context-based tasks. This directive teaching approach was mostly used in the comprehension and transformation stages of problem solving, which are crucial stages of mathematical literacy. After identifying Indonesian students' difficulties and their possible reasons, the CoMTI project focussed on designing a way to improve students' mathematical literacy. For this part of the study an intervention programme was developed comprising a consultative teaching approach and a set of context-based tasks with metacognitive prompts. An examination of the effect of the intervention on students' errors showed a positive influence of the opportunity-to-learn on reducing students' errors. Students who received the opportunity-to-learn could better understand the instruction for a context-based task and had improved performance in selecting relevant information (Wijaya, Van den Heuvel-Panhuizen, Doorman, & Veldhuis, 2018).

The results of KLM and CoMTI show potential for improving Indonesian students' mathematical literacy. Of course, it should be highlighted that developing students' mathematical literacy is not the work of an individual person or organisation. Supports from the government such as P4TK Matematika's participation in KLM, and also the commitment of IP PMRI and P4MRIs are crucial to sustaining the programme for improving students' mathematical literacy. The CoMTI project was conducted in the Province of Yogyakarta. Therefore, it is important to incorporate the project into a programme of P4MRIs so that the data can be more representative for Indonesia in general. Furthermore, the investigation into possible reasons for Indonesian students' poor mathematical literacy emphasised only factors that are related to cognitive aspects: textbooks and teachers' teaching practices. However, as pointed out by Leron and Hazzan (1997), students' thinking is influenced not only by cognitive factors, but also by affective factors. Therefore, investigating emotional factors such as students' motivation might provide a comprehensive picture of possible factors that influence student performance.

18.3.4 Development of a Web Portal on PMRI

In about 22 provinces in Indonesia, the P4MRIs have set up their website or blog. The main goal of these blogs is to support users with information about PMRI and its development from each area. To connect and link all blogs from all over Indonesia, a P4MRI web portal was developed by Zulkardi in 2011; see http://p4mri.net/new/. This web portal functions as a clearinghouse for PMRI information, documentation for activities, and resources.

The P4MRI web portal contains:

– Content about PMRI such as examples of learning materials, teacher guides on PMRI, examples of student works and assessment problems.
– Resources on PMRI for teachers, student teachers and researchers such as papers, thesis, dissertations, images, applets, and videos.
– Links to all websites PMRI from all PMRI centres in Indonesia as well as from other countries.
– Other resources including the curriculum of the master's programme and the doctoral programme on RME, scholarships, conferences, PISA, mathematics contests and journals on mathematics education.

With the recent growth in the number of internet users in Indonesia, the P4MRI web portal is a useful tool in for disseminating PMRI in a big country such as Indonesia.

18.3.5 Course on Realistic Mathematics Education for Junior Secondary School Mathematics Teachers in Southeast Asia

One of the interesting effects of PMRI in Indonesia is that it became the main content for the professional development programme, the Course on Realistic Mathematics Education for Junior Secondary School Mathematics Teachers in Southeast Asia or the SEA-RME course. The course is developed by the PMRI team, and was launched for the first time in October 2012. The goal of the course is enhancing junior secondary school mathematics teachers' competence in mathematics teaching and learning using RME.

The SEA-RME course contains the following modules: *Introduction to RME, Indonesian Experience in Disseminating RME, Designing RME Lesson, Assessment, RME, PISA/TIMSS, Lesson Study, Classroom Observation* and *Teaching Practice in the School*. These modules are delivered by several facilitators from some prominent universities in Indonesia (Sanata Dharma University, Sriwijaya University, Padang State University and Lambung Mangkurat University, Yogyakarta State University). An example of a 10-minute-video on introducing PMRI to training participants from ASEAN countries can be viewed at https://www.youtube.com/watch?v=fjXyNmNTBWg.

18.3.6 A New International Journal on Mathematics Education

In 2010 a new journal on mathematics education was initiated by Zulkardi, the vice president of the Indonesian Mathematical Society (IndoMS). The *Indo-MS Journal on Mathematics Education* (JME) was launched during the opening of the Fifteenth National Conference on Mathematics (KNM15) at the University of Manado, North Sulawesi, on July 31, 2010 by the President of IndoMS, Professor Widodo. *JME*, which is the first international journal on mathematics education in Indonesia, is devoted to school mathematics teachers, teacher educators, and university students who want to publish their research articles about mathematics education. Some of the contributors are also well-known researchers in mathematics education such as:

– Lee Peng Yee and Berinderjeet Kaur from Singapore
– Kaye Stacey and Tom Lowrie from Australia
– Koeno Gravemeijer, Frans van Galen and Dolly van Eerde from the Netherlands

– Christa Kaune and Edyta Nowinska from Germany
– Fou Lai Lin from Taiwan.

After five years, in September 2015, this journal was successfully accredited by DIKTI and the Minister of Research, Technology, and Higher Education in Indonesia. This accreditation is an indication that the journal has been managed in a good and a consistent way. Surprisingly, up to Volume 7, released in January 2016, 47 (58%) of the 81 published articles were about RME or PMRI. One might say that *JME* could also be called 'JRME' (Journal on Realistic Mathematics Education). On top of that, one can say that the increase in publications on RME shows the sustainability of research on RME in Indonesia. The journal has also been indexed in DOAJ, ERIC Database, and Google Scholar. All articles can be freely accessed at www.jims-b.org or http://ejournal.unsri.ac.id/index.php/jme.

18.4   New Developments on PMRI

In 2014 a small-scale joint research project on PMRI was started between UNSRI and Utrecht University. This research project was supported by the Rector and the Dean of UNSRI. The goal of this initiative is a way to sustain the academic relationship between the two universities. The two topics addressed in this project are socio-mathematical norms in mathematics teaching in primary school, and mathematics and science literacy in teacher education. The main goal of the first topic is to support teachers in how to manage an interactive PMRI classroom (Putri, Dolk, & Zulkardi, 2015) and the goal of the second topic is to develop a PISA centre in Indonesia and to improve the quality of mathematics and science education at the undergraduate level (Zulkardi, 2015).

In 2015, UNSRI and Utrecht University started a new IMPoME programme. The scholarship will be supported by LPDP-Lembaga Pengelola Dana Pendidikan, a department of the Ministry of Finances that is involved with the educational budget. As in the previous IMPoME programme, in the first semester students will take basic courses on RME at UNSRI. Then, they will take their main courses on RME at Utrecht University at the Freudenthal Institute for two semesters. In the fourth semester, they have to do research on RME in Palembang. Finally, they have to defend their thesis before graduating the programme and getting a M.Sc. degree.

A new doctoral programme on mathematics education, that uses the IMPoME model, has also been created. This means that first students will be recruited by a joint team from both universities. Students will then spend a year taking four courses and writing a good research proposal at UNSRI. In the second year, there will be two groups of doctoral students, namely one group who will continue at Utrecht University for three years and another group who will continue for two years at UNSRI and will take their doctorate there.

18.5   PMRI Continues

Some questions about the untold stories about PMRI that were asked in the introduction have been answered in this chapter. For instance, what was the history of PMRI before, during and beyond the PMRI project? Some development and research activities about PMRI are still continuing and need to be supported.

There is also a new initiative on PMRI, namely developing a Centre of Excellence of PMRI at the University of Sriwijaya Palembang. It will have a role as a national centre of PMRI, and will manage all local centres of PMRI from all provinces in Indonesia.

At the end of this chapter, the story of PMRI from ICMI 1994 in Shanghai to ICME 2016 in Hamburg will stop, but activities related to PMRI are still continuing in Indonesia. These activities support stakeholders such as teachers, student teachers, learners, teacher educators, researchers, and book writers in reforming mathematics education in Indonesia and can be seen as proof that the movement of PMRI as an innovation in mathematics education sustains.

All these activities on PMRI have implications for policies on and further research in mathematics education in Indonesia. They inspire student teachers, teachers, and researchers for teaching mathematics. These activities need to be managed and supported by all parties to make it possible that in the coming decades, they will help and encourage many people to learn about PMRI in mathematics education in Indonesia.

Acknowledgements   The authors wish to express their gratitude to the colleagues who brought their support in the preparation of this chapter, and in particular to the head of the PMRI team, R. K. Sembiring.

References

Ekholm, M., & Van den Hoven, G. (2010). Summary of PMRI-Majulah! A report of the International Advisory Board of PMRI. In R. K. Sembiring, K. Hoogland, & M. Dolk (Eds.), *A decade of PMRI in Indonesia* (p. 88). Jakarta, Indonesia/Utrecht, the Netherlands: APS International.

Leron, U., & Hazzan, O. (1997). The world according to Johnny: A coping perspective in mathematics education. *Educational Studies in Mathematics, 32*(3), 265–292.

OECD. (2013). *PISA 2012 results: What students know and can do. Student performance in mathematics, reading and science.* Paris: OECD.

Pusat Kurikulum [National Curriculum Centre]. (2003). *Kurikulum 2004. Standar kompetensi mata pelajaran matematika Sekolah Menengah Pertama dan Madrasah Tsanawiyah* [The curriculum 2004: The competence standards for mathematics in Junior High School and Islamic Junior High School]. Jakarta, Indonesia: Departemen Pendidikan Nasional.

Putri, I. I. P., Dolk, M., & Zulkardi, Z. (2015). Professional development of PMRI teachers for introducing social norms. *Indonesian Mathematical Society Journal on Mathematics Education, 6*(1), 11–19.

Sembiring, R. K., Hadi, S., & Dolk, M. (2008). Reforming mathematics learning in Indonesian classrooms through RME. *ZDM Mathematics Education, 40*(6), 927–939.

Sembiring, R. K., Hadi, S., Zulkardi, Z., & Hoogland, K. (2010b). The future of PMRI. In R. K. Sembiring, K. Hoogland, & M. Dolk (Eds.), *A decade of PMRI in Indonesia* (pp. 189–190). Utrecht, the Netherlands: APS International.

Sembiring, R. K., Hoogland, K., & Dolk, M. (Eds.). (2010a). *A decade of PMRI in Indonesia.* Utrecht, the Netherlands: APS International.

Stacey, K., et al. (2015). PISA's influence on thought and action in mathematics education. In K. Stacey & R. Turner (Eds.), *Assessing mathematical literacy—The PISA experience* (pp. 275–306). Cham, Switzerland: Springer International Publishing.

Van den Heuvel-Panhuizen, M. (2003). The didactical use of models in realistic mathematics education: An example from a longitudinal trajectory on percentage. *Educational Studies in Mathematics, 54*(1), 9–35.

Van den Heuvel-Panhuizen, M., & Drijvers, P. (2014). Realistic Mathematics Education. In S. Lerman (Ed.), *Encyclopedia of mathematics education* (pp. 521–525). Dordrecht, the Netherlands: Springer. https://doi.org/10.1007/978-94-007-4978-8.

Widjaja, W. (2011). Towards mathematical literacy in the 21st century: Perspectives from Indonesia. *Southeast Asian Mathematics Education Journal, 1*(1), 75–84.

Wijaya, A., Van den Heuvel-Panhuizen, M., Doorman, M., & Robitzsch, A. (2014). Difficulties in solving context-based PISA mathematics tasks: An analysis of students' errors. *The Mathematics Enthusiast, 11*(3), 541–554.

Wijaya, A., Van den Heuvel-Panhuizen, M., & Doorman, M. (2015a). Opportunity-to-learn context-based tasks provided by mathematics textbooks. *Educational Studies in Mathematics, 89*(1), 41–65.

Wijaya, A., Van den Heuvel-Panhuizen, M., & Doorman, M. (2015b). Teachers' teaching practices and beliefs regarding context-based tasks and their relation to students' difficulties in solving these tasks. *Mathematics Education Research Journal, 27*(4), 637–662.

Wijaya, A., Van den Heuvel-Panhuizen, M., Doorman, M., & Veldhuis, M. (2018). Opportunity-to-learn to solve context-based mathematics tasks and students' performance in solving these tasks – Lessons from Indonesia. *EURASIA Journal of Mathematics, Science and Technology Education, 14*(10), em1598; https://doi.org/10.29333/ejmste/93420.

Yap, K. T. (2011). Realistic Mathematics Education in a project approach. In R. K. Sembiring, K. Hoogland, & M. Dolk (Eds.), (2010). *A decade of PMRI in Indonesia.* Utrecht, the Netherlands: APS International.

Zulkardi, Z. (2002). *Developing a learning environment on realistic Mathematics Education for Indonesian Student Teachers.* Published doctoral thesis of the University of Twente. Enschede, the Netherlands: PrintPartners Ipskamp. Available online at http://doc.utwente.nl/58718/1/thesis_Zulkardi.pdf.

Zulkardi, Z. (2015). *Using PMRI and PISA for improving research and learning on mathematics literacy of Indonesian students.* Paper presented as Invited Speaker at the International Conference on Mathematics, Natural Sciences and Education (ICoMaNSed 2015), State University of Manado, 7–8 August 2015.

Zulkardi, Z., Nieveen, N., Van den Akker J., & De Lange, J. (2002a). Implementing a 'European' approach to mathematics education in Indonesia. In *Proceeding of Second International Conference on Teaching Mathematics.* Crete, Greece, July 1–6, 2002. [Online]. Available at: http://www.math.uoc.gr/~ictm2/Proceedings/pap81.pdf.

Chapter 19
Intervening with Realistic Mathematics Education in England and the Cayman Islands—The Challenge of Clashing Educational Ideologies

Paul Dickinson, Frank Eade, Steve Gough, Sue Hough and Yvette Solomon

Abstract In this chapter, we discuss the issue of implementing Realistic Mathematics Education (RME) in the English education system over a number of years and education sectors. We also consider the experience of one of us in the Cayman Islands, a British overseas territory with an education system that is influenced by British tradition, but is distant from many of its politically driven accountability pressures and measures. We illustrate first the challenges of developing an RME approach which is operable within the English system, highlighting the issues of student expectation, dominant didactic practices and assessment, all of which influenced what we were able to do. Second, we describe the outcomes of interventions in England at early secondary school level (age 12–14, Key Stage 3) and at General Certificate of Secondary Education (GCSE) level (normally age 15–16, Key Stage 4, but also available in post-16 education). Finally, Frank Eade describes his experience of building on our early work to develop an RME approach in the Cayman Islands. We conclude with a discussion of the lessons learned from these challenges. We argue that despite the problems we encountered there are reasons to remain optimistic about the potential of an RME approach in the English system.

Keywords Accountability pressures · Assessment · Student expectations · Progressive formalisation · Classroom cultures

P. Dickinson · F. Eade · S. Gough · S. Hough · Y. Solomon (✉)
Manchester Metropolitan University, Manchester, UK
e-mail: y.solomon@mmu.ac.uk

P. Dickinson
e-mail: p.dickinson@mmu.ac.uk

F. Eade
e-mail: frankeade@outlook.com

S. Gough
e-mail: s.j.gough@mmu.ac.uk

S. Hough
e-mail: s.hough@mmu.ac.uk

© The Author(s) 2020
M. van den Heuvel-Panhuizen (ed.), *International Reflections on the Netherlands Didactics of Mathematics*, ICME-13 Monographs, https://doi.org/10.1007/978-3-030-20223-1_19

19.1   Translating Realistic Mathematics Education into the English System: Dealing with Student Expectations, Didactic Practice and Assessment Systems

Over the past ten years, we have led a number of projects working with teachers and their students to develop classroom approaches based on Realistic Mathematics Education (RME). Our early work included a Gatsby Foundation funded Key Stage 3 project Developing Mathematics in Context and an Esmée Fairbairn Foundation funded Key Stage 4 project Making Sense of Maths. Over 40 schools, 80 teachers and 2000 students took part. Evaluations of these projects (Dickinson & Hough, 2012; Searle & Barmby, 2012) comparing the progress of project students and control students have shown them to have a lasting impact in terms of teacher development and student achievement. Of particular note is the way in which these approaches have enabled students to develop methods which make sense to them, which they can apply in new situations and for which they do not need to rely on memory. This is described in Dickinson, Hough, Searle and Barmby (2011, p. 51):

> Teachers noted that using RME encourages an intuitive approach, in which pupils can visualise problems, try things out for themselves, and think about different approaches to a problem, rather than having a teacher demonstrate an algorithmic technique, which pupils then practise, probably with little understanding.

More recently, we have taken an RME approach into post-16 classrooms, funded by the Nuffield Foundation. Our students have been those who had failed to gain a 'pass' grade in the public General Certificate and Secondary Education (GCSE) examinations in mathematics. This particular context has brought to the fore a number of issues which arise in implementing RME in England, in particular the impact of education policy on both teachers and students. In this section, we discuss the key features of the English context that our work has needed to address. In particular, radical differences between the Dutch and English education system and their effect on teachers' and students' experiences and expectations have presented us with considerable challenges in terms of assessment and the pace of movement towards formalisation.

19.1.1   Classroom Cultures in England: Students' Expectations and Experiences of Mathematics

English mathematics education traditions have had a well-documented impact on classroom cultures and on student experiences and expectations, all of which present challenges for the implementation and impact of an RME approach. In particular, student performance in public examinations is used in systems of school measurement and accountability, often leading to 'transmissionist' classroom cultures that emphasise getting right answers over understanding (Noyes, Drake, Wake, & Murphy, 2010; Wake & Burkhardt, 2013). Many young people consequently see mathematics as a question of learning rules which lead to answers based on received wisdom and the authority of the teacher (De Corte, Op't Eynde, & Verschaffel, 2002). It is seen as irrelevant to everyday life, and as meaningless and abstract (Boaler, 2002). The prevalent practice of grouping by ability in England often contributes to a general disaffection from mathematics for a large majority of students, in both higher and lower ability groups. In lower ability groups, they are likely to experience a reduced curriculum, which limits exposure to mathematics and the grades they can attain in public examinations at age 16 (Boaler & Wiliam, 2001; Boaler, Wiliam, & Brown, 2000). Students in higher ability groups do not necessarily fare any better: the high speed of coverage and competitive context reinforces students' beliefs that doing well in mathematics is a question of ability rather than effort. This situation alienates some students, particularly girls (Boaler, 1997; Solomon, 2007).

The patterns of classroom interaction that are fostered by a traditional transmissionist approach to teaching mathematics can lead students to have lower expectations of themselves as well as of mathematics. Zevenbergen (2005) argues that lower performing students' awareness of the restrictions on them in terms of curriculum and pedagogy leads them to develop a predisposition towards mathematics as negative and to behave in ways that contribute further to their reduced participation. Higher performing girls are often anxious, and many drop out of mathematics study at the post-compulsory level (Forgasz, Becker, Lee, & Steinthorsdottir, 2010). An RME-based approach presents not just a challenge to teachers but also to students who have become used to particular mathematics classroom cultures, which, while they might not like them, are at least predictable situations in which they have developed strategies for coping. An approach whereby students need to explain their thinking and make connections, ask questions and generally take more risks instead of simply 'learning the rules' can meet resistance (Brantlinger, 2014; Lubienski, 2007); this was particularly relevant in our more recent intervention, detailed in Sect. 19.2.2 below.

19.1.2 Didactic Practice in England and in RME: Pressure to Move to Early Formalisation

As highlighted above, teachers in England are very aware of the pressure to move towards formal mathematics as quickly as possible. Any contexts are quickly dropped to allow for abstraction and for the development of the desired formal methods. Progression is seen as the learning and practising of these methods, the use of them in more complicated situations (often 'bigger' numbers), and the application of the methods to answer 'contextual' questions. So, for example, in the teaching of fractions, formal notions of equivalence through 'doing the same to numerator and denominator' are quickly developed with halves and quarters and then extended to thirds, fifths, etcetera. The idea of a common denominator is also introduced early in the curriculum, and becomes the sole method for comparing and ordering fractions and then for addition and subtraction.

Quite early in our work with RME, on a visit to the Netherlands, we asked a group of 13-year-olds to compare $\frac{2}{3}$ and $\frac{3}{4}$ and say which was the larger. We knew from our classroom experience that this question would often prove difficult for students in England, with many saying that the fractions were equal because of the difference between the individual numbers. We were struck not just by the confidence with which the Dutch students gave a correct answer, but also by the variety of justifications that they gave. Some used an appropriate whole number (a 'mediating quantity'; Streefland, 1991) to argue that $\frac{3}{4}$ of 60, say, was greater than $\frac{2}{3}$ of 60; some used a percentage or decimal argument; and a significant number compared with a whole one, arguing that $\frac{3}{4}$ needs only an extra $\frac{1}{4}$ to make it up to a whole one and is therefore the larger. Such methods would simply not have been available to U.K. students at the time.

One possible reason for this is given by looking at the lesson plans produced by the Primary Strategy launched by the Department of Education in 1999 for year 6 (11-year-old students). The first lesson for this age group begins with the question "How do you know that $\frac{2}{5}$ is more than $\frac{1}{4}$?" This is followed immediately with advice to the teacher to "Establish the need to change to a common denominator" and then "Discuss other examples such as comparing $\frac{1}{4}$ and $\frac{1}{3}$, $\frac{3}{4}$ and $\frac{7}{10}$ etcetera" and "Repeat with other examples if appropriate" (Department for Education, DfEE, 1999). While we now have a new primary curriculum (DfE, 2013), it is still dominated by formal notions of equivalence and the need to use common denominators.

In the initial stages of working with RME, it was challenging to teachers as well as students to compare fractions without using a common denominator, and the work of Streefland (1991) was critical to our development here. This gave us a framework within which we could structure lessons, and design a range of developmental questions that could be asked. It was heartening, at a later stage of the project, to see a student justify why $\frac{2}{5}$ was bigger than $\frac{1}{4}$ by picturing a restaurant where "if four people only have one pizza, it will need one new person with a whole pizza if they are to have as much as the other table. So, the $\frac{2}{5}$ have much more at the moment!"

One difficulty at this point, particularly with higher achieving students, was that they had the formal knowledge (or at least could remember the methods), but not the understanding to accompany this. So, for example, when previously asked why three pizzas shared between 4 people gave the same amount of pizza as 6 shared between 8, these students could only justify this by referring to procedures such as "you double the numerator and double the denominator." The 'iceberg model' (Webb, Boswinkel, & Dekker, 2008) and the 'landscape of learning' (Fosnot & Dolk, 2002) were very important to our work at this time, particularly in the development of 'milestones' on the journey towards more formal mathematics.

Influenced by RME, we began to define mathematical progress differently, with two important issues emerging. Firstly, our view of how the use of context can aid abstraction was completely changed. Before, we had always believed that we needed to take away the context in order to work on more formal mathematics. Now we came

Fig. 19.1 Progression from
'model of' to 'model for'

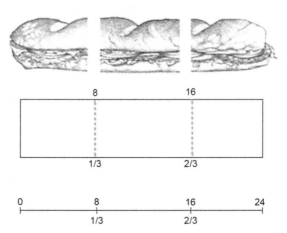

Progressive formalisation of models

to see that adding more contexts, allowing students to see the 'sameness' of different situations, was actually a far more powerful route to abstraction. Secondly, we saw how progress could be defined through the progressive formalisation of models (Van den Heuvel-Panhuizen, 2003). In terms of fractions, this progression can be seen in Fig. 19.1, where a drawing of a sandwich eventually becomes a model for the formal comparison of fractions.

Again, the work of Streefland (1985, 1993) and his notion of progression from 'model of' to 'model for' was crucial here. Although as teachers we came to re-define how we saw progression, we struggled to articulate this within the U.K. curriculum. For example, the work in Figs. 19.2 and 19.3 is from two different students who have studied areas of rectangles and triangles and are then given an unfamiliar shape to work with. We would argue strongly that Student 2 in Fig. 19.3 has made more progress in understanding the notion of area, but the challenge is how to describe and validate this progress within a given assessment system: the notion of 'progressive formalisation' never seems to sit easily within the English curriculum. Despite numerous revisions, we remain locked in a teaching system which values 'little and often', with each 'little' aimed at the tip of the iceberg (Webb, Boswinkel, & Dekker, 2008) or the 'horizon' (Fosnot, 2007), and achieving as much formality as possible. Even with recent moves to spending more time on a topic, and working with the issue of mastery (NCETM, 2014), there is little evidence of any willingness to slow down the process of formalisation.

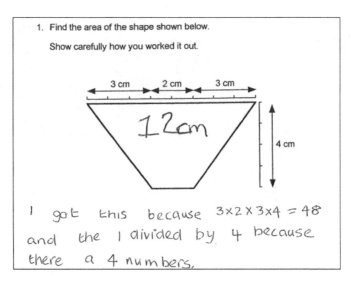

Fig. 19.2 Progression in the understanding of area (Student 1)

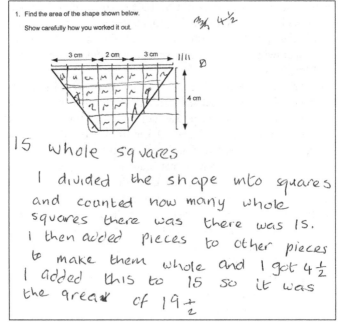

Fig. 19.3 Progression in the understanding of area (Student 2)

19.1.3 Assessment Systems in England and in RME: Dealing with Accountability Pressures

In 1988, a statutory National Curriculum was introduced in England and Wales with programmes of study outlining what students should be taught and attainment targets indicating the expected level of student performance. Over a seven-year period from 1990, Standard Assessed Tests (SATs) were phased into state schools in order to measure students' levels of attainment at Key Stage 1 (age 7), Key Stage 2 (age 11) and Key Stage 3 (age 14). This was in addition to the national GCSE (General Certificate of Secondary Education) examinations for all 16 year olds at Key Stage 4. Although the statutory requirement for students to sit external examinations at Key Stage 1 and Key Stage 3 was later replaced by internal teacher assessment of the students' level, the increased frequency of national testing saw a dramatic increase in the amount of curriculum time given to teaching to the test.

Detailed prescription of what students should be taught, year by year, came with the introduction in 1999 of the Primary National Numeracy Strategy Framework followed by the Key Stage 3 National Strategy in 2001. These documents not only described what should be taught and when, but also exemplified the sorts of activities which should take place in lessons. Sample medium term plans formed the backbone of a school's scheme of work and itemised unit plans provided teachers with daily lesson objectives. The latest version of the National Strategy, launched in September 2013, has a deliberate emphasis on reducing the amount of itemised prescription. However, the practice of teachers setting specific content-loaded objectives at the start of every mathematics lesson is still prevalent.

In addition to prescribing, as never before, the detail of what should be taught, the U.K. government also set about transforming the systems by which schools were monitored. In 1992, the Office for Standards in Education (OFSTED) was established in order to ensure a rigorous and transparent process of school inspection (Elliott, 2012). The OFSTED framework for inspections has undergone many changes with increasing emphasis given to students' achievements and the quality of teaching. Expectations are that students will typically make the equivalent of two whole levels of progress from one Key Stage to the next and schools are required to evidence this. This has led to schools adopting rigorous student tracking systems with students being tested regularly in mathematics and interventions provided for those who are not making the required progress.

Increasing the amount of curriculum time devoted to teaching to the test presents a number of challenges for the implementation of an RME approach. Likewise, the U.K. practice of overtly stating content-focused objectives at the start of every lesson is contradictory to the deliberately slow route to formal mathematics that is characteristic of RME. These two clashing ideologies are discussed in detail below.

19.1.3.1   Lesson Objectives in England and in RME

When the first trial of RME began in England in 2004, the notion of setting lesson objectives was relatively new. However, as the pressure from OFSTED with regard to students making required levels of progress increased, the practice of setting lesson objectives and sharing these with the students at the start of a lesson was seen as extremely important. This gave a way of indicating whether progress had been made during the course of one lesson towards those particular objectives. The National Strategy documentation (DfE, 2013) provides teachers with lists of objectives that students should be taught. They refer to very specific mathematical content focussing on the formal methods students need to learn. So, for example, in the geometry and measures strand of the latest version of the Key Stage 3 (age 12–14) programmes of study, it is stated that "[p]upils should be taught to derive and apply formulae to calculate and solve problems involving: perimeter and area of triangles, parallelograms and trapezia, ..." (ibid., p. 8). The Key Stage 2 programmes of study refer to "use formulae for area" and "calculate" (ibid., p. 43). Consequently, most teachers in England adopted the practice of setting lesson objectives which referred to acquisition of a formal process.

In RME, the importance of engaging with particular contexts, as well as the significance of enabling students to work with a range of informal strategies, is apparent in a different kind of lesson objective. This can be seen in *Mathematics in Context* (MiC) (NCRMSE & Freudenthal Institute, 1997–1998), the textbook series developed at the University of Wisconsin in collaboration with the Freudenthal Institute. In the MiC module entitled "Reallotment" (Gravemeijer, Pligge, & Clarke, 2003), which includes work on area, students are asked to "compare the areas of three tulip fields and determine using a variety of strategies which field has the most tulips" (p. 9). Another lesson requires that "students price tiles of different shapes and sizes by comparing their areas to the area of the $5 tile" (p. 15). These lesson objectives make specific reference to particular contexts, and highlight that there are various ways to answer the problems. Although the second objective does direct students to the specific strategy of comparing sizes, this is not a standard formal method for finding areas.

This creates major tensions for English teachers embarking on the use of RME. Their expectations relate to students learning how to perform a mathematical procedure within the course of one or two lessons. In RME, progress to that particular procedure may involve engaging with several contexts over the course of many lessons, which could be spread over a number of years, thus enabling students to gain conceptual understanding of how the procedure works, where it might be used, and how it connects to other areas of mathematics. In all our project work supporting English teachers to trial RME, we found that many teachers were anxious about when students would be shown the formal procedure and, if unsupported, some teachers may intervene and demonstrate the formal procedure after only one contextual problem. These concerns were particularly apparent in our most recent RME project (described in Sect. 19.2.2) working with post-16 students who had not achieved a grade C, where the course is designed so that the teacher and their students should re-visit as much of the GCSE syllabus as they can in nine months.

19.1.3.2   The Use of Assessment in the United Kingdom and in RME

Test-oriented teaching is an understandable consequence of placing such an important emphasis on the performance of students and their teachers and on using such thresholds to judge schools. Teaching to the test requires teachers to focus their teaching towards a particular body of knowledge, even a specific style of questioning. According to Bell (1994), it is widely practised and often results in short-term learning which soon fades away. Recent evidence from school inspections carried out in England indicates that too much lesson time is devoted to the teaching and practising of GCSE examination style questions, with an emphasis on memorising and replication of procedures at the expense of understanding (Ofsted, 2012). This effect was exacerbated when schools, in an effort to increase the number of students achieving the required standards at GCSE, embarked on the practice of entering students for examinations early and on numerous occasions.

As De Lange (1992) points out, it is the nature of the style of test questions which dictates the focus of learning in the classroom. Until recently, the style of GCSE examination questions used in England has been to place a heavy emphasis on the recall of mathematical procedures, and as a direct consequence the focus in lessons tends to be on teaching procedures rather than developing conceptual understanding. In addition, the style of questions varies very little from year to year which means that practising past examination questions would appear to be a worthwhile means of preparing students. It is therefore understandable that teachers will devote a considerable amount of time to this.

Much has been written about the role of assessment in RME. Van den Heuvel-Panhuizen (2005) highlights a number of criteria which are required for problems to be considered suitable for assessment in RME. These can be summarised as follows:

– A problem must be accessible and worth solving.
– A student should be able to take ownership of a problem because it requires a decision to be made.
– A problem should enable students to demonstrate a full range of mathematical approaches from basic recall to higher order thinking.
– A problem situation should be unfamiliar so that rather than offer a standard procedure, students have an opportunity to formulate their own constructions and routes to a solution, on different levels.
– A problem situation should be imaginable so that students can apply their own knowledge and experiences and it should be suitable for mathematisation.

The contrasting style of GCSE assessment questions compared with questions designed in an RME frame can be seen in the examples illustrated in Figs. 19.4 and 19.5.

6 Here is a list of numbers.

11 8 11 14 11 15 13 14

(a) Find the mode.

(a)......................... [1]

(b) Find the range.

(b)......................... [1]

(c) Find the median.

Fig. 19.4 GCSE Question 6

20   The stem and leaf diagram shows some information about the speeds of 25 cars.

```
2 | 9
3 | 1  3  5  6  7  8  8  9
4 | 2  3  3  4  5  6  8  8  9  9
5 | 1  2  4  5  6
6 | 0
```

Key:

2 | 9 means 29 miles per hour

(a) How many of the 25 cars had a speed of more than 50 miles per hour?

....

(1)

(b) Find the median speed

.... miles per hour

(1)

(c) Work out the range of the speeds

.... miles per hour

(2)

Fig. 19.5 GCSE Question 20

The first example, shown in Fig. 19.4, is not uncommon. The techniques of mode, range and median are associated with analysing data, which inevitably is a real-life context, and yet the question presents the figures as merely a set of bare numbers, completely devoid of any context or meaning. It seems likely that students might wonder why they are answering questions of this kind, other than the fact that they are on a GCSE paper. The question does not provide any opportunities for students to make decisions, to make sense of their answers, or to demonstrate higher-order thinking. Instead, the purpose of this question is to test whether students can regurgitate the steps of a series of procedures.

The second example, shown in Fig. 19.5, does refer to a real-life context, but this is not presented in such a way that students need to engage with it. A common approach to answering this question is for students to ignore the first sentence, skip onto the key words and treat the data as a set of numbers. There is no need for students to make decisions or take ownership of the problem. In many ways, this problem is really a bare number question in disguise. The strategy of highlighting the key words and numbers is a tactic promoted by teachers and revision guides alike. This in itself sends a message that the context of the question is of little or no importance.

In 2011, Hodder Education, a well-established U.K. publisher, commissioned us to write a series of textbooks based on RME principles, suitable for the U.K. market. The series, called *Making Sense of Maths* (Dickinson, Dudzic, Eade, Gough, & Hough, 2012), was aimed at preparing students in the middle to low ability range for the GCSE examination. One of the challenges of writing these textbooks was to make sure that students were sufficiently prepared to answer GCSE questions of the type shown in Figs. 19.4 and 19.5, whilst staying true to the design principles of RME. Whilst we would have avoided writing questions of the type illustrated in Figs. 19.4 and 19.5, sometimes we would adapt and extend the ideas. For example, the speed camera question in Fig. 19.5 could be made much more purposeful if the question included car speed data for two different roads and a traffic surveyor who needed to decide which of the two roads was more in need of a speed camera. Students could be asked to find an average speed for each stretch of road using a method that they considered the most appropriate for this situation. They could also be asked to justify their choice of method and make recommendations to the traffic surveyor as to which road they believe warranted a speed camera. Setting up the context in this way where a person who needs to make a decision is introduced in the question provides the learner with a problem situation which is 'imaginable'; inviting the learner to select which average to use means that there are various 'routes to a solution'; and the fact that a decision is required encourages the learner to take 'ownership' of the problem (Van den Heuvel-Panhuizen, 2005). Writing questions which we considered to be purposeful, and which provided students with opportunities to make comparisons (between, say, two data sets, or between two different people's strategies) were two of the ways in which we were able to adapt traditional GCSE style questions so that they satisfied some of the criteria required for RME assessment.

The latest re-structuring of GCSEs to begin teaching in 2015 sees a greater emphasis on problem solving with the use of more open-ended questions set in real world contexts (OCR, 2014). This creates a greater need for teachers in England to teach in ways which develop a student's ability to genuinely solve problems, and may lead to less emphasis being placed on the teaching and regurgitation of formal mathematical procedures.

Despite the issues outlined above with regard to student expectations, pressure to meet lesson objectives and an examination system that promotes knowledge of formal mathematical procedures, there have been some successes in implementing RME in England. In the section that follows, we describe three RME trials in English classrooms, and exemplify ways in which students made considerable progress in developing a relational understanding of mathematics through sustained engagement with RME.

19.2   RME Interventions and Outcomes in England

19.2.1   The Early Interventions: Success at Key Stages 3 and 4

A number of influential reports published just after the turn of the century high-lighted concerns in the teaching and learning of mathematics in the United Kingdom. In particular, the report *Making Mathematics Count* (Smith, 2004) recommended the increased use of applications of mathematics, and a number of research papers (Anghileri, Beishuizen, & Van Putten, 2002; Brown, Askew, Millett, & Rhodes, 2003; Hodgen, Küchemann, & Brown, 2009) reported that although there had been improvements in students' end of school assessments, longer term conceptual under-standing and the ability to apply mathematics remained an issue. It was against this background that our interest in RME evolved.

In 2004, the Gatsby Foundation funded Manchester Metropolitan University (MMU) to trial the RME approach using the MiC textbook series. The trial lasted three years and involved over 400 project students aged between 11 and 14 in 12 schools. Lessons in these project classes were delivered using MiC books, selected by tutors at MMU to meet the requirements of the U.K. mathematics curriculum. For the purpose of comparison, each project student was matched with a control student. Results showed that project and control students performed at approximately the same level in traditional examination questions; this was in spite of the fact that control students experienced lessons that were specifically designed to allow them to succeed with this type of question. In comparison, project students had received a diet of MiC problems that had little resemblance to the examination and yet their results matched those of their assessment-led peers. Although this alone reinforced our confidence in the RME approach, the results of our problem-solving tests were even more interesting. These tests were designed to assess students' ability to mathematise an unfamiliar problem. We found that over twice as many age-12 project students as control students in the lower quartile ability range were able to answer this type of questions successfully (36% project, 17% control). In the middle range a smaller but still significant positive difference occurred (55% project, 43% control),

Fig. 19.6 Example of a
question eliciting
mathematical understanding

Find $\frac{1}{4}+\frac{1}{2}$
Do you think you have got this right? Explain why.

Table 19.1 Key stage 4 (age 14–16) results of the fractions addition question shown in Fig. 19.6

	Target GCSE Grade C (middle ability) % correct	Target GCSE Grade D/E (lower middle ability) % correct	n
Project students	83	57	50
Control students	72	30	50

and in the upper quartile results for project and control students were similar. There was "evidence that project pupils' approach to problem solving changed and this influenced how they understood the mathematics" (Searle & Barmby, 2012, p. 9). What was particularly striking was the willingness of the project students to 'have a go' at the problems, indicating confidence in their ability to make sense of a problem and to apply their mathematics in different contexts. These findings confirmed the need to re-define our own understanding of progress in mathematical development, while a corresponding shift in teachers' beliefs resulted in requests from project teachers for classroom materials for students aged 14–16 years.

In response, in 2007 we began producing our own resources for the 14–16 years age group, initially in collaboration with the Freudenthal Institute and then more independently, drawing on our experiences from our initial project. These materials were trialled in 16 schools and published by Hodder Education as a series of books for use with GCSE students (Dickinson et al., 2012). As the students involved in this new project were approaching their final GCSE examinations, there was a need to accelerate the learning trajectory to allow them to answer more formal, abstract questions within two years of teaching. There was also an issue of convincing students brought up on a diet of teacher exposition followed by student consolidation that what we were offering them was real mathematics. Again, our research involved project and control students, but in this instance, we focused our trial on the middle and lower middle ability range, the group of students that had benefitted most in our previous study. Their achievement in the formal GCSE examinations at the end of the trial was again broadly similar but there were remarkable differences in their ability to answer problem-solving questions. To illustrate this, we will look in detail at one of the questions (Fig. 19.6).

Although this does not immediately present itself as a problem-solving question, for the many students who had forgotten the method it required an application of their mathematical understanding, and provided many insights into their understanding of fractions. Table 19.1 displays the results for the 50 project students and 50 control students.

The project students were able to use a range of strategies to answer the question. Their explanations often involved a drawing (usually a bar or a circle) to illustrate and make sense of the mathematics. Contexts such as cakes and pizzas were utilised to justify their solutions. Those control students who could remember the algorithm they had been taught were able to achieve the correct answer. However, those who had forgotten the method, or some part of it, were unable to engage in the question in any other way, having no mathematical resources to fall back on. This was particularly true of lower middle ability control students, half of whom gave $\frac{2}{6}$ as the answer, whereas none of the project students offered this answer. Generally, the control students justified their solution by describing their numerical method and the procedure that they had used. This question, and others like it, suggested that RME provided strategies that would be remembered for longer and were underpinned by informal and intuitive mathematical understanding. These findings resonated with comparative studies of the relative progress of British and Dutch students, for example, Anghileri et al.'s (2002) research into students solving problems involving division. We felt that, despite the challenges of implementing RME in England, continuing to develop this approach was worthwhile.

19.2.2   Intervening in GCSE Resit Classes: Student Resistance and Success

Following on from our interventions at Key Stage 4, our most recent project (Nuffield Foundation, 2015) has presented some of the toughest challenges for the use of an RME approach in an English education policy climate. Since September 2013, students who have not achieved an acceptable pass grade in GCSE mathematics by the age of 16 are now required to work towards this as part of a 16–19 study programme. This requirement raises multiple issues. Firstly, the short duration of post-16 GCSE resit courses (6–9 months only) means that teachers feel a particular tension between covering content and taking the time to develop understanding (Swan, 2006). Consequently, a large proportion of GCSE resit teaching focuses on examination practice, transmission teaching, and memorisation of rules and procedures. Secondly, students on GCSE resit courses are amongst the most disaffected in terms of studying mathematics; their prior experience of expected low attainment impacts on their predisposition to study and their attitudes towards, and beliefs about, mathematics (Boaler et al., 2000; Dalby, 2013). Indeed, resit examination success rates are poor—latest statistics relating to the academic years 2012–2017 show that between 2012 and 2016 an average of just 8.6% of students leaving school at age 16 without an acceptable pass in GCSE mathematics went on to achieve an acceptable grade during 16–18 education, with a rise to only 13.3% between 2016 and 2017 (DfE, 2018).

We were interested to explore whether a slower-paced intervention based on supporting understanding through an RME approach could have a positive impact on students' achievement, understanding and engagement, and their general attitudes towards mathematics. Teaching number and algebra in four GCSE resit classes, we employed sustained use of context and models in order to help students imagine problems and to support the process of increasing but very gradual formalisation while retaining sense-making. Interventions in number and algebra based on this approach were trialled in four project and four parallel control classes spread across three different post-16 education sites, with a total of over 100 students. We encountered a number of difficulties in working with this group. Host teachers were not always willing to allow us our planned time, student attendance was poor, and there was wide variation in their prior achievement (some had barely missed a pass grade in the past, while others came to the course with a history of multiple failure grades). In particular, our work with algebra came under pressure due to its proximity to the GCSE examination—teachers were anxious to cover the syllabus and were reluctant to allow us to proceed at the pace we felt was necessary.

We did find small but significant gains for the project group on the number module ($F(1,93) = 4.55$, $p = 0.035$, partial eta squared $= 0.047$), and some indications of associations between participation in the project group and attitudes towards mathematics, but these did not reach significance. We also collected a variety of qualitative data (we interviewed case-study students about their experience of learning mathematics and conducted post-test videoed discussions about their work) which have enabled us to obtain a clearer picture of the impact of RME for this group. Alongside close analysis of their test scripts, these data show that, while some students gain from the RME approach, changing their overall beliefs about mathematics learning is difficult, especially within the context of education systems which put pressure on both students and teachers to learn and teach rules without meaning in order to make short-term progress. These issues are illustrated in the case of one student, Joel, who was able to gain from the RME approach, but needed more time to develop his understanding. His score in the number tests moved from $\frac{1}{17}$ to $\frac{10}{17}$. Figure 19.7a–d shows Joel's working in Questions 4 and 7. Sections b and d in this figure illustrate how he used the RME bar model productively in the post test. Question 7 in particular is considered to be quite challenging for this group.

However, in his post-test interview Joel's security with the RME modelling process came under scrutiny in discussion about his post-test solution to Question 2, illustrated in Fig. 19.8. The fact that the bar had to be divided into seven led to problems for Joel as he tried to apply his (often successful) strategy of halving to solve the problem. While his post-test answer to Question 7 shows real sense-making, his solution to Question 2 shows him dropping back into an algorithmic approach to mathematics in which he persists in applying halving, apparently without thinking about its usefulness or how the model will work. In his post-test interview, Joel needed heavy scaffolding to help him think about the problem, and like other students, he showed a tendency towards using the bar as the basis for an algorithmic strategy rather than as a model for making sense of the problem. Despite the obvious advantages of drawing diagrams that the RME approach provided him with, and which he acknowledged, Joel found it hard to move away from his previous ways of engaging with mathematics. In interview, he said:

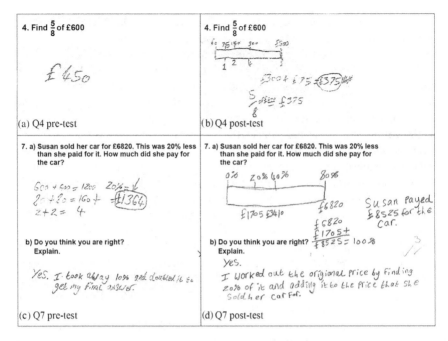

Fig. 19.7 Joel's pre- and post-test attempts to solve Question 4 and Question 7; in the post-test Joel used the bar model with halving

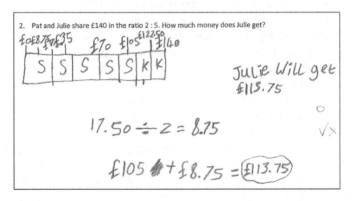

Fig. 19.8 Joel's post-test solution to Question 2

I always kind of do it in my head. I never really put it down on paper. Although everyone says that you should because you can get extra marks. … But I've never really put my working out on paper… I find it easier just to do it in my head…

Nevertheless, Joel was amenable to using the bar. However, some students, especially those on the pass grade boundary, can be unwilling to engage with methods that they see as unnecessary and too slow, when faster learned alternatives are available. Clare prioritised speed and was reluctant to spend time representing problems diagrammatically:

I think the pictures thing, … I just think it's wrong to do it and the other people in the class, they try and explain it. It just confuses me, because I did it. I think my way is an easier way, because I just go straight to it. … I only find it confusing when the rest explain it and they try and get to the answer and then they'll be finding half and they have to add another one when they could just do a division and then it would give their answer.

Joel and Clare were not untypical. The RME approach provided students with strategies that they could and would use, but the legacy of their previous experience of learning mathematics presented particular problems in terms of (1) their tendency to understand the RME approach as 'just another (algorithmic) method', and (2) their resistance to, or lack of belief in, sense-making in mathematics. These issues underline the importance of moving slowly towards formalisation, and of maximising opportunities for visualisation. While these requirements provide the greatest possibility for success, they also increase the amount of class time required, and the possibility of resistance from students (and even teachers) who may be unwilling to engage with methods that they see as unnecessary and too slow, instead of faster rote-learned alternatives. The 'risks' of investing in a slower-paced didactical trajectory which emphasises understanding and engagement (and perhaps higher grades) are high. One host teacher commented on the dilemmas that giving the team time to teach the RME approach created:

With every other group I am three or four weeks ahead of [the RME one] and where am I going to squeeze in this and this and this? But you're right about the underlying understanding being really really important, so I'm pulled two ways. … I really like what you do and buy into it, and the other side of me is saying "damn, with this group I've still got to cover this, this and this, and when am I going to do it?", because when I start teaching again I've still got things on the scheme of work to do…

19.3 Moving to Another Education System: Taking Lessons Learned in England to the Cayman Islands

In September 2011, Frank Eade moved from higher education in England to become a mathematics adviser in the Cayman Islands. The Cayman Islands adopted the English National Curriculum in 2008, uses the OFSTED framework for inspections and uses a primary mathematics textbook that is very popular in England. In what follows, Frank writes about his experiences of introducing an RME-based approach at primary and secondary education levels.

19.3.1 Primary Education

Initial observations indicated that teachers taught very formally and struggled to cope with students' difficulties. Students were expected to learn rules given to them by the teachers, and many fell increasingly behind and participated little in lessons. Consequently, they constantly asked for help, afraid to take any mathematical risks or to use their intuitions. It also became clear that even relatively able students struggled to relate money to number, with little understanding of how money worked. For example, in a lesson with 9-year-olds using 25 cent coins lined up in groups of four to represent a dollar, the class struggled to use the coins to represent $1.25. It became clear that teachers rarely used imagery to support mathematical development and, perhaps because of this, students had very poor number sense. In one lesson with students aged 10 years, a teacher was attempting to teach subtraction by adding on and addition by compensation. For example, he wanted the students to solve 136 + 195 by thinking of 195 as close to 200. The students struggled with the problems. When I drew a number line with 0 and 200 marked on it and asked them to indicate where they thought 195 was, they tended to place it somewhere close to the middle. So, two major initiatives in Cayman were to utilise models and imagery in lessons and to get teachers to simulate the use of money in the classroom and to encourage parents to take children to the shops—not a common practice, as it turned out—and get them used to using money.

Because of the high number of struggling students, we introduced the Mathematics Recovery training programme (Wright, Stranger, Stafford, & Martland, 2014), which makes extensive use of images such as 10-frames, the Rekenrek (arithmetic rack), the 100-bead bar and arrays to support mathematical development, but little use of contexts. Through gradual but sustained exposure to these images as well as the empty number line, a group of teachers who were training to become leaders in primary mathematics developed their understanding of N10, N10C, A10 and 1010[1] (Beishuizen, 1997) and started to use these. Although it took time, they began to use contexts as a means of entry to mathematics and some did their best to use context throughout. We began to develop study units to help teachers with classroom ideas but also to support them in understanding how the mathematics would develop. Where teachers' thinking and experience related to the teaching and application of rules, change required considerable effort not only in developing activities, but also

---

[1]N10 = The first number is kept whole, the second number is split into tens and units and the tens of the second number are added to the first number followed by the units.

N10C = The first number is kept whole, the second number is rounded up to a multiple of ten and this number is added to the first number followed by an adjustment or compensation for the rounding.

A10 = The first number that is kept whole, the second number is split so that a number of its units are added to the first number to arrive at a multiple of ten and then the remainder is added to the first number.

1010 = Both numbers are split into tens and units and then the tens are added together, then the units, then the combined tens and units are added together.

Fig. 19.9 Explanation of
how the subtraction 91 − 37
is solved

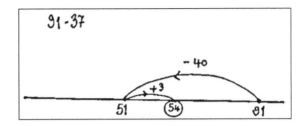

in developing the 'big picture' and a sense of how the mathematics developed over time.

In my first year in Cayman, in 2011, I tested students to find out how they solved number problems. Given 154 + 49, the facility for Year 4 was 45% and for Year 6 was 78%. No student solved the problem by adding 50 and subtracting 1. Following the interventions described above, facilities in 2013 increased to 70 and 85% respectively. However, although the number of students using compensation increased, it was still very low. In another problem, shown in Fig. 19.9, students had to explain how 91–37 was solved. In 2011, only 16% of Year 6 students, the vast majority of these being high attaining, could provide a reasonable explanation of how it was solved and understood the use of the number line. In 2013, the facility for year 6 was now 46%. Considering the responses to 154 + 49, this does suggest that students become aware of a strategy before they actually use it strategically.

Another question in 2015 asked students to solve 315–180 and about 20% used an empty number line with some also using it to confirm the accuracy of their formal answer. So, change was taking place, albeit slowly. This change was further evidenced by work on division, where between 2011 and 2013 the proportion of Year 6 students successfully answering a standard problem rose from 31 to 61%. There was also evidence of more students using less formal methods such as 'chunking' (Anghileri & Beishuizen, 1998). Figure 19.10, showing some of the strategies used by Year 5 to solve the problem 222 ÷ 3, evidences further the changes that we began to see. Students were starting to make strategic decisions about how to solve problems rather than just following a procedure provided by the teacher.

19.3.2 Secondary Education

The position in secondary was very similar to primary in that teachers taught the syllabus formally with little regard to whether students grasped the ideas or not. Because of a substantial private school sector of over 30%, the ability range in state schools is skewed towards the middle and lower end. The standardised assessments, however, demonstrated very clearly that students were not making the gains that they should be and, in particular, the lowest achieving students were falling rapidly behind.

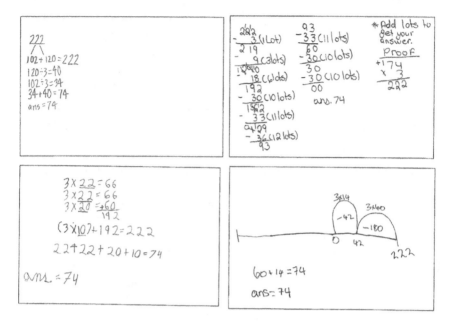

Fig. 19.10 Year 5 students' strategies for the division problem $222 \div 3$

Building on the intervention in primary schools, I tried to initiate change by providing activities for teachers to use in the classroom. Informal activities based around Cayman were introduced (see Fig. 19.11) and generally teachers warmed to the idea that working more informally was worth exploring.

Although the teachers used these activities and students really seemed to enjoy the lessons, teachers would usually revert to traditional teaching unless I provided the activities, and clearly this was not sustainable. As an alternative, teachers began to trial some MiC textbooks (Abels, Burrill, & Wijers, 2010) with lower and middle Year 7 classes, with a particular focus on fractions, decimals and percentages. As always, some teachers were enthusiastic about the possibilities, but others agreed with some reluctance. It was clear that we needed a rigorous approach to evaluation, so among other things we developed a test to be taken in 2014 by all Year 7 students who had no MiC experiences and in 2015 by two groups (Group 2 and Group 3) who had experienced MiC and one group (Group 1) who had not.

The teachers were provided with a number of professional development sessions in preparation for using the materials. I met with them once every two weeks during implementation to discuss progress, and also observed lessons weekly. Table 19.2 summarises the outcomes.

It can be seen that there are only minor changes in the Group 1 (control group) scores but major gains for the Groups 2 and 3. In addition, these students also made major gains in the standardised tests used in Cayman, making close to two years gain in the year when normally they would be struggling to make a year's gain. A

The person in the photograph is 5 ft tall. How tall is the tower?

The bricks in the library are the same as in the tower. How tall is the library door?

Fig. 19.11 Example of Cayman-based context problem

Table 19.2 Outcomes of the MiC intervention

Question	% correct					
	Group 1		Group 2		Group 3	
	2014	2015	2014	2015	2014	2015
1	38	41	0	42	0	9
2	30	34	5	8	0	7
3	57	67	29	49	18	33
4	43	47	5	19	0	5
5	80	81	42	64	23	54
6	47	55	11	8	5	12
7	70	60	24	32	13	7
8	35	26	13	28	3	10
9	52	49	4	21	0	5
10	55	70	35	45	5	40
11	13	11	2	4	0	2
12	17	11	2	4	0	0
13	32	29	4	15	3	7
Mean (%)	44	45	14	26	5	15

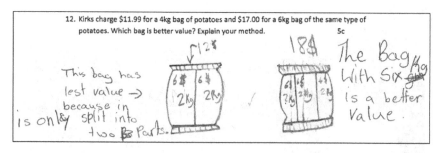

Fig. 19.12 A solution by a Group 3 student

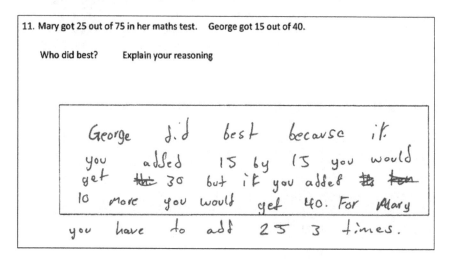

Fig. 19.13 A solution by a Group 2 student

feature of the answers given by Groups 2 and 3 was the range of solution strategies in evidence, and the confidence with which students offered such strategies. Two of the most striking of these are given in Figs. 19.12 and 19.13.

In interviews and questionnaires, students were very positive about the experience and wanted to continue using MiC in Year 8. The teachers have agreed to continue using the materials in Year 8 and also to trial some algebra materials with higher ability groups in Year 7. The teachers also indicated that they were using the contexts with other year groups, adopting more interactive approaches and being more inclined to use models to support problem solving rather than focusing on formal algorithms.

Observations, however, have also highlighted a number of challenges that need to be worked on in the coming year, and which resonate with the experience of the teachers in England when first working with RME:

– Teachers want to continue with a problem until all understand, and feel uncomfortable in moving on.

- Teachers tend to believe that when students solve a problem in context, then they understand the associated content; later, in subsequent lessons teachers realise that the skills do not transfer.
- Teachers tend to spend too long in whole class mode rather than letting students solve problems in pairs or groups first. Moving in and out of group work seems to collide with the normal practice of whole class teaching followed by exercises.
- Teachers want to formalise the content rather than allowing students a more gradual journey to formal mathematics.

For both primary and secondary education, there have been some major shifts both in the teaching and in teachers' more subtle understanding of mathematical development. However, there is still a long way to go and there is still a danger that, if the political/educational climate changes, then it would be very easy to destroy the fragile advances that have been made.

19.4 Conclusions and Implications

This chapter has outlined a number of initiatives aimed at implementing RME in an English system. It was clear from the outset that there would be barriers to these initiatives, and that the main principles of RME were significantly different from dominant didactic practices. In addition, these practices, along with student expectations, were often the result of external pressures such as an increasingly frequent external assessment pattern and a rigorous inspection regime. In particular, the notion of progressive formalisation, essentially for many students the slowing down of the move to formal mathematics, proved difficult to adopt. So, while teachers (and students) were enthusiastic about trialling RME, embracing it fully proved too much of a challenge for many schools.

Results, however, showed that classes who did work with RME materials produced sizeable gains, both in problem solving and in examinations. This has led teachers to continue to try to adapt RME principles to the English setting. So, while we cannot claim that RME has been implemented fully in schools, it is clear that many of the principles have been. The mathematics departments we have worked with are now far more likely to use models such as the ratio table and the empty number line, to use contexts throughout a topic, and to invoke visualisations and imagery in their lessons. There is also currently a move in schools to spend more time on topics before moving on to the next one; this does at least open up the possibility of delaying the journey to more formal mathematics, and embracing progressive formalisation. While some of the challenges we face are inevitably unique to England, others are more general issues faced by anyone attempting to develop a new approach in the classroom. Hence, when one of our colleagues attempted to develop RME in the Cayman Islands, many of the issues encountered were of a similar nature to those met in England. Those of us involved in these projects remain committed to the principles of RME, and believe that the results from the projects justify this commitment. The challenge remains as to how to continue to develop these principles within the constraints of our education policies and frameworks.

References

Abels, M., Burrill, G., & Wijers, M. (2010). *Mathematics in context. Key to success. Level 1. Teacher's guide.* Chicago, IL: Encyclopedia Britannica, Inc.

Anghileri, J., & Beishuizen, M. (1998). Counting, chunking and division algorithm. *Mathematics in School, 27,* 2–5.

Anghileri, J., Beishuizen, M., & Van Putten, K. (2002). From informal strategies to structured procedures: Mind the gap. *Educational Studies in Mathematics, 49,* 149–170.

Bell, A. W. (1994). Teaching for the test. In M. Selinger (Ed.), *Teaching mathematics.* London, UK: Routledge.

Beishuizen, M. (1997). Two types of mental arithmetic and the empty number line. *Informal Proceedings BSRLM [British Society for Research in the Learning of Mathematics], 17*(1&2), 18–22.

Boaler, J. (1997). When even the winners are losers: Evaluating the experiences of 'top set' students. *Journal of Curriculum Studies, 29*(2), 65–182.

Boaler, J. (2002). Experiencing school mathematics: Traditional and reform approaches to teaching. Mahwah, NJ: Lawrence Erlbaum.

Boaler, J., & Wiliam, D. (2001). "We've still got to learn!" Students' perspectives on ability grouping and mathematics achievement. In P. Gates (Ed.), *Issues in mathematics teaching.* London, UK: Routledge Falmer.

Boaler, J., Wiliam, D., & Brown, M. (2000). Students' experiences of ability grouping-disaffection, polarisation and the construction of failure. *British Educational Research Journal, 26*(5), 631–648.

Brantlinger, A. (2014). Critical mathematics discourse in a high school classroom: examining patterns of student engagement and resistance. *Educational Studies in Mathematics, 85*(2), 201–220.

Brown, M., Askew, M., Millett, A., & Rhodes, V. (2003). The key role of educational research in the development and evaluation of the National Numeracy Strategy. *British Educational Research Journal, 2,* 655–672.

Dalby, D. (2013). An alternative destination for post-16 mathematics: Views from the perspective of vocational students. In C. Smith (Ed.), *Proceedings of the British Society for Research into Learning Mathematics (BSRLM)* (Vol. 33, Issue 3, pp. 13–18).

De Corte, E., Op't Eynde, P., & Verschaffel, L. (2002). "Knowing what to believe": The relevance of students' mathematical beliefs for mathematics education. In B. Hofer & P. Pintrich (Eds.), *Personal epistemology: The psychology of beliefs about knowledge and knowing* (pp. 297–320). Mahwah, NJ: Lawrence Erlbaum.

De Lange, J. (1992). Critical factors for real changes in mathematics learning. In G. C. Leder (Ed.), *Assessment and learning of mathematics* (pp. 305–329). Hawthorn, Australia: Australian Council for Educational Research.

DfE. (2013). *National curriculum in England: Mathematics programmes of study.* https://www.gov.uk/government/publications/national-curriculum-in-england-mathematics-programmes-of-study. Accessed October 20, 2015.

DfE. (2018). *A level and other 16 to 18 results: 2016 to 2017 (revised) National Tables SFR03/2018.* https://www.gov.uk/government/statistics/a-level-and-other-16-to-18-results-2016-to-2017-revised. Accessed July 31, 2018.

DfEE. (1999). *The National numeracy strategy framework for teaching mathematics from reception to year 6.* London: DfEE.

Dickinson, P., Dudzic, S., Eade, F., Gough, S., & Hough, S. (2012). *Making sense of maths.* London, UK: Hodder Education.

Dickinson, P., & Hough, S. (2012). *Using realistic mathematics education in UK classrooms*. http://www.mei.org.uk/files/pdf/rme_impact_booklet.pdf.

Dickinson, P., Hough, S., Searle, J., & Barmby, P. (2011). Evaluating the impact of a Realistic Mathematics Education project in secondary schools. *Proceedings of the British Society for Research into Learning Mathematics (BSRLM), 31*(3), 47–52.

Elliott, A. (2012). Twenty years inspecting English schools-Ofsted 1992–2012. *RISE Review*, November. London, UK: RISE.

Forgasz, H., Becker, J. R., Lee, K.-H., & Steinthorsdottir, O. (Eds.). (2010). *International perspectives on gender and mathematics education*. Charlotte, NC: Information Age.

Fosnot, C. T. (2007). *Contexts for learning mathematics*. Portsmouth, NH: Heinemann.

Fosnot, C. T., & Dolk, M. (2002). *Young mathematicians at work: Constructing fractions, decimals, and percents*. Portsmouth, NH: Heinemann.

Gravemeijer, K., Pligge, M. A., & Clarke, B. (2003). Reallotment. In National Center for Research in Mathematical Sciences Education & Freudenthal Institute (Eds.), *Mathematics in context*. Chicago, IL: Encyclopaedia Britannica.

Hodgen, J., Küchemann, D., & Brown, M. (2009). *Secondary students' understanding of mathematics 30 years on*. Conference presentation at the British Educational Research Association Conference, September 2–5.

Lubienski, S. T. (2007). Research, reform, and equity in U.S. mathematics education. In N. S. Nasir & P. Cobb (Eds.), *Improving access to mathematics* (pp. 10–23). New York, NY: Teachers College Press.

National Centre for Excellence in the Teaching of Mathematics (NCETM). (2014). *Mastery approaches to mathematics and the new national curriculum*. https://www.ncetm.org.uk/public/files/19990433/Developing_mastery_in_mathematics_october_2014.pdf.

National Center for Research in Mathematical Sciences Education (NCRMSE) & Freudenthal Institute. (1997–1998). *Mathematics in context: A connected curriculum for grades 5–8*. Chicago, IL: Encyclopaedia Britannica Educational Corporation.

Noyes, A., Drake, P., Wake, G., & Murphy, R. (2010). *Evaluating mathematics pathways. Research Report DFE-RR143*. London, UK: Department for Education.

Nuffield Foundation. (2015). *Achievement and attitudes in GCSE Resit Classes* Project. http://www.nuffieldfoundation.org/achievement-and-attitudes-gcse-mathematics-resit-classes.

OCR (2014). *GCSE (9-1) Mathematics*. www.ocr.org.uk/gcsemaths.

Ofsted (2012). *Mathematics*. www.ofsted.gov.uk/resources/110159.

Searle, J., & Barmby, P. (2012). *Evaluation report on the Realistic Mathematics Education pilot project at Manchester Metropolitan University*. Durham, UK: Centre for Evaluation and Monitoring (CEM), Durham University. http://www.mei.org.uk/files/pdf/RME_Evaluation_final_report.pdf.

Solomon, Y. (2007). Experiencing mathematics classes: How ability grouping conflicts with the development of participative identities. *International Journal of Educational Research, 46*(1–2), 8–19.

Smith, A. (2004). *Making mathematics count: The report of Professor Adrian Smith's inquiry into post-14 mathematics education*. London, UK: The Stationery Office.

Streefland, L. (1991). *Fractions in realistic mathematics education*. Dordrecht, the Netherlands: Kluwer Academic Publishers.

Streefland, L. (1985). Wiskunde als activiteit en de realiteit als bron [Mathematics as an activity and reality as a source]. *Nieuwe Wiskrant, 5*(1), 60–67.

Streefland, L. (1993). The design of a mathematics course. A theoretical reflection. *Educational Studies in Mathematics, 25*(1–2), 109–135.

Swan, M. (2006). *Collaborative learning in mathematics: A challenge to our beliefs and practices*. Leicester, UK: NIACE.

Van den Heuvel-Panhuizen, M. (2003). The didactical use of models in Realistic Mathematics Education: An example from a longitudinal trajectory on percentage. *Educational Studies in Mathematics, 54*, 9–35.

Van den Heuvel-Panhuizen, M. (2005). The role of contexts in assessment problems in mathematics. *For the Learning of Mathematics, 25*(2), 2–23.

Wake, G. D., & Burkhardt, T. H. (2013). Understanding the European policy landscape and its impact on change in mathematics and science pedagogies. *ZDM Mathematics Education, 45*(6), 851–861.

Webb, D., Boswinkel, N., & Dekker, T. (2008). Beneath the tip of the iceberg: Using representations to support student understanding. *Mathematics Teaching in the Middle School, 14*(2), 110–113.

Wright, R., Stanger, G., Stafford, A. K., & Martland, J. (2014). *Teaching number in the classroom with 4–8 year olds*. London, UK: Sage Publications.

Zevenbergen, R. (2005). The construction of a mathematical habitus: Implications of ability grouping in the middle years. *Journal of Curriculum Studies, 37*(5), 607–619.